Gendering Politics, Feminising Political Science

Joni Lovenduski

ecpr PRESS

First published by the ECPR Press in 2015

Cover: Art by Favianna Rodriguez

The ECPR Press is the publishing imprint of the European Consortium for Political Research
(ECPR), a scholarly association, which supports and encourages the training, research
and cross-national co-operation of political scientists in institutions throughout
Europe and beyond.

ECPR Press
Harbour House
Hythe Quay
Colchester
CO2 8JF
United Kingdom

Typeset by Lapiz Digital Services

Printed and bound by Lightning Source

British Library Cataloguing in Publication Data

A catalogue record for this book is available from the British Library

ISBN: 978-1-910259-14-6
PDF ISBN: 978-1-785521-60-7
EPUB ISBN: 978-1-785521-61-4
KINDLE ISBN: 978-1-785521-62-1

www.ecpr.eu/ecprpress

Related reading from ECPR Press

Deeds and Words: Gendering Politics after Joni Lovenduski
(ISBN: 9781907301520) Rosie Campbell and Sarah Childs

Gender, Conservatism and Political Representation
(ISBN: 9781907301711) Karen Celis and Sarah Childs

Gender and the Vote in Britain: Beyond the Gender Gap?
(ISBN: 9780954796693) Rosie Campbell

Representing Women? Female Legislators in West European Parliaments
(ISBN: 9780954796648) Mercedes Mateo Diaz

Why Aren't They There? The Political Representation of Women, Ethnic Groups and Issue Positions in Legislatures
(ISBN: 9780955820397) Didier Ruedin

Please visit www.ecpr.eu/ecprpress for information about new publications.

For Joseph and Karen Lovenduski and Alan Ware whose many years of support made it possible for me to do the work I wanted to do.

Contents

List of Figures and Tables   vii

Introduction   1

THE SELECTION

Selection of Articles and Acknowledgements   11

PART 1: POLITICAL REPRESENTATION

Chapter One – Women in Parliament: Making a Difference   17
    with Azza Karam

Chapter Two – Westminster Women: The Politics of Presence   41
    with Pippa Norris

Chapter Three – Political Representation   63
    with Marila Guadagnini

Chapter Four – Feminising British Politics   99

PART 2: POLITICAL PARTIES

Chapter Five – The Dynamics of Gender and Party   109

Chapter Six – Will Quotas Make Labour More Woman-Friendly?   121

Chapter Seven – Women's Equality Guarantees and the Conservative Party   131
    with Rosie Campbell and Sarah Childs

Chapter Eight – Obstacles to Feminising Politics   143

Chapter Nine – United Kingdom: Male Dominance Unbroken?   169

PART 3: GENDER AND PUBLIC POLICY

Chapter Ten – The New Politics of Abortion   195
  with Joyce Outshoorn

Chapter Eleven – Sexing London: The Gender Mix of Urban Policy Actors   199
  with Stefania Abrar and Helen Margetts

Chapter Twelve – Feminism, Violence, and Men   229

Chapter Thirteen – Feminist Ideas and Domestic Violence Policy Change   265
  with Stefania Abrar and Helen Margetts

PART 4: GENDERING THE POLITICAL SCIENCE AGENDA

Chapter Fourteen – Toward the Emasculation of Political Science:
  The Impact of Feminism   293

Chapter Fifteen – Gendering Research in Political Science   311

Conclusion: Does Feminism need Political Science?   **337**

Index   349

List of Figures and Tables

Figures

Figure 2.1: Women in Public Office, UK   42

Figure 9.1: Women's Representation in House of Commons,
   Scottish Parliament and National Assembly for Wales, since 1945   172

Tables

Table 1.1: Four Areas of Change that will Impact on Women's Participation   21

Table 1.2: Women: Making Impact through Parliament   21

Table 2.1: Factor Analysis of Political Attitudes Amongst all Candidates
   in 2001 BRS Survey   50

Table 2.2: Mean Scores on the Value Scales by Party and Gender   54

Table 2.3: Regression Model Predicting Support for Affirmative Action
   Values Scale   56

Table 3.1: Women's Movement Actor Intervention by Institutional Base
   and Issue   71

Table 3.2: Policy Agency Interventions by Debate Issue and Percentages   73

Table 3.3: Representation in Priority Issue Debates and Percentage of
   Interventions   76

Table 3.4: Representation in Nonpriority Issue Debates and Percentage of
   Nonpriority Issue Interventions of All Interventions by Actor   77

Table 3.5: Issue Frame at the End of Debate by Issue Frame Fit   83

Table 3.6: Ordinal Regression of Women's Movement Actor
   Presence Model   88

Table 3.7: Ordinal Regression of the Achievement of Both Substantive
and Descriptive Representation   89

Table 6.1: Women's Share of Parliamentary Candidacies and Seats in 1992   124

Table 9.1: Electoral Systems in the UK   171

Table 9.2: Number of Labour Women Nominated and Elected as MPs
on All-Women Shortlists, 1997–2010   178

Table 9.3: Women and Men in the UK Political Leadership   187

Table 9.4: Election Rates of Women Candidates in 2010 by Party   188

Table 11.1: Distribution of Women's Employment by Industrial Sector,
Greater London and Great Britain, Including Self-Employment   202

Table 11.2: Unemployment Rates by Sex (February 1995)   203

Table 11.3: Women Departmental Directors, England and Wales, 1993   209

Table 11.4: Members of Council Across Eight London
Boroughs, 1974–94   210

Table 11.5: Executive Elites Across Seven Boroughs, 1992–93   210

Table 11.6: Total Executive and Legislative Policy Elites Across Seven
Boroughs, 1992–93   211

Table 11.7: Reputational View of Women's Groups, July 1992 to
July 1993   217

Table 13.1: Domestic Violence Policy Beliefs of Feminist Coalition and
Traditionalist Coalition — Deep Core, Policy Core and Secondary
Aspect   271

Table 13.2: Domestic Violence Policy Beliefs of Traditionalists 1975
and 1995   287

Introduction

The central theme of my research is the way gender is embedded in political institutions, mainly but not exclusively as expressed in patterns of political representation in democracies. In common with other academics of my generation who were interested in politics, I started as a political scientist, though a sceptical and critical one, with a strong commitment to broader notions of social science as an integrated project. Early on I was particularly doubtful about the 'science' part of the term, largely because there were so many competing versions of it around but also because many political scientists almost wilfully adopted the narrowest possible uses of the term. The idea of political science was so contested that the founders of the UK Political Studies Association (PSA) avoided the term, preferring the more anodyne and inclusive 'Political Studies'. I have often thought they might better have chosen the term science and defended it as systematic inquiry, observation and thinking. For me, political science is the systematic study of politics, a project that is impossible without feminism.

Why feminism?

Feminism was an influence from the earliest stages of my research. My way of studying and thinking about politics was slowly moulded into a fairly consistent approach to problems developed in response to the challenges of concept formation and research design that I encountered and, of course, the other researchers I worked with on different projects. My work covers gendering research into politics and its impact on the theorisation of political representation, the nature of women's and feminist movements, political recruitment, research design including the supply and demand framework for analysing political recruitment, equality agencies, equality strategies and their contexts including especially political parties, all in an increasingly articulated framework of feminist institutionalism.

Why politics?

The term politics has a number of different meanings that include activities, organisations and conflicts in which the allocations of resources are decided. Harold Lasswell's famous definition which stated that politics is who gets what, when and how is a common starting point. It is both succinct and much criticised. It misses at least two important questions (where and why) and overemphasises outcomes at the expense of process. Even so, it is a good place to start. For me, understanding politics turns on the idea of power and is a matter of understanding the interplays of ideas, institutions and interests that constrain and permit the use of power in making authoritative effective decisions. In democratic systems, politics is often described in terms of politicians, governments, assemblies, elections and power. Democratic politics and processes that entail political representation and are ultimately a matter of the political arrangements and practices, especially the elections that permit leaders to decide the answers to Lasswell's questions. Authoritative decision making turns on electoral success which is achieved through the competition of ideas and interests organised by political institutions that include the political parties and the media. However, even where there are democratic trappings, all modern political systems are dominated by elites, by the few who have the capacity to manufacture the consent of the many.

Such institutional manifestations of politics are the tip of a very substantial iceberg. The central concept, if there is one, is power. For my generation of political scientists, power was a high concept, the essential component of authoritative decisions about public issues located variously in political institutions. Traditionally it was problematised by distinctions between power over, power to, affect, effect, power as a resource or capacity and, of course, distinctions between consent and coercion. But, however articulated, it was always present as a concept that required definition and operationalisation.

It is the centrality of power to its concerns that makes political science worthwhile for feminists, a point to which I return in the concluding chapter. The focus on power is what makes political science at its best a worthwhile discipline for feminists. As a political scientist, my understanding of political power emphasises the processes and contexts that sustain dominance of some groups or individuals by others. As a feminist I always consider the gender dynamics of the relationships between the dominant and dominated parties. Today, feminists draw on a range of theories of power, highlighting the foundation of public power in the 'private' sphere and contend that the exercise of power in the state and the economy depends on private arrangements. The gendering of those arrangements conceals the interdependencies of public and private life. But distinctions between public and private life in common articulations of politics have a major effect on the design, membership and agendas of political institutions.

These insights are founded in a longstanding feminist understanding of the state. For some time the feminist approach to political power was oblique as scholars worked through the implications of their insights into the smokescreen of the assumed split between public and private life that relegated women mainly to the private sphere. In the 1980s feminists were preoccupied with the state, much engaged in its 'deconstruction'. The early 1990s saw a shift from the notion of the state as a political entity that had knowable boundaries and functions to one of shifting networks of power and dominance (Watson 1990). This change coincided with the 'institutional turn' in political science which saw calls to 'Bring the state back in …' (Evans *et al.* 1985). The subsequent emergence of the 'new' institutionalism brought a new emphasis on the rules (formal and informal) processes and practises through which power operated. The shift highlighted the very dynamics through which masculine dominance is created and recreated, creating space for gender analysis. Feminist institutionalism, which I discuss in the concluding chapter, is founded on the gendering of these analytical movements.

One implication of these contentions is that the exercise of political power cannot be understood in isolation from an understanding of private life. It logically follows that the interactions between public and private life are central to research on political power. This, of course, affects the research agenda. Research employing such a widely drawn notion of political power sacrifices parsimony and may be awkward to operationalise. It is necessarily mixed method and multi-level, including not only the political science basics of state institutions and observed political behaviour, but also discourse and ideas and sources of behaviour in 'private' life. Feminists have developed a considerable portfolio of concepts and ideas for this project in the course of which they have developed a feminist political science. Central to this political science are two concepts –political representation and gender.

Why political representation?

Since the nineteenth century women's movements have made claims that all women should be citizens, are entitled to political representation and to positions of public power. Processes of political representation are central to the fortunes of competing interests in democracies. A key question is whether women need women to represent them. Whilst logically it is possible for men to represent women, it is evident that they do not do so unless women are present in decision making institutions. Historically many of the more feminised areas of social life found no reflection in political institutions which were made to suit the men who designed them. Ever since Anne Phillips (1995) argued so effectively for a 'politics of presence', feminists have contended that a necessary condition for the representation of women's interests is the presence of women in decision-making bodies. Phillips contended that interests are realised in the course of deliberation and decision-making as various options, implementation strategies, and competing concerns are discussed. Only those who take part in the deliberation can benefit from such realisation and insert their interests. Leaving aside the vexed question of identifying 'valid' group interests, the logic of Phillips' claim is inescapable. Presence is sometimes termed descriptive (or microcosmic) representation and is often discussed in conjunction with substantive representation. Feminist advocates of descriptive representation hold that women (in their diversity) should be present in representative institutions in proportion to their presence in the electorate. Substantive representation refers to the ideas that get represented and the policies that get made. Most feminists would prefer to vote for a representative who promoted feminist goals, hence do accept that in some circumstances women may be represented by men.[1] Both are important to the way I understand political representation. To recap, the institutions of political representation are gendered, and the underrepresentation of women in politics is a matter neither of accident nor choice, but a product of that gendering.

Why Gender?

Why women? The dichotomy between women and men is apparent in any analysis of power. All you have to do is look. Read the foundational political theory texts in which authors assume the political actor is male (Pateman 1988). Historically one of the most reliably consistent differences between women and men is the male dominance of access to positions of political power that is more acute as one ascends recognised hierarchies of power. I am not sure it is essentialist (in a bad way) to acknowledge this difference even though it clearly affects different men and women differently. Of course most people do not have much political power but those who do are more likely to be men, albeit certain groups of men.

Making sense of politics entails the understanding of gender as a social construction in which power is implicated. While the relationships between the concepts of gender and sex are contested in feminist theory, I nevertheless argue here that the concept of gender captures more conceptual sophistication than is expressed in the 'biological' distinction between two sexes. Gender is both an idea and an institution. It can be thought of as culturally and socially based differences in characteristics located on parameters of masculinity and femininity according to which individuals are socialised in various ways. It is expressed in the gender relations on which systems of public power are founded. Non-feminist political scientists mainly ignore this project. They do not 'get' gender and tend to use the term interchangeably with sex. The need to correct the distorted analyses that result are the starting point of my arguments that political science needs feminism.

To expand on these points I argue that the phenomenon that not all men have political power and only a few women do is accommodated by abandoning the dichotomous notion of 'biological' sex and employing the concepts of gender and gender relations. The question 'why gender?' is at least two questions. The first is why should students of politics be interested in gender? The answer turns both on power and difference. In democracies political power is a public (if not always transparent) matter. It is gendered in the sense that men have predominated. Not

---

1. Both concepts are drawn from Hannah Pitkin's typology of representation, *The Concept of Representation* published in 1967. Her four types of representation are: (1) authorised, where a representative is legally empowered to act for another; (2) descriptive representation, where the representative stands for a group by virtue of sharing similar characteristics such as race, sex, ethnicity, or residence; (3) symbolic representation, where a leader stands for national ideas; and (4) substantive representation, where the representative seeks to advance a group's policy preferences and interests. A number of feminists including Sarah Childs, Karen Celis and Johanna Kantola have recently begun to explore the concept of symbolic representation.

all men have been powerful but the powerful have normally been men, certain types of men. So, throughout the histories of democracies many more men than women have been politically powerful in public life. Why? I argued in 1986 and still contend (*Women and European Politics* 1986, pp 209–211) that the sources of power for women and men differ and are of different value. In democratic societies both women and men have social resources that are convertible and expandable. Until recently most women have had access only to the social resources that are available in private, domestic life. Normally such resources cannot be converted outside of the private sphere. For centuries women were not citizens, did not have political rights, could not vote or hold public office, and were regarded as being represented via families through male heads of household, even in democracies. This does not mean that women had no political power, rather that authoritative public political positions were visibly and obviously overwhelmingly dominated by men. In contrast, men developed networks, skills and organisations in the public spheres of work and politics that were converted into the resources necessary to political power. Although this traditional pattern is changing, a well-established set of institutions with a considerable afterlife (path dependence) continues to support it.

The second question illuminates the first - why gender instead of sex? The answer is that making sense of political relationships between women and men requires more than a simplistic male-female dichotomy. In terms of difference, historically only *some* men have been powerful in the established order. Feminists understand this and are sensitive to the political dominance of particular kinds of public masculinity. Difference of course creates the potential for alliances between and among groups of women and men, a contingency that explains why not all women are feminists and why some (but not that many) men are.

To put it another way, feminists know that some men have power over and are able to dominate other men and almost all women in the who gets what, when and how (and where and why) decisions. Thus the evident distinction between women and men turns out not to be dichotomous, but something more like a continuum. The concept of gender, and especially of its logical extension, gender relations, provides a conceptual sophistication that is lacking in most of contemporary political science. Though also socially contingent, gender is logically prior to, but affected by the other key variables in political analysis such as class, race, religion and region. Recognising that different masculinities and femininities characterise political actors exposes, permits and encourages the analysis of the relationships that support political power and underpin political domination. As a concept that illuminates difference it alerts us to the possibilities that distinctions are not simply between the powerful men and powerless women but of the distribution of different kinds of power among women and men in particular societies.

How, exactly, does the assumption of a feminist perspective affect approaches to the study of politics? What might political scientists gain/want from feminism? Broadly there are two possibilities – the explanation of gendered outcomes of political processes and predictions of future developments in politics that give proper weight to gender dynamics. Both entail the specification of contexts, the collection and analysis of evidence and the theorisation of political relationships. For feminists these are inevitably gendered in some way, whether biased, neutral or balanced. Too often gender relations are not considered in studies of political behaviour yet may be of crucial importance to understanding political phenomena. For example, failures to consider respondent sex in voting studies obscured major developments in patterns in women's voting in the UK and the USA. The result of ignoring gender has all too often been bad science, poor explanation and unreliable prediction, points that have been made repeatedly by feminist critics of the conventions of the formal study of politics. Feminism fixes bad political science by bringing to it a combination of ideas about power and its gendered aspects.

Although sometimes difficult, the reconfiguration of political science to accommodate the impact of gender is feasible. Gender is an institution nested in other institutions. A considerable corpus of traditional political science was the study of public political institutions. That tradition was revisited during the 1980s as 'new' institutionalists extended and reworked their approach, to include more informal and hidden but still powerful institutions, a project that has attracted many feminist political scientists. Feminists claim that gendered asymmetries of power are often embedded in institutions. An example is the rules and conventions of a political party that favour traditional masculine life styles (e.g. evening meetings in pubs, bars or men's clubs.) Political institutions are a crucial site of gendered power relations whose workings must be understood if the gendered nature of political power is to be exposed to view.

Political science needs feminism. Political explanation shows how power is implicated and used in ideas, interests and institutions that affect most people's lives. While most students of politics agree that such answers require empirical investigations of institutions and their effects on political decisions and outcomes, feminists go further, insisting that those institutions are gendered in various ways.

Feminist investigate political institutions for the ideas they express about women and men, masculinity and femininity showing how the practice of these ideas produces and reproduces power relations that we would otherwise take for granted and leave unquestioned. Feminists therefore bring to the study of political institutions a specific lens that makes visible its constitutive gendered power relations and the processes that support and undermine them. In identifying changing gender relations as a potential cause of institutional change, feminism increases the capacity to model causality. Without an understanding of gender the intellectual project of understanding politics must fail.

Unfortunately the shared interest that feminists and political scientists have in how institutions work in general has not to date extended to a common interest how that working is gendered. This has huge scientific consequences. For the most part political scientists do not use a gendered approach, for the most part they ignore feminist research altogether. But the exclusion of consideration of gender risks ignoring crucial elements of ideas, interests, rules and processes, portents and causes of change, instances of agency and the everyday operation of power as it plays out in political and social practice.

Why does (most of) political science overlook the feminist contribution? It is tempting to say that it is because so many of its practitioners have lost interest in the nature of power, but that is probably not correct. More likely they think they so well understand power that they do not any longer think it necessary to define, problematise, excavate, examine or report on it. Hence it is more difficult than it should be to consider the import of its gendered nature. This is a serious error that not only reduces the explanatory power of much political analysis but also impedes the projects of explanation and prediction of change.

References

Evans, P. B., Rueschemeyer, D. and Skocpol, T. (1985) *Bringing the State Back In*, Cambridge: Cambridge University Press.

Pateman, C. (1988) *The Sexual Contract*, Cambridge: Polity Press.

Phillips, A. (1995) *The Politics of Presence*, Oxford: Oxford University Press.

Pitkin, H. (1967) *The Concept of Representation*, Berkeley: University of California Press.

Watson, S. (1990) *Playing the State: Australian Feminist Interventions*, London: Virago.

THE SELECTION

Selection of Articles and Acknowledgements

When I was first asked[1] to put this volume together I was hesitant, because it seemed to be going backwards. I have tended to think of my work as an organic, slowly but logically growing project with an incrementally developing intellectual agenda. I wanted to carry on to the next work and continue as I always had done, researching two or three areas at once, then publishing, then doing it again. I was eventually persuaded, partly by an argument that some of my ideas seem to have been misunderstood and partly because I mistakenly thought it would be a fairly easy thing to do. As it turned out I have benefitted from the process of looking through the old essays and thinking about what they had in common and how my ideas developed. Considering what to select forced me to think about why I thought the things I researched were important and how it all fits together. One important selection issue was that so much of my work was collaborative. My memories of working with Rosie Campbell, Sarah Childs, Marianne Githens, Marila Guadagnini, Jill Hills, Helen Margetts, Amy Mazur, Pippa Norris, Joyce Outshoorn, Vicky Randall, Diane Sainsbury, Birgit Sauer, Dorothy McBride and others are of very intensive theoretical discussions and interactive, iterative work on design as well as of shared field work and sometimes seemingly endless drafting and redrafting of the results. It is therefore almost impossible to separate out who contributed what to the publications that resulted. Thus I am especially grateful to my co-authors not only for allowing our joint works to be reproduced here, but also for making me think more clearly about various aspects of gender and politics.

Selection of articles

The essays reproduced in this volume address two related questions: does political science need feminism? And does feminism need political science? All the essays included here are based on theoretical understandings derived from comparative research, whether over time, space or practice. After quite a lot of looking through files, advice from colleagues and thinking about what I am proud of, what I may have changed my mind about and what I still want to do, I decided to organise this volume into four sections: Political Representation, Political Parties, Gender and Public Policy and Gendering the Political Science Agenda, and to include examples of writing on each theme. All are on gender with a mainly UK and/or European focus. All the work raises questions about

---

1.   By Dario Castiglione for ECPR Press. Dario has also commented on and made helpful suggestions for the structure of the volume and, after reading earlier drafts, for improving this and the concluding chapter. I am also grateful to the two anonymous readers who commented on my original proposal.

democratic inclusion and/or equality. I have also included discussions of the gender blindness of political science and the consequent feminist interventions. On the advice of the series editors and the reviewers of my original outline, I have concentrated on including only more theoretical and consciously reflective examples of my writing. These have the advantage of being shorter and more self-contained than my empirical work. But the reflection and theorisation took place in the context of some forty years of empirical study in which the operationalisation for research of feminist ideas about politics was a constant concern. For me the research process is always iterative, a constant interplay between ideas and practices, hence the separation of empirical and theoretical work is inevitably artificial.

Political Representation

The four articles in this section take up some of the key issues that arise from demands for the equal representation of women and men. The Insitute for Democracy and Electoral Assistance (IDEA) essay *Women in Parliament: Making a Difference* is practitioner directed. From a variety of sources, it assembles what we knew in the 1990s about what happened when women entered legislatures in order to offer advice and identify good practice about what they should do. This article makes use of the term 'critical mass' not as a mechanistically applied threshold, but to aid description of the changes we could see in legislatures as more women entered. The advice was 'learn the rules, use the rules, and change the rules'. It would not be so different now. Both the *Westminster Women* and *Political Representation* essays consider what our reasonable expectations of elected women representatives should be. The *Westminster Women* article (which has been widely misquoted) revisits the critical mass argument that women can make a difference only when a certain number of them are present in the context of what we knew in 2003 about the UK House of Commons. It reaffirms Drude Dahlerup's 1988 contention that numbers are only important insofar as they permit the critical acts that make a difference. *Political Representation* is a close exploration, using the Research Network on Gender and the State's (RNGS) cross national data set of what women legislators contribute to the politics of equality. Finally *Feminising British Politics* unpacks the (often hidden) case against women's political representation.

'Women in Parliament: Making a difference' (with A. Karam), in J. Ballington and A. Karam (eds) *Women in Parliament: Beyond numbers. A revised edition*, Stockholm, International IDEA, 1998, pp. 125–158.

'Westminster women' (with P. Norris), *Political Studies*, 2003, 51(1), pp. 84–102.

'Political Representation' (with M. Guadagnini), in D. E. McBride and A. G. Mazur (eds) *The Politics of State Feminism: Innovation in comparative research*, Philadelphia, PA, Temple University Press, 2010, pp. 164–193.

'Feminising British politics', *The Political Quarterly*, 2012, 83(4), pp. 697–702.

Political Parties

Every political scientist knows that in almost all, if not all democracies, it is political parties, not voters who decide who our representatives are. Nomination processes may be more or less transparent (almost always less), more or less regulated and more or less women friendly. These five essays trace my longstanding preoccupation with this issue, a preoccupation that began with research conducted with Pippa Norris at the end of the 1980s and the early 1990s.

'The Dynamics of Gender and Party', in J. Lovenduski and P. Norris (eds) *Gender and Party Politics*, London, Sage, 1993, pp. 1–15.

'Will quotas make Labour more woman-friendly?', *Renewal*, 1994, 2(1).

'Women's equality guarantees and the Conservative Party' (with S. Childs and R. Campbell) *Political Quarterly*, 2005, 77(1), pp.18–28.

'Obstacles to Feminizing Politics', Ch. 3, in *Feminizing Politics*, Cambridge, Polity Press, 2005, pp. 45–82.

'Male Dominance Broken' in D. Dahlerup and M. Leyenaar (eds) *Breaking Male Dominance in Old Democracies*, Oxford, Oxford University Press, pp. 72–96.

Gender and Public Policy

Public policy is a theme of most of my research and writing. The first two academic articles I published (with Paul Byrne at Loughborough University) were analyses of the UK Equal Opportunities Commission. My interest in gender equality policy, broadly defined, informs everything else I have done and is reflected in the above listed articles about political representation and party candidate selection as well as the many years spent working on the RNGS research. The four essays here cover other issues and reflect different ways of thinking about the gendered aspects of policy, and especially how to marry political science and feminist approaches to the gendered essence of so much of public policy.

'Abortion and the Political System' (with J. Outshoorn), in J. Lovenduski and J. Outshoorn (eds) *The New Politics of Abortion*, London, Sage, 1986, pp. 1–4.

'Sexing London: the gender mix of urban policy actors' (with S. Abrar and H. Margetts), *International Political Science Review*, 1998, 19(2), pp. 147–171.

Selection from 'Feminism, Violence and Men' in J. Lovenduski and V. Randall (eds) *Contemporary Feminist Politics*, Oxford, Oxford University Press, 1993, pp. 305–351.

'Feminist ideas and domestic policy change' (with S. Abrar and H. Margetts), *Political Studies*, 2000, 48(2), pp. 239–262.

Gendering the Political Science Agenda

Both these essays were commissioned by the volume or series editors. Dale Spender asked me to write the political science contribution to *Men's Studies Modified*, a cross-disciplinary view of what political science and feminism had to offer each other. Nearly twenty years later, Nelson Polsby asked me to write a state of the field essay about gender for his *Annual Review of Political Science*. I am grateful to both of them as I never otherwise would have done it! Yet the ideas in these two essays set the terms of my research agenda for the subsequent decades and clarified my thinking on a number of disciplinary issues, forcing me to think about developments in both gender analysis and political science and, I hope, helped me to acquire a voice of my own.

'Toward the Emasculation of Political Science', in D. Spender (ed.), *Men's Studies Modified: The impact of feminism on the academic disciplines*, Oxford, Pergamon, 1981, pp. 83–98.

'Gendering research in political science', *Annual Review of Political Science*, 1998, Vol. 1, pp. 333–56.

PART 1

POLITICAL REPRESENTATION

Chapter One

Women in Parliament: Making a Difference*

with Azza Karam

Although women remain significantly under-represented in today's parliaments, they are now looking beyond the numbers to focus on what they can actually do while in parliament — how they can make an impact, whatever their numbers may be. They are learning the rules of the game and using this knowledge and understanding to promote women's issues and concerns from inside the world's legislatures. In so doing, they are not only increasing the chances of their own success, but they are also paving the way for a new generation of women to enter the legislative process. How can women maximise their impact on the political process through parliament? What strategies are most useful in increasing their effectiveness? What lessons can women MPs share with those aspiring to enter the field? In what ways have women impacted on political processes? This is our focus in this chapter, as we move from the road to parliament to making inroads in parliament.

Making Inroads in Parliament

In the Beijing Platform for Action (United Nations 1995), more than 180 governments agreed that 'Achieving the goal of equal participation of women and men in decision-making will provide a balance that...is needed...to strengthen democracy and promote its proper functioning'. When women in different parts of the world struggled to win the right to vote, they expected that this would inevitably lead to greater women's representation. Their expectations were not always met, as chapters in this volume have illustrated [these refer to the original volume]. Instead, women embarked on another long and difficult struggle to actually get women elected to parliament. Part of this effort involves convincing women voters to support women as their representatives. In most countries, much of the work centres on political parties, the typical channels of entry to national legislatures. Women inside and outside political parties organise and mobilise themselves to change long-established party methods of political recruitment.

Once women enter parliament, their struggle is far from over. In parliament, women enter a male domain. Parliaments were established, organised and dominated by men, acting in their own interest and establishing procedures for

---

*   'Women in Parliament: Making a difference' (with A. Karam), in J. Ballington and A. Karam (eds) *Women in Parliament: Beyond numbers. A revised edition*, Stockholm, International IDEA, 1998, pp. 125-158.

their own convenience. There was no deliberate conspiracy to exclude women. It was, in most cases, not even an issue. Most long-established parliaments were a product of political processes that were male-dominated or exclusively male. Subsequent legislatures are, for the most part, modelled on these established assemblies. Inevitably, these male-dominated organisations reflect certain male biases, the precise kind varying by country and culture.

Until recently, this 'institutional masculinity' has been an invisible characteristic of legislatures; it is embedded, pervasive and taken for granted. Only recently have legislatures' masculine biases come under scrutiny. Indeed, in most countries, the political role of women in legislatures became a public issue only in the second half of the twentieth century.

In 2005, women constitute 16 per cent of members of parliaments (MPs) worldwide. In the Nordic countries, their numbers are highest at 40 per cent, while in the Arab states their representation (as of January 2005) was only 6.5 per cent (Inter-Parliamentary Union 2005).

As with previous efforts to try to get women elected to parliament, today women inside parliament are organising, mobilising, motivating and advancing women from inside the world's legislatures. They are devising strategies and taking action to promote issues relevant to women and facilitate changes in legislation.

The actual impact women parliamentarians can make will depend on a number of variables that vary from country to country. These include the economic and political context in which the assembly functions, the background, experience and number of the women who are in parliament, and the rules of the parliamentary process. Each of these factors has a significant bearing on the extent to which women MPs can make a difference once elected. Because these factors vary significantly from country to country, it is difficult to make generalisations that are universally relevant regarding how women MPs can maximise their impact.

In addition, there is relatively little research and information available on what sort of impact women have made. Underscoring the need for more knowledge and understanding in this particular field of women and decision-making, the United Nations' Beijing Platform for Action, together with the Commission on the Status of Women (CSW), call for more documentation on 'women making a difference' in politics.[1] Extrapolating from what is available in this field and on the basis of interviews and discussions with women MPs around the world, we have identified some of the strategies and mechanisms women are using and can use to impact on the process. We have formulated a strategy, what we refer to as the 'rules strategy', to organize and present these ideas. The case studies that follow illustrate some of these strategies in action.

Presence

The extent of women's impact will depend very much on the number of women in parliament who are motivated to represent women's issues and concerns.

Feminists often argue that pioneer women parliamentarians became surrogate men — that they were socialised into the legislature and became indistinguishable from the men they replaced. We doubt this. Men are known to behave differently when women are absent. Because it upsets gender boundaries, the presence of even one woman will alter male behaviour; the presence of several women will alter it even further. West European experience shows that where women MPs have a mission to effect change even small numbers can produce significant results.

While the presence of even one woman can make a difference, it is most likely that long-term significant change will only be realised when there is a substantial number of women in parliament who are motivated to represent women's concerns. Buoyed by their colleagues, women MPs may then elicit the active partnership of their male counterparts. However, change does not simply result from numbers; rather it is a complex process of overcoming resistance to women in which presence is only one part of the necessary mixture. According to Drude Dahlerup, the test that a critical mass of women is present is the acceleration of the development of women's representation through acts that improve the situation for themselves and for women in general. These actions are critical acts of empowerment.

Once present in larger numbers, and willing to act together on behalf of women, women MPs can overcome the 'tokenism' phenomenon, that is, move beyond the perception they are subjected to, as well as be enabled to form interactive and strategic partnerships both within the legislatures and outside them. Within the legislatures, a critical mass makes it easier to cross party lines, and particularly to reach out to their male colleagues — the other half of an important equation for social transformation. Their presence as a critical mass also multiplies the possibilities and extent of their outreach to civil society organisations, which, in turn, enhances the momentum required in impacting on the legislature and its policies. In her studies of women MPs in Scandinavia and elsewhere, Dahlerup found that women politicians worked to recruit other women and developed new legislation and institutions to benefit women. As their numbers grew it became easier to be a woman politician and public perceptions of women politicians changed (Drude 1988; *see* also Lovenduski 2005). In 2005, Mercedes Mateo Diaz found in her study of Belgian and Swedish legislators that as the presence of women MPs increases so does their social representativeness (Mercedes 2005). When the numbers of women were low, at around 15 to 20 per cent, women MPs were less like women voters than male MPs are like male voters. The differences are due to distortions caused by recruitment procedures that were designed to select suitable men. To succeed in such processes women have to display 'male qualifications'; hence they are more likely to have characteristics associated with male MPs. For example, they may have careers in male-dominated professions such as business or law. To display such characteristics they may have sacrificed domestic lives, and hence are less likely than men or women in the general population to have children. However, as the proportion of women in parliament nears parity it becomes more likely that they will reflect the social characteristics of women in the electorate.

Rules Strategy

In this chapter, we have formulated a strategy to help maximise women's impact on the legislative process. The full development of this rules strategy requires a critical mass of women working on and promoting women's concerns.

Simply put, the strategy consists of three parts: **learning the rules, using the rules and changing the rules.** By rules we mean the customs, conventions, informal practices and specific regulations that govern the way a legislature functions. These include law-making processes, the division of labour in the assembly, hierarchy structures, ceremonies, disciplines, traditions, habits and the norms of the assembly including its internal functioning and its relationship to other parts of the government and to the nation it has been elected to serve.

This strategy of learning, using and changing the rules is based on the belief that there is a need for change and that an objective in electing women MPs is to secure change. There are essentially four types of change that will make a difference to women. They can be categorised as institutional/procedural change, representation change, influence on output and discourse.

1. **Institutional/procedural change** refers to measures that alter the nature of the institution to make it more 'woman-friendly'. Greater gender awareness should be accompanied by procedural changes designed to accommodate women members. This is a product of an increased sensitivity to the fact that class, age, ethnicity, race, physical ability, sexuality, parenting and life stage have a determining effect on women's lives, in much the same way as they do on men's lives.

2. **Representation change** involves specific actions to secure women's continued and enhanced access to the legislature. These include the encouragement of women candidates; conscious use of role model capacities when applicable; the promotion of sex equality legislation, or parity or equality regulations; and appropriate changes in electoral and campaigning laws. Representation change also includes actions in parliament that are designed to place women in important parliamentary positions and to secure their presence in government. It must also include changes in political parties that bring more women to legislatures. Women MPs often use the power their representative status gives them to support the improvement of political opportunities for women in their parties, as well as organising to support women for higher office. Parliaments constitute a crucial pool of recruitment to higher office.

3. **Impact/Influence on output** refers specifically to the 'feminisation' or regendering of legislation and other policy outputs, that is the extent to which laws and policies have been altered or influenced in women's favour. This includes both putting women's issues on the agenda and ensuring that all legislation is woman-friendly and gender-sensitive.

4. **Discourse change** involves changes both inside and outside parliament. Not only should efforts be made to alter parliamentary language so that women's perspectives are actively sought and normalised; it is also necessary to make use of the parliamentary platform to alter public attitudes and to change the discourse of politics so that a political woman becomes as frequent a fixture of the political space as a man. Such 'speaking out the window' uses the parliamentary opportunity of greater access to the mass media and to the general public to raise awareness of women's issues and of women's political capacities in public debate.

Table 1.1: Four Areas of Change that will Impact on Women's Participation

Institutional/Procedural	Making parliament more 'woman-friendly' through measures to promote greater gender awareness.
Representation	Securing women's continued and enhanced access to parliament, by encouraging women candidates, changing electoral and campaigning laws and promoting sex equality legislation.
Impact/Influence on Output	'Feminising' legislation, by making sure it takes into account women's concerns.
Discourse	Altering parliamentary language so that women's perspectives are sought and normalised, and encouraging a change in public attitudes towards women.

Table 1.2: Women: Making Impact through Parliament

	Institutional/Procedural and Representation	**Influence on Output and Discourse**
Learning the Rules	Participate in training and orientation exercises on internal parliamentary codes of conduct (e.g. how to ask for the floor); develop public speaking and effective communication; and relate to and lobby male colleagues. Network with women's organisations. Mentoring and shadowing by more senior MPs. Understand and handle the media.	Distinguish between women's perspectives, women-specific needs, and gender issues. Caucus with media, national and international organisations. Draw attention to sexist discourse. Establish a presence within different committees (e.g. budget, defence, foreign affairs). Clarify the value and importance of 'soft' committees.

Table 1.2 (Continued): Women: Making Impact through Parliament

	Institutional/Procedural and Representation	Influence on Output and Discourse
Using the Rules	Make a point of nominating and voting for women in internal elections and within parties. Draw attention to absence of women in key positions. Invest in committee work. Push for and establish government equal opportunity positions and women's ministries. Campaign to expand existing structures to include women's concerns. Set up networks to train in more convincing and less adversarial types of debate.	Influence parliamentary agendas: introduce women-sensitive measures (e.g. changes in parliamentary work schedules to suit working mothers). Establish public enquiries on women's issues and use findings to place issues on government agendas and within legislative programmes. Speak for, co-sponsor and sponsor bills. Seek partnership with male colleagues. Make public issue out of certain concerns by cooperating with the media (e.g. on ways of referring to women in parliament, sexual harassment issues). Link gender inequalities to other inequalities. Form alliances with other excluded groups to seek representation. Use the media as a part of the effective outreach strategy to widen women MPs' constituencies and public support bases.
Changing the Rules	Change candidate selection rules for the entire party, especially for leadership positions. Introduce quota systems on certain committees or issue of proportionality for men/women representation. Establish a women's whip. Establish gender equality committees. Establish national machinery to monitor implementation and ensure accountability; institutionalise regular debates on progress into the parliamentary timetable. Establish mechanisms to encourage female speakers (e.g. giving them priority over male colleagues). Participate in institutional and procedural reform and modernisation processes to ensure the resulting changes are women-friendly.	Encourage the provision of financial incentives to programmes/projects designed to facilitate women's decision-making endeavours (e.g. for leadership-training schools, increasing government subsidies to political parties with more women in leadership positions/ candidates; introducing a specific women's budget earmarked for enhancing women's decision making). Cooperate with the women's movement and the media to change the image of women as 'only' housewives, to portray them as effective and efficient politicians and to normalise the image of a woman politician. Be proud of identity as a woman, instead of attempting to imitate men and hide or deny womanhood. Expand legislation to include emerging issues of importance to women (e.g. conflict resolution and peace-making, human rights, special women's budgets).

Learning the Rules

Legislatures debate policies, make laws, examine their implementation and effects, provide a recruitment pool for government and scrutinise the activities of government. Most legislatures have a budgetary function; they are responsible for both the formal allocation of the budget and auditing government spending. They are organised into front and back benches, government and opposition, and functional and procedural committees. Through such structures, debate, monitoring, interrogation and interpolation are organised. MPs tend to specialise in particular issue areas and make their parliamentary reputations on the basis of their performance in the various structures and processes of the legislatures.

For women to be effective parliamentarians, they must clearly understand the functions of the legislature and they must learn the rules of the game — both the written and unwritten codes, and the procedures and mechanisms for getting things done in parliament. They must first learn the internal practices of parliament in order to equip themselves to utilise these rules better and to devise effective strategies to change the rules to advance women's interests and goals. These ideas are elaborated below, grouped under each of the four main areas of change, namely institutional/ procedural, representation, influence on output and discourse. In the margins, to facilitate easy access and readability, we highlight some of the specific strategies that we suggest within each area.

Institutional/Procedural

The first step is for women MPs to understand how the legislature works in order to be able to use this knowledge to operate more effectively within the legislature. MPs can acquire this knowledge in a variety of ways, including specific training and orientation programmes as well as more general socialisation processes. For example, it is common for legislative leaders and other officials to offer orientation to new members on how the assembly works. Often, political parties also provide such training.

Training by political parties is particularly useful since it offers insight into how the MP's party understands the procedures and how the party itself fits into the procedures. Since the organisation of legislative work often depends on party composition, parties have a significant influence on procedures. In some parts of the world political parties offer special skills training especially for women, since they may be less experienced in legislative procedures than men. However, in many parts of the developing world most parties do not have the resources, or the willingness, to offer such training. In fact, as many of the case studies point out, very often party allegiance can handicap the development of political discourse in general and of any assistance to women MPs in particular. Political parties in some of the Arab and Latin American countries, for example, do not allow for any structural improvements and still operate on the assumption that women's perspectives and women's issues do not deserve any specific priority. This has repercussions within parties both in and out of the legislature.

Networking is a crucial training and socialisation mechanism for women MPs. Networking provides quick access to knowledge that may otherwise take years of experience to acquire and enables women MPs to come together to discuss their concerns and share their knowledge and expertise, thus greatly enhancing their potential for effectiveness. Such networking takes place both within and (less frequently) across party lines. Cross-party alliances of women MPs have been successful in a number of countries including Sweden, France, the Netherlands, South Africa, Croatia and Egypt. The issues are as diverse as rape laws, electoral reform, institutional reform, personal status and other country-specific issues (such as women's rights to apply for passports without their husbands' permission in Egypt, and social, political and economic rights for Dalits (or scheduled castes, formerly called 'untouchables') in India). Also noteworthy is the formation of 'support groups' composed of women professionals and MPs, a phenomenon especially apparent in European countries. In the words of one Finnish MP, Riitta Uosukainen, 'The fact that these women are able to get together across party lines, across professional areas and support each other not only personally, but also seek to do so professionally, is invaluable'. Mentoring (i.e. supervising, befriending and giving advice and guidance) by more experienced women MPs is another important way of providing special training for women MPs. In the Netherlands, for example, a system of 'shadowing' was developed whereby women who were hesitant to be nominated for elected office were assisted by elected members to gain confidence.

One global structure that seeks to provide a space for women to exchange ideas and strategies across nations is the Inter-Parliamentary Union (*see* the case study that follows this chapter) [this refers to the original volume]. This body works to enhance the visibility and effectiveness of women locally, regionally and internationally and also provides women MPs with mentoring, capacity-building support and information.

In addition to programmes specially geared for women, orientation exercises involving both men and women are important. In joint training sessions, women are encouraged to address their areas of interest and to network with male counterparts, as well as to learn how to break through established 'codes of conduct'. At the same time, male MPs are made aware of women's issues and the importance of enabling women MPs to act effectively in the legislature. The latter in particular is an important step in overcoming the sense of threat that many male deputies feel vis-à-vis women colleagues, since it provides an opportunity not only to raise awareness of gender issues, but to indicate the extent to which they are interlinked with most other social, economic and political concerns. Thus training and orientation of male parliamentarians play an important role in the mainstreaming of women's issues and perspectives.

In addition to information about both the written and the unwritten rules and procedures of parliament, women may also find training in voice and image projection and public speaking particularly helpful. Many women have difficulty speaking authoritatively and arguing convincingly, and some find it difficult to make themselves heard in large legislative chambers. New entrants, in particular in developing democracies, confess that they find it difficult to be given the opportunity to speak and to know the ins and outs of parliamentary speaking procedures. The effectiveness of former actress Glenda Jackson in the British House of Commons, for example, proves that a trained woman's voice can have as much impact as a man's.

Some women MPs in established democracies have also organised media training sessions. This involves, among other things, seminars and workshops where MPs are informed about 'media-speak' (i.e. what kind of information the media are interested in and how best to deliver it) and advised on how to network with media personalities and on which ones are more sympathetic to women's issues.

Representation

Institutional rules, customs and procedures (in addition to party politics) are key to determining the legislative positions and functions, such as committee assignments and participation in debates on the floor. Recruitment to these important positions may depend on any one or a combination of factors including party position, seniority, faction, ability, support for the government, national or local profile and issue expertise. While the appropriate strategy will depend to some extent on the number of women in the legislature, at a minimum women should identify key interests, positions and functions and strategise about ways to get women into the relevant forum. If existing channels are not open to promoting women into key positions, new avenues should be developed.

Gender Equality Committees

In some countries, such avenues could be parliamentary or governmental women's committees or broader equality committees that include women's rights in their mandate. Formal and informal gender equality committees were successfully established in Sub-Saharan Africa and the Netherlands, while the assemblies of Scotland and Wales have broadly-based equality committees which, under pressure from women representatives, take a close interest in equality. Also effective are committees of women legislators such as those found in New Zealand, Australia and the USA. In other cases, nationwide umbrella organisations (non-governmental) or strong grass-roots organisations can act as catalysts to get women into key areas. Further avenues could be opened through training and educational programmes, or through pressure for representation by the media. International pressure could also be used to encourage governments to include women at all levels of power and decision making.[2] Knowledge about these positions and about ways to get women in can be shared by mentoring, caucusing and networking both among women and with male colleagues.

Women in key positions not only enhance their own ability to make an impact; they also facilitate opportunities for other women to speak out. For example, a study of the Colorado State legislature measured differences in the speaking behaviour of members of legislative committees by sex, seniority, interest and party. It was found that women did better at controlling the dialogue and making themselves heard when other women were present, visible (sitting where they could be seen) and in positions of authority (Kathlene 1995). This research also showed that male dominance of conversation, discussion and meetings enhanced men's power and undermined that of some women even where the formal positions of men and women legislators were equal.

One way of building women's careers and thus their advancement into key positions is by learning how to use the media to increase the visibility and confidence of women parliamentarians. Since women employed in the media have their own problems of self-establishment and advancement they may be sympathetic to MPs interested in women's concerns. In fact, one of the key problems in most media is the lack of women in decision-making posts, which effectively means that decisions concerning editorial content and production issues are largely controlled by men. As the presence of women in the media expands, so do the possibilities for women MPs and politicians, journalists and other broadcasters and writers to network on the basis of common interests and concerns.

Typically, women's interests have led them to what is still perceived as the less prestigious (and possibly less powerful) social policy areas of specialisation, that is, committee assignments such as education, health and family affairs. Many women MPs believe it is necessary to establish women's presence in traditionally influential sites within parliaments, such as finance, defence and foreign affairs. Others argue that the distinction itself cannot be justified. European political scientists have made the important point that describing social issues as 'soft' caricaturises them as unimportant and ignores the facts that these areas, in which European women are most active, account for the largest share of public expenditure — education, health and social services at local and regional levels. Women choose these areas because they prefer them and they accept making the very difficult decisions such as whether to prioritise care of the elderly or day care (Raaum 1995). The traditional distinction between 'hard' and 'soft' issues is old-fashioned and inaccurate and should be contested by women representatives. Ideally a twofold strategy must be developed: on the one hand, the importance of such areas needs to be continually stressed; on the other hand, simultaneous efforts should be made to ensure women's active participation in all policy areas.

Impact/Influence on Output

To discuss the impact of women representatives it is useful to make a distinction between women's issues and women's perspectives. Women's issues are issues that mainly affect women, either due to largely physical concerns (e.g. breast cancer screening, reproductive rights) or for social reasons (e.g. sex equality or childcare policy). Women's perspectives are women's views on all political concerns. Some research indicates that, although broadly the same issues are significant for both sexes, women's perspective on issues differs from that of men. For example, research carried out in Britain in 1996 showed that, although both women and men prioritised economic issues, women were more concerned about part time work, low pay and pension rights, while men were more concerned about unemployment.

MPs need to have knowledge and understanding of both women's issues and women's perspectives — if only, as most contributors to this volume [this refers to the original volume] have expressed, to see the other half of reality — in order to produce output that has a favourable impact on women. The kind of impact MPs will wish to have will inevitably vary by party. In her research on Sweden (in this volume) [this refers to the original volume] for instance, Lena Wängnerud reports that women representatives from different political parties tend to emphasise women's issues and concerns.

But the need for knowledge and information exists regardless of party perspective. Women MPs have successfully used various means of becoming informed about women's issues and perspectives. Most important in this regard is what contributors to this volume [this refers to the original volume] have repeatedly highlighted — maintaining close links with women's organisations of all kinds and drawing on their expertise and resources. Such linkages with women's movements also enhance the legitimacy of MPs and keep them in touch with changing, often varying, women's concerns and policy needs. European parliamentarians have made use of the goodwill and knowledge of academic experts to draft policies on such matters as domestic violence, female bondage, trafficking in women, care of children and the aged, pensions and women's health issues. Research on policy issues is a major political tool and can be gathered and used by MPs by participating in conferences organised by women's organisations, experts and politicians and by caucusing with other MPs who have similar interests. Caucusing is part of both learning and using the rules. MPs interested in a particular issue, for example employment or women's health, might meet to identify important upcoming votes and committee discussions and decide on tactics and strategies to influence the outcome. Another strategy is to facilitate the access of women voters to their legislators. In Scotland a crèche was established for visitors to the assembly to ensure that those with childcare responsibilities (usually women) can seek out and meet their representatives.

Discourse

Parliaments have their own distinct language, a product both of their specialised tasks and functions and of their culture and their traditional male membership. In the United Kingdom (UK), for example, the House of Commons had a discourse characterised by a formal set of titles, modes of address and rules of debate, as well as a barracking, sexist and scatological 'humour', from many years of male domination, that women MPs found offensive, especially when it was used on them. Familiarity with speaking and debating techniques can help to curtail such 'yahoo' heckling. British women have successfully used the media to draw attention to the sexism in the House of Commons by revealing these practices to women in the media and to other journalists eager to criticise ill-behaved MPs.

The result has been a series of press and broadcasting items about the childish and sexist behaviour of male MPs. The public, previously unaware of this, disapproved of their MPs' behaviour.

Using the Rules

By learning how to use the rules, women can seize opportunities to participate on key committees and positions, make themselves heard in discussions and debates, and fully utilise their skills and abilities.

Gaining familiarity with the rules is the first part of a longer-term process to enhance women's position and to highlight women's issues and perspectives. The next step is to learn how to use the rules for maximum impact. One of the problems many women parliamentarians face is that they are not allocated time in discussions and debates and they find it difficult to be selected for participation on key committees and in key positions. Thus they are not able to fully utilise their skills and abilities and their contribution cannot be accurately assessed. By learning how to use the rules, together with other women deputies and the media, women can break this vicious circle. Many of the tactics for using the rules, discussed below, can be shared across national boundaries.

Intergovernmental organisations such as the Council of Europe, the Commonwealth Secretariat, the European Union and the United Nations and international non-governmental organisations (NGOs) can and do play a vital role in helping women learn how to use the rules by facilitating the sharing of information. Their meetings bring together experts and politicians to network and exchange ideas and their publications make these discussions about women's needs, strategies and achievements available to a wider audience.

Institutional/Procedural

Formal and informal parliamentary roles are often allocated by established rules and procedures. There is, nevertheless, some room for influence and intervention which women should maximise. For example, women MPs should make a point of nominating and voting for women in internal elections, of suggesting women's names for informal positions, and of drawing attention to the absence or relative absence of women in key positions. Particular attention should be given to opportunities available in committee work, as there is considerable evidence from the long-established democracies that women do better in committee work than in debating chambers. Having said this, women should not abandon debating chambers since this is where parliamentary reputations are often made and where the media often direct their sustained attention. The skill of debating in general is a particularly important one and can be encouraged and sponsored through parliamentary networks linked up to schools, that is, through the curricula, as well as through leadership institutions. Women's parliamentary networks can also play a crucial role in supporting women speakers and in changing to less adversarial styles of debate.

Since government careers tend to follow from legislative careers, the advancement of women through the range of committees and through the legislative hierarchy is an important component in their qualification for high office. Equal opportunity positions in government and ministries for women's affairs and their shadow counterparts in opposition parties are other positions that have been well used by women politicians to advance their interests and their careers.

For example, between 1992 and 1997 four Labour women MPs in the UK were shadow ministers for women. All four were appointed to important government positions (two at cabinet level) when Labour won the election in 1997. They proved reliable advocates of gender equality and were supporters of women's concerns in their departments. Their numbers expanded in 2001. This indicates (a) that such positions need not be a ghetto for women, but may instead be a means of advancement, and (b) that they can facilitate the mainstreaming of gender sensitivity across government.

Representation

Rules have been used to increase women's representation in a number of ways. In this area, a three-track strategy has proved effective:

- pressure political parties to ensure that women are nominated for winnable seats in the legislature;
- design procedural mechanisms to ensure the presence of women in the full range of parliamentary positions; and
- design legislation that creates new structures to ensure that women's interests are represented.

The expansion of political structures, whether by creating new ministries or expanding the size of the cabinet for instance, has proved a useful means of securing women's representation. Modernisation and reform of existing legislatures or the creation of new legislatures offers opportunities to secure or enhance women's representation. A good example is Scotland where feminists intervened in the process of constitutional change to secure a Scottish legislature in which women were fairly represented. Under the umbrella of the Scottish Women's Co-ordination Group they lobbied the Constitutional Convention and the political parties to gender the debate on devolution. They became involved in debates about institutional design and the recruitment of legislators. When the first Scottish Parliament was elected in 1999, 37 per cent of its members were women, as were 30 per cent of ministers, and 41 per cent of committee members, including six out of seventeen chairs. All the numbers increased in the subsequent election in 2003. However, constitutional change is an opportunity, not a guarantee, as experiences in Eastern and Central Europe and with the European Convention indicate (Lovenduski 2005: 85–88).

In Costa Rica, a practice that the vice-president should be a woman has been established. The experience of the Netherlands shows that the creation of parliamentary committees on women's issues is one way of making positions available for women. Such committees scrutinise all legislation for their gendered content and thereby aid the extension of women's agendas. They also enhance awareness of the gendered nature of many political issues. The committees feed into the legislative process and also play a part in generating public discussion on such issues.

Concern has been expressed by women deputies in many countries that such devices may serve only to separate and 'ghettoise' women's issues and the politicians who support them. Although 'ghettoisation' may be a risk in the short term, experience indicates that over time such work becomes accepted and, in fact, affirms and legitimises broader gender issues. Moreover women gain valuable experience by serving on women's committees, in reserved places and in women's ministries. They may then extend their influence by working with other committees on different issues, for example by monitoring the implementation of the Beijing Platform for Action or other international treaties. Women's committees need not be seen as permanent structures, but while in existence they can enable women to display their skills and thus serve as launching platforms for careers in other political areas. Moreover women who have experience of sex equality portfolios carry this increased awareness and knowledge of women's issues to other ministries, thus advancing the process of mainstreaming women's concerns (Skjeie 1991).

Impact/Influence on Output

Knowledge of the procedural rules has frequently been used to influence the parliamentary agenda by introducing women's concerns into otherwise gender-blind debates — forcing debates on issues such as reproductive rights, equal pay, childcare and child rights — as well as by proposing sex equality legislation and amendments. Parliamentarians have established public enquiries into women's status and condition, and then used the results to push through legislative programmes. Once the issues are on the agenda, the behaviour of other politicians changes. After all, it is more difficult politically to come out against equality for women than it is to prevent equality issues from getting onto the agenda in the first place. An example in the UK is the Sex Discrimination Candidates Act of 2002 which permits political parties to use affirmative action to increase the number of women MPs and candidates. The bill was passed with all-party support and almost no dissent because its opponents were silent, unwilling to oppose women's representation in public. For similar reasons many male opponents abstained from participating in the French *parité* debate in the National Assembly in 2000.

In some cases, activities such as co-sponsorship, speech-making and sponsorship of bills by women have been much more effective than their actual votes. One study looking at the support for women's issues in the French legislative structures found that women were more likely than men to co-sponsor feminist bills, to make speeches on behalf of feminist legislation and to sponsor feminist legislation. A study of early day motions, which are devices for drawing attention to issues in the UK House of Commons, found women

MPs much more active than their male colleagues in supporting women's concerns (Childs and Withey 2004).

There are many instances in some parts of the developing world, however, where women MPs shy away from any association with bills on women. This is largely due to their sense that such arguments would lack support and endorsement from their fellow colleagues and may contribute to their marginalisation, as well as to a certain stigma associated with being 'feminists'. This further underscores the need for mainstreaming women's concerns, or raising awareness about the interlinkage between women's issues and every other issue handled by parliament. Budget and economic interests, for example, are not and should not be seen as only male concerns since they affect everyone. Similarly, health, social welfare and education do not only affect women.

Discourse

In certain countries, cultural norms of equality between men and women, or discourse on rights, meritocracy and conventions about representation, may be avenues that can be used to alter parliamentary balances. For example, Danish women MPs have succeeded in altering the parliamentary discourse. Drude Dahlerup notes how, prior to the entry of significant numbers of women into the Scandinavian parliaments, most politicians did not have the vocabulary to speak about issues such as discrimination, inequality, sexual harassment or sexual violence. Most had problems even using the word for women and preferred to use euphemisms. Over time in the Nordic states the increased presence of women has altered the style of campaigning, bringing in expressions of warmth and compassion as well as references to the family (Karvonen *et al.* 1995). This does render campaigning less adversarial. In the Netherlands, study of legislative debates reveals how women's interventions have been associated with changing the way in which abortion policy is debated, notably its shift from a medical or religious issue to an issue of choice (Outschoorn 1986). Research from the UK shows that the interventions of women MPs are more likely than those of men to refer to examples of how policies and decisions affect individuals and families, while male MPs invoke abstract concepts such as citizens or constituents (Lovenduski 2005).

The participation of women politicians in major international conferences has also had an important effect on challenging public notions of what women can do. One example is the way in which perceptions about the women's movement in Egypt and in other Arab countries changed following the International Conference on Population and Development (ICPD) that was held in Cairo in September 1994. Prior to this conference, many Egyptian women MPs, and indeed the general public, had at best been ignorant of the women's movement and at worst been downright disdainful of its capabilities. Those involved in the women's movement held a similar view of women parliamentarians. The ICPD was an opportunity for women MPs to actually witness what women's NGOs had managed to accomplish and to network with them on issues of common interest. It also enabled the women's movement to realise that they could have potential allies in women MPs since they shared many interests and goals. Regardless of what may have actually happened later on, at least there was a perceptible change in awareness on the part of both the MPs and the women's organisations. Equally important was a shift in public awareness and perception of women as activists and as politicians. The ICPD and subsequent international networking opportunities demonstrated to the general public that women's issues (whether it was changes in family law, reproductive rights or female circumcision) were part of their general concerns and that, rather than a bunch of loose women clamouring for change, those articulating these concerns were capable and intelligent women who deserved to be listened to and taken seriously.

Changing the Rules

The presence of women and the introduction of women's concerns will inevitably challenge existing arrangements and procedures. At a minimum, parliamentary timetables, places of meeting, childcare provisions, working hours and travel arrangements may be changed to make them more suitable for women.

One of the most significant changes that we have noted is the networking of women across party lines. This underscores the now more frequent cross-party cooperation by women legislators found in the European Parliament, South Africa, the USA, the Netherlands, France, Belgium and Italy on issues such as women's representation policy, forced marriage, domestic violence, reproductive rights, rape and employment equality (Lovenduski *et al.* 2005).

Women's experiences in a variety of parliamentary roles will build up political capital which can be used to secure further advancement, to help change existing rules and structures, and to assist new generations of women politicians.

Institutional/Procedural

Changes in parliamentary structures and procedures might include the introduction of proportionality norms for men's and women's membership in committees, the establishment of women's whips (responsible for organising the parliamentary votes of women in a particular party) and formal or informal quotas for women in various legislative positions. Internal voluntary party quota systems have been used effectively in Germany at the local and national levels, and have been introduced in France by means of legislation. In countries where compulsory quotas are politically difficult, voluntary targets can be set. At their most effective such policies include deadlines and realistic timetables for implementation.

Mechanisms to monitor the implementation of quotas that are accountable to the assembly should be established. This ensures that regular discussions on progress are part of the parliamentary timetable. Setting up committees on women's issues and national women's policy agencies that are also accountable to parliament have similar effects. Accountability to parliament ensures that their work is scrutinised, debated and publicised, providing numerous additional opportunities for discussion of women's concerns. For example, the South African Government has implemented a national gender machinery which proposes changes in legislation and supervises and ensures implementation. The case of South Africa reveals how simultaneous functions, both inside and outside parliament, can operate: in South Africa a new constitution was drafted, a woman's empowerment programme was set up in consultation with women parliamentarians and an Office for the Status of Women was created to mainstream women's concerns and ensure follow-up. A Commission on Gender Equality was also established in 1997 to promote gender equality and to advise and make recommendations to the legislature about how proposed legislation affects gender equality and the status of women (*see* the case study) [this refers to the original volume]. An important challenge is to ensure that these institutional mechanisms maintain their links with grass-roots activists, so that MPs are aware of what takes place outside the parliamentary walls.

Changes in procedure can be effective in and of themselves and can also have a wider impact on society. One such practice is in place in the German Bundestag: when a woman raises her hand to speak in discussions she is automatically shifted to the top of the list of male speakers. This practice seeks to overcome women's diffidence about speaking in male-dominated groups by maximising their opportunities to participate. It has become so ingrained in MPs that they repeat the practice even when they are outside parliament.

More fundamental changes involve changing the way in which certain issues, namely those closer to women's concerns and in which women have an expertise (e.g. education, welfare policy, family policy), are viewed in the parliamentary hierarchy. As we have mentioned, the distinction between 'hard' and 'soft' issues is difficult to sustain and is likely to break down. This process will develop from increased interest in 'soft' issues by all politicians, as women deputies become more successful in pushing them up the parliamentary agenda. Agenda changes are closely related to output changes.

Representation

Networks of women MPs have been successful in changing candidate selection rules to assist women's access to political office. Special measures such as quotas or minimum proportion rules for both sexes on candidate lists, reserved places for women and earmarked public funds for political parties have been operationalised. Political parties have been at the centre of most of the effective strategies to enhance women's representative capacities. Parties have developed strategies to promote women internally into decision-making positions in the party organisation and externally into elected assemblies and public appointments. Generally they have been more radical, committed and imaginative in devising policies to bring women into internal party positions than to nominate women as candidates for elected office. Their most effective action has been the introduction of various kinds of quotas.

Quotas are, in most cases, temporary measures designed to overcome imbalances that exist between men and women. They are an effort to change the political equilibrium between women and men.[3]

Another important representation strategy is to expand definitions of representation to include all public decision-making bodies, and to campaign for women's inclusion in the senior civil service and the judiciary. Such campaigns have been undertaken in Austria, Finland, the Netherlands, the UK and elsewhere. A difficult but necessary further step will be the extension of such demands to the private sector, as has happened in Finland.

Impact/Influence on Output

One clear indication that women have influenced output is the fact that quotas exist for women in political parties and parliament. Output changes are inevitable as women become more and more effective in promoting women's issues and concerns. Once women's issues are raised and sustained on the agenda, they rapidly secure the interest of all politicians. This interest can apply to a wide host of issues — political, economic, social and even cultural.

Recent research indicates that the most effective way to influence output and promote women's equality is to provide financial incentives to programmes geared towards women. For example, to enhance the education of girls, the Indian Government pledged to match and double any contribution made to the building of girls' schools. The Dutch Government previously used the system of public funding of political parties to earmark special funding for the promotion of women candidates by all parties. South Africa introduced a women's budget to fund projects that cater to the particular needs and interests of women. Financial incentives may be targeted directly at women's representation by tying the public funding of political parties to their numbers of elected women legislators. This policy has been implemented in Italy, for elections to the European Parliament, and France, for elections to the National Assembly so that parties which do not nominate or return a certain number of women legislators forgo some of their public funding.

Discourse

The most important change affecting discourse has been the overturning of implicit rules limiting appropriate topics of debate to matters in the 'public' sphere. In cooperation with women's movements, parliamentarians in some countries have extended the agenda of legislatures to discussions of domestic violence, stalking, rape, forced marriage, female genital mutilation, consent in marriage and the rights of lesbian mothers.

Further change in the area of discourse can come about once women themselves become increasingly proud of their identities as women. Former member of the European Parliament (MEP) Hedy D'Ancona surveys some of the most influential women MEPs of the 1990s and argues that by not being shy of their 'womanhood', but rather being proud of their identity as women, they have enhanced their work, impact and performance (D'Ancona 1997). Women are often apologetic about rather than proud or assertive of their identity as women. A change in a woman politician's self-perception, Nadezhda Shvedova maintains remains key to changing public perception and reaction to women and their contributions.

A woman's sex identity and her 'outsider' status can even enhance electoral attractiveness, particularly in times of constitutional crisis. As relatively new political entrants, women are often not associated with the corrupt and autocratic practices of collapsing regimes. Instead they can become symbols of modernity, honesty, democracy and caring, all images that are invaluable to reform movements.

The process of increasing the proportion of women in legislatures is part of a larger phenomenon of changing political images so that politics starts to be regarded as a normal activity for women. To take hold, such an attitude shift requires significant reinforcement in the mass media, and support from within the women's movement.

Criteria for Measuring Success

'I am convinced that when we have established and are working with a system based on real equality, then the quality of women's participation will be raised.' *Birgitta Dahl, former Speaker of Parliament, Sweden*

To claim that women representatives make a difference in political processes, it is necessary to establish clear criteria to measure their impact. A fundamental component of such criteria is that women parliamentarians act, at least some of the time, in women's interests. In formulating such criteria, it should also be recognised that: (a) there are many, sometimes conflicting, women's interests to be represented; and (b) the very presence of women in a traditional male environment creates gender awareness and alters expectations.

As we have mentioned, what women can actually achieve will vary according to their numbers in parliament. Numbers form an important, necessary if not sufficient condition for sustained impact. It takes a substantial minority of women to ensure that critical acts of representation are undertaken. As the numbers of women grow we should expect increased participation by women in all aspects of parliamentary life, including interventions in debate, the proposing and sponsoring of legislation, access to parliamentary resources and occupancy of leading positions.

Another criterion for determining success is that women's impact must be detectable in legislation on women's issues. With women's growing effectiveness, and enhanced representation, all legislation will increasingly take women's perspectives into account as a matter of course. An especially telling indication of women's impact will be an increase both in men raising women's issues and in men's deferring to women's voices on all legislative debates which would exhibit a concern for women's perspectives.

An important facet of success will involve interaction between the different agents of change — governments, women MPs, women's organisations and other members of civil society, locally, regionally and internationally. It should always be remembered that partnership between women and men is a key ingredient in the process of change and impact. Many women MPs openly acknowledge that to attempt to work alone, without men, is not feasible.[4]

Strategies to Enhance Impact

The following are some of the main strategies to help women maximise their power and effectiveness as representatives.

1. **Raise awareness.** Campaigns with the media should focus public attention on the importance of balanced participation and representation of women and men. Political parties or women's organisations could be financed to mount such campaigns and related activities. NGOs interested in encouraging the participation of women in political life have often been active in awareness raising. To encourage such campaigns, women and men politicians must be proactive in identifying and establishing relations and promoting these issues with key members of civil society as well as with media producers and presenters. An example of this is the Movement for Equal Rights–Equal Responsibilities in Cyprus which aims to promote public awareness that women can be politicians.

2. **Work in partnership with men.** This entails designing programmes, whether inside or outside specific political forums, that take into account men's concerns and perspectives with respect to solidarity with women politicians. This idea is now gaining credibility with the growing realisation that women need the support of their male colleagues, partners and electorate to enhance the effectiveness of their strategies and increase the value of their social and political message.

3. **Enlarge the pool of eligible, aspirant women.** This means enhancing women's interest in becoming politicians as well as increasing their involvement in politics. Eligibility for and involvement in politics are partly a matter of access to general resources such as education, income and time, and partly a matter of specific resources such as knowledge and information about politics and political experience. Policies to enhance women's access to higher education, to paid employment and to various social and economic organisations provide a context for political participation that is increasingly hospitable to women. However, even where they lack adequate resources to participate politically, women are devising creative strategies to mobilise resources that would facilitate their access. For example, in India some women draw upon transitional networks of extended family, neighbourhood links and other 'women-centred' spheres to enable them to gather the resources they may require.

4. **Take positive action.** Quotas have been particularly effective in increasing women's presence in legislatures. Both incremental and 'fast-track' models have been used effectively. An example of the incremental model is Sweden, where women used several means to press their parties to nominate women candidates and place them in favourable positions on party lists. One way was to simply put forward women's names, a tactic that was very important in the early stages. They also conducted campaigns to promote women candidates and issued proposals to get women into better positions on party lists. Finally, they acted as watchdogs and protested whenever reversals occurred. This process of securing substantial increases in women's electoral fortunes was achieved without recourse to formal compulsory quotas. Recommendations, arguments and the threat to press for quotas succeeded in setting targets requiring women to get 40 per cent of the nominations. Once these targets were set, considerable progress was achieved (Sainsbury 1993). Fast-track models have been more commonly used in transitional or democratising countries.

5. **Amend laws to allow positive discrimination.** Such practices were once rare in politics. In the past governments did not use the law to compel parties to promote women, not least because such policies often ran against other legal principles. But this is an area of change as governments have legislated to compel (Belgium), to provide incentives (France, Italy) or to permit (the UK) measures to guarantee better representation of women legislators. Moreover, some countries have introduced laws requiring that women hold a certain proportion of seats on government-appointed bodies. Such laws were introduced in Denmark in 1985, Finland in 1987, Sweden in 1987, Norway in the 1980s, the Netherlands in 1992 and Germany in 1994. Published statistics in these countries indicate that women's participation in such bodies has risen steadily since. Governments can also use incentives. This is particularly easy where there is state funding of political parties. For example, the Dutch Government was able to make financial support for political parties dependent on their efforts to increase the proportion of women in their electoral bodies.

6. **Raise the general standard of living and access to resources of all women.** The high achievements of Scandinavian women stem from a combination of government policy, party initiative and demographic changes. The remarkable position of women in Scandinavian politics rests on social/demographic foundations involving considerable changes in the structure of women's family, economic and social lives. These are probably irreversible. The policies on equality of representation have included government equality reforms operating in conjunction with the influence of the women's movement, functioning both autonomously and through the political parties. To some extent there is feedback between demographic and political change as policies have included explicit attempts to change demographics and the gendered division of labour both in the family and in paid employment.

7. **Build and maintain links with women's organisations and civil society institutions as a whole.** The maintenance of ties to the women's movement is crucial both for their support and for information on issues; similarly, the women's movement needs bases in political parties and in the legislature.

8. **Caucus and network.** This allows women MPs to share information, ideas, resources and support. Networks may be party-based, cross-party (very rare), local, regional and international. Meetings, conferences, seminars, newsletters and electronic mail links are useful networking devices. Consultations with women's organisations and research gauging the needs of women (demand) and their practical constraints (supply) enable women MPs to target their efforts to activities that will be most useful and effective. In this regard, training on the use of information and communication technology, and eventually also on an introduction to and efficiency in emerging e-government practices, will become increasingly necessary to place women firmly at the cutting edge of governance as a whole.

9. **Use the mass media effectively.** Women MPs must use the mass media, particularly the resources offered by women broadcasters, editors and journalists, to communicate their concerns and highlight relevant issues. As well as enhancing the image of women MPs and promoting their political ideas, the mass media are instrumental in educating and mobilising voters, particularly in rural areas — an important concern particularly in developing countries where women, with limited resources, may have difficulty reaching out to these voters.

10. **Establish women's committees** and other machinery accountable to the legislature. This provides opportunities for women deputies to gain experience and for women's issues and perspectives to be debated and publicised.

11. **Collect, monitor and disseminate statistics and facts about women's political participation and representation.** This enables women's advocates in parliament to analyse the position of women in decision making and to define problems, devise appropriate solutions and seek political support for their preferred solutions. In particular, a collation of data on how women MPs have actually managed to make a difference through their legislatures is an ongoing need.

12. **Mainstream gender issues.** Ensure that gender issues are integrated within different political, social and economic concerns, in order to reveal the interdependence and linkages with other issue areas.

The ultimate objective of enhancing the quality of women's political participation is a goal that must be worked towards constantly. In much the same way as men's political input is in constant need of improvement, women should not be complacent about their contributions to the political process; nor should they take whatever gains are achieved for granted. Political participation is a process that is evolving and developing. The actors involved in this process should be prepared always to strive to keep ahead of the changes. The women and men involved in this process should work together to be agents of change, constantly aware that obstacles are but means to realise new and evolving strategies. Women and men politicians have achieved a great deal in the area of women's participation. Politicians of both sexes have contributed to advancing women's political participation in general and within legislative structures in particular. Although the road ahead is long, the lessons learned from the accumulation of experiences can, and will, significantly illuminate and smooth the many paths ahead.

Notes

1. Excerpted from the moderator's summary published as UN document ECN.6/1997/lL.2/ Add.2.
2. *See* also chapter 4 on how quotas can help this process [this refers to the original volume].
3. The different types of quotas, and their consequences, are detailed by Drude Dahlerup in chapter 4 [this refers to the original volume].
4. *See* the Inter-Parliamentary Union's references to this in the case study that follows [this refers to the original volume].

References

Childs, S. and Withey, J. (2004) 'Women Representatives Acting for Women: Sex Equality and the Signing of Early Day Motions in the 1997 Parliament', *Political Studies*, 52 (3): 552–564.

Dahlerup, D. (1988) 'From a Small to a Large Minority: Theory of Critical Mass', *Scandinavian Political Studies*, 11 (4): 275–298.

D'Ancona, H. (1997) 'Politieke diva's rekenen af met de haantjestcultuur in Brussel' [Political divas reckon with the working culture of Brussels], Opzij, December.

Inter-Parliamentary Union, 2005. 'Women in National Parliaments: Situation as of 31 July 2005', http://www.ipu.org/wmn-e/world.htm.

Karvonen, L., Djupsund, G. and Carlson, T. (1995) 'Political Language', in L. Karvonen and P. Selle (eds) *Women in Nordic Politics: Closing the Gap*, London: Dartmouth Press, pp. 343–379.

Kathlene, L. (1995) 'Position Power versus Gender Power: Who Holds the Floor?', in G. L. Duerst-Lahti and R. M. Kelly (eds) *Gender Power, Leadership and Governance*, Ann Arbor, Michigan: University of Michigan Press, pp. 167–194.

Lovenduski, J. (2005) *Feminizing Politics*, Oxford: Polity Press.

Lovenduski, J., Baudino, C., Guadagnini, M., Meier, P. and Sainsbury, D. (eds) (2005) *State Feminism and Political Representation*, Cambridge: Cambridge University Press.

Mateo Diaz, M. (2005) Representing Women? Female Legislators in West European Parliaments, Colchester: ECPR Press.

Outschoorn, J. (1986) 'Women in Nordic Politics. The Rules of the Game: Abortion Politics in the Netherlands', in J. Lovenduski and J. Outschoorn (eds) *The New Politics of Abortion*, London: Sage, pp. 5–26.

Raaum, N. C. (1995) 'The Political Representation of Women: A Birds Eye View', in L. Karvonen and Per Selle (eds) *Women in Nordic Politics*, pp. 25–55.

Sainsbury, D. (1993) 'The Politics of Increased Women's Representation: The Swedish Case', in J. Lovenduski and P. Norris (eds) *Gender and Party Politics*, London: Sage, pp. 263–290.

Skjeie, H. (1991) 'The Rhetoric of Difference: On Women's Inclusion in Political Elites', *Politics and Society*, 19 (2): 233–263.

United Nations, 1995. 'The Beijing Platform for Action: Women in Decision Making', para. 181, available at http://www.un.org/womenwatch/daw/beijing/platform/decision.htm.

Chapter Two

Westminster Women: The Politics of Presence*

with Pippa Norris

The rising tide of women in elected office has raised expectations about their role as political leaders. Some hope, and others fear, that this development could alter the predominant political culture, the policy agenda, and the representation of women's interests in public life. This growth has occurred in many democracies and it is exemplified by dramatic developments at Westminster where the June 1997 election saw the entry of 120 women members into the UK House of Commons (18 per cent), double the number elected in 1992. This trend forms part of a larger phenomenon evident in the United Kingdom during the late-1990s where growing numbers of women entered other legislative bodies, thereby becoming 37 per cent of the Scottish Parliament and 40 per cent of the Welsh Assembly, 24 per cent of British MEPs in the European parliament, 16 per cent of the House of Lords, and 27 per cent of local councillors (*see* Figure 2.1). The change experienced in Britain represents part of a larger shift in cultural attitudes towards the political and social roles of women that has been sweeping through many postindustrial societies (Norris and Inglehart 2003).

What are the political consequences that flow from this development? And, in particular, did the entry of a substantial number of women MPs in the 1997 election, and their subsequent re-election in 2001, alter the predominant culture at Westminster? This chapter compares survey evidence drawn from a representative sample of almost 1,000 national politicians in Britain (including parliamentary candidates and elected members) to examine whether women leaders display distinctive attitudes and values which have the capacity to make a substantive difference for women's interests. The first part briefly explains the theoretical framework based on the politics of presence and outlines a model to test it empirically. Three sources of evidence are available to examine the theoretical claims. We argue that, given the serious constraints on back bench activities at Westminster, *behavioural* measures, such as roll-call data based on legislative voting rebellions, provide an unduly limited yardstick for examining the capacity of women politicians to offer a distinctive contribution to politics. *Self-reported* measures taken at face value without independent verification, such as interviews where women politicians claim to act for women, are equally suspect given the electoral self-interest embodied in such claims. In contrast, *cultural* measures provide the most suitable, systematic and reliable evidence, where any gender

* 'Westminster women' (with P. Norris), *Political Studies*, 2003, 51(1), pp. 84–102.

Figure 2.1: Women in Public Office, UK

Women MPs in the UK Parliament, 1918–2001

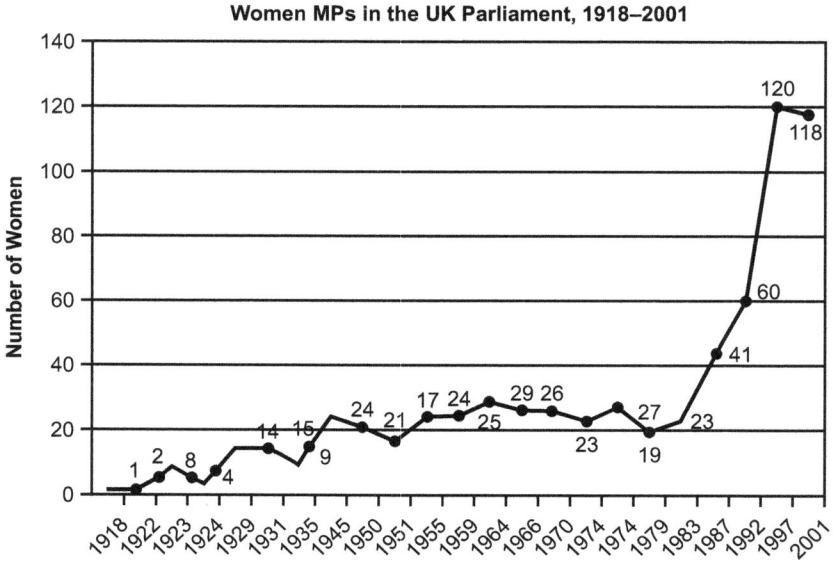

**% Women in different kinds of Public Office
in the UK, January 2000**

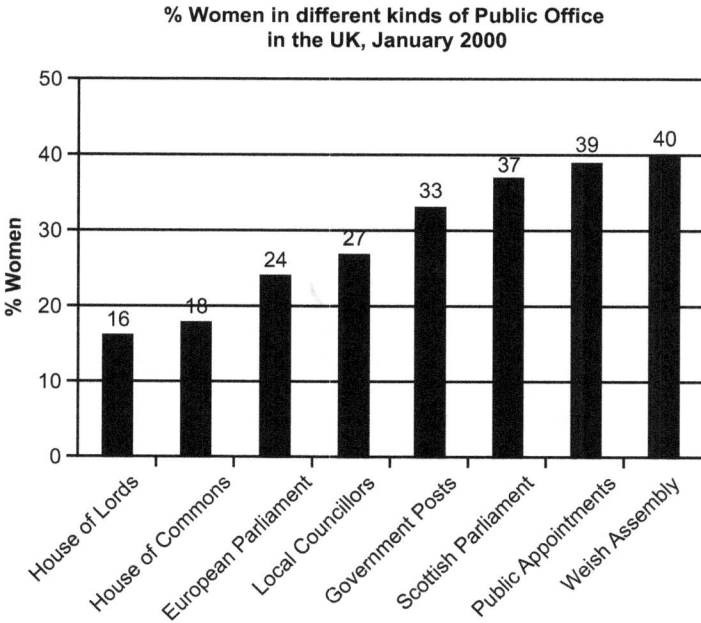

differences in attitudes and values can be regarded as a *necessary*, although not *sufficient*, condition for women representatives to act for women as a group. If women and men MPs share similar attitudes and values, then it seems unlikely that the election of more women backbenchers has the potential to make any sort of substantive policy difference, whether through legislative votes, parliamentary activities, or influencing the policy process behind the scenes. We theorise that the values of women and men politicians can be expected to prove similar on many traditional left-right issues that have long divided British party politics, but that they can be expected to display the most significant contrasts towards the key issues that most directly affect women's ability to lead an independent life. The second part describes the data and measures, including the British Representation Study survey of 1,000 candidates and members conducted in the 2001 general election. The third part examines the evidence for gender differences concerning five scales measuring attitudes and values that commonly divide British party politics. The results confirm that once we control for party, there are no significant differences among women and men leaders across the value scales measuring support for the Free Market economy, for European Integration and for Traditional Moral values. Yet on the values and attitudes that are most closely related to women's autonomy — namely the Affirmative Action and the Gender Equality scales — women and men express significantly different values within each party. This pattern persists even after controlling for other social variables that commonly influence attitudes, such as age, education and income. The conclusion summarises the main findings and considers why and under what conditions they may have important consequences.

Theoretical Framework

The flourishing and extensive literature on women and public office has developed two central strands. The first focuses on '*descriptive* representation', seeking to identify the reasons why so few women are elected to legislative bodies and the importance of barriers such as the electoral system, the role of party recruitment processes and the resources and motivation that women bring to the pursuit of elected office (*see* Darcy *et al.* 1994; Lovenduski and Norris 1993, 1996; Norris and Lovenduski 1995). Descriptive representation can be regarded as intrinsically valuable, for example Mansbridge (1999) argues that for African-Americans and for women, both historically disadvantaged social groups, the entry of representatives into public office improves the quality of group deliberations, increases a sense of democratic legitimacy, and develops leadership capacity. The second approach pursues the related question of whether, if elected, women will 'make a difference' in legislative life and political leadership, or if they will offer '*substantive*' representation of women (Diamond 1977; Thomas 1994; Norris 1996; Tremblay 1998; MacDougal 1998; Carroll 2001; Swers 2001). Feminist theorists suggest that the presence of women in the House of Commons offers possibilities that women are not just 'standing as' women but also 'acting for' women as a group (Phillips 1995; Lovenduski 1997). This argument is commonly heard when it is assumed that, due to their particular life-experiences in the home, workplace and public sphere, women politicians prioritise and express different types of values, attitudes and policy priorities, such as greater concern about childcare, health or education, or a less conflictual and more collaborative political style (*see*, for example, Brooks *et al.* 1990; Perrigo 1996; Phillips 1995, 1998; Short 1996; MacDougal 1998). Although these issues are of long-standing theoretical interest, in Britain until recently there have been so few women serving in most levels of public office that it seemed premature to ask what impact they may have on the policy process. The changing situation during the 1990s, however, calls for these issues to be re-examined.

How might such a distinctive contribution be identified and tested? The theoretical framework in this study draws on accounts of 'the politics of presence' developed by Phillips (1995, 1998). Acknowledging that mechanisms of accountability (the politics of ideas) are necessary to representative democracy, Phillips argues that women have a distinctive group identity based upon shared common interests on issues such as abortion, childcare or equal opportunities in education and the labour force. There is nothing particularly novel about these type of claims, after all the analogy can be drawn with many other groups which have sought to secure legislative representation within established or separate parties to articulate and defend their interests. Such a process is exemplified in the early twentieth century by the creation of the British Labour Party by trade unions to advance collective labour organisations and the legal right to strike (Pelling 1968). Acknowledging that men and women have complex sets of interests that both diverge and overlap, and that women as a group are far from monolithic, Phillips points out that '... the variety of women's interests does not refute the claim that interests are gendered. ... The argument from interest does not depend on establishing a unified interest of all women: it depends, rather, on establishing a difference between the interests of women and men' (Phillips 1995: 68). If, however, women are divided by predominant crosscutting cleavages, such as those of social class, region, ethnicity or religion, and by ideological divisions between left and right, then these factors may override any common or shared interests associated with gender. Indeed, the classic account of the evolution and consolidation of parties in Western Europe, by Lipset and Rokkan (1967), argued that other cleavages in the electorate were the primary building blocks of party competition — including those dividing the core and periphery regions, Catholics and Protestants, and workers and the bourgeoisie. Lipset and Rokkan assumed that any residual differences between women and men were subsumed under these primary social cleavages.

Before we can test the claims of the politics of presence thesis it is necessary to establish a clear definition of 'women's interests'. Although this concept is common, it remains controversial in feminist scholarship. As Wängnerud notes, problems include the relationship between 'objective' and 'subjective' interests, as well as the relationship between gender and other social divisions like race and class (Wängnerud 2000: 68). Defined broadly, if 'women's interests' are understood to include all political issues where women and men may disagree, for example, in their attitudes towards the deployment of armed forces, the protection of the environment, or the desirability of a strong and effective welfare safety net, then it becomes unclear how to define the boundaries of 'women's interests'. Instead it seems preferable to adopt a strong but narrower definition of women's interests since such a formulation will improve its possibilities for effective theorising and measurement. In line with Wängnerud (2000: 70), we define women's shared interests to be in those policies that increase their autonomy. The recognition of such interests is a *process* of politicisation that can be treated as a number of steps in which (1) women are recognised as a social category, that is the gender neutrality of politics is contested; (2) the inequalities of power between the sexes are acknowledged; and, (3) policies to increase the autonomy of women are made. In her analysis of interview data on successive cohorts of Swedish legislators, Wängnerud shows how each step influences the political process and concludes that women's presence in the Riksdag has brought about a shift of emphasis whereby women's interests have become more central in politics. She found differences in attitudes between women and men across a wide range of issues and showed how these differences provoke political changes that lead to an increased legislative sensitivity to women's interests by all politicians. Wängnerud shows that the articulation and mobilisation of such interests in the Riksdag is the work of women politicians (Wängnerud 2000).

We recognise that the effects of women's presence in politics do not happen automatically but exist and become explicit under certain conditions. Instructive here is the work of Rosabeth Moss Kanter (1977) on gender relations within industrial corporations. Kanter's argument is that the size of a minority matters. *Uniform* groups contain only men or only women. *Skewed* groups contain a large imbalance of men or women, up to about 15 per cent of the minority group. *Tilted* groups contain about 15–40 per cent of the opposite sex. Lastly, *balanced* groups contain 40–50 per cent of each sex. Kanter suggests that once a group reaches a certain size — somewhere in the tilted group range — the minority starts to assert itself and from this assertion there eventually follows a transformation of the institutional culture. This argument implies that rather than steady evolution, there is a critical 'tipping point' that depends upon numbers. When a group remains a small minority within a larger society its members are tokens who will seek to adapt to their surroundings, conforming to the predominant rules of the game. They will not act to increase the size of their group. If anything their various available strategies ('queen bee', assimilation and so on) will tend to keep the number of tokens appropriately and conveniently small. Once the group reaches a certain size, however, their available strategies change and lead to a qualitative shift in the nature of group interactions, as the minority starts to assert itself and thereby transform the institutional culture, norms and values. Kanter fails to explain why change in the relative numbers of women and men leads to institutional, cultural or policy change. Such effects are not a simple result of increasing numbers, they are an effect of the processes of mobilisation that are made possible by the presence of women in a traditionally masculine institution. In the language of feminist scholarship it is an effect of gender, defined as the socially ascribed characteristics of women and men.

Even so, we should not expect an increase in the presence of women politicians to bring immediate change. In a critical assessment of Kanter's argument, Janice Yoder drew attention to the gendered processes that take place as the balance between the numbers of women and men change. Where women are in gender-inappropriate occupations, as defined by traditional norms, then an increase in their numbers may generate a backlash. When this occurs, it makes it difficult for women to influence the wider society or organisation, at least initially (Yoder 1991, *see* also Dahlerup 1988). Taken together, this body of work suggests that to understand what happens when the numbers of women rises, it is necessary to understand under what conditions change can be expected to occur and how institutional effects will distort or delay this process.

Measures, Data and Methods

In sum, 'presence' theory highlights gendered interests as the cause of the political change that occurs when women enter a legislature. If women and men politicians differ in their underlying interests, then when parliaments include more women politicians this could contribute towards a transformation in the institutional culture, political discourse and policy agenda. The expectations are explicit in Clare Short's claims: 'As more women come into the Commons, the culture will change, the agenda of politics will broaden, and the institution itself will be transformed' (quoted in MacDougal 1998). The entry of more women politicians into the House of Commons following the 1997 election generated high expectations of what they could achieve. Are such expectations likely to be met? The 'presence' argument suggest that, beyond a certain threshold, as the numbers of women change, so also will other elements of the legislature because men and women bring different interests to politics. Yet the precise consequences are left implicit, albeit with some agreement about what they *might* be.

There are at least three alternative ways in which any latent gender 'difference' among politicians could be expressed and measured, namely through (i) the legislative voting record of MPs; (ii) the roles and activities of backbenchers; and (iii) the underlying cultural attitudes and ideological values of politicians.

MPs' Legislative Voting Record

The first and strongest measure of political impact could be if women and men MPs differed in their voting record on key bills, for example if women were more likely to rebel against Labour initiatives to cut back on welfare or childcare benefits. This approach has often been used in the USA, where gender differences have been established in studies examining roll call data in Congress and state houses (Vega and Firestone 1995; Dolan 1997; Swers 1998). This yardstick was also commonly used to evaluate the 1997 cohort of women MPs by the British press. As a result, within a few months of their entry in 1997, popular commentary in the media often adopted a critical and sceptical tone, suggesting that initial hopes for women as agents of change failed to be realised (Perkins 1999). Far from altering parliament, 'Blair's Babes', as they were quickly dubbed by the tabloids, appeared more quiescent towards the leadership, less willing to rebel, and therefore unlikely to make a distinctive contribution to the legislative agenda (Cowley and Childs 2001; Thomson 1999). Criticism was particularly strong in the 1997 Parliament when Labour cuts in benefits for lone mothers were more likely to be supported by women than men MPs. Research by Phillip Cowley and Sarah Childs confirmed that Labour women MPs were slightly less likely to rebel than men although these gender differences diminished to near insignificance after controls for cohort of entry were introduced (Cowley and Childs 2003). Press criticism of the newly elected Labour women was sustained and frequently vicious. It was also reflected in comments by MPs on both sides of the house. Thus Brian Sedgemore, Labour member for Hackney South and Shoreditch, famously referred to the new Labour women MPs as 'Stepford Wives' (*The Observer* 1 April 2001) while the leader of the Conservatives, Iain Duncan Smith, accused them of being second rate politicians (*Financial Times* 4 August 2001). The stigma of 'Blair's Babes' continued throughout and beyond the life of the parliament elected in 1997.

Roll call analysis is perhaps better suited to the US Congress. In European parliamentary democracies where party constraints on back bench MPs are common (Bowler *et al.* 1999) legislative votes are a limited and too strict test of political effectiveness. The ability of elected members to rebel on most legislative votes at Westminster remains highly constrained, due to the sanctions of strict discipline by party whips, especially during an era of strong parliamentary management by the governing party. 'Free' votes, such as moral issues on which party managers give no instructions to their backbenchers, provide an exception, but these issues remain atypical of Westminster politics, and high levels of party discipline and cohesion persist even when the party whips are 'off' (Cowley and Stuart 1997). British MPs who commonly rebel on whipped votes can face severe penalties in terms of lack of ministerial advancement, or even loss of further nomination, effectively ending their political careers (Norton 1993). As a result, in systems of party government we should expect the political expression of any potential differences among women and men members of parliament to be inhibited by the institutional context.

MPs' Political Roles and Activities

The second, weaker claim is that the parliamentary activities of back bench women MPs could still differ in many other regards beyond legislative votes, such as in the priority that they give towards constituency service (Norris and Lovenduski 1995), or in their style of politics in committee work, parliamentary debates, Private Members Bills, or Early Day Motions. American research, for example, has often found that women in Congress and state houses promote women's issues through lobbying, committee work and bill sponsorship (Tamerius 1995) as well as finding that women and men differ in their rhetorical style during committee hearing debates (Kathlene 1994; Rosenthal 1997). The literature in the USA suggests that women officeholders give greater attention than their male colleagues of the same party to women's rights, as well as to concerns reflecting women's traditional roles as caregivers in the family and society (Carroll 2001). Similar patterns have been established in the Nordic states, where women leaders have raised distinctive concerns, through parliamentary questions and debates (Karvonnen and Selle 1995; Skjeie 1993; Bergqvist 2000), as well as affecting the agenda-setting process on issues like day-care coverage (Bratton and Ray 2002). Elsewhere Georgia Duerst-Lahti and Rita Mae Kelly (1995) provide evidence of different leadership styles and practices by male and female legislators in the USA. In the Australian parliament women representatives have also been found to bring a distinctive contribution to parliamentary debates on issues such as euthanasia (Broughton and Palmieri 1999). Yet while some studies suggest that women do make a distinct contribution to the policy agenda in legislatures elsewhere, such as in North America, Western Europe and Scandinavia, the evidence remains under debate (*see*, for example, discussions in Thomas 1994; Karvonnen and Selle 1995; Tremblay 1998; Carroll 2001; Reingold 2000).

In Britain, anecdotal reports suggest that women MPs work effectively on behalf of women behind the scenes, for example in influencing party policies or articulating women's concerns in discussion with ministers (Lovenduski 2001). In discussions women MPs also commonly make similar claims (Ross 2002). For example, interviews with half the newly elected Labour women MPs in 1997 found that two-thirds identified themselves as feminists and expressed support for the values of women's autonomy and equality, suggesting that there might be the potential for the articulation of a distinctive voice in parliament (Childs 2001a, 2001b). Yet without independent verification it is difficult to evaluate the validity of self-reported claims. Such claims cannot simply be accepted at face value, given that members may have an interest in making such arguments when seeking to maximise their electoral support. Nevertheless this research strengthen our scepticism about the analysis of MPs' voting records. Critics of the conformity of 'Blair's Babes' use a yardstick that may well prove too narrow to monitor the full range of legislative activities and back bench roles where men and women may differ at Westminster.

Political Attitudes and Values

Lastly, even if we assume that there are no *behavioural* differences because the parliamentary votes of women MPs conform to the bidding of party whips, and if women and men backbenchers adopt similar legislative roles and activities in the House of Commons, the third claim that the underlying attitudes and values of women and men politicians could still differ in some important regards may hold. After all an extensive body of literature has established that women legislators in America commonly express slightly more liberal attitudes across a range of social and economic issues, after controlling for their type of party and district (Thomas 1994; Duerst-Lahti and Kelly 1995; Thomas and Wilcox 1998; Carroll 2001). Could such findings be replicated at Westminster? In the UK parliament the existence of strong party discipline and the predominant parliamentary culture might make it difficult for women backbenchers to articulate a distinctive set of perspectives and interests, as a minority, although they may differ substantially from men members on many core attitudes and values, especially on issues concerning women's interests. Yet on the other hand, if women and men MPs share similar attitudes and values, due to either the selection process in parties or to the socialisation process at Westminster, then it seems unlikely that women backbenchers will be motivated to make a substantive policy difference, whether through legislative votes, parliamentary activities, or influencing the policy process behind the scenes. Attitudinal differences can therefore be regarded as a *necessary* although not *sufficient* condition for women representatives to act for women as a group.

The British Representation Survey, 2001

To measure attitudinal differences, this study analyses a representative sample of national politicians (including British parliamentary candidates and elected Members of Parliament). Evidence is drawn from the 2001 British Representation Studies (BRS), a mail survey sent to all parliamentary candidates and MPs standing in the British general election for all parties with parliamentary representation.

In early spring 2001, before the official campaign got underway, the BRS was mailed to 1,859 candidates selected by the main British parties (excluding the Greens, BNP, UK Independence party, and other minor parties or independent candidates without parliamentary representation). In total 1085 politicians had replied by the end of June 2001, representing a response rate of over 58 per cent (for full details and the questionnaires *see* http://www.pippanorris.com). Although the response rate was (as usual) higher among parliamentary candidates than MPs, the study includes about one third of the current House of Commons and it is broadly representative by party. The results can be compared with other surveys in this series, the 1997 British Representation Study (N=999), and the 1992 British Candidate Study (N=1658) (for full methodological details of previous research see Norris and Lovenduski (1995)). Initial analysis of the results in terms of patterns of party ideology is available elsewhere (Norris and Lovenduski, 2001).

This study focuses on whether women and men politicians differ within each party in terms of a wide range of political attitudes and values. We monitored attitudes towards major economic, social and foreign policy issues commonly dividing British party politics, exemplified by attitudes towards Britain's membership of the European Union, support for values such as the redistribution of wealth, and support for traditional moral values, as well as towards explicitly gendered issues such as the use of affirmative action for women candidates and equal opportunities policy. The BRS contains multiple items measuring these values, with most derived from long-standing questions contained in the British Election Study. Principal component factor analysis with varimax rotation was used to examine the underlying ideological dimensions in responses to twenty-six items. The results in Table 2.1 show that the items fell into five dimensions that divided

Table 2.1: Factor Analysis of Political Attitudes Amongst all Candidates in 2001 BRS Survey

	Free Market Economy	Affirmative Action	Liberal Gender Equality	Europe	Moral Traditionalism
Big business benefits owners at worker's expense	0.822				
Ordinary people do not get their fair share of wealth	0.799				
Management will always try to get the better of employees	0.798				
There is one law for rich, one for poor	0.793				
Government should redistribute wealth	0.649				
All-women shortlists		0.818			
Reserved seats for women		0.805			
Positive quotas/ affirmative action for women		0.791			
Opinion on gender quotas		−0.665			
Financial support for women candidates		0.649			

Table 2.1(Continued): Factor Analysis of Political Attitudes Amongst all Candidates in 2001 BRS Survey

	Free Market Economy	Affirmative Action	Liberal Gender Equality	Europe	Moral Traditionalism
Men better suited for politics than women			0.733		
Husband's job is to earn money, wife's is at home			0.711		
Family life suffers when wife has full-time job			0.679		
Should Parliament have more women MPs?			−0.607		
Government should ensure that women have equal chances			−0.522		
Attempts to give equal opportunities to women			0.491		
Opinion on single European Currency				0.757	
Long-term policy on the EU should be. .				0.742	
Feel about				0.741	
Britain's membership of the EU					

Table 2.1(Continued): Factor Analysis of Political Attitudes Amongst all Candidates in 2001 BRS Survey

	Free Market Economy	Affirmative Action	Liberal Gender Equality	Europe	Moral Traditionalism
Schools should teach children to obey authority					0.617
Censorship is necessary to uphold moral standards					0.611
The law should be obeyed even if wrong					0.584
Young people lack respect for traditional values					0.584
People who break the law should be given stiffer sentences				−0.428	0.546
Being a housewife is just as fulfilling as working for pay					0.409
% Variance explained	35.6	8.8	7.2	5.1	4.2
Cronbach's Alpha for each scale	0.90	0.86	0.80	0.87	0.80

Extraction Method: Principal Component Analysis. Rotation Method: Varimax with Kaiser Normalisation. Rotation converged in 7 iterations. Coefficients less than .40 were excluded. Cronbach's Alpha was used to test the reliability of each of the scales.
Source: British Representation Study 2001 (N=999).

British politicians, reflecting attitudes towards the classic left-right dimension of support for the free market economy, affirmative action towards women, liberal gender equality, Europe and moral traditionalism. The factor analysis accounted for over half (59 per cent) of the variance in attitudes towards these items. As shown in Table 2.1, each of the five scales proved consistent and reliable when tested using Cronbach's Alpha (all scoring 0.80 or above). The scales were standardised to 100-points for ease of interpretation, where low equals minimal support and high represents maximum support. We first compared the mean score on each scale by gender and party, testing the significance of any difference in the group means by ANOVA. We then employed OLS regression analysis to see whether the gender differences that we established on some scales persisted after controlling for other factors that commonly predict political attitudes, including age, income and education, as well as party and incumbency status.

Results and Analysis

Differences in the mean scores on these scales among women and men within each party are shown in Table 2.2. The results show that once we control for party, there are almost no significant differences in the values of women and men leaders concerning the core scales measuring support for free market left-right economic values, attitudes towards Britain's role in the European Union, and moral traditionalism. On all these values women and men politicians displayed common agreement within each party. The only exception concerns the economic values of Labour women that were significantly more moderate or centrist than their male colleagues. In all these regards, contrary to some of the evidence in studies of gender differences in the American Congress and state houses (Vega and Firestone 1995; Dolan 1997; Swers 1998), there is no support for the stronger claims that women leaders in British politics are consistently more liberal or more conservative than men towards the traditional left-right issues such as crime, moral censorship, or the redistribution of income that have long divided party politics at Westminster. Nor are women politicians in each party significantly more or less 'internationalist' in orientation towards the EU than men, another set of issues that generates sharp inter- and intra-party clashes. On all these issues, in Westminster politics it is party not gender that demarcates the predominant pattern of ideological beliefs and values. Moreover these findings suggest one possible reason helping to explain why women backbenchers proved less likely to rebel during the first Labour administration than their male colleagues (Cowley and Childs 2001), namely their attitudes towards a range of social and economic values were fairly moderate and therefore largely in tune with the centrist position of the Blair government.

In contrast, when we measure attitudes and values directly relating to women's interests, we find significant differences between women and men politicians, and differences that are consistently found within each of the major parties. The results confirm that on the scales concerning support for equal opportunities and affirmative action there are strong and significant gender differences among Conservative, Labour and Liberal Democrat politicians, and the affirmative action scale also divides women and men nationalist politicians. The scale measuring attitudes towards affirmative action includes items where women candidates might be expected to have a direct interest in

Table 2.2: Mean Scores on the Value Scales by Party and Gender

PARTY	Gender market (N)		Pro-free market economy scale	Pro-affirmative action scale	Pro-liberal gender equality scale	Pro-European scale	Pro-moral Traditionalism scale
Con	Men	194	78	9	66	29	57
	Women	38	80	14	75	28	58
	Eta		0.07	0.16***	0.23***	0.03	0.02
Lab	Men	165	40	34	85	54	41
	Women	58	45	50	90	53	38
	Eta		0.17***	0.40***	0.17**	0.05	0.09
L. Dem	Men	189	44	25	82	61	38
	Women	55	45	36	87	62	37
	Eta		0.04	0.28***	0.17***	0.02	0.05
Nat	Men	75	38	28	81	58	36
	Women	14	38	35	89	61	36
	Eta		0.01	0.16	0.26**	0.08	0.02

Note: The figures represent the mean score on each of the value scales among 999 British politicians (parliamentary candidates and elected members) by party and gender, without any controls. See Table 2.1 for the items includes in each of these scales. Each of the scales has been summed and standardised to 100 points for ease of interpretation, where low equals minimal support and high equals maximum support. The difference between groups is measured by ANOVA and the strength of association coefficient is Eta. Significance P. *** =0.01 **=0.05, 0.10. Due to the smaller number of cases, 'Nat' combines members of the SNP and Plaid Cymru parties.

Source: British Representation Study 2001.

the outcome, including support for all-women shortlists, the use of reserved seats, or the use of positive quotas to get more women candidates nominated. In some ways the gender difference within the Labour party is not surprising, it reflects long-standing debates in the party. But the fact that there is a significant gender gap on affirmative action within the Conservative party is both striking and unexpected, running directly counter to the official policy and mainstream ideology of the party. Conservative politicians prove least supportive of the use of affirmative action, but men are significantly less in favour than women politicians within the party. There are also consistent gender differences in each major party towards the scale measuring 'liberal' gender equality, reflecting issues such as more general support for equal opportunities policy for women, the items concerning men and women's roles in the family and workforce, and attitudes towards the suitability of women for public office. The comparison of means shows that male Conservatives prove least approving on this scale, while female Conservative politicians are positive; indeed on this scale they prove slightly more positive than male Labour politicians.

Of course these gender differences could be due to differences in other characteristics of men and women politicians. Tables 2.3 and 2.4 therefore use multivariate regression analysis to see whether these gender differences persist on these two scales even after controlling for factors that can be expected to shape political attitudes, such as the incumbency status, education, income and the age of politicians. Among the different factors, age does prove important, with the younger generation of politicians more favourable towards gender equality, as might be expected. The contrasts between the Labour and Conservative parties remain important. Nevertheless the results confirm that the gender gap continues to be significantly related to the affirmative action and the liberal gender equality value scales even with these prior social controls, suggesting that the gap reflects deep-seated attitudinal differences between women and men leaders that cannot simply be explained away as due to their social background.

Conclusions and Implications

Westminster provides a suitable case to analyse how far the entry of more women into elected office has the capacity to make a substantive difference in the context of a European parliamentary democracy characterised by strong party discipline. The 1997 British general election saw the proportion of women MPs doubling overnight, from 9.2 to 13.2 per cent of the House of Commons. In the governing Labour party, women became one quarter of the MPs. The 2001 election returned only 118 women MPs, a drop that is attributable to the abandonment of Labour's All-Women shortlist policy in half their target seats (Lovenduski 2001). Nevertheless their substantial presence in Parliament makes women MPs more able to form alliances and act as a coherent force to affect the dominant culture of their institution, as well as being in a position to perform the 'critical' acts that Dahlerup (1988) argues are necessary to the feminisation of political institutions.

Table 2.3: Regression Model Predicting Support for Affirmative Action Values Scale

	Unstandardised coefficients B	Std.	Standardised coefficients Beta	T	Sig.
(Constant)	32.32	4.27		7.57	0.00
Woman politician (1/0)	10.75	1.18	0.23	9.11	0.00
Year of birth	−0.07	0.05	−0.04	−1.51	0.13
MP elected in 2001	1.18	0.68	0.05	1.73	0.08
Conservative	−13.57	1.95	−0.45	−9.54	0.00
Labour	7.43	1.97	0.17	3.78	0.00
Liberal Democrat	−2.31	1.90	−0.06	−1.22	0.22
Total household income	−0.04	0.22	−0.01	−0.19	0.85
Education	−0.29	0.75	−0.01	−0.38	0.70
Adjusted R2	0.40				

Note: The OLS regression model has the standardised 100-point Affirmative Action value scale as the dependent variable. *See* Table 2.1 for the items included in this scale. The figures in bold are significant at the conventional level. Total household income, as a proxy for class, is measured using a 10-category scale. Education is measured on a 4-point scale from primary school to university or polytechnic degree. N=970 respondents.
Source: British Representation Study 2001.

Yet despite extensive popular interest, and the publication of some qualitative studies, so far little previous research has presented systematic attitudinal evidence about the impact of women as legislators at Westminster. As argued earlier, the party discipline that characterises Westminster politics means that any evidence based on roll call voting provides an unduly limited and conservative indication of gender differences. Other behavioural measures, such as rhetorical analysis of debating styles or content analysis of Early Day Motions, so far unavailable, would provide alternative indicators of the existence of any gender differences at Westminster. Without independent verification, self-reported claims expressed during interviews that women politicians will prioritise women's interests and concerns more than men cannot be accepted at face value, any more than we would accept without demonstrable evidence any claims that Labour MPs speak for and defend the interests of the poor, or that Conservative MPs represent the business community.

Attitudinal differences concerning the issues that affect women's autonomy are the necessary but not sufficient condition for women to act 'for women'. The claim that increasing the numbers of women will bring qualitative change, or that descriptive representation will lead to substantive representation, depends upon the existence of underlying differences in the values and attitudes of the groups concerned. If women and men MPs are similar in these respects, then even if women gradually became the majority at Westminster, British parliamentary politics will continue in familiar ways. The public face of politics will become feminised, but the political culture and the substantive policy agenda will remain unchanged. Qualitative change will follow quantitative change only if female politicians differ significantly from men, for example if they give greater priority to public spending on education rather than defence, or if they raise more parliamentary questions about childcare than about Europe, or if they pay more attention to constituency service rather than parliamentary debate.

From the standpoint of feminist theory, the most important changes expected from women's entry into public office would be those that support the goals of increased women's autonomy by acknowledging and redressing gender inequality. Such change will follow from different values among women and men that were tested using British Representation Study data. As expected, in the system of strong, cohesive and disciplined party government that prevails at Westminster, the evidence confirms that men and women's attitudes and values within each party coincide on many issues where party competition reflects the traditional left-right ideological spectrum. Legislative discipline and the culture of party unity may exaggerate agreement between women and men in each party. Thus, the entry of more women into Westminster cannot be expected to alter policies where the major parties remain deeply divided, such as Britain's role with the European Union, the traditional role of the state in the economy, or moral traditionalism. Yet this does not mean to say that the only impact of more women in parliament will be symbolic. The results indicate that within each party women and men politicians differ most significantly over issues that directly affect women's autonomy, that is, in their attitudes towards positive action and liberal sex equality policy.

The idea that increasing women's representation will change politics has public resonance. Much of the popular rhetoric supporting the selection of more women candidates prior to 1997 stressed that, while a clear case for positive discrimination in favour of women candidates could be made on the grounds of equity alone, in addition the entry of more women into Westminster would help to change policy priorities. The lack of any obvious evidence of radical change in terms of back bench voting rebellions led towards the popular view that the new women at Westminster were conformist and would be unlikely to lead towards radical change. This popular conclusion rests on exaggerated expectations and faulty premises. The results of this study suggest that the expansion of women's representation at

Westminster does promise to alter the balance of interests, not on all economic and social issues, but most clearly on the issues of women's autonomy.

What are the implications of these findings? This study is limited to examining differences between women and men politicians in terms of their attitudes and values, which represents only one dimension of legislative life. The next step is to link attitudes to behaviour, a project that is being undertaken by the Study of Gender and Parliament Group. We plan to examine whether these value differences have important consequences for legislative behaviour, for example in terms of parliamentary questions, committee debates, Early Day Motions, perceptions of legislative roles, and back bench activities such as constituency work. Further research is needed on all these issues. Nevertheless, theoretically, there are at least four distinct ways in which the value differences that we have established between women and men politicians could potentially alter the UK House of Commons.

First these differences could generate changes in the political leadership. British MPs constitute the pool from which all elected government leaders are drawn, including members of the Cabinet and the opposition front benches. Changes in the composition of parliament may ultimately be expected to percolate upwards to the highest offices of state; studies have established that in Western Europe the proportion of women in parliament is one of the best predictors of the proportion of women in Cabinet (Davis 1997; Siaroff 2000).

Second, legislative priorities may alter. As discussed earlier, like many other parliaments in Western Europe, the UK House of Commons is characterised by strong party discipline, seriously limiting the autonomy of back bench MPs on whipped votes affecting government legislation. As Phillips has noted. 'If the field of politics has already been clearly demarcated, containing within it a comprehensive range of ideas and interests and concerns, it might not so much matter who does the work of representation. But if the range of ideas has been curtailed by orthodoxies that rendered alternatives invisible, there will be no satisfactory solution short of changing the people who represent and develop the ideas' (Phillips 1995: 70). Women backbenchers can play an important role in developing and debating public policy, in shaping and revising legislation, in scrutinising the actions of government departments, and in linking citizens and government (Norton 1993). The most obvious direct impact of gender differences in values may be in legislative activities where backbenchers have the most autonomy, such as in the choice of Parliamentary Questions or Private Members Bills.

Third, party politics may be changed. Conservative MPs determine the choice of the candidates, who can be elected as party leader by the wider membership, while Labour MPs help select the leader and shadow cabinet. Parliamentarians play a leading role in determining official party policy, as embodied ultimately in the official party manifesto, as well as shaping the nature of the party image in the public's mind. Comparative research by Caul (2001) indicates that the presence of women in senior party positions is a major factor in the adoption of measures to promote sex equality in political representation. Even if women members adopt back bench roles that are similar to men, they could still work effectively behind the scenes, influencing matters such as the contents of party manifestos, the government's legislative agenda, the policy priorities in committees, or the tone and issues raised by parliamentary debate. If these claims are valid, then the entry of more women into parliament could subtly alter the predominant culture and policy agenda at Westminster, a process affecting both women *and* men members equally. Such a shift would not be revealed by comparison of women and men MPs, but rather by changes in the parliamentary culture over time. Yet such a development would be difficult to detect in the UK House of Commons through any systematic means because the dramatic rise in the proportion of women members at Westminster in 1997 coincided with the entry of the new Labour government.

The findings are particularly relevant for the reform of party selection processes, and therefore the opportunities available for women candidates in future elections. In 2001 the *Sex Discrimination (Election Candidates) Act* became law, allowing British parties to use affirmative action to increase their complement of women representatives. As drafted, the legislation is permissive. It removes the possibility of prosecution for affirmative action under British law. It does not indemnify parties from prosecution under European law. But whether parties will take advantage of this legislation depends upon their predominant culture and how far they favour such measures. The presence of women who support such measures in the senior ranks of the party will affect how parties react (Caul 2001). The parliamentary selection processes used by parties could therefore be influenced by the attitudes of women candidates and MPs who are pressuring for new opportunities for women in elected office.

Lastly, as Mansbridge (1999) suggests the composition of parliament could have a significant impact on the articulation and defence of group interests within representative democracy. Women's presence as elected representatives signals the legitimacy of their concerns and may bring a wider recognition of those interests. It therefore seems plausible that the value differences documented here among women and men politicians on issues of women's autonomy, combined with the increased feminisation of public office that has occurred in Britain during the last decade, are likely to have broad long-term consequences for representative democracy.

We can conclude that the entry of more women into Westminster will not generate a radical revolution in the predominant culture at Westminster, as the more optimistic scenarios suggest. But nor are there grounds to believe that the entry of more women into Westminster merely led to 'politics as usual'. The evidence consistently suggests that women politicians in all the major British parties (not just Labour) do bring a different set of values to issues affecting women's equality, in the workplace, home and public sphere. While it may take some time, if these attitudes gradually come to shape party manifestos, political debates and ultimately legislative action, for example by influencing policies towards equal pay, reproductive rights, and the adoption of affirmative action strategies in the recruitment of women within parties, then the entry of more women into Westminster has the capacity to make more than simply a symbolic difference to the face of British representative democracy.

References

Bergqvist, C. (2000) *Equal Democracies*, Dartmouth: Aldershot.

Bowler, S., Farrell, D. M. and Katz, R. M. (1999) *Party Discipline and Parliamentary Government*, Columbus OH: Ohio State University Press.

Bratton, K. A. and Ray, L. P. (2002) 'Descriptive Representation, Policy Outcomes, and Municipal Day-care Coverage in Norway', *American Journal of Political Science*, 46 (2): 428–37.

Brooks, R., Eagle, A. and Short, C. (1990) *Quotas Now: Women and the Labour Party*, London: Fabian Pamphlet.

Broughton, S. and Palmieri, S. (1999) 'Gendered Contributions to Parliamentary Debates: The Case of Euthanasia', *Australian Journal of Political Science*, 34 (1): 29–45.

Caul, M. (2001) 'Political Parties and the Adoption of Candidate Gender Quotas: A Cross-national Analysis', *Journal of Politics*, 63 (4): 1214–29.

Carroll, S. J. (ed.) (2001) *The Impact of Women in Public Office*, Indiana IN: University of Indiana Press.

Childs, S. (2001a) '"Attitudinally Feminist"? The New Labour Women MPs and the Substantive Representation of Women', *Politics*, 21 (3): 178–85.

Childs, S. (2001b) 'In Her Own Words: New Labour Women and the Substantive Representation of Women', *British Journal of Politics and International Relations*, 3 (2) June: 173–90.

Cowley, P. and Childs, S. (2001) 'Critical but not Rebellious? New Labour Women in the House of Commons', paper presented at the annual meeting of the American Political Science Association, San Franscisco CA.

Cowley, P. and Childs, S. (2003) 'Too Spineless to Rebel?', *British Journal of Political Science*, 33 (3) July: 345–365.

Cowley, P. and Stuart, M. (1997) 'Sodomy, Slaughter, Sunday Shopping and Seatbelts: Free Votes in the House of Commons, 1979 to 1996', *Party Politics*, 3 (1): 119–30.

Dahlerup, D. (1988) 'From a Small to a Large Minority: Women in Scandinavian Politics', *Scandinavian Political Studies*, 11 (4): 275–98.

Darcy, R., Welsh, S. and Clark, J. (1994) *Women, Elections and Representation*, 2nd edn, Lincoln NB: University of Nebraska.

Davis, R. H. (1997) *Women in Power in Parliamentary Democracies*, Lincoln NB: University of Nebraska Press.

Diamond, I. (1977) *Sex Roles in the State House*, New Haven CT: Yale University Press.

Dolan, J. (1997) 'Support for Women's Interests in the 103rd Congress: The Distinct Impact of Congressional Women', *Women & Politics*, 18 (4): 81–94.

Duerst-Lahti, G. and Kelly, R. M. (eds) (1995) *Gender, Power, Leadership and Governance*, Michigan MI: University of Michigan Press.

Kanter, R. M. (1977) 'Some Effects of Proportion of Group Life: Skewed Sex Ratios and Responses to Token Women', *American Journal of Sociology*, 82 (2): 965–90.

Karvonnen, L., Djupsund, G. and Carlson, T. (1995) 'Political Language', in L. Karvonnen and P. Selle (eds) *Women in Nordic Politics*, Aldershot: Dartmouth, pp. 333–79.

Karvonnen, L. and Selle, P. (1995) *Women in Nordic Politics*, Aldershot: Dartmouth.

Kathlene, L. (1994) 'Power and Influence in State Legislative Policy-making: The Interaction of Gender and Position in Committee Hearing Debates', *American Political Science Review*, 88 (3): 560–76.

Lipset, S. M. and Rokkan, S. (1967) *Party Systems and Voter Alignments*, New York: Free Press.

Lovenduski, J. and Norris, P. (1993) *Gender and Party Politics*, London: Sage.

Lovenduski, J. and Norris, P. (eds) (1996) *Women in Politics*, Oxford: Oxford University Press.

Lovenduski, J. (1997) 'Gender Politics: A Breakthrough for Women?', *Parliamentary Affairs*, 50 (4): 708–19.

Lovenduski, J. (2001) 'Women and Politics: Minority Representation or Critical Mass?', in P. Norris (ed.) *Britain Votes 2001*, Oxford: Oxford University Press, pp. 179–184.

MacDougal, L. (1998) *Westminster Women*, London: Vintage.

Mansbridge, J. (1999) 'Should Blacks Represent Blacks and Women Represent Women? A Contingent "Yes"', *Journal of Politics*, 61 (3): 628–57.

Norris, P. (1996) 'Women Politicians: Transforming Westminster?', *Parliamentary Affairs*, 49 (1): 89–102.

Norris, P. and Inglehart, R. (2003) *Rising Tide: Gender Equality and Cultural Change around the World*, New York: Cambridge University Press.

Norris, P. and Lovenduski, J. (1995) *Political Recruitment: Gender, Race and Class in the British Parliament*, Cambridge: Cambridge University Press.

Norris, P. and Lovenduski, J. (2001) *The British Representation Study 2001*.

Norris, P. and Lovenduski, J. (2001) 'The Iceberg and the Titanic: Electoral Defeat, Policy Moods and Party Change', paper given at the 2001 annual meeting of the Elections, Parties and Public Opinion Group (EPOP), University of Sussex.

Norton, P. (1993) *Does Parliament Matter?*, London: Harvester Wheatsheaf.

Pelling, H. (1968) *A Short History of the Labour Party*, London: Macmillan.

Perkins, A. (1999) 'Women: So Far, So What?', *The Guardian* 29 April.

Perrigo, S. (1996) 'Women and Change in the Labour Party 1979–1995', in J. Lovenduski and P. Norris (eds) *Women in Politics*, Oxford: Oxford University Press, pp. 116–129.

Phillips, A. (1995) *The Politics of Presence*, Oxford: Clarendon.

Phillips, A. (ed.) (1998) *Feminism and Politics*, Oxford: Oxford University Press.

Pitkin, H. (1967) *The Concept of Representation*, Berkeley CA: University of California Press.

Reingold, B. (2000) *Representing Women: Sex, Gender, and Legislative Behavior in Arizona and California*, Chapel Hill NC: University of North Carolina Press.

Rosenthal, C. S. (1997) 'A View of their Own: Women's Committee Leadership Styles and State Legislatures', *Policy Science Journal*, 25 (4): 585–600.

Ross, K. (2002) 'Women's Place in "Male" Space: Gender and Effect in Parliamentary Contexts', *Parliamentary Affairs*, 55 (1): 189–94.

Short, C. (1996) 'Women and the Labour Party', in J. Lovenduski and P. Norris (eds) *Women in Politics*, Oxford: Oxford University Press, pp. 17–25.

Siaroff, A. (2000) 'Women's Representation in Legislatures and Cabinets in Industrial Democracies', *International Political Science Review*, 21 (2): 197–215.

Skjeie, H. (1993) 'Ending the Male Political Hegemony?', in J. Lovenduski and P. Norris (eds) *Gender and Party Politics*, London: Sage, pp. 231–62.

Swers, M. L. (1998) 'Are Women More Likely to Vote for Women's Issue Bills than their Male Colleagues?', *Legislative Studies Quarterly*, 23 (3): 435–48.

Swers, M. L. (2001) 'Understanding the Policy Impact of Electing Women: Evidence from Research on Congress and State Legislatures', *PS: Political Science and Society*, 34 (2): 217–20.

Tamerius, K. (1995) 'Sex, Gender and Leadership in the Representation of Women', in G. Duerst-Lahti and R. M. Kelly (eds) *Gender, Power, Leadership and Governance*, Michigan MI: University of Michigan Press, pp. 93–112.

Thomas, S. (1994) *How Women Legislate*, Oxford: Oxford University Press.

Thomas, S. and Wilcox, C. (eds) (1998) *Women and Elective Office*, Oxford: Oxford University Press.

Thomson, M. (1999) 'Blair's Babes: Gender Governance and Power', in S. Millns and N. Whitty (eds) *Feminist Perspectives on Public Law*, London: Cavendish.

Tremblay, M. (1998) 'Do Female MPs Substantively Represent Women?', *Canadian Journal of Political Science*, 31 (3): 435–65.

Vega, A. and Firestone, J. M. (1995) 'The Effects of Gender on Congressional Behavior and the Substantive Representation of Women', *Legislative Studies Quarterly*, 20 (2): 213–22.

Wängnerud, L. (2000) 'Testing the Politics of Presence: Women's Representation in the Swedish Riksdag', *Scandinavian Political Studies*, 23 (1): 67–91.

Yoder, J. (1991) 'Rethinking Tokenism: Looking Beyond Numbers', *Gender and Society*, 5 (2): 178–192.

Chapter Three

Political Representation*

with Marila Guadagnini

Feminist empirical and theoretical work on representation has largely proceeded along separate paths.[1] The RNGS project offers a corrective, as it permits the simultaneous consideration of the effects of formal and informal channels of participation, patterns of women's presence in decision-making arenas, movement activities, and policy outcomes. Thus, it provides a rich source of data that can be analysed to illuminate both substantive and descriptive representation, a distinction that is central to current feminist debates. We find evidence that feminists should not give up on presence, that women's substantive and descriptive representation are linked through the critical acts of women legislators and agency officials.

Our findings challenge various aspects of previous research on women's representation, four of which are contentious. First, they raise questions about the relationships between descriptive (procedural) and substantive representation. Second, they suggest a model of effective policy advocacy that does not quite correspond to the idea of the policy triangles of movement, agency and legislature, or of autonomous and integrated women's movements and agency or legislature. Third, they suggest that the debate over critical mass–critical actor–critical acts should be revisited and respecified. Fourth, they raise important questions about accountability.

In this chapter, we first examine the varying dimensions of political representation found in recent feminist research and summarise these concerns into a series of nine researchable questions. Second, we show how we draw on RNGS concepts and data in an attempt to refine and provide initial answers to these questions. Third, we use the RNGS data to answer the questions. We conclude with a discussion of the relationships between different kinds of representation and different actors in contemporary policy debates.

Dimensions of Political Representation:

Much of feminist political representation scholarship that we address here draws heavily on Pitkin's four-part typology of representation (1967) and attempts to develop it theoretically for the analysis of instances of representation in particular, usually legislative, settings (Bratton and Ray 2002; Celis *et al.* 2008; Dovi 2002, 2007; Lovenduski 2005; Lovenduski *et al.* 2005; Mansbridge 1999, 2003; Phillips

---

* 'Political Representation' (with M. Guadagnini), in D. E. McBride and A. G. Mazur (eds) *The Politics of State Feminism: Innovation in comparative research*, Philadelphia, PA, Temple University Press, 2010, pp. 164–193.

1995; Schwindt-Bayer and Mishler 2005; Wängnerud 2000; Weldon 2002). Such scholarship implies that the gender-blind standard operating procedures of research on representation mask the exclusion of women and women's interests from authoritative political deliberation and decision making.

This feminist scholarship is largely driven by a common concern to characterise representation in such a way as to allow a systematic assessment of contemporary experiences of women's representation. For example, recent studies include work that highlights the neglected interconnections among all of Pitkin's categories (Schwindt-Bayer and Mishler 2005), studies focusing on the relationships between substantive and descriptive representation (Bratton and Ray 2002; Lovenduski *et al.* 2005; Weldon 2002), reformulations of Pitkin's categories in the light of feminist theories of representation and the requirements for research (especially on the United States; Dovi 2007), and proposals for new categories that consider the requirements of deliberative democracy particularly in an American political setting, but also in Great Britain (Campbell *et al.* 2010; Mansbridge 2003).

A central problem is the measurement of the extent to which the interests of particular groups of voters (normally more or less differentiated groups of women) are represented in legislative decisions. Since Phillips (1995) argued so effectively for a 'politics of presence,' feminists have contended that a necessary condition for the representation of women's interests is the presence of women in decision-making bodies. Phillips contends that interests are realised in the course of deliberation and decision making as various options, implementation strategies, and competing concerns are discussed. Only those who take part in the deliberation can benefit from such realisation and insert their interests. Leaving aside the vexing question of identifying 'valid' group interests, the logic of Phillips' claim is inescapable. However, it has proved difficult to demonstrate empirically that the representation of women's interests necessarily follows from the presence of women representatives in legislatures, although a great deal of circumstantial evidence that this is the case has been assembled and presented (Chaney *et al.* 1998; Childs 2004, 2005, 2007; Childs and Krook 2006; Lovenduski 2005; Mateo Diaz 2005). Repeated demonstrations of a strong association between increases in the presence of women legislators and enhanced agenda status of variously described women's issues or preferences does not convince some scholars, who insist (unfairly, we believe) that such studies merely read off substantive from descriptive representation.[2] Others reckon that the associations between presence and policy substance are limited and argue that it makes most sense to consider all four of Pitkin's dimensions of representation together (Schwindt-Bayer and Mishler 2005). Still others stress the necessity to move beyond legislatures as sites of representation to understand the totality of women's representation (Weldon 2002). Finally, a repeating debate among feminist political scientists turns on the relationship between critical mass and critical acts. Briefly, the fundamental question is whether the presence of at least a certain number of women legislators will lead to a better representation of women's interests in politics. At the time of writing, the matter seems to be settled around agreement that it is the critical acts of representatives and not their numbers that matter (Childs and Krook 2006). Such agreement brings the debate back to its starting point in 1988, when

Dahlerup argued that acts, not numbers, are critical (Dahlerup 1988). Agreement that acts matter has not yet been accompanied by much empirical testing of their relationship to numbers, however, RNGS data can be used to explore this relationship and move the debate forward.

Feminist scholars are concerned with differences between and among women, and have recently been especially concerned with intersectionality. Women are thought to be fully represented when deliberations about public policy explicitly consider the potential impact on different groups of women. In practice, the processes of making effective and properly differentiated claims to increase the representation of women in political processes are rudimentary. For the most part, institutionalised political processes were designed to aggregate politically salient differences among men. Hence, incoming women and women's interests are assumed to coincide with those of men and tend to be treated as unproblematic. We attribute this to the relatively early stage of the campaigns for the equal representation of women in most countries; such claims are not irrevocably essentialist but instead are starting points on the basis of which different identities will acquire political purchase as the processes of women's representation develop.

Feminist political scientists are attracted to the potential of descriptive representation to deliver at least a measure of substantive representation. However, there remains a division between those who allegedly claim that descriptive representation will lead to substantive representation and those who see no connection. To us, this argument represents a position that can be constructed in theory but for which no advocates can be found. Most students of political representation are all too aware of possible discrepancies between the characteristics of representatives and their actions. Pitkin herself is dismissive of descriptive representation, because she rejects its implicit assumption of such a conjunction. She believes that, in hands less competent than hers, concentration on descriptive representation leads to a focus on presence at the expense of action. If this were ever true, it no longer is. While she may be correct to identify such a danger, it is not an inevitable error, and if it was ever a common mistake, it no longer is. These days in empirical study, any curiosity about the relationship between action and personal characteristics is regarded as a topic for empirical research, not an assumption. Even so, the literature is awash with instances of feminists constructing fictional opponents from scholarship that allegedly reproduces mindlessly the error of simply assuming that women's presence in decision-making bodies is a good thing for women's interests. It is something of a trope, one that offers a convenient launching pad for an argument that might otherwise be more difficult to make.[3]

Representation takes place in the state and in civil society on executives, boards, and commissions, as well as in political parties, trade unions, and international organisations. Only a fraction of these positions are directly elected; many are appointed, and some are self-selected. Such representation is highly sensitive to context and is not necessarily democratic.

Several feminist scholars have attempted to research representation beyond legislatures. In a pathbreaking study, Weldon (2002) claimed that representation in state bodies in conjunction with women's movement activism, in circumstances where the state body consults the women's movement, does outperform what she terms *descriptive representation,* but by which she clearly means legislative representation. Her formulation raises key issues about representation, as it equates accountability with consultation, a problem we discuss later in the chapter. Despite its theoretical value, this work only minimally considers political context, uses the terms *descriptive* and *legislative representation* interchangeably, and covers only the year 1994, when there was much less variation in women's legislative presence in her thirty-six countries than in the following decade; hence, a later study might have produced different conclusions.[4] In contrast, in their study of thirty-one countries over time, Leslie Schwindt-Bayer and William Mishler (2005) provide powerful evidence that increases in women's representation in legislatures tend to be associated with increased policy responsiveness to women's concerns.

Women's movement actors make alliances both within movements and between movements and civil society and the state. Such activity is recounted in feminist research, which reveals policy cooperation between women's policy agencies and movement advocates located in different arenas, such as autonomous women's movements, the media, political parties, trade unions, legislatures, government and public administration. The literature includes discussions of strategic partnerships between women's movements and women's policy machinery (Holli and Kantola 2005). A common metaphor is that of the triangle, capturing the idea of an alliance linking movements, the state and some other entity. Different terms have been used, including *strategic partnership, triangle of empowerment, velvet triangles,* and *feminist advocacy coalitions* (Halsaa 1999; Vargas and Wieringa 1998; Mazur 2002; Woodward 2003). Although there is no agreement on the definition of the triangle, its components, or its strategic location, most include state actors, legislators, and women's movement actors who are linked to each other through different organisations and political processes.

Thus, research demonstrates that representation is not confined to legislative structures and also identifies the variety of possible alliances between movement and state actors. It distinguishes between different sources of representation and draws attention to their combined impact on policy processes. In showing that a strong women's movement improves the representative function of policy agencies, it highlights the importance for movements of having allies in the state, combining and making more systematic the findings of previous studies of women's movements and the state. Although the metaphor is limited and may obscure complex processes of alliance making, it has considerable analytical utility if used sensibly (Holli 2008).

Arguably, both the theory and the practice of representation are in a complex phase of change that poses huge challenges for research. The divide between theoretical and empirical research has been recognised by scholars who call for detailed strategies of investigation that take into account the range of questions theorists have raised about women's representation. A good example is found in the work of Celis *et al.* (2008), and others who draw attention to the requirements of empirical research on political representation that they argue must answer at least four questions: Who represents or claims to represent women, what policies are put forward by representatives, where and why are they put forward? Our reading of feminist representation theory suggests five additional questions:

Which women are represented (capturing difference and intersectionality); when does the representation take place; what are the processes through which claims are formulated, refined, and advanced (indicative of political context); to whom are the representatives accountable (a classic concern of representation theory); and to what extent are they made an indicator of effectiveness? The logical order of the questions becomes *how* is representation done, *who* does it, in relation to *which* women, *what* policies, *where, when, why*, and *to whom* accountable, and *how effective* is the representation?

Concepts, Data, and Definitions

We focus here on each question about representation in turn using RNGS data, which we contend offers new answers to many of the questions. RNGS supplies new data on representation in different kinds of institutions including movements, bureaucracies, agencies and parties in conjunction with legislative representation, as well as in the context of temporal and specific policy settings. The RNGS project extends well beyond simply correlating the characteristics of representatives with their activities. The key innovation is the research design, in which the unit of analysis is the policy debate.[5] Debates were selected using criteria that included their importance at the time in terms of the issue. While it has its limitations (Celis 2008), the design generates a sample size sufficient for quantitative analysis, often impossible in studies of individual countries. It also offers a cleaner view of the existence and effectiveness of movement representation. Simply asking what movements achieve risks exaggerating their effects; in contrast, starting with debates allows empirical observation of movement actor intervention and effectiveness.

In this chapter, we use a common distinction between autonomous and integrated women's movements and organisations. Autonomous women's movements are a form 'of women's mobilisation that is devoted to promoting women's status and well-being independently of political parties and other associations that do not make the status of women their main concern. Autonomous organisations must be self-governing and recognize no superior authority nor be subject to governance of other political agencies' (Weldon 2002: 1161). By contrast, 'integrated women movement(s) [are] individuals and groups inside non women's movement organisation (women in political parties, in trade unions, media, academia, etc.)' (Weldon 2002: 1161). Women's movement actors, like social movements actors, may adopt a strategy of working within a variety of state institutions. Following Ferree and Mueller (2007), only when actors have *links* to organised collective women's movement entities may they be considered women's movement actors. Independent individuals (free of movement constraints) who happen to use feminist rhetoric are not movement actors. In the RNGS study, movements are diverse but may be thought to contain actors from either or both autonomous and integrated movements.[6] Both make claims for women. The RNGS definition of women's movement stipulates that all such actors must be women. Representation is fully successful when the state both includes movement actors in the policy process and makes decisions that reflect movement preferences (Dual Response), is partly successful when the state accepts either procedural or substantive representation by movement actors (Co-optation and Preemption), and is unsuccessful when the state makes no response (No Response).[7]

To explain political representation in relation to the theories discussed above, we developed several additional measures from the datasets. These are women's movement actor *presence* at the beginning and end of the debate, *legislator presence* in the debate, women's *policy agency representativeness,* women's movement actor *agreement, feminism of agency leadership, debate gendering,* and *legislator intervention.*[8]

- Women's movement actor *presence* is a scaled measure of procedural (or descriptive) representation defined as participation by movement actors at the beginning and end of the debate. It is a measure of the extent to which movement actors are accepted in the policy subsystem and is not exhaustive of those movement actors who put forward microframes in a debate.
- *Legislator presence* indicates whether one or more movement actors who were legislators took a stand in the debate.
- Women's *policy agency representativeness* scale is a simple measure of agency attempts to represent. Here we distinguish between strategic and delegate representation, where strategic representation is the independent advocacy of women's interests as understood by agencies and delegate representation is the strict advocacy of women's movement preferences. Thus, the highest point on the agency representativeness scale is delegate representation, capturing the occasions when agency officials advocate expressed movement preferences. The (perhaps arbitrary) placement of delegate above strategic representation reflects feminist concern with accountability to movements, discussed later in this chapter.
- *Women's movement agreement* simply distinguishes between debates in which both autonomous and integrated actors intervened and those in which only one or the other did.
- *Feminism of agency leadership* indicates any women's movement background of the agency head.[9]
- *Debate gendering* identifies the point at which a debate became gendered.
- *Legislator intervention* counts the number of legislators who intervened in each debate. It is the performance of a public act in the debate, including the public expression of an opinion.

These additional indicators enable us to distinguish the input and effectiveness of different participants in policy debates. Movement actors, agency officials and legislators are corners of a hypothetical policy triangle. We determine the circumstances under which each participates, the relative contributions of each to the substantive and procedural representation of women, and the extent of links between the three groups. In short, we can determine if such triangles operated in the debates.

The remainder of this chapter follows the questions and distinctions developed above through the RNGS datasets. We next explore the activities and effects of movement actors, women's policy agencies and legislators. We use both quantitative (bivariate correlations) and qualitative evidence to inform our discussion of the representation questions and use the findings to draw conclusions about both the nature of women's political representation in various policy environments and the relationships between different policy actors.

Answering the Nine Questions about Representation

1. How Is Representation Done?

Representation is performed by elected and appointed actors, movements and individuals operating in different and changing circumstances at different stages of policy debates. In our data, representation is conceptualised in terms of processes of framing. Women's representatives put forward gendered ideas in attempts to frame or reframe a debate so that its discourse is gendered or regendered in line with women's interests. These gendered frames may be feminist but are not necessarily so. Debates on public policy issues have several sources. They may emerge from public debate and be taken forward by individuals working in different institutions and arenas. They may, for example, begin in discussions inside sections of political parties, interest organisations, social movements, or parts of the civil service, or within the political leadership, and later find their way into manifestos and achieve priority in political programmes.

What does gendering do to a discourse? Most issues have gender dimensions, as they implicitly or explicitly reflect some notion of relations between women and men, and between masculinity and femininity. The strategy of gendering exposes the biases of debates by drawing attention to their gendered content or by offering a regendering of an already gendered debate. Women's representatives act in these processes. Although practices vary considerably, the case studies presented in Box 3.1 provide clear evidence of such involvement. Movement actors attempt to establish and maintain consultative relationships with policy agencies; policy agencies seek movement support and occasionally establish consultative groups that include movement actors. Recently, for example, Great Britain's Women and Equalities Unit established a Muslim women's forum to facilitate government consultation with this group of women (Lovenduski 2007). Probably the most common relationship between agencies and movement turns on the research and expertise of movement actors. Contribution to policy research by expert movement actors is one of several forms of lobbying and a major site of framing. It feeds into deliberation in terms of content, and discourse, hence, is an attempt to gender subsequent debate.[10]

As predicted, movement actors, agencies, and women legislators attempted to gender debates. Agencies intervened in eighty debates, movement actors operating autonomously or together with other organisations did so in 110 debates, and legislators intervened in forty-six debates. The initial answer to the 'how' question is that representation is done by all three sets of actors through standard repertoires of political intervention, both separately and together.[11]

2. Who Represents Women?

Movement actors prioritise women's movement concerns to the exclusion of other interests. Women legislators may present their party's view of women's interests, while, normally, the brief of a policy agency is to advocate for women's interests as conceived by the appointing government when designing the agency's remit.

Table 3.1 classifies 217 representative acts found in the debates. It shows the number of interventions by women representatives in the most important decisional arenas of the 114 debates and indicates that actors from free-standing women's movement organisations (autonomous) made the most interventions.[12] However, these eighty-seven interventions were still a minority of the total number of interventions.

Box 3.1 Two Case Studies on Diversity

The Debate on Ending Entitlements for Poor Families in the United States, 1992–1996
The U.S. welfare reform debates of the 1980s and 1990s were gendered with a focus on poor women. The Personal Responsibility and Work Opportunity Reconciliation Act of 1996 'instituted a paradigm shift in welfare policy, holding the poor individually responsible for poverty and for ending it' (McBride 2007: 293). This welfare-to-work policy was enacted after a protracted set of debates. The policy was aimed at poor single mothers. The discourse mainly named single mothers as the proposed targets. Race was a subtext, and many of the participating welfare advocacy organisations were black women's groups. The long-term welfare recipients in the United States were mainly black. Hence the debate was saturated with class, race and gender meanings. Women's movement actors made explicit the gender and class but not the race meanings. In the recorded testimony of actors, there are many accusations that middle-class feminists acquiesced to the plan to deny support to poor women, an accusation that McBride (2007: 292) regards as founded. Antifeminist gendering came from both right-wing movements and fathers' rights groups. In this debate, although the interests of poor black women were under threat, attention was focused mainly on class and gender interests. Despite long-standing and general recognition that campaigns against welfare benefits in the United States are racist, race does not appear to have been a preoccupation of the movement actors in the debate. The issue was not a priority for the movement, which was also divided about the goals of welfare policy. The near-silence on race may have reflected public discourse on race more generally. However, McBride argues that movement failure on the issue reflects a failure to focus on the interplay of race, gender, and class.

Canadian Jobs Strategy to Combat Unemployment, 1984–1985
Diversity was built into the debate on Canadian job training strategy. By the mid-1980s in Canada, state institutions were organised to take responsibility for diversity effects. Hence the initiating document on job training strategy stressed the 'importance of addressing the specific needs of disadvantaged groups in particular women, people living with a disability, aboriginal people and immigrants' (Teghtsoonian and Grace 2001: 242). Provision was made for women's movement actors to participate in the debate, including representatives of immigrants and minority women. The final policy contained a fair number of elements that both matched their preferences and incorporated diversity. For example, the law included provision for participation targets for women and minority groups. In Canada at that time, the founding logic of agencies required them to consider diversity, and this was reflected in movement organisation and debates (Teghtsoonian and Grace 2001: 242).

Table 3.1: Women's Movement Actor Intervention by Institutional Base and Issue

	INSTITUTIONAL BASE					
Issue	Parliament/ Legislature	Political Party	Trade Union	Other Non–Women's Movement Organisations	Autonomous	Total
Abortion	14	10	1	6	29	60
Job training	5	7	11	9	10	42
Prostitution	7	4	0	7	24	42
Political representation	14	11	2	8	15	50
Hot issue	6	3	1	4	9	23
Total	46	35	15	34	87	217

Policy agencies were also active. At least one intervened in more than half (seventy-one) of the debates. In practice, the claims of agencies to speak for or to act for women are necessarily indirect. Agency relationships to women's movements are often left unspecified, given that RNGS concept definitions *assume* that movement actors speak for women.[13] Therefore, when other actors, like women's policy agencies, articulate ideas that coincide with those of movement actors, they represent women. For the agencies, such claims derive from mandates made by governments, usually on the basis of fairly specific briefs,[14] and may or may not involve regular consultation with movement representatives. Weldon (2002) argues that agency interventions facilitate movement representation when reliable arrangements for consultation with autonomous movements are in place. Although we lack systematic evidence of the patterns of consultations with women's movements, we do have data on the presence of movement ideas in agency microframes and also on the presence of women's movement experience in the form of officials with movement experience. In sixty-three of the sixty-six cases for which we have evidence both on agency representativeness and on movement actor and agency microframe fit, agency microframes either match or are compatible with those of movement actors. In thirty-eight such cases, the microframes match; hence, agencies are representative of movement actors. The data also provide evidence that agency leaders may be influenced by women's movement and feminist ideas or may have backgrounds in women's movements.

Statistical correlations suggest the existence of a policy triangle linking some women legislators, movement actors and agencies. Agency representativeness associates positively with movement actor presence at the end of the debate (.275*), which is also positively associated with the presence of women legislators in the debate (.429**), the number of women legislators who intervened (.412**), and with movement agreement (.347**), but not with the percentage of women in the lower house of the legislature — a finding that warrants further research.[15] Technically, women legislators are also movement actors and appear in the dataset as such. This raises the question of overlap in the data and means that we cannot be confident of the correlations. When the cases in which women legislators intervene are removed from the dataset, the correlations between agency representativeness and movement actor presence disappear — an effect that may suggest that those legislators who intervene are a key element to the relationships on which policy triangles are based. Although we are stretching the data beyond its reach, these findings suggest that intervention by women legislators enhances movement participation but the percentage of women in the legislature does not. Is this preliminary evidence of critical acts that enhance the representation of women? We return to these discussions in our conclusions.

3. Which Women Are Represented?

The question raises issues of difference among women. The data presented here describe instances of both feminist and nonfeminist representation, whereas the two case studies (*see* Box 3.1) include some consideration of diversity but not intersectionality, as such. To construct an answer to this question, we read off claims about who is represented in the different debates from their responsibilities to their organisation or movement. In each debate, movement actors advocate for those women's movements interested in the issue, including sometimes feminist movements. Because the perceived interests of different groups of women vary by debate issues, so also does the pattern of intervention.

Table 3.1 indicates that interventions in abortion debates mobilised a range of movement actors concentrated in free-standing groups and, to a lesser extent, in parliaments. Job training debates predictably mobilised trade unions; eleven of the fifteen interventions by trade union movement actors were in job training debates. Prostitution debates most often engaged autonomous movements. Political representation debates engaged women legislators as well as party and autonomous movement actors, while hot-issue debates attracted the attention of autonomous and parliamentary women. Autonomous movement actors were the most consistently active, often speaking for issue-specific groups. Actors in legislatures, in trade unions, and with other institutional affiliations may have responsibilities to represent women within the context of their organisation but will normally also be required to be responsible to wider membership, electors, and the goals of their organisation. In other words, they operate within the normal lines of political contestation and are thereby constrained. In so doing, they may have responsibilities to act on behalf of particular groups of women and in opposition to the interests of other women.

As Table 3.2 shows, in thirty-six debates, agencies either did not represent women's movements or they advanced frames that threatened those of the women's movements. Agencies attempted representation in seventy-two debates, gendering thirty-eight of them. They were least likely to intervene in hot-issue

Table 3.2: Policy Agency Interventions by Debate Issue and Percentages

Issue	No Intervention or Intervention Does Not Advance Movement Actors' Frames	Intervention Advances Movement Frames But Not Gender Debate	Intervention Advances Movement Frames and Gender Debate	Total Number of Debates
Abortion	11 (40.7%)	7 (25.9%)	9 (33.3%)	27
Job training	6 (27.2%)	12 (54.5%)	4 (13.2%)	22
Prostitution	6 (23%)	10 (33.5%)	10 (33.5%)	26
Political representation	6 (23.6%)	3 (14.2%)	12 (57.1%)	21
Hot issue	7(53.3%)	2 (16.7%)	3 (25%)	12
Total	36	34	38	108

debates. To interpret these findings in terms of the question of which women are represented, we need to turn to our qualitative evidence, which shows that the groups of women for whom claims to representation were made varied by debate and type of representative. This tells us a little about the different groups of women who are represented. Interventions in job training debates were designed to improve the position of employed women or women seeking employment (Mazur 2001). In the abortion debates, women's rights were framed in a variety of contexts. In Great Britain and the United States, some attention was given by advocates to the needs of those women who were dependent on public provision for abortions (poorer, therefore more likely to be young and to belong to an ethnic minority) (McBride Stetson 2001a and 2001b). In Great Britain, minority women's movement actors explicitly asserted separate interests in abortion debates. In prostitution debates, some movement actors and some agencies advocated on behalf of prostitutes and of trafficked women and children and against their clients, but frames did not normally highlight differences among women. In a few cases, however (the Netherlands, Italy, Finland), it was noted that many prostitutes were foreign (Outshoorn 2004). In political representation debates, different roles, social characteristics, and interests of women were sometimes highlighted, as attention was drawn to the requirements of mothers, the relationships between women's claims and those of others (e.g. ethnic or linguistic minorities) (Lovenduski 2005). In the smaller sample of hot-issue debates, references to different groups of women varied by the issue under consideration (Haussman and Sauer 2007). Parliamentary women, often divided along party lines, were most likely to express movement microframes on political representation and abortion debates.

Because difference has been a consistently important concern in feminist movements, we expect that feminist interventions were sensitive to it. Feminist concerns were advanced by fifty-five agencies. To the extent that feminist and women's movement discourse was imbued with ideas about difference, and this was reflected in representation, then we can infer that ideas about different groups of women were taken into account. But this is an imperfect process, and we are not in a position to make a systematic quantitative assessment of which of the various categories of women were represented in discourse, in terms of their class, race, education, marital status, and so forth. While we can only infer so much from the classification of frames as feminist, we can explore the issue of diversity further, by looking at the two case studies described in Box 3.1.

Discourses of gender diversity seem to be confined mainly to considerations of class in the debates, with an occasional genuflection to race. The data do not suggest that diversity issues were central to representation. Though advocates did not deny, and indeed frequently affirmed, the diversity of women — with the exception of some of the political representation debates — and despite some mobilisation of minority women's movements, intersectionality did not receive much attention. On these issues and at this level of decision making, women's movement actors are ineffective when they express concerns about diversity, and women continue to be treated as a unitary category. Outshoorn and Johanna Kantola note the slowness of governments to 'recognise diversity among women and to take it into account in policy' and the tendency for 'agencies to take women as an undifferentiated category ... with the attendant danger of paying too little heed to minority voices' (2007: 279–280). Religious, class and regional differences may be reflected in party systems that are more or less responsive to their women's advocates. However, in systems where the state and party institutions do not reflect a difference among women — often because there is no corresponding politically salient difference among men — neither does the agency. This is a pattern that began to change in the 2000s, especially after European legislation to protect various diversity strands came into force; but most of our debates took place before this change, and few of them portend it. The ideally gendered representation of diversity that is so central to feminist concerns translates only poorly through institutional political structures, which are designed to aggregate and not to differentiate interests.

4. What Policies Are Put Forward by Representatives; What Representations Are Made?

Feminist scholars argue that representatives should advance women's interests but falter when it comes to producing a reliable and accepted definition of those interests. Frequently, expressed preferences are treated as proxies for interests. Following this logic, the relevant research question here becomes: Do representatives put forward claims that are made by women's movements? In classic representation theory, representatives advance the interests of the represented either as delegates who act *as* those they represent, putting forward the policies advocated by their voters (or whoever appoints or elects them), or as trustees who act *for*, that is, attempt to learn and advance, or even to construct, the interests of those they claim to represent. Although we cannot determine if representatives see themselves as delegates or trustees without asking them, we can observe their interventions in relation to movement issues and infer from our observations that expressed movement interests are (or are not) represented.

The policies that are put forward by representatives are a significant part of the basis of their claims to represent. Our data indicate (1) the top five movement priorities at the time of the debate; (2) whether the interventions of movement actors were made on issues that were movement priorities; (3) which categories of movement actors intervened; and then (4) whether movement concerns were expressed by each category of representative.

Accordingly, we identify actor, agency, and legislator presence in each debate that took place while they were among the top five women's movement priorities. We then compare these with interventions on issues that were not top priorities. For each debate, we identify which types of actors participated. Finally, we inspect the content of the interventions to determine whether movement actor and agency official interventions were congruent and how congruence varied by type of actor.

All three expressed gendered microframes in both priority and nonpriority debates. These are presented in Tables 3.3 and 3.4.

Table 3.3 shows that in most of the seventy-nine debates that were on priority issues, agencies advanced gendered microframes; autonomous and integrated movement actors and legislators intervened in just under half of them, but separate interventions by autonomous and integrated actors were much less frequent.

In the thirty-five nonpriority debates shown in Table 3.4, the pattern is not the expected mirror image. The last row of the table gives interventions by each category of actor on nonpriority issues as a percentage of their total interventions. While this calculation is admittedly crude, it is quite instructive. If we could verify the patterns suggested by the tables, then the percentages would suggest that on the debate issues studied by RNGS, women legislators and coalitions of autonomous and integrated movement actors are more likely to act as delegates who put forward women's movement priorities than agencies and movement actors acting separately, who in turn are more likely to act as trustees taking a position on issues that were not movement priorities. This does not mean that the positions are in movement interests, which may have been under construction. It means only that movements were not at the time giving priority to the issue being debated and may have preferred representatives to be spending their time on the issues that were priorities.

To deepen our understanding of the representativeness of the interventions, we also inspect the content of the microframes. Where both agencies and movement actors have microframes on debate issues, we can inspect their fit with each other. Policy agencies mainly attempted to gender debates that were about movement priority issues. In the majority of cases, agency officials attempted to represent the preferences expressed by women's movement actors by inserting matching microframes into policy debates, and, in a substantial minority of cases, the shared microframes were feminist.

Table 3.3: Representation in Priority Issue Debates and Percentage of Interventions

Issue	Agency Advances Gendered Microframe	Autonomous Movement Actors	Integrated Movement Actors	Autonomous and Integrated Movement Actors	Legislators	Number of Debates
Abortion	19 (31%)	11 (58%)	1 (8%)	18 (38%)	14 (37%)	30
Job training	12 (19%)	3 (16%)	6 (46%)	4 (9%)	3 (8%)	13
Prostitution	7 (11%)	1 (5%)	0 (0%)	6 (13%)	4 (11%)	7
Political representation	16 (25%)	1 (5%)	3 (23%)	14 (30%)	12 (32%)	8
Hot issue	8 (13%)	3 (16%)	3 (23%)	5 (13%)	5 (13%)	11
Total	62	19	13	38	38	79

Table 3.4: Representation in Nonpriority Issue Debates and Percentage of Nonpriority Issue Interventions of All Interventions by Actor

Issue	Agency Advances Gendered Microframe	Autonomous Movement Actors	Integrated Movement Actors	Autonomous and Integrated Movement Actors	Legislators	Number of Debates
Abortion	1 (3%)	0	1 (10%)	0	0	1
Job training	9 (31%)	2 (17%)	5 (50%)	1 (11%)	2 (25%)	9
Prostitution	15 (52%)	10 (83%)	2 (20%)	7 (78%)	3 (38%)	20
Political representation	4 (14%)	0	2 (20%)	0	2 (25%)	4
Hot issue	0	0	0	1 (11%)	1 (13%)	1
Total of nonpriority interventions	29	12	10	9	8	35
Percentage of all interventions	36% (N=81)	39% (N = 31)	43% (N = 23)	19% (N = 47)	17% (N = 46)	N = 228

The pattern is clear. Agencies seemed more likely to advance movement frames on those movement priority issues on which both autonomous and integrated actors were active, and they did not intervene in cases where autonomous movements acted alone. Similarly, women legislators were most likely to express movement microframes where both autonomous and integrated movements and organisations were engaged. Otherwise, they expressed microframes in debates in which integrated movements acted alone but did not speak in support in those debates in which autonomous movements acted alone.[16] Initial statistical testing of the associations indicates that more women legislators intervened when the issue was a movement priority (.207*). Movement actor presence at the end of the debate rose with movement actor agreement (.347**). However, although agency representativeness varied with movement actor presence (.275*), it did not vary consistently and significantly with movement issue priority or with movement actor agreement.

5. Where Are the Policies Put Forward?

Affecting representation are the political system or country in which the debate takes place, the institutional sites (especially their proximity to power) at which the debate is conducted, and the bases from which the debate's participants operate. We propose that the citizenship model, the policy environment, the institutionalisation of the women's movement, the type of institution, and the proximity of agencies to power all affect actor behaviour in debates.

Most of the debates took place in Western and Northern European democratic systems. Reasoning that citizenship models were important to the framing of representation debates, we classified these systems in ascending order according to their responsiveness to claims for group representation, with republican systems least likely, followed by liberal, hybrid and consociational corporatist (Krook et al. 2009).[17]

We found significant and strong positive associations between citizenship type and the percentage of women in the lower house (.457**). This is an expected effect of the tendency of hybrid and corporatist systems to have relatively high numbers of women in the parliament. The positive association of citizenship model with legislator presence in these debates is weaker but nonetheless significant (.233*), as it is with the intervention of women legislators (.234*). But we found no associations with movement presence in policy subsystems or agency representativeness, suggesting that women's representation is not well provided for via established systems of extraparliamentary group representation, and that women are outsiders in established interest group politics.

As several earlier chapters [this refers to the original volume] have indicated, theories of public policy highlight the policy sector as a crucial determinant of the nature and outcome of policy debates. Access to the policy subsystem is a crucial group resource. Where systems are closed, only those inside have access; hence, the relative openness of the policy subsystem in which a decision is made is an important element of the ability of movements to participate. As expected, women's movement presence in the policy subsystem was positively associated with the openness of the policy subsystem (.331**), a finding that was unaffected by the political complexion of the government in power at the time of the debate. The representativeness of the policy agency is not associated with the degree of openness of the policy subsystem. However, in cases in which the policy subsystem is closed, there is a strong association between movement actor presence and women legislator intervention (.664**). When compared to the correlation of .412** of these variables in all debates, this finding suggests that in closed systems, where access is at a premium, women legislators will be important points of access.

Debates were conducted and, in practice, were decided upon in a variety of locations, but for the most part, were eventually decided in the legislature (92 of 114), at least on a formal basis. In most legislatures, both women and men are likely to be represented by men who in all but a few countries operate in contexts that are constrained by party discipline and party manifestos, institutions that historically are dominated by men and male concerns. In such systems, women's movements and agency officials may actually have more scope to represent women than legislators bound by party discipline. For example, party discipline affects the behaviour of parliamentary women, who may vote with their party and against movement preferences that they have otherwise supported, as did the women legislators of the Centre Right in the Italian debate on constitutional reform between 1992 and 2001 (Guadagnini 2007).

The RNGS research strategy of debate tracing brings the legislature to the fore through its requirement that the debate must have an end point in an official authoritative decision. Constitutionally, this is often the legislature. However, in European party democracies, where legislatures do not necessarily hold the ultimate decision-making power, it is normal to give legitimacy to decisions made whether publicly or behind the scenes elsewhere in the system by the executive or the political parties, or both. Thus, the very high proportion of issues that were debated in parliament may be more an indicator of system type than of decision point, and we should, therefore, assume that other institutions were involved, especially political parties; this issue, for reasons of space, is not discussed in this chapter.[18] Although intervention by parliamentary women is important, it is only one aspect of the decision system.

In the ninety-two debates that were wholly or partly conducted in parliament, neither the presence of movement actors in the policy subsystem nor the interventions of women legislators were associated significantly with the percentage of women legislators. This finding suggests that numbers determine neither acts nor effectiveness, and, hence, has implications for the critical-mass debate. Have we demonstrated conclusively, then, that critical acts are independent of numbers? We return to this question in our conclusions.

Women's movement institutionalisation is a measure of the relative degree of presence of movement activists representing ideas and agendas of the collective women's movement inside social, political and authoritative state institutions. It refers to the extent to which movement actors are in legislatures, well-established lobby coalitions, bureaucratic and legislative commissions, political parties, unions, interest groups, academia, media, and formal campaigns. This conceptualisation treats institutionalisation in terms of levels or degrees. It is effectively a count of presence across an extensive range of key decision-making institutions and is, therefore, an indicator of descriptive representation.[19] The institutionalisation of the women's movements was not significantly associated with movement actor participation or with agency representativeness. However, our expectation that high levels of women's movement institutionalisation might overcome the barriers of a closed policy subsystem to movement actor presence in policy subsystems was confirmed with a significant positive association between them of $.332^{**}$ in closed policy systems.

In terms of their proximity to government power, most women's policy agencies were part of the top echelon of decision-making power in their institutional context. The closeness of the agency most involved in the debate to the centre of power co-varies with the presence of women legislators ($.204^{*}$) but is not associated with the number of women legislator interventions, movement actor presence or agency representativeness.

To summarise, that citizenship models are associated with the presence of women in the legislature does not predict movement actor presence in the policy subsystem or agency representativeness. Open policy subsystems benefited movement actor presence. Debates in parliament provided a useful site to test arguments about critical mass. In such debates, the interventions of parliamentary women enhanced movement actor presence, but this effect was not associated with the percentage of women legislators. Women legislators were more likely to intervene in debates in which both autonomous and integrated movement actors engaged, one of several associations that support claims that cross-movement cooperation is more powerful than feminist separatism. Finally, neither movement institutionalisation nor agency proximity to the centre of power predicted movement participation or agency representativeness.

6. When Does Representation Take Place?

Political time is complex; hence, this question has several dimensions, including proximity to election years; the phases of the world and national economies; the public opinion cycle; the timetable of the decision process and sequence, or whether the debate followed a victory or defeat for the movement; favourable political climate and consensus around priorities, issues and policy content. The most straightforward usage is the dates of debates. The RNGS sample of debates was selected to be representative of each decade since the emergence of the new women's movements in the 1960s. This period extends from the 1960s to the early 2000s, with some concentration of debates in the 1990s.[20] If policy agencies become more likely to act in concert with movement actors over time, we expect to see an increase in the degree to which they express the same microframes on movement priority issues. We found no statistically significant relationship between the fit of the movement actor and agency microframes and the decade in which the debate takes place.

The issue books offer insight into some aspects of sequence, the effects of which vary by issue type. For example, while the analysis of job training debates revealed a widespread context characterised by movement away from male breadwinner models of employment, this was not reflected in a change over time in the success of women's movements in gaining substantive and descriptive representation. Nor did the data on this issue suggest a link between economic cycles and variation in agency performance over time (Mazur 2001: 309–310). Sequence effects vary by issue. McBride Stetson found that sequence had some effect in abortion debates. Once debates were gendered, the frame tended to last through subsequent debates on the same issue, although this pattern was not universal (2001a: 274–275). On the issue of prostitution, however, the achievement of representation does not ensure access in subsequent debates (Outshoorn 2004: 270). No systematic sequential cross-national patterns were found in debates on political representation either (Lovenduski *et al.* 2005: 291).

We can infer changes in the political climate from the position of the government on the Left-Right political spectrum and the ideological and organisational closeness of the women's movement to the Left. We found that the ideological and organisational closeness of the movements to the Left increased over time ($.270^{**}$ and $.267^{**}$, respectively) and expected that when the Left was in power and movements were close to the Left, they would have both procedural access and the benefit of having their microframes advanced by policy agencies. However, this prediction proved unfounded.

7. Why Are Representations Made?

Decisions to represent, like any decisions to undertake political action, are based on motivation, obligation, or opportunity — or a combination thereof. Motivation follows from interests and desire, obligation from legal and/or moral responsibility, and opportunity from a combination of capacity and position. For all actors, we expect motivation, obligation and opportunity to vary by debate issue, citizenship model, the number of women in parliament, and the position on the Right-Left spectrum of the government in power.

The obligation of movement actors to represent movement interests is moral and in this research is a matter of definition. Agency obligations are legal and may also be moral; they do not necessarily include representation of women's movements but may vary with the feminism of the leadership. Legislators have opportunity in the sense that so many debates are decided in parliaments but, as we have seen, may be constrained by their party and perhaps by institutional convention and procedures. We explore the patterns for each category of actor.

There are at least four ways in which actor motivation to intervene may vary: according to cohesion, threat, feminism and priority. If an issue is of high priority to the women's movement, we expect that its actors will make claims, and we hope that agencies and legislators will support them. Movement cohesion did not have predictive value. At least half of movement actors were in agreement on all but one issue, and on most issues there was complete agreement within the part of the movement that was interested in the issue. Despite their theoretical promise, motivation variables of cohesion, priority, and degree of threat did not add to the explanation of movement actor participation.

The concept of opportunity had more predictive value. We understand opportunity as a feature of the political configuration at the time of the debate and of the associated winnability of the debate. Relevant here are the relationships of the movement to the Left, the party in power, the proportion of women parliamentarians, the institutionalisation of the movement, and the winnability of the debate. Movement actor presence rises with some indicators of the political opportunity structure but not others. In addition to legislator intervention and agency representativeness (already discussed), we found that actor presence in policy subsystems co-varies with the institutionalisation of the women's movement $(.235^*)$ but not with the percentage of women in parliament or closeness of the movement to the Left or the presence of a left-wing party in government.

The winnability of the debate is a difficult condition to quantify in a convincing way. Arguably, some debates are more winnable than others, which may affect strategic decisions to intervene by representatives. Some issues are more susceptible to gender reframing. One aspect of debate winnability is that some policy subsystems are amenable to explicitly gendered debate frames. How well do the frames of movement actors match the frames of the policy subsystem in which the debate is resolved? It could be said that where movement and subsystem frames are matching or compatible, the debate is more winnable for the movement; yet tests for correlation do not confirm this notion. RNGS measures the compatibility of the microframe of movement actors with the issue frame that initially shapes the debate in the policy subsystem. In more than half the cases (58 per cent), movement actors' frames were compatible with those of the policy subsystem actors. Table 3.5 shows that issue frames were most likely to be gendered at the end of debate when the initial subsystem frame matched that of the movement actors, while compatible frames predicted a less than even chance of debate frame gendering. Movement actor presence in the policy subsystem was not significantly associated with the frame fit between actors and policy subsystems, but it correlated strongly with the gendering of the issue frame by the end of the debate $(.417^{**})$. These seemingly perverse findings may result from a greater reluctance on the part of decision makers to adjust policy when frames are compatible but not matching, a possibility that requires further investigation.

The data include observations of feminist issue frames at both the beginning and end of the debate. Twenty-five debate frames were feminist at the beginning of the debate and forty-five at the end. Movement actor presence in the policy subsystem was positively correlated to feminist frames at beginning $(.395^*)$ and at end of the debates $(.369^*)$.

We discussed priority at length in question 4 above. Here we extend that discussion to consider the question of why movement actors might support

Table 3.5: Issue Frame at the End of Debate by Issue Frame Fit

Issue Frame Fit	Issue Frame Gendered at End of Debate		Total
	Yes (%)	No (%)	
Threatening	10 (71)	4 (29)	14
Mixed	27 (77)	8 (23)	35
Compatible	23 (48)	25 (52)	48
Matching	15 (88)	2 (12)	17
N	75 (66)	39 (34)	114

issues that are not among movement top priorities. This occurred most often in prostitution debates, where 56 per cent of agency and 32 per cent of movement nonpriority interventions were made. An issue that is difficult for women's advocates to ignore, prostitution, touches on aspects of sexuality and, once under consideration, highlights the state habit of regulating sexual behaviour, a habit of considerable importance to feminists. As Outshoorn (2004) and others have shown, prostitution debates feature many gradations of gender content that are stressed by women's movements seeking to gender debates on this issue. It is also an issue on which women's movements are not cohesive. Prostitution debate frames are polarised and controversial. The rights of prostitutes are interpreted either as sex work or in terms of sexual oppression. Outshoorn points out that the few women's movements that did give high priority to the prostitution issue did so in debates that took place after 1990. Prostitution debates tend not to be high priorities for movements, which find it difficult to agree to a common problem definition and to maintain agreement once achieved. The relationship between agreement and priority is well illustrated by the Italian debate on prostitution that took place in 1998 presented in Box 3.2.

When we consider the contested and complex frames of the prostitution issue and its conjunction with the importance to movements of what is at stake, it becomes more understandable why movement actor presence, agency representativeness and movement priority may not coincide. As already discussed, opportunity for agencies is related to their capacity and their location. Policy agency representativeness may also be affected by motivation, obligation, and opportunity. Officials may be *motivated* by the beliefs of their leadership at the time of the debate. They may be *obliged* to intervene by their terms of reference; they may, as professionals charged with advancing women's interests, seek to advance women's movement concerns especially where issues are of high priority to the movements. They may respond to a particular *opportunity* when a public debate of some kind illuminates a women's concern — including those not currently on the movement agenda. Policy agency officials may be inhibited or encouraged by their capacity.

Policy agencies rarely act when the debate is outside of their remit; only ten put forward microframes during debates outside of their remit. Agency representativeness could not be explained by agency capacity, movement issue priority, or feminist leadership.[21] Nor could it be explained by any of the political opportunity variables, except the organisational closeness of the movement to the Left, with which it was negatively associated (−.200*).

For women legislators, opportunity is a function of whether a debate is decided in parliament and of the views of their party on the issue. Legislator intervention was associated with the organisational closeness of the movement to the Left (.221*) and could possibly be explained by the impact of party affilitation on motivation and opportunity.

Box 3.2 Case Study: Criminalisation of Clients of Underage Prostitutes in Italy, 1998

Changes in ideas during the years before the debate seem to explain women's movement ambivalence about the policy. By the early 1990s, blaming clients for the existence of prostitution was common among both Catholics and feminists, an awkward political combination at best. From 1994 onward, many city mayors ordered municipal traffic police to fine clients in order to reduce street prostitution. At first, feminists welcomed the shift in blame from women to men. However, as the effects of such policies became apparent, feminists withdrew their support, arguing that the resulting measures worsened the working conditions of women on the streets. So, by the time the 1998 bill was debated, punishment of clients was not on the movement agenda, and neither women's movement actors nor women's policy agencies participated in the debates (Danna 2004).

To summarise, except when microframes are feminist at the beginning or end of the debate, movement presence is not predicted by indicators of motivation or opportunity. Agency representativeness is not explained by changes in the opportunity variables, but legislator intervention may depend on opportunity.

8. To Whom Are the Representatives Accountable?

Although not an explicit focus of the RNGS project, the data include useful information about the accountability of representatives to movements. RNGS defines women's and feminist movements in terms of ideas and identifies women's movement actors accordingly. Accountability to ideas may potentially be a powerful constraint but raises questions about who determines what criteria need to be met and if the requirements are satisfied. Representatives have two main modes of acting, which we conceptualise as the poles of a parameter of representativeness. At one pole, we find representatives who are specifically mandated by those represented on an issue to be debated — the delegates. At the other pole, representatives are mandated to act on behalf of those represented by discovering their interests if these are not already agreed upon — the trustees. In practice, delegate representation would be secured only by regular and effective consultation between movements and representatives, including between movement actors and other members (*see* Weldon 2002).

At the system level, accountability is a function of the institution in which representatives act. So, where movement actors are in the legislature they are accountable to their electorate, their parties, and their constituencies. Where movement actors are in trade unions, they are accountable to their members and co-workers, whereas in parties they are answerable to their fellow members but also more indirectly to the electorate and to the interests that are the basis of party support. The accountability of a representative to women's movements is not normally constitutionally specified and may or may not figure large in decision making.

While policy agencies may be accountable to women's movements at the level of ideas, movements do not have legal purchase over agency officials; hence, there is very little formal or legal basis for agency accountability to women's movements. Most policy agency leaders owed their jobs not directly to women's movements, but to elected governments; almost all were political appointments. In general, the recruitment of staff and lower level appointments in the agencies followed the appointments conventions of the relevant system (e.g. civil service procedures or corporatist nominees). Thus, whereas women's movements may have been influential in getting agencies established and are often involved in the formal or informal nomination of leaders, they do not have the last word about who are the decision makers and are not in a position to recall unsatisfactory officials. There are exceptions; some agencies are committees of movement representatives or include designated places for movement representatives (Guadagnini and Dona 2007). In addition, many agency officials try to represent women's movements, if only as a means of legitimating their activities by securing movement support.

To return once again to the distinction between trustees and delegates, if agency officials are movement delegates, then we expect them to advance issues that are movement priorities using microframes that match those of movement actors, and in so doing advocate for the movement except when the discourse is adopted solely for symbolic reasons. We have shown that agency officials sometimes do this. At such times, they directly support movement goals. On other occasions, however, agencies make claims on issues that are not movement priorities or advance frames that are not congruent with those of movement actors. On such occasions, they may be acting as trustees — that is, discovering or constructing interests that movements have not yet expressed. Alternatively, they may decide to advocate interests expressed by some movement actors on non-priority issues. Either way, agencies act as trustees. They might also, of course, act against women's interests and express frames that are opposed to those of women's movement actors.

When agencies intervene on issues that are movement priorities and advance microframes that are congruent with those of movement actors, they are advocates for the women's movement. May we infer accountability because ideas match? This seems a step too far, as crucial elements of accountability are missing. As stated above, generally movements are not invited to select officials and are not in a position to recall them from their roles in state decision-making positions, so traditional accountability is not present. Indeed, autonomous movements are especially constrained, as they have by definition no formal part in the powerful established decision-making institutions and can control only their own delegates where they have such delegates.

Integrated movements may well be in a different position. Party and trade union women's organisations, for example, often determine who are the movement actors within that institution, whereas organised-party women sometimes have considerable influence over who the legislative representatives are and sometimes over who is appointed to a policy agency. Integrated movement actors, by virtue of their presence in channels of representation, have some purchase over traditional levers of accountability. We can stretch this a little farther and state that when women's movements are institutionalised into the traditional institutions that are formally accountable to the electorate via the legislature, they may be able to influence levers of accountability through the activity of movement actors in these contexts. Thus, we can illuminate some dimensions of accountability by exploring the institutionalisation of women's movements into decision-making structures.

'Institutionalisation is the process by which claims-making by social movements becomes repetitive, revitalised and self-sustaining in response to the internal dynamics of social movements and the imperatives of the external environment' (Mueller and McCarthy 2003: 233). This is not a unitary concept, and different movements achieve different levels of institutionalisation that may vary by policy subsystem, by issue type, and by country. We measure this on two related scales: Our distinction between autonomous and integrated movement actors captures some of the variation in women's movements' institutionalisation into civil society, while the RNGS institutionalisation variable can be used to probe presence in civil society and state institutions together. The data show that only a few movements enjoyed relatively high levels of institutionalisation (7 of 114); most movements (79) were at a medium level of institutionalisation, and 28 were at a low level of institutionalisation.[22] Movement institutionalisation rose consistently with the openness of the policy subsystem (.194*), with the ideological (.419**) and organisational (.192*) closeness of the movement to the Left, and with movement presence in the policy subsystem at the end of the debate (.235*), but not with agency representativeness, the receptivity of the citizenship model to group representation, or the presence of the Left in government. The variation with the openness of the policy subsystem suggests that movement actors, who are often outsiders, may benefit from the greater political hospitality of open policy sectors. Of course, relatively greater institutionalisation may also portend relatively greater access in closed policy systems.

To summarise, although attention to women's movement ideas about women's interests may affect the representativeness of policy agencies and definitionally inform the microframes of movement actors, ideas are porous channels of accountability. Strictly speaking, agencies are accountable to movements only insofar as the working of the particular democratic system in which they are embedded provides for them to be so accountable. In most democratic systems, that provision is via the legislature and is normally indirect.

9. How Effective Is the Representation?

So far, we have explored the connections predicted by feminist representation theory, testing associations where the data permit by running bivariate correlations. This exploratory research suggests that women's movement actor presence in policy subsystems is explained by movement actor agreement, intervention by women legislators, policy agency representativeness, issue priority, the openness of the policy subsystem, and relative movement institutionalisation. The percentage of women in the lower house of the legislature at the time of the debate seems to have no explanatory power for either movement presence or agency representativeness. However, because of its theoretical importance to the critical-mass debate, we will test it in our final models.

To conclude our analysis, we entered each variable into an Ordinal Regression or PLUM, an extension of the linear model to ordinal categorical data.[23] The full model was not substantiated by further statistical testing, which found only the number of women legislator interventions and agency representativeness to be significant, confirming that the acts of women legislators and policy agencies increase the presence of women's movement actors. This result is reported in Table 3.6. As explained in Chapter 4 [this refers to the original volume], the last column of the table shows the exponential ratio, EXP (β), for each level of the predictor variables. An EXP (β) of less than 1 indicates a negative effect, whereas an EXP (β) of greater than 1 is a positive effect. Table 3.6, thus, shows that the absence of agency representativeness has an independent negative effect and that legislator intervention has an independent positive effect on movement presence. The likelihood of women's movement actor presence in the policy subsystem at the end of the debate is more than twice as great when women legislators intervene in the debate than when they do not. When the policy agency neither supports nor contradicts movement microframes, the likelihood of movement actor presence is about 80 per cent less than when agency and movement actors' frames match and about 89 per cent less likely than when the agency does nothing. Thus, we confirm that movement actor presence is enhanced by the acts of legislators and policy-making officials.

Finally, we turn to the interplay between substantive and descriptive representation to consider whether policy agencies and legislators also facilitate substantive representation. The variable State Response counts the occasions when movements achieve either a procedural or a substantive response, neither, or both.[24] Exploratory bivariate analysis indicates that one or more interventions by women legislators is associated (.213*) with the achievement of substantive and descriptive representation—full success for the movement—and this effect is also positively associated (.200*) with the percentage of women in the lower

Table 3.6: Ordinal Regression of Women's Movement Actor Presence Model

Independent Variable Measures	Parameter Estimate	EXP(β)
Legislator intervention	.846**	2.253
No legislator intervention	Reference category	N/A
Policy agency representativeness: agency microframe incompatible with women's movement actors	−.484	Not significant
Policy agency representativeness: agency does nothing	−2.145***	.1171
Policy agency representativeness: agency advances microframe neither matching nor conflicting	−1.568*	.2008
Policy agency representativeness: agency matches movement actor's microframe	Reference category	N/A

Pseudo R^2: Cox and Snell, .299; Nagelkerke, .359; McFadden, .199.

house of parliament. However, there is no association between women's policy agency representativeness and the successful achievement of both substantive and descriptive representation together.

To unpack this further, we created indicators of outcomes of substantive representation (defined as the state meeting movement actor demands without permitting their participation, i.e. Preemption) and descriptive representation (defined as the state permitting movement actor participation without meeting their policy demands, i.e. Co-optation). There were twenty-two cases of substantive representation only and twelve cases of descriptive representation only. These outcomes were not associated with agency representativeness, parliamentary intervention, characteristics of the policy system, or movement institutionalisation. Half of the substantive representation debates were on prostitution, underlining the points made above about this issue, but otherwise there was no particular issue-based pattern.

Hence, the final step in our analysis is to test the impact of agencies, legislators, and movements on the achievement of both substantive and descriptive representation, again using the PLUM Ordinal Regression technique and State Response as the dependent variable. We entered movement actor agreement, the presence of women legislators, intervention by women legislators, policy agency representativeness, issue priority, the openness of the policy system, movement institutionalisation, and percentage of women in the lower house of the legislature into the regression, finding that only agency representativeness was independently positively associated with successful movement actor representation on both descriptive and substantive representation. However, legislator intervention was almost as significant, and, when entered into a streamlined model, it proved to be a predictor of movement success independently of agency representativeness.

Table 3.7 shows a significant positive association between women legislator presence and the achievement of both procedural and substantive movement success in systems in which a women's policy agency exists. Where one or more women legislators take a stand in the debate, movements are more than twice as likely to achieve both substantive and descriptive representation than when no legislators do so. Where an agency does nothing, movements are about one third less likely to achieve both kinds of representation than when agency frames match movement frames.

Conclusion

One version of the policy triangle model is partly supported by our research, which identifies three important components: movement actors, policy agencies and women legislators. But the linkages within this triangle exist only under certain conditions. Intervention by women legislators is not associated with agency representativeness. The pattern is not triangular but consists of converging lines in which agencies act independently, while movement actor success is boosted by the acts of women legislators. The association between interventions by parliamentary women and the agreement of autonomous and integrated movement actors suggests yet a different type of linkage and indicates that effective action is most likely to come from a division of labour between autonomous and integrated feminists and other feminist policy actors, including politicians and state officials.

Table 3.7: Ordinal Regression of the Achievement of Both Substantive and Descriptive Representation

Independent Variable Measures	Parameter Estimate	EXP(β)
Women legislators present	.835*	2.305
Women legislators not present	Reference category	N/A
Policy agency representativeness: agency microframe incompatible with women's movement actors	Not significant	N/A
Policy agency representativeness: agency does nothing	-1.158*	.3141
Policy agency representativeness: agency advances microframe neither matching nor conflicting	Not significant	N/A
Policy agency representativeness: agency matches movement actor's microframe	Reference category	N/A

Pseudo R^2: Cox and Snell, .09; Nagelkerke, .104; McFadden, .047. Link function: Logit.

Thus, we add to the evidence that substantive and descriptive representation are linked through the critical acts of women legislators and of policy agencies that assist their achievement by women's movement actors, independently of the nature of the policy system and the percentage of women in the legislature. We suggest that the standard critical-mass account of representation does not pay enough attention to the nature of the institutions in which representation takes place. The political affiliations and preferences of women legislators may be crucial to their position and capacities as critical actors. Our research reinforces the contention that it is critical acts and not critical mass that determine movement success, but it also points to the need for further work that is sensitive to the interplay between actors in different institutional contexts. Moreover, the full RNGS dataset provides some evidence that the percentage of women legislators in conjunction with their political party affiliations may be especially important to policy success, although this discussion is beyond the scope of this chapter.[25] The analysis in Chapter 4 [this refers to the original volume] confirms that important alliances are formed between left-wing legislators and women's movement actors.

Accountability is the hidden dragon of feminist representation theory, some of which can be read as a catalogue of justifications for demands for the accountability of state actors to women's movements. But that is not how democratic political systems are constructed. Accountability exists through imperfect, formally democratic processes, in which movement voices are absorbed into aggregating electoral politics that were not designed to take account of the interests of women. Women's movements aim to correct the resulting imbalances, but their effectiveness is limited by the nature of the systems in which they operate. There is very little feminist political representation theory that acknowledges this problem in real political systems. Jane Mansbridge's discussion of accountability is an honourable and useful exception (2003). However, although her theories are advanced as though they are of general applicability to democratic deliberation, it is difficult to fit them to the cases of party government that are characteristic of the eleven European democracies in our research, in which voters have little choice of candidate and legislators are subject to party discipline. Policy agencies cannot make up the shortfall. The accountability of movement to agency is rarely direct and is generally a matter of the arrangements in whatever part of the state women's policy agencies are located.

The claims of movement actors also raise accountability issues. The representativeness of movement actors observed in the research is an issue frequently raised by RNGS critics, who argue that the project does not take account of all parts of the women's movement but only of those active on a particular issue (Squires 2007). This, it is argued, privileges certain kinds of actors and certain parts of the movement. In fact, the concern with movement actors who have a microframe on the issue results from the debate focus of the research design. We study movements in relation to debates because it gives a clearer picture of the existence and effectiveness of movement representation. This specificity has the advantage of accuracy. By starting with debates and naming movement actors within them, we keep the question of movement actor intervention a research question, a matter for empirical observation.

Does our analysis support the contention that the descriptive representation of women is necessary for their substantive representation? It seems so. We find that legislator and agency interventions enhance the achievement of movement representation. Such interventions depend on the presence of women legislators. Moreover, combinations of autonomous and integrated women's movement actors are more effective than either acting independently. It is difficult to resist the conclusion that for successful political representation, the women's movements need both presence and action in representative institutions to achieve their goals.

Although this chapter has provided some of the answers to all of the questions it raises, it has inevitably highlighted new avenues of research. Each research question suggests an extensive research project of its own and generates a set of data requirements, some of which require new survey instruments and fieldwork. Yet each also offers a starting point for extending research on political representation. Viewed through the lenses of representation theories, the RNGS research contributes to knowledge of processes and effects of the intervention in policy debates by movement actors, agency officials, and women legislators, and offers some support for movement engagement with the state.

Definitions of key terms

Symbolic agencies: Women's policy agencies that are in a position to participate in a policy debate but take no position and have no influence.

Transformative State Feminism: The outcome where women's policy agencies ally with feminist movement actors to gender policy debates with feminist ideas and demands-that is, recognise patriarchy and gender-based hierarchies and promote gender equality; the alliance results in procedural access for feminist movement actors and policy outcomes that reflect feminist movement goals.

Type: One of the characteristics of women's policy agencies that classifies them according to form; the most common types are ministry, administrative office, commission, and advisory council.

Women's movement: Discourse that uses gendered language to express identity with women and represents women in public life and the actors who present that discourse.

Women's Movement Actor dataset: Compiled by Joyce Outshoorn for her analysis in Chapter 7 [this refers to the original volume] and containing information on activities of all women's movement actors in the RNGS policy debates.

Women's Movement Actors' Frames dataset: Developed by Birgit Sauer, the dataset classifies the substantive content of microframes expressed by women's movement actors in policy debates in the RNGS dataset Text Appendices.

Women's Movement Location dataset: Developed by Joni Lovenduski and Marita Guadagnini, the dataset that identifies the specific institutional location of 217 women's movement actors in policy debates in the RNGS dataset Text Appendices.

Women's Movement Resources: One of three clusters of explanatory conditions and variables that includes women's movement activism and institutionalisation, priority of the issue to the movement as a whole, and the cohesiveness of women's movement actors in the debate.

Women's policy agencies: A structure that meets both of the following criteria: (1) any agency or governmental body formally established by government statute or decree, and (2) any agency or governmental body formally charged with furthering women's status and rights or promoting sex-based equality.

Notes

1. We are grateful to Rosie Campbell, Karen Cells, Fiona Mackay, and, as always, Dorothy McBride and Amy Mazur, who gave valuable feedback on earlier versions of this chapter.

2. For a discussion of these arguments, *see* Squires (2007).

3. A recent example is Dovi (2007), who draws attention to this apparent problem, but names none of its putative practitioners.

4. Weldon's argument depends on an intervening variable that indicates an interaction between movement and policy agency. While this intervening variable explains everything that her model does not explain and is, thus, an important part of her argument, unfortunately its description does not allow one to test it for validity and reliability. Even so, the work has analytical potential and implicitly alerts us to the potential importance of policy triangles.

5. The principles of debate selection are explained in Chapter 2 [this refers to the original volume].

6. *See* Chapter 2 for more on the operational definition of women's movements from RNGS used here and throughout the book [this refers to the original volume].

7. For more on these four types of movement representation, see discussion of the State Response Typology in Chapter 1 [this refers to the original volume].

8. A new dataset was developed of the specific location of the women's movement actors active in policy debates: parliament, political party, trade union, autonomous women's movement groups, and other non-women's movement groups. The Women's Movement Actor Location dataset classifies 217 women's movement actors and their activities into these different locations. *See* the Web Appendices for Chapter 8 [this refers to the original volume] for full details of the scales and measurements discussed in these paragraphs.

9. Unlike the analysis in Part II [this refers to the original volume], this operationalisation does not differentiate between women's movement leadership and feminist leadership; agency leaders with either feminist experience or women's movement experience are counted here.

10. Sauer, in Chapter 9 [this refers to the original volume], draws attention to the importance of gender experts, as well as many of the country-based analyses in the five RNGS issue books (McBride Stetson 2001b; Mazur 2001; Outshoorn 2004; Lovenduski et al. 2005; Haussman and Sauer 2007).

11. This is an operational definition; hence, these findings do not take into account undiscovered women's interests, which are beyond the scope of the RNGS project.

12. Interventions are instances where women's policy agencies or women's movement actors expressed a position or a microframe in policy debates.

13. The RNGS definition of women's movement actor is based on discourse. If an actor is a woman, articulates movement discourse in public by expressing explicit identity with women as a group, uses explicitly gendered language, and claims to be representative of women, then she is acting for women.

14. For more on the formal mandates and briefs of the agencies in this study, *see* Chapter 3 [this refers to the original volume] and our analysis below. For a more general discussion of women's policy machineries, *see*, for example, Outshoorn and Kantola (2007).

15. All bivariate significance tests discussed in this chapter are nonparametric bivariate correlations. The test of significance is Spearman's rho: * significant at .05; ** significant at .01; *** significant at .001. *See* the Web Appendices for Chapter 8 for full correlation tables [this refers to the original volume].

16. *See* the Web Appendices for Chapter 8 for details of frequency and cross-tabulation of microframe fits [this refers to the original volume].

17. Liberal models are Canada, Ireland, Great Britain, and the United States; hybrid ones are Sweden and Finland; a republican one is France; and consociational corporatist models are Belgium, Italy, the Netherlands, and Spain.

18. Party debates from the RNGS study are examined in Chapter 10; party women's policy agencies, (usually what RNGS calls quasi agencies), are discussed in Chapter 3 [these refer to the original volume].

19. For more on how institutionalization is operationalized in this book, *see* Chapter 2 [this refers to the original volume] or the RNGS *Codebook*, Concept 22 (RNGS 2007).

20. This concentration is partly an effect of the hot-issue debates, which were intended to capture issues of importance in the 1990s and were mostly resolved in the 2000s; hence, the full dataset does not adequately reflect debates in the 2000s, which were, therefore, subsumed into the 1990s category.

21. Feminist leadership varied negatively with agency capacity (−.224*), suggesting that the less powerful agencies were more likely to have leaders with feminist experience.

22. The institutionalization measure is of movements in relation to each other. The three different levels of low, moderate, and high were calculated from the 10-point scale developed by RNGS, where low instances of institutionalization scored 1–3; moderate, 4–7; and high, 8–10 points. For the correlations, the full 10-point scale was used.

23. Polytomous Universal Model in SPSS. *See* Chapter 4 [this refers to the original volume] for a more in-depth discussion of its use in this book and Norušis (2007) for a useful guide to Ordinal Regression in SPSS. To run the regression, we collapsed movement institutionalization and percentage of women in the legislature into bands of low, moderate, and high.

24. State Response: 0 = state does nothing (No Response); 1 = movement actors achieve policy change or procedural access (Preemption or Co-optation); 2 = movement actors achieve policy change and procedural access (Dual Response).

25. The full RNGS dataset includes an additional sixteen debates that were excluded from this analysis either because there was no policy agency at the time of the debate or because the debate was decided in a political party or at the subnational level. If we run the same statistical tests using the 130-case dataset, the percentage of women legislators is a significant predictor of State Response. *See* the Chapter 8 Web Appendices for these results [this refers to the original volume].

References

Bratton, K. and Ray, L. (2002) 'Descriptive Representation, Policy Outcomes and Municipal Day-Care Coverage in Norway', *American Journal of Political Science*, 47 (2): 428–437.

Campbell, R., Childs, S., and Lovenduski, J. (2010) 'Do Women Need Women Representatives?', *British Journal of Political Science*, 40 (1): 171–194.

Celis, K. (2008) 'Representation', in G. Goertz and A. G. Mazur (eds) *Politics, Gender, and Concepts: Theory and Methodology*, Cambridge: Cambridge University Press, pp. 71–93.

Celis, K., Childs, S., Kantola, J., and Krook, M. L. (2008) 'Rethinking Women's Substantive Representation', *Representation*, 44 (2): 101–110.

Chaney, C., Alvarez, M. R., and Nagler, J. (1998) 'Explaining the Gender Gap in U.S. Presidential Elections', *Political Research Quarterly*, 51 (2): 311–339.

Childs, S. (2004) *New Labour's Women MPs: Women Representing Women*, London: Routledge.

Childs, S. (2005) 'Feminising British Politics: Sex and Gender in the 2005 General Election', in A. Geddes and J. Tonge (eds) *Britain Decides: The UK General Election 2005*, Basingstoke, England: Palgrave, pp. 150–167.

Childs, S. (2007) 'Representation', in V. Bryson and G. Blakeley (eds) *The Impact of Feminism on Political Concepts and Debates*, Manchester: Manchester University Press, pp. 94–118.

Childs, S. and Krook, M. L. (2006) 'Should Feminists Give Up on Critical Mass? A Contingent "Yes"', *Politics and Gender*, 2 (4): 522–530.

Dahlerup, D. (1988) 'From a Small to a Large Minority: Women in Scandinavian Politics' *Scandinavian Political Studies*, 11: 275–298.

Danna, D. (2004) 'Italy: The Never-Ending Debate', in J. Outshoorn (ed.) *The Politics of Prostitution: Women's Movements, Democratic States and the Globalisation of Sex Commerce*, Cambridge: Cambridge University Press, pp. 165–184.

Dovi, S. (2002) 'Preferable Descriptive Representatives: Will Just Any Woman, Black or Latino Do?', *American Political Science Review*, 96 (4): 729–743.

Dovi, S. (2007) 'Theorizing Women's Representation in the United States', *Politics and Gender*, 3 (3): 297–319.

Ferree, M. M. and Mueller, C. (2007) 'Feminism and the Women's Movement: A Global Perspective', in D. A. Snow, S. A. Soule, and H. Kriesi (eds) *The Blackwell Companion to Social Movements*, Oxford: Blackwell Publishing, pp. 576–607.

Guadagnini, M. (2007) 'The Reform of the State in Italy', in M. Haussman and B. Sauer (eds) *Gendering the State in the Age of Globalization*, Lanham, MD: Rowman and Littlefield, pp. 169–188.

Guadagnini, M. and Dona, A. (2007) 'Women's Policy Machinery in Italy between European Pressure and Domestic Constraints', in J. Outshoorn and J. Kantola (eds) *Changing State Feminism*, New York: Palgrave Macmillan, pp. 164–181.

Halsaa, B. (1999) 'A Strategic Partnership for Women's Policies in Norway', in G. Lyclama a Nijeholt, V. Vargas, and S. Wieringa (eds) *Women's Movements and Public Policy in Europe, Latin America, and the Caribbean*, New York: Garland, pp. 157–169.

Haussman, M. and Sauer, B. (eds) (2007) *Gendering the State in the Age of Globalization. Women's Movements and State Feminism in Postindustrial Democracies*, Lanham, MD: Rowman and Littlefield.

Holli, A. M. (2008) 'Feminist Triangles: A Conceptual Analysis', *Representation*, 44 (2): 169–85, doi: 10.1080/00344890802080407.

Holli, A. M. and Kantola, J. (2005) 'A Politics for Presence: Finland', in J. Lovenduski (ed.) *State Feminism and Political Representation*, Cambridge: Cambridge University Press, pp. 62–84.

Krook, M. L., Lovenduski, J., and Squires, J. (2009) 'Gender Quotas and Models of Political Citizenship', *British Journal of Political Science*, 39 (4): 781–803.

Lovenduski, J. (2005) *Feminizing Politics*, Cambridge: Polity Press.

Lovenduski, J. (2007) 'Unfinished Business: Equality Policy and the Changing Context of State Feminism in Great Britain', in J. Outshoorn and J. Kantola (eds) *Changing State Feminism*, New York: Palgrave Macmillan, pp. 144–163.

Lovenduski, J., Baudino, C., Guadagnini, M., and Meier, P. (eds) (2005) *State Feminism and Political Representation*, Cambridge: Cambridge University Press.

McBride, D. E. (2007) 'Welfare Reform: America's Hot Issue', in M. Haussman and B. Sauer (eds) *Gendering the State in an Age of Globalization: Women's Movements and State Feminism in Postindustrial Democracies*, Lanham, MD: Rowman and Littlefield, pp. 281–300.

McBride Stetson, D. (ed) (2001a) *Abortion Politics, Women's Movements and the Democratic State: A Comparative Study of State Feminism*, Oxford: Oxford University Press.

McBride Stetson, D. (2001b) 'Women's Movements Defence of Legal Abortion in Great Britain', in D. McBride Stetson *Abortion Politics, Women's Movements and the Democratic State: A Comparative Study of State Feminism,* Oxford: Oxford University Press, pp. 41–61.

Mansbridge, J. (1999) 'Should Blacks Represent Blacks and Women Represent Women: A Contingent "Yes"', *Journal of Politics*, 61 (3): 628–657.

Mansbridge, J. (2003) 'Rethinking Representation', *American Political Science Review*, 97 (4): 515–528.

Mateo Diaz, M. (2005) *Representing Women? Female Legislators in West European Parliaments*, Colchester, England: ECPR Press.

Mazur, A. G. (ed.) (2001) *State Feminism, Women's Movements, and Job Training: Making Democracies Work in the Global Economy*, New York: Routledge.

Mazur, A. G. (2002) *Theorizing Feminist Policy*, Oxford: Oxford University Press.

Mueller McClurg, C. and McCarthy, J. D. (2003) 'Cultural Continuity and Structural Change: The Logic of Adaptation by Radical Liberal and Socialist Feminists to State Reconfiguration', in L. A. Banaszak, K. Beckwith, and D. Rucht (eds) *Women's Movements Facing the Reconfigured State*, Cambridge: Cambridge University Press, pp. 219–242.

Outshoorn, J. (ed.) (2004) *The Politics of Prostitution: Women's Movements, Democratic States, and the Globalization of Sex Commerce*, Cambridge: Cambridge University Press.

Outshoorn, J. and Kantola, J. (eds) (2007) *Changing State Feminism: Women's Policy Agencies Confront Shifting Institutional Terrain*, New York: Palgrave Macmillan.

Phillips, A. (1995) *The Politics of Presence*, Cambridge: Oxford University Press.

Pitkin, H. F. (1967) *The Concept of Representation*, Berkeley: University of California Press.

RNGS (2007) *Codebook*, Available at http://libarts.wsu.edu/polisci/rngs.

Schwindt-Bayer, L. A. and Mishler, W. (2005) 'An Integrated Model of Women's Representation', *The Journal of Politics*, 67 (2): 407–428.

Squires, J. (2007) *The New Politics of Gender Equality*, Basingstoke, England: Palgrave.

Teghtsoonian, K. and Grace, J. (2001) '"Something More Is Necessary": The Mixed Achievements of Women's Policy Agencies in Canada', in A. G. Mazur (ed.) *State Feminism, Women's Movements, and Job Training: Making Democracies Work in a Global Economy*, New York: Routledge, pp. 235–270.

Vargas, V. and Wieringa. S. (1998) 'The Triangle of Empowerment: Processes and Actors in the Making of Public Policy for Women', in G. L. Nijeholt, V. Vargas, S. Wieringa (eds) *Women's Movements and Public Policy in Europe, Latin America, and the Caribbean*, New York: Garland, pp. 3–23.

Wängnerud, L. (2000) 'Testing the Politics of Presence: Women's Representation in the Swedish Riksdag', *Scandinavian Political Studies*, 23 (1): 67–91.

Weldon, L. (2002) 'Beyond Bodies: Institutional Sources of Representation for Women in Democratic Policymaking', *Journal of Politics*, 64 (4): 1153–1174.

Woodward, A. E. (2003) 'Building Velvet Triangles: Gender and Informal Governance' in T. Christiansen and S. Piattoni (eds) *Informal Governance in the European Union*, Cheltenham: Edward Elgar, pp. 76–93.

Chapter Four

Feminising British Politics*

Progress on increasing the political representation of women in the United Kingdom has stalled. At the 2010 election just 22 per cent of returned MPs were women — an increase of less than 4 per cent over the three elections since 1997 when the proportion of women MPs doubled from 9.2 to 13.2 per cent. The average increase in the proportion of women MPs over the last fifteen years is around 1.3 per cent per election. Initially, the tiny 2010 increase was ludicrously framed by commentators as a robust indicator of inevitable improvement. Only when advocates pointed out that at the current rate it would take over 100 years for women MPs to reach parity with men did the faux euphoria subside and a sober assessment begin. Feminist politicians, think tanks, equality advocates and women's movement activists expressed anger and frustration that the claims for equality of political representation were so little heeded. So, too, did individuals who had not previously been engaged in the campaigns for women's presence. Women's advocates repeatedly drew attention to the consequences of poor representation — not least the coalition government's public expenditure decisions. Since the 2010 emergency budget, these seem almost to target women to bear the brunt of public sector and benefit contraction.

It was almost impossible after the election to generate public discussion and debate on equal political representation. Equality advocates report encountering a false but persistent belief that the problem of women's representation is now solved, that enough has been done and if the number of women's in decision-making positions still lags behind that of men, it is only a matter of time before equality is reached. Recognising these developments it seemed a good moment to revisit the issue of women's political representation. With the sponsorship of *The Political Quarterly,* the Centre for the Study of British Politics and Public Life organised a workshop to explore the problems. Held at Birkbeck College on 4 November 2011, the day-long workshop brought together activists, journalists, experts and politicians. The event was very lively and very productive, generating a wide-ranging discussion. Here I do some ground clearing and try to draw out the main arguments and concerns covered at the workshop and highlight key points in the articles that follow.

*   'Feminising British politics', *The Political Quarterly*, 2012, 83(4), pp. 697–702.

What is the problem?

The workshop discussed women's presence and roles in all areas of United Kingdom decision making, including government, the House of Commons, local and devolved councils and assemblies, public appointments, honours lists, the House of Lords, quangos and committees, and corporate boards. A common concern was the simple question of how any reasonable person could honestly believe the problem of women's underrepresentation is all but solved when two of the main political parties have yet to establish gender-neutral and reliable candidate recruitment mechanisms, when the heart of government is entirely male, when the House of Commons remains a stubbornly sexist institution, and while the press continues to take pot shots at women politicians on the basis of their appearance. One possible explanation is found in Nirmal Puwar's concept of the 'amplification of numbers'. In her excellent *Space Invaders* (Puwar 2004), she argues that any presence of a previously excluded group appears to be larger than it is because the members of that group are so visible in their otherness. Thus when Margaret Thatcher was Prime Minister opinion polls routinely reported that the public (mistakenly) thought there were many more Conservative than Labour women in the House of Commons. In other words, more than a few women somehow comes to be perceived as many women — too many perhaps.

Participants in the workshop wondered why the political under-representation of women in the United Kingdom is not treated as the public disgrace that it is. Undoubtedly there is continuing resistance to sex equality, but from whom? Who opposes increases in women's political representation? I can think of at least eight types of opponents. The *uninterested*, who think it does not matter; the *complacent*, who, if they think about it at all, believe women's interests are well represented; the *traditionalists*, who believe that politics is about the representation of class interests, hence other inequalities are a diversion; the *diversity advocates*, who argue that gender is only one of many identities; their mirror image, the *anti-essentialists*, who think that claims for more women ignore the great differences among women; the *optimistic*, who think it is just a matter of waiting; and the *dinosaurs*, who think politics is best left to men. Each of these in different ways contributes to the eighth type: the *mistaken*, who misread or misconstrue data about women in politics.

The uninterested simply ignore the issue. They are probably the majority of political commentators and are dangerous because they are part of the reason why sex inequality is so often below the radar of discussion of political events, behaviour, issues, electoral forecasts and so on. When pressed, they may opine that it simply does not matter (Campbell and Edwards 2012). The complacent, if they argue at all, hold that under-representation does not really matter because the United Kingdom does well on issues of sex equality. That is not the case. The United Kingdom's ranking in the World Economic Forum's Annual Gender Gap Report has fallen steadily since the first report in 2006. The Report measures inequalities between women and men in economic and political participation, health and education. In 2011, the United Kingdom was 16th out of 135 countries;

in 2006 it was 9th out of 110 countries. This is a real fall; the United Kingdom has not been pushed down the rankings by new entrants to the list. It is 34th in the rank order of economic participation, and 23rd in political participation — rankings that are disguised at the aggregate level by relatively more equality in education and health. The data show that in each case except education where it ranks first, the position of British women is improving relative to that of men, but more slowly than in comparator countries where women's political participation is higher.[1]

The United Kingdom's position on other league tables is worse. Using the simple indicator of the percentage of national legislators who are women, the Inter-Parliamentary Union places the United Kingdom at a wretched 54th behind not only the worthy Scandinavian states, but also Canada, Mexico, Latvia, the Philippines and Malawi.[2]

The optimistic will have to wait a long time. At the current rate of increase in each party and assuming a normal election cycle, it will be at least 100 years before parity of women is reached in the House of Commons — not a fast track to equality by any reasonable standards.

Traditionalists probably operate on the assumption that political inequality is a zero-sum game. Often they argue that more women means more middle-class women and fewer working-class men. This impression almost certainly reflects party candidate selection regimes in which, in order to be successful, women aspirants must be more 'qualified' than their male opponents. However, it is selector stress on particular 'qualifications' that squeezes working-class aspirants, not prioritisation of women. Class and gender interact. A wealth of social research shows that it is women who bear the brunt of class inequality, and that gender and class are so intertwined that treating inequalities of sex simultaneously treats those of class.

Some diversity advocates and antiessentialists make similar assumptions, failing to recognise that identities such as race, class, sexuality and disability cross cut each other. They also fail to recognise that with more women representatives there are more opportunities for those who are working class, members of ethnic minorities, disabled and so on.

Political dinosaurs are not quite extinct. Many thrive in British politics sometimes as eccentrics who take pride in their exaggerated outdated prejudices. They are useful for equality advocates because they are so easy to discredit, as is the sexist behaviour that characterises their condition. Like the smile of the Cheshire cat, their influence may be evident even as they fade from view. Their attitudes leave an afterglow that encourages sexist remarks, which are then excused as parliamentary humour. While David Cameron is probably not a dinosaur, he sometimes behaves like one. Examples include his 'calm down, dear' remarks to Angela Eagle and his accusation that Nadine Dorries' interventions took place because she was 'frustrated' — not exactly hilarious comments, for which Cameron apologised. Press dinosaurs are very much in evidence. As recently as April 2011, the *Telegraph* ran an item entitled 'Whose boobs are these?', using photos of a woman MP sitting behind Ed Miliband during Prime Minister's Questions.[3]

Finally, the mistaken come in various forms. Some argue that women candidates cost votes for parties who select them. Yet data from the United Kingdom on voter preferences for different types of candidates consistently shows that votes do not penalise women candidates (Campbell and Cutts 2009). Another common mistake is making unsubstantiated assertions about women's political preferences, implying that they differ from men's. An example is the widely reported Netmums claim that women were turning to the Tories in 2012, based on a survey only of women — that is, with no male comparators.[4] Contrast this with contemporary evidence that women are turning away from the Tories.[5] Women may be turning right, or to the left, but the evidence was flawed. Often commentators use data and/ or design research badly to draw unsound conclusions. Common errors are women-only samples, badly framed questions and mixed samples that are too small. It is bad science to design and use social surveys or other studies that examine only women to claim that women are distinctive in some way without systematically comparing them to men. It is bad science to collect evidence from such a small number of respondents that variations within groups are not reflected.

The case for more women in parliament more or less mirrors the arguments of its opponents with one exception. Current absolute and relative numbers are low, policy is often unfavourable to women, but concealed by gender blindness, the rate of progress is glacial, traditional roles are no longer sustainable — not least because demography shows they are rarely found. To this we must add the argument from justice. The representation of women in political decision making is vital not because it will necessarily make a difference for women, though it often does, but because justice demands it. Equal representation should be taken for granted, part of the institutional fabric. Women should not have to claim political presence on any other basis than justice. To do so puts a special burden of representation on women MPs who become subject to scrutiny and pressure that male politicians largely avoid — a point well made by Ruth Fox in this issue [this refers to the original volume]. Yet as Rosie Campbell (also in this issue) [this refers to the original volume] shows there are subtle but important differences in men's and women's political attitudes that warrant representation. Political parties, not voters, are responsible for the male domination of politics. This is sometimes defended by the assertion that men can and do represent women's interests. While true, it begs the question of which particular version of women's interest is being represented. Moreover, evidence from more balanced legislatures than ours shows that as membership of women increases, so does the sensitivity of male MPs to the range of women's concerns. So men can act for women, but they may be more likely to do so when there are more women around.

Guaranteeing political equality

What needs to be done? The crucial place for action is the political parties because they are responsible for choosing candidates. It is impossible to overstate this point. Parties select, voters elect. Voters are amenable to women candidates, parties less so, especially when it comes to nomination for winnable seats. Parties can and do change. The long march of women through the Labour party continues; next year it will implement a rule that holders of the two leadership positions must include both sexes. That this rule change went through conference almost without comment is testament to real attitude change. That it was thought necessary shows both that there is some way yet to go and illustrates the importance of properly designed institutional provision for equality.

The new Labour party leadership rule is a simple quota policy. Experience of raising women's political representation worldwide consistently shows that guaranteeing women's equality through quotas works and works well, either to accelerate slow progress or to overcome inertia. Often temporary, their effect is to disrupt prevailing male dominance pending the establishment of a new 'taken for granted' equilibrium in which balanced candidates lists are normalised. Sarah Childs and Liz Evans in this issue [this refers to the original volume] list the well-rehearsed arguments that are typically mobilised against quotas and show each to be unfounded. Quotas are controversial, but despite inevitable resistance and even sabotage, they work, so we need to use them.

Effective candidate quotas must be designed to fit the system in which they are applied. Design tends to be a process as loopholes are closed over successive elections. The two main types are party quotas which require a minimum of nominations of women and men in winnable seats or list positions and voluntary quotas. Legislative quotas reserve seats for women MPs. There may be some overlap between party and state responsibilities. States may enforce quotas directly — for example, by refusing to accept nomination lists that are unbalanced. Quotas work best when they are part of a wider strategy that treats institutional resistance to women, including targeting traditional and sexist attitudes, institutional cultures and political processes designed around the lives of men and media preferences for adversarial politics. According to the IDEA (International Institute for Democracy and Electoral Assistance) quotas project database, eleven of thirty-two European countries currently have such legislation.[6]

The main alternative to mandatory quotas is voluntary party quotas. Britain is already one of the twenty-two European countries with such quotas as permitted by the Sex Discrimination Candidates Act 2002. However, the failure of most parties to use them suggests that something more powerful is necessary to accelerate change to a reasonable speed. Party leaders are aware of the uses of quotas. Quota politics are discussed by Rainbow Murray, Sarah Childs and Liz Edwards and Ruth Fox in this [this refers to the original volume] — all of whom now call for the constitutionalisation of quotas in the United Kingdom. In other words, they support the introduction of legislation to mandate parties to nominate a minimum number of women and men. In 2010, David Cameron told the Speaker's Conference that his party would adopt all-women shortlists, a form of quota, if that is what it took to achieve equality of political representation for women and men.[7] The Liberal Democrats have played with the idea in the past, but are currently divided, though officially opposed to the policy. However, Nick Clegg also promised improvements when he testified to the Speaker's Conference. Both were making rhetorical commitments. Neither implemented them and neither is expected to. Their perceived unreliability may be at the root of the call by the Speaker's Conference for compulsory candidate quotas to be legislated if substantial progress is not made by the 2015 general election.

Few believe that such progress will be made. And time is already running out. Boundary changes and the reduction in the number of seats have generated fierce contests in candidate selection. In such environments, the issue of women's representation tends to slip down the agenda. Knowledge of these political realities is why the stakes are being raised. Repeated failure by parties to deliver on women's representation has united feminist advocates in the view that legislative quotas with severe sanctions for uncooperative parties are necessary for real change.

How likely are legislative quotas?

The received wisdom is that there is not much public appetite for quotas. However, good data on attitudes to quotas is hard to find. One source is the Eurobarometer,[8] which reports high levels of support among Europeans for the feminisation of politics, but finds that only 16–19 per cent support the use of quotas to bring it about. However, as Childs and Evans argue in this issue, quotas can be implemented ahead of attitude change, as the Labour party experience shows. Such a strategy requires determined political leadership.

The call for legislative quotas is a very big demand requiring fundamental political change. One telling implication is the probable impact on party–state relations. Over time, the constitutionalisation of women's representation may also entail a constitutionalisation of political parties. To implement quotas, the state must require that parties revise their selection procedures — a step in the direction of party regulation that will be fiercely resisted. However, in strategic terms, the very threat of increased regulation may be enough to generate change.

Many barriers to women representatives remain. The activities in which potential politicians are made are still not organised on family-friendly lines, the institutional culture of politics stubbornly favours certain kinds of men. Traditional practices put women off and impede change. Rosa Malley shows vividly in this issue [this refers to the original volume] how intimidating the anachronistic Westminster culture can be to observers and visitors, and contrasts it to the more open and accessible Holyrood — an observation reinforced by Fiona Mackay and Laura McAllister (also in this issue) [this refers to the original volume]. Moreover, on current trends, the expansion of the numbers of women who are available cannot be assumed. There may be an emerging supply problem as a result both of the inhospitable culture of British politics and previous failures to recruit women to political leadership. Peter Allen shows that in local elected office, women are more likely to serve fewer terms and to leave local politics for more informal (and less powerful) activities. The experience of the Scottish Parliament suggests that after their initial success, women are not coming forward to be candidates as the first generation of elected women retires.[9] Claire Annesley and Francesca Gains report that the political executive pipeline is also short of women.

Moving beyond legislatures

Representation in decision making is not only a matter of elected office. Most democracies use various public-appointed boards and commissions to make decisions, and these interact with the private boards of the corporate world from which they draw many of their members and a substantial part of their agendas. This live issue is currently giving the government some difficulty. Its very timid exhortations to business to improve the sex balance of their boards are falling on deaf ears. Moreover, the government appears reluctant to act even where it is in a position to do so, as Kate Jenkins argues.

Many seminar participants remarked on the exclusion of women from consultative processes by the coalition government. It was argued that the coalition do not appear to be concerned about listening to women. One victim of its 'quango cull' was the Women's National Commission, the official voice of women's organisations in the United Kingdom. As Fiona Mackay remarked:

> Despite the shortcomings of the WNC, its abolition has left a structural gap and leaves the UK women's sector without a formal voice to central government. . . . [Its closure means] we have lost the coordinating structure across the four nations which further intensifies fragmentation and the centrifugal dynamics of devolution for the women's movement and solidarity across the UK. (MacKay personal communication)

Remedies

Overall the picture is mixed, but tilting downward. The various dismal performances outlined here are indicative of resistance to gender equality across most of the spectrum of United Kingdom institutions. We do not have a full understanding of the current order. While there are some examples of good practice, it is widely known that monitoring is inadequate. Policies to monitor the relative positions of women and men in political parties and in the financial sector are simply not being implemented. Arguably, good routine monitoring is central to the effectiveness of any equality policy and is therefore as radical as the quota policy toward which it often leads. What is clear is that the crucial responsible institutions are the political parties and it is for that reason that the participants in the workshop concluded that the issue cannot any longer be left to the parties. More direct solutions are required.

At the end of the workshop participants attempted to formulate an agenda for change that would remove or act to remove barriers to women's representation. The *constitutionalisation of gender equality* was the strongest proposal made on the day. Other suggestions were:

- A limit on the number of executive directorships an individual can hold.
- A limit on the number of public body appointments an individual can hold.
- Pay for all local councillors.
- Reconstitution of the Women's National Commission — or equivalent.

- Reconvening the Speaker's Conference on parliamentary representation.
- Legislation to require equality of outcomes in selection/appointment of women, to include effective sanctions.
- Draft legislation or rules of public broadcasting to require media/public broadcasting to gender balance political images and so on during elections and more.
- House of Lords reforms to include requirements of gender parity.
- Modernisation of parliamentary sitting hours.
- A debate about the possibility of offering job shares to MPs.
- The establishment of an equalities select committee in the House of Commons.

These are modest proposals that reflect a continuing, if perhaps misplaced, underlying trust in the democratic political institutions of the United Kingdom. Even so, there was a real sense of outrage among participants that the coalition has sidelined women and a real fear that recent collective efforts to equalise political representation could well slip backwards, creating the conditions for a new generation of dinosaurs to dominate our political institutions.

Notes

1. http://reports.weforum.org/global-gendergap-2011/
2. http://www.ipu.org/wmn-e/classif.htm
3. http://blogs.telegraph.co.uk/culture/lucyjones/100053061/pmqs-whose-boobs-arethese/
4. http://www.independent.co.uk/news/uk/politics/cameron-winning-female-vote-fortories-1881337.html
5. http://www.dailymail.co.uk/news/article-2054973/Alarm-Cameron-falls-favour-womenvoters.html
6. http://www.quotaproject.org/aboutQuotas.cfm
7. http://www.parliament.uk/business/committees/committees-a-z/othercommittees/speakers-conference-onparliamentary-representation/
8. http://ec.europa.eu/public_opinion/index_en.htm
9. http://www.hansardsociety.org.uk/blogs/downloads/archive/2010/05/24/hasdevolution-delivered-for-women.aspx

References

Campbell, R. and Cutts, D. (2009) 'Do women vote for women?', unpublished conference paper, Chicago, IL: Midwest Political Science Association.
Campbell, R. and Edwards, J. (2012) 'Men's voting behaviour: it's a hunter-gatherer thing apparently!', 12 January, http://www.csbppl.com/blog/
Puwar, N. (2004) *Space Invaders: Gender and Bodies Out of Place*, Oxford: Berg.

PART 2

POLITICAL PARTIES

Chapter Five

The Dynamics of Gender and Party*

The issue of the political representation of women has changed substantially since women first secured the franchise. When nineteenth century feminists sought the right to vote they also wanted the right to stand in elections because they were convinced that changes in women's condition would come about only when women themselves became members of elected legislatures. In contrast, during the 1960s and 1970s many second wave feminists were cynical about political institutions and electoral politics, preferring the political autonomy they found in new social movement organisations. By the early 1980s, however, there had been a reconsideration of the importance of mainstream politics and feminists became active members of political parties. Meanwhile some of the women who were already established in their parties began to claim parity of political representation. The struggle for equal pay was a watershed. Once parties became committed to the policy of equality at work it was only a matter of time before more substantial demands for equal political representation than 'one person, one vote' were made. During the 1980s support for getting more women into politics grew in each of the countries discussed in this book [this refers to the original volume]. There was a shift in the agendas of both the parties and their women members.

Over the same period political parties were a major site of women's activity. There was a clear challenge to parties by women who claimed a voice in decision-making and pressed for changes in the political agenda. Women demanded and secured party reforms with varying degrees of success. In some countries this led to the appearance of new issues in party programmes, new systems of candidate selection, new means of policy making, and the establishment of new structures of government such as ministries for women, equal opportunities ombudspersons and publicly funded women's committees. In response to pressure from women activists, members and voters, gender became an explicit issue for many political parties. This took place in contexts affected by different kinds of party politics. The extent and the manner of party accommodation of gender has been influenced by increased party competition via the entry of new parties and/or the decline of established parties, the erosion of established coalitions, modernisation strategies devised to replace or renew declining constituencies, system level constitutional change and altered party–state relationships.

Demands for women's representation have had the most dramatic success in Scandinavia. Norwegian feminists were early in advocating the integration of

* 'The Dynamics of Gender and Party', in J. Lovenduski and P. Norris (eds) *Gender and Party Politics*, London, Sage, 1993, pp. 1–15.

'Will quotas make Labour more woman-friendly?', *Renewal*, 1994, 2(1).

women into the existing party structure as a strategy of empowerment. It has now been more than twenty years since the 'women's coup' overturned agreed party preferences on candidates lists for local authority elections and returned three local councils with a majority of women. The implications of this initial display of women's solidarity were understood rapidly by parties and the progress that Norwegian women have made since then is remarkable. As Hege Skjeie recounts in Chapter 10 [this refers to the original volume], the representation of women grew from below 10 per cent of elected representatives in the 1960s to about 25 per cent in local and national assemblies by the end of the 1970s, and 35 per cent in the early 1980s. At least 40 per cent of the members of every Norwegian government since 1986 have been women. Moreover, much of the women's agenda that has emerged in other countries is complete or well advanced in Norway where a new and wider-ranging equality agenda has developed.

Near the other end of the scale is Britain, where demands for equality in women's representation came later, gathering force in the opposition parties only in the early 1980s and becoming a feature of the ruling Conservatives' strategies of representation as late as the early 1990s. By then women comprised fewer than 10 per cent of members of the House of Commons. Of course, the timing of demands for representation is only part of the story. The Norwegian and British political systems present different possibilities for women. In general the rules of the game in Norway favour the representation of women while in Britain they do not.

This raises the question of what we mean by political representation. In democratic societies, the representation of a group's interests has two dimensions: the presence of its members in decision-making arenas and the consideration of its interests in the decision-making process. An implication of the first dimension is that, to be democratic, the composition of the elected assemblies should mirror the composition of the society it serves. But the second dimension implies that it is enough that an assembly takes into account the interests of all its electors. There have been intense theoretical arguments about which of the two formulations should prevail and these arguments have been reflected in debates amongst feminists who have disagreed sharply about the nature of women's interests and the political strategies required to press them. In practice, the demands women have made to be represented in party politics reflect both programmatic and organisational concerns. Thus parties have been under pressure to promote policies to attract women voters, to undertake campaigns to recruit women members, to promote women into key positions in the party organisation and to nominate women candidates. Party programmes have been expanded to include policies on equal opportunities and reproductive rights, as well as to revise traditional party positions on family policy to take into account new understandings of gender and power.

Our objectives in compiling this volume [this refers to the original volume] are to explain how gender has affected party politics and how the imperatives of party politics influence the patterns of women's political representation. We argue that liberal democracies offer women the means to claim equality of representation by utilising the political opportunities offered by the party system. Party systems have responded to women's demands, but to varying degrees. Women's share of parliamentary seats ranges from 5.7 per cent in France to 38 per cent in Sweden, of party candidacy from 9 per cent in the USA to over 40 per cent in Sweden, of government from 6 per cent in Italy to over 45 per cent in Norway. These contrasts have both general and particular explanations. They indicate changes in party politics to accommodate women's demands for political representation but they also reflect different social, cultural and historical circumstances. And there are common patterns here as well. Women's demands for political representation inevitably affect party politics, party politics inevitably affects the strategies that women employ to press their claims. A continuous process of adjustment and accommodation takes place on both sides. We need to look beyond the particular and specific cultures in which that adjustment takes place if we are to gain a good overview of women in contemporary party politics. To do this we have, as far as possible, separated the two sides of the process. In this chapter, I discuss the development of the demands that women have made on political parties. In the concluding chapter [this refers to the original volume], Pippa Norris assesses the factors that condition party responses. In the intervening substantive chapters [these refer to the original volume], the interplay between gender and party politics is examined in detail in eleven countries. The central focus of each chapter is the political representation of women in programmatic and organisational terms. The contributing authors describe a variety of party systems and a range of strategies to represent women. They include multi-party, one party dominant, two and two-and-a-half party systems, centralised and decentralised party organisations and the full panoply of political ideologies. In each of the eleven countries demands have emerged from within the political parties to increase the political representation of women. An important purpose of this book is to account for those demands in their particular political context. In order to offer such an account we asked each of the contributors to describe the particularities of the country about which they were writing and to explain the roles and status of women in its political parties. For each country our authors describe unique elements of the way women have struggled for representation and parties have responded.

The development of women's claims

Women have made demands on political parties since the issue of female suffrage was first raised. In this discussion I consider three aspects of their development:

1   How women have made their claims.
2   How they intervened in party politics.
3   The mutual accommodation between parties and women claiming increased political rights.

The development of party gender politics in recent years is an effect both of the infiltration of feminist ideas and the attention women influenced by those ideas have paid to the imperatives of party politics. There are four identifiable components to the strategies such women devised. First, women's issues were brought to the political agenda. Prominent party women, supported by women's organisations and networks raised issues of sex equality in the parties. Often they began with demands for policies to secure sex equality in employment, but the implications of equality for childcare, reproductive rights and family policies were also issues. Secondly, seeking to avoid accusations of sectionalism, they sought to transform women's issues into universal issues. Thirdly, women used a dual strategy of working within women's networks and in male-dominated areas of the party. Finally, women paid close attention to the rules of the game. They sought to transform gender relations in politics from within, hence they were careful to affirm their commitment to their parties.

The gains made during the 1970s and 1980s must be considered in the light of a large mobilisation of women. This background gave credence to efforts to get women's issues on the political agenda. The emergence of the second wave of feminism after the end of the 1960s had important effects. Even in countries in which a widespread and radical women's liberation movement did not appear, ideas about sex equality were in the air and women began to seek inclusion in a variety of areas of social life. Gradually campaigns for equality gained support and parties began to respond. But the momentum built up by wide-ranging movements in support of equal rights would not have been enough to secure changes in party policies. Political parties moved on women's issues when they were pressed to do so. What Diane Sainsbury terms 'women's agency' is of great importance. Sweden, for example, has a widespread egalitarian ethos and the several features of its electoral system favour women but these cannot account by themselves for the increase in women's representation at all levels of the system since the 1960s. There, it was women who changed, who made new claims on the party system.

Once a party committed itself formally to the principle of gender equality in one sphere, then party women were able to use this commitment in their arguments for increased representation. In Ireland awareness of the gender dimension in politics came with the appearance of equality in employment on the political agenda. In Norway a similar process occurred until, by the beginning of the 1990s, high levels of women's representation had been achieved and all but one of its political parties offered a comprehensive sex equality strategy that encompassed the range of public policy concerns.

An implicit goal of feminist infiltration of parties is to secure changes in attitudes about gender, mainly by increases in understanding and awareness of gender differences and their implications for power relations. Women in the Italian parties, especially the Democratic Left (the largest successor party to the Communists) were not only active in forcing the implementation of party initiatives favouring women's concerns, but also developed a debate (called the *rappresentanza sessuata*) about the necessity of a gender-based viewpoint in politics. A similar strategy was employed by feminists who entered the British Labour party and by women in the German Social Democratic party during the 1980s. In Norway the challenge to attitudes was particularly successful, apparent in the recognition that has been given by policy-makers to women's various roles. In the early 1970s Norwegian party feminists led a political recognition of women's search for paid employment. Later, women politicians were regarded as responsible for bringing the politics of women's care and career roles to the political agenda.

In almost all of the parties that are considered here, women kept to the rules of the political game. Party divisions outweighed gender divisions. Cross-party alliances are exceptional within and outside legislatures. Party women have primarily sought change from within the parties except in the USA where party loyalties are exceptionally weak and the rules of the game allow greater flexibility in making coalitions.

Attention to party imperatives presents a dilemma for feminists who seek to transform parties into more women-friendly entities, but risk incorporation as they adapt to the rules of the game. A great dilemma for second wave feminism has been whether women will change institutions before institutions change women. Originally, some feminists were dismissive of party structures with their hierarchies and rituals, preferring separate autonomous organisations that sought political change from outside the established political structures and institutions. However, the cost of such separatism was low effectiveness. Understanding this, many feminists acknowledged the necessity of party politics, implicitly by their activism and explicitly in their publications and debates.

Party change

The justification for such a strategy is that parties will adapt to accommodate the new demands, and in so doing will become carriers of feminist ideas. This raises a number of questions, the most obvious of which is whether parties do adapt. To answer we need to look at the main sites of women's interventions in the parties. This requires us to examine the ways that parties differ in their policies to represent women. Here we must consider both the programmatic and the organisational dimensions of representation: how parties differ in their treatment of women's issues and in their strategies to promote women's representation.

Programmatic change

Parties devised gender policies to respond to the claims of women voters, members and activists. Over the past twenty years the sort of sex equality policies women demand has developed from a set of fairly straightforward employment laws to a wide-ranging programme affecting the whole of society. Most political parties have accommodated these demands in ways that are congruent with their ideologies. There was a tendency for parties to converge in the sense that, eventually, they all adopted particular policies to satisfy women voters and members, for example by making laws about equal pay or childcare, but the policies themselves reflect the ideology of the party.

Norway is a good example of this syndrome. Hege Skjeie's analysis of the priorities of the Norwegian political parties shows how gender issues are filtered through the ideological preferences of the parties (1993). So, parties of the right prefer policies that are more supportive of the 'caring mother' while parties of the left prefer to strengthen the position of the 'woman worker'. The new policies brought to the political agenda by women have been subjected to established political cleavages, in this case, the left–right ideological division. In Canada too we have further evidence of the relationship between the kind of changes the parties have made to represent women and the ideological position of the parties. The right of centre party, the Progressive Conservatives, was slower to adopt new reforms and more voluntaristic in its approach to increasing women's representation. Liberals were more responsive to the feminist movement and to demands for gender parity. On the centre left the NDP (New Democratic party) was more responsive still, offering a comprehensive programme of affirmative action to promote women in the party hierarchy. These differences were congruent with the attitudes of party activists except over the issue of abortion where the religious dimension confused the left–right polarities.

The activity of party women is vital if such changes are to be secured. There is considerable evidence now that, within political life, women take an active part in creating definitions of reality that support efforts to make new policies. In Norway there were two differences that women made to party politics: first, they got parties to address gender issues which then became arenas of political competition; secondly, as the initial policies were implemented and debates were developed shifts in attitude about the types of solution that were possible and the costs that might be paid took place. Parallel to women's integration into party politics, new agendas were established including strategies to get more women into political office.

Organisational change

Parties have developed strategies to promote women internally into decision-making positions in the party organisation and externally into elected assemblies and public appointments. Generally they have been more radical, determined and imaginative in devising policies to bring women into internal positions than to nominate women as candidates for elected office. There appear to be three party strategies for increasing the proportion of women in decision-making positions. These are:

1. *Rhetorical* strategies whereby women's claims are accepted in campaign platforms and party spokespersons make frequent reference to the importance of getting more women into office.
2. Strategies of *positive* or *affirmative action* in which special training is offered to aspirant women, targets are set for the inclusion of women and considerable encouragement, including, sometimes financial assistance, is given to enable women to put themselves forward to be considered.
3. Strategies *of positive discrimination* in which places are reserved for women on decision-making bodies, on candidate slates, on shortlists. In addition, special women's committees with significant powers may be

set up parallel to or within existing party decision-making structures and institutions. All three strategies may be controversial, but most parties now have rhetorical strategies to promote women and many have adopted strategies of positive action. Positive discrimination, however, is much less common and tends to be restricted to women's access to internal party structures.

Rhetorical strategies

Rhetorical strategies often begin as a pious set of public statements that women are necessary to party politics by leaders who have little intention of devising and implementing policies to include them. Political parties in France, for example, have wholeheartedly accepted French women's claims in their campaign rhetoric, and they actively compete for women's votes, but they are considerably less enthusiastic about strategies to promote the participation of women in party affairs. Often announcements of party interest in sex equality are accompanied by assertions that women are not interested in political office and that, anyway, they are satisfied with what the party offers. Sometimes party leaders claim, with some degree of truth that they do not have the power to influence the choice of officials, delegates or candidates. But this does not mean that such strategies are invariably insincere or doomed to failure. A commitment to women's representation in party rhetoric may be the beginning of a process that will lead to more substantial policies of inclusion. Once the public commitment to equality is made, women then start to expect effective action. Such a process is apparent in the British Conservative party where pressure from women for a greater share of candidacies during the 1980s has led to several informal, but significant attempts by Central Office to encourage women to seek nominations, and to encourage constituencies to nominate women. The result so far is a small increase in the proportion of women nominated, combined with slightly greater attention by the party to the presentation of its women activists, leaders and MPs.

Positive action

In many parties rhetorical strategies have been the first step towards the introduction of strategies of positive action. Programmes have been implemented to encourage women, provide special training, and aid searches for women to fill vacant positions. But the adoption of targets has been more difficult. Initially targets were introduced for internal party boards and executives and later extended to party candidacies.

Most political parties have long had some kind of internal or associated women's organisation. These have been a site of women's campaigns for political equality and, often, debates about women's roles in the party turn on the issue of the status of the women's organisation. Such strategies are important, but they are most effective when accompanied by women's activity in the main party decision-making bodies, that is, a *dual* strategy is required. Otherwise opponents may claim that women's organisation leaders are not representative of the party, and, in some cases, of its women. During the 1970s and 1980s women struggled to obtain places in delegations to party conferences, on executive committees and councils, regional boards and local management committees. The responses varied, often by the political fortunes of the party, but also by party ideology. For example, the Australian Labor party adopted affirmative action at its special national conference in 1981. Their poor performance in the 1977 elections gave women the opportunity to push for better representation. The party constitution was altered to call for a minimum of 25 per cent women in each state delegation and to declare that women should be represented on decision-taking bodies in proportion to their membership. The new rules stopped short of requiring parties to undertake positive discrimination to implement them — they were targets rather than quotas. But they had some effect. As a result the proportion of women delegates rose from 4 per cent (two of forty-nine women) in 1979, to at least 25 per cent of the total in 1982 and 40 per cent by the end of the 1980s.

In many countries by the 1980s internal party debates about targets and quotas were widespread as parties sought to feminise their image in response to perceptions of the demands of their women voters and to the explicit demands of their women members and activists. These debates often took place in the context of struggles to modernise the party. In the British Labour party, decisions to introduce quotas for women in the various ruling committees at different levels of the party structure, to be implemented by the mid-1990s, were taken in the context of an overhaul of party structures designed to reduce the power of the Trade Unions and control its left wing. These objectives were incorporated in a modernisation and democratisation strategy that offered opportunities for women to press claims for representation.

Party change also offered opportunities for German women. Eva Kolinsky (1993) notes shifts in the nature of membership in German political parties in the post-war years. Party membership became more individual, more clearly linked to political interest and to a motivation of shaping the course of politics, contributing to the policies of a given party and holding political office. For men activists, she writes, these changes simply intensified business as usual, but for women the meaning of membership was transformed and one result was that the women's track of membership started to become integrated into the party mainstream, leading inevitably to demands for inclusion that spread across the party spectrum from the left to the right, a process that was accelerated by the rise of the Greens and the subsequent increase of political competition during the 1980s. As a result the German parties adopted positive discrimination strategies in the form of quotas for women at different levels of the party structure. These were soon followed with requirements for quotas of women on the candidates' lists.

Positive discrimination

The form of positive discrimination that has been most controversial in political parties is mandatory quotas for women. These are regarded as reverse discrimination and are often opposed on ideological grounds. The more important the office or position in question, the more opposition the policy meets, and parties are particularly reluctant to introduce positive discrimination into their candidate selection procedures. Indeed it would be impossible for some parties to do so. In the USA for example, the widespread use of primaries means there is virtually no conventional selectorate in the sense of a group of party gate- keepers who make decisions about candidacy. The problems to be overcome by women candidates in the USA are the obstacles of a political marketplace in which many significant resources are controlled by political action committees (PACs), rather than party organisations. In Canada imposing gender requirements on individual constituency organisations is viewed as a limitation on local organisations. The situation is similar in the British Conservative party. But other systems are more flexible. In Germany during the 1980s all the parties except the CSU set targets of women legislators and the SPD adopted temporary quotas of women candidates. Their idea is that once the barrier is broken, once women have experience in political positions, quotas will no longer be necessary. Temporary quotas are likely to be easier to justify than permanent ones. Another idea is the 'negotiable quota'. In the Netherlands a form of negotiable quotas has been implemented in which the localities and the party centre agree the quotas they will meet. This 'thin end of the wedge' approach has the merit that local selectors agree in principle to accept quotas and they have a responsibility to nominate women.

In this sensitive area of party activity, virtually all of the obstacles to women's representation come into play as do most of the strategies party women have devised to improve their representation. The fortunes of women's demands for representation as candidates and in legislatures have varied significantly in the countries we consider here. But there is a common dynamic to the claims and responses which suggests a logic to the process itself. Once a party accepts a demand for sex equality it is vulnerable to arguments that the political under- representation of women is unjust. The first step is to secure agreement that more women should be nominated. Then strategies must be devised to overcome obstacles to such an increase. Many of the obstacles are specific to a party or party system. Sometimes rules have to be changed to allow women access. Often resources must be reallocated to facilitate access. Demands for the selection of more women candidates for good seats tend to begin with pressure to get more women with 'standard' qualifications nominated. In the course of getting an increase in women's nominations accepted and implemented, questions about the appropriateness of the standard qualifications get raised and debates about the desired composition of the legislature begin. At the same time selection procedures are scrutinised and strategies of elite insulation whereby male party members protect their monopolies of power are identified and criticised.

The rules of the game: ideology, organisation, political careers and gender

The claims that women make and the strategies they employ are considerably affected by the kind of party they seek to influence. All political parties have decision-making procedures consisting of formal rules, informal practices and customs. These reflect the party's political environment and patterns of internal conflict as well as expressing its ideology and goals. They also structure the party's organisation. When women become political claimants, when they seek political representation, they must take the rules into account and pay attention to the ideology and organisation of their party. All their claims will be contested in the party, but the most intense opposition will occur when the inevitable claim for an increased women's presence in the national legislature is made. Seats in the legislature are the political prize towards which much of party politics is directed, hence access to them is usually carefully guarded.

The pattern of the political careers of party parliamentarians tells us a great deal about the rules of the game. In the past, in many systems, women's political careers have differed from those of men, and in many systems women have not been nominated because they do not have appropriate 'qualifications'. Inhibitions about the appropriateness of their qualifications may stop women from seeking candidacy. The qualifications a party requires of its candidates are, of course, a function both of ideology and organisation. This is an area of some variation. Different countries and parties have developed different political apprenticeships and it is clear that some are more accessible to women than others. In Ireland the traditional route for women to elected office was (and in Fianna Fail continues to be) kinship with the previous incumbent. This used to be termed the 'widow factor' in the USA and Australia. In the Netherlands and in the Italian PCI (Partito Comunista Italia) and its successors, the long party career is the main qualification for candidacy to the legislature. Requirements for continuous and lengthy apprenticeships in firms are thought by equal opportunities experts to favour men as employees. In politics the effect appears to be similar.

But requirements for *local* experience need not have a negative effect on women. It has long been argued that women's political concerns tend to be centred on the locality and the community, hence an emphasis on local experience should benefit them. In Sweden, which has the highest proportion of women legislators in the liberal democratic world, this is borne out. The political qualification for the Riksdag is local elected office. This is the case across the political parties and men's and women's career paths do not diverge. A similar tendency is becoming apparent in the British Labour party. In Italy, where pre-parliamentary careers are important, candidates in good positions tend to have held local or party elected office simultaneously. Italian women's political careers are coming to resemble men's. By contrast, in France, the absence of women in elected office may in part be explained by their exclusion from local politics. Local political bases are essential to the careers of French politicians and there is great competition amongst men for likely offices. Women have been largely excluded from these competitions and have not therefore been able to make the first steps of a standard French political career.

When party rules alter to facilitate women's candidacy they may well upset normal career paths. Eva Kolinsky (1993) notes that the adoption of quotas of candidates in the German SDP has changed the nature of the political apprenticeship there. It has sharply reduced the *Oschentour* (slaving like an ox), the long haul necessary to become qualified as a candidate. The backlog of 'qualified' women who sought careers was very quickly cleared after which novices became candidates. Quotas broadened access routes and increased the pool of women who were 'eligible'.

Parties of the left have traditionally been more willing than parties of the centre and the right to make agreements to nominate women and they also appear to be more able to deliver on such agreements. But ideology is a less reliable indicator of party support for women's representation than it once was. Today the trend is for parties across the ideological spectrum to seek ways of promoting women.

Party organisation is another variable that we must take into account. As we have seen, weak or decentralised party organisation means that party centres are less able to implement policies to promote women because they have low levels of control over their local branches and constituency organisations. Federal party organisations embracing affiliates of various kinds are similarly impeded. In the British Labour party, it is difficult to exercise effective control over the way that affiliated trade unions exercise their considerable selection powers. Marila Guadagnini makes use of Panebianco's work on party organisation in her chapter on Italy [this refers to the original volume] to argue that the way a party is structured has considerable impact on the capacity of its leadership to influence the composition of the candidates list. This is both because of the power that the centre has over the localities and because centralised parties with relatively large bureaucracies are able to recruit, develop and support officials who constitute a corps of professional politicians. The bureaucracy also offers the security of paid employment for politicians who lose their seats. But she also remarks that in Italy's factionalised parties with weak bargaining structures (notably the Christian Democrats), it is still the core elite who are in control, the difference between the two types is that the elite is fragmented rather than cohesive. In practice the localities in almost all parties have some bargaining power in the candidate selection process, but the amount of local power will vary considerably by the type of electoral system and by the strength of the party. The level of competition for candidacy also varies considerably by party and is closely associated with party fortunes. But other factors are also important. In Italy, high levels of political competition for candidacy impede women's chances of securing nominations. In Canada, where levels of turnover are high and there are comparatively few safe seats, women have relatively high rates of entry. In most countries minor parties with lower chances of electoral success are more likely to nominate women, but this is not a reliable indicator that they wish to see more women in power. Such parties are generally more likely to nominate atypical candidates because they have a limited choice of applicants.

The disadvantages that women candidates may experience are sometimes transformed by political circumstances. In the USA in the 1990s women have the advantage of being perceived as outsiders by the public at a time when it is a 'plus' to be outsiders. Similarly in Italy, the contemporary crisis is essentially about political representation, hence the issue of women's representation is readily incorporated into the current debates about restructuring the party system.

There is no party in which efforts to nominate more women have occurred without an intervention by women making claims. In Sweden, organised women pressed their parties to nominate women candidates and place them in favourable positions on party lists by several means. At first, they simply put women's names forward, a tactic that was very important in the early stages. They also conducted campaigns to promote women candidates and made proposals to get women into better positions on party lists. Finally they acted as watchdogs and protested whenever reversals occurred. The task of securing substantial increases in women's electoral fortunes has been achieved without recourse to formal quotas. Recommendation, arguments and the threat to work for quotas achieved agreements to set targets of 40 per cent of nominations going to women. Once these targets were set, considerable progress was made.

The dynamic of gender and party politics

In conclusion, it is evident that there is a dynamic between women's claims and party responses whereby initiatives on women's representation lead to more radical such initiatives by both sides. When parties fail to respond or, as is the case when they adopt rhetorical strategies, they respond only minimally, women increase their demands. As a result rhetoric leads to positive action strategies which by the same dynamic become more comprehensive as time passes. When positive action strategies lead to good results women become more integrated into their parties and thus better positioned to secure and maintain adequate levels of representation. When insufficient change results from positive action, demands for positive discrimination are made and these have been adopted in many countries

In the rest of this volume [this refers to the original volume] examples of the claims that women have advanced and the responses parties have made in particular liberal democratic systems are explained in detail. They demonstrate clearly that the way a party responds to women's claims is a product both of the nature of those claims and the strategies used to press them. But it is also conditioned by the party's place in its political environment. Accordingly, in the concluding chapter [this refers to the original volume], Pippa Norris discusses the party responses and considers the effect of systemic factors on party strategies to represent women.

References

Kolinsky, E. (1993) 'Party Change and Womens Representation in United Germany' in J. Lovenduski and P. Norris (eds) *Gender and Party Politics*, London: SAFE.

Skjeie, H. (1993) 'Ending the Male Political Hegemony: The Norwegian Experience in J. Lovenduski and P. Norris (eds) *Gender and Party Politics*, London: SAFE, pp 231–262.

Chapter Six

Will Quotas Make Labour More Woman-Friendly?*

The current controversies over the legality of quotas and the beginning of the parliamentary selection round make this a good time to rehearse the debate over positive action strategies. The arguments surrounding the autumn conference decision to introduce all-women shortlists in half of all Labour marginals and vacant Labour seats is a version of a controversy that has been running for some time, not only in the Labour Party, but also in the socialist (and other) parties throughout Europe, the Anglo-American democracies and in most of the parties of the Socialist International. The Labour Party has come late to these arguments which were made, resolved, re-made and re-resolved across the whole spectrum of socialist parties, unions, firms and workplaces in the early 1980s. The pattern in party politics is pretty clear (Lovenduski and Norris 1993): experience since the 1960s suggests that, once a party addresses and devises policies about equal pay and opportunities for men and women at work, the issue of equality of women's political representation will inevitably become more insistent; and if other measures fail, quotas will be introduced. The resistance to quotas is equally inevitable. There are clear gainers and losers in such strategies which attempt to correct generations of past discrimination in a comparatively short space of time.

Promoted by feminist activists and their supporters, Labour's quotas are meeting with resistance from male aspirants who themselves may not be responsible for unfair discrimination against women, and therefore do not see why they should bear the burden of its redress. They are joined, of course, by diehard sexists and other defenders of the status quo, including some Party women who fear either a backlash or that participation in a political world structured by men will merely make them behave as the men do or both. Backlash there certainly is: quotas are vituperatively described as 'assisted places' schemes or 'gendered gerrymanders', and there is a widespread assumption that the women who are selected and elected as a result of their implementation are less able than the men who would otherwise have been chosen. But it is more likely that increased powers for women will change the Party than the other way around. The experience of Scandinavian women shows that party cultures and practices can and do change.

Setting quotas of women candidates should be seen in the context of Labour's policies to promote women and assessed in the light of experience in other countries. Although Britain's first-past-the-post electoral system presents special problems to the way quota strategies are devised, the principles and politics are

---

*   'Will quotas make Labour more woman-friendly?', *Renewal*, 1994, 2(1).

broadly similar in other systems. In the following discussion I will attempt to do both, first outlining Labour's array of quotas, then rehearsing the arguments about what quotas will achieve for Labour's women and the Party itself, drawing on the experience of promoting women in comparable political systems. Separating the 'woman' question from the 'party' question is somewhat artificial and, in practice, virtually impossible. I am well aware that the fate of the Party is entangled with its capacity to address its whole membership and the entire electorate, and that changes in the Party have brought feminist standpoints into most areas of policy and debate. I try to make the distinction, nevertheless, because it highlights different aspects of the controversy over women's representation and party change.

Labour's sex equality strategies

In common with other political parties Labour has devised gender strategies to respond to the claims of women voters, members and activists. The new gender policies were developed during a period of Party change and modernisation. As Party feminists have become better organised and more insistent, and Labour's fortunes, particularly among women voters, have faltered, the approach has become progressively more radical in both programmatic and organisational terms.

It is organisational change which is at issue here. Typically there are three party strategies to promote women. These are: first, rhetorical strategies whereby women's claims are accepted in campaign platforms, and party spokespersons make frequent reference to the importance of getting more women into office; second, strategies of positive or affirmative action in which special training is offered to women office-seekers, targets are set for the inclusion of women and considerable encouragement is given to women to come forward for posts of various kinds; and finally, strategies of positive discrimination in which places are reserved for women on decision-making bodies, on candidate slates, and in party leadership positions. Positive discrimination (sometimes pejoratively called reverse discrimination) — essentially the use of compulsory quotas of one kind or another — is always controversial and tends to be adopted only as a last resort, when other methods fail to deliver parity, yet women continue to insist on representation. It is not always necessary. In Sweden, party women were able to increase their presence as candidates through the use of voluntary targets, combined with the explicit threat that if these were not met, mandatory quotas would be implemented. However, in Germany, Norway and the Netherlands, quotas have been an important part of party strategies to increase the political representation of women (Lovenduski and Norris 1993).

In addition to its various women's sections, committees, councils, conferences and officers, Labour now has gender quotas throughout its organisation. The rulebook decrees that two of the four statutory branch officers must be women and the delegation from the branch to the constituency shall have a quota of 50 per cent women. Constituency Labour Parties (CLPs) are now required to elect a woman as their delegate to conference at least every other year, and affiliated trade unions will by 1994–95 be required to include women in their delegations to conference in proportion to their memberships. The twenty-five person National Executive Committee has three different quotas: there are five places reserved for women; and, by 1995, three of the seven members elected by CLPs must be women and four of the twelve members elected by trade unions must be women. Voters in shadow cabinet elections must now cast four votes for women. And since the 1993 conference, half of all Labour's vacancies in Parliament must be filled by women. These are very radical policies and there are real fears they will prove impossible to implement. It is therefore difficult to escape questions about what they may reasonably be expected to achieve.

What will quotas of women do to and for Labour women?

The expressed goal is to bring more women into public office. Britain ranks low in the tables on the political representation of women.

The obvious and central goals of quotas are to empower women, to feminise the Party and, as a result, to feminise politics. In their support it is argued that, in a party shaped and dominated by men, women's voices are heard only insofar as they conform to the rules, follow the customs and practices men have generated, and promote the priorities men have established. Promoting a few women will not be enough to change this culture. Women have diverse interests and for these to be expressed their representation must be large enough to make critical acts likely (Dahlerup 1988). Critical acts are measures which change things for women in general, to ensure that more women will be empowered. An example of this phenomenon, at least in its intentions, is the foundation last year of the Women's Group Parliamentary Labour Party and its action to increase the number of women's places on the Shadow Cabinet. In the Scandinavian countries where women's representation is relatively high there are numerous examples of Dahlerup's critical acts: women deputies generate, monitor and develop legislation to secure parity for women in employment, education, to expand child-care provision and to enhance their position in legislatures, councils and other decision-making bodies (Dahlerup 1988; Lovenduski and Norris 1993). As the numbers of women it is less likely they will 'pull the ladders up' after them.

Quotas mean both having more women around and encouraging women to seek power. These newly empowered women are unlikely to behave like the men they have succeeded, not because women politicians will have a different genetic structure, but, it is argued, because women have a culturally different approach to debate and negotiation, and to politics in general. This is the thinking behind the view that when the numbers and powers of women increase, the culture of the Party will change. It is far too early to tell whether, in Britain, the empowerment of women will alter the established contours of political practice. However, there is every reason to wish and hope that at least some of the macho ethos and posturing fraternalism of the Labour Party will dissipate, and that women will be encouraged to believe and behave as if it is their Party too.

Table 6.1: Women's Share of Parliamentary Candidacies and Seats in 1992

	Percentage of candidates	Percentage of MPs
Sweden	41	38
Norway	41	36
Holland	na	21
Germany	na	20
Canada	19	13
Italy	16	13
USA	12	11
Britain	18	9
Ireland	14	8
Australia	18	7
France	12	6
All	21	16.5

Source: Interparliamentary Union.

What will quotas of women do to and for the Labour Party?

Labour's adoption of positive discrimination is a tough political decision and it was taken for tough political reasons. An intractable and much discussed gender gap whereby women voters in the largest age groups do not support the Party has been one of the main pressures to feminise its image. Another is the key role Party women have played in the coalitions supporting modernisation and democratisation within the Party. This support was predicated on a *quid pro quo* of measures to increase women's representation. Third, there is the phenomenon of women's agency: organisation by women on behalf of women in the Party has grown and strengthened during the years of opposition. The skills and sophistication of the women's networks were one of the most striking features of the 1993 conference.

Of course, getting decisions through conference is only one step in the process of adopting quotas. The implementation of all-women shortlists will inevitably affect the balance of central, local and regional power. In addition to the programmatic implications mentioned above, these three related political pressures have organisational, representational and cultural implications. For many years now, when selecting their candidates for general elections, CLPs have had all but the very last, formal word in selection decisions, provided they operated according to the rather complicated rules. The conference decision increases NEC powers to press a shortlist on selecting CLPs, and imposes on regional organisations the responsibility to negotiate which constituencies will or will not have all-women shortlists.

The organisational implications will be felt at all levels of the Party, creating many opportunities for opponents to destroy or distort the policies. But under the current British electoral system it is hard to see another way of increasing women's candidacies. This strategy is not unique: in the Canadian New Democratic Party regional clusters of riding associations create plans for achieving affirmative action goals, individual associations implement them. All associations where an incumbent is not seeking reselection are required to take part and the national Party will take direct responsibility for drawing up affirmative action plans if such action proves necessary. But in Canada there are often problems of finding any candidates at all. The highly competitive nature of seeking candidacy for winnable seats in Britain is reinforced by the independent attitudes of many CLPs and makes the success of such negotiations less certain.

Organisational obstacles may be sufficient to prevent a full implementation of the quotas. The consultation exercise by the NEC found some 75 per cent of CLPs disagreed with women-only shortlists, although 71 per cent were prepared to support them as a voluntary option. It is far from clear that there is enough support to make the quotas work. There were, for example, many reports at conference that constituencies were ignoring rules about branch officer and constituency delegate quotas.

Decisions to increase women's representation in the Party have come at the same time as the structure of representation itself has been under discussion. The debate about the power of trade union affiliates and the role of individual members opened a space in which women activists were able to press claims to get more women into key positions. The feminisation of the Party is now associated with its capacity to present a modern image and is a consistent feature of arguments about programmes and policy. This is more than mere window-dressing. Party research has repeatedly shown that its masculine image puts off women voters, prevents women members from becoming activists and inhibits interested women from joining the Party (Radice 1992; Hewitt and Mattinson 1989). The male ranks of the faithful at conference are only part of the offending image. Presentation, style and culture have all been revealed as part of the fraternalism that characterises Labour's particular brand of patriarchy.

The quotas will undermine that patriarchy in a number of ways. For example, a substantive effect of efforts to improve women's representation may be changes in 'political apprenticeship', in the qualifications which are required to enter Parliament. In Germany the backlog of 'qualified' women who had undergone the traditional long political apprenticeship for qualification as a Social Democratic Party candidate (the *Oschentour*) cleared soon after quotas were introduced and women with less traditional qualifications began to be selected.

Although there are large numbers of able women who seek candidacy in Britain, it is possible that a similar effect will eventually become apparent. And trade unions, if they are to maintain their current levels of sponsorship, will have to address the qualifications for their panels. In other words, quotas will bring new kinds of politicians into Parliament and into the leadership of the Party — a prospect that raises questions about what are the appropriate qualifications of politicians. An audit of the qualifications for parliamentary careers should form an important part of the debate about feminising political representation. There is a widespread assumption that women who are elected through the use of quotas will be 'unqualified'. This, in turn, assumes that the qualifications according to which men get selected are the appropriate, indeed the *only* appropriate, qualifications. But it takes just a few televised parliamentary debates to show how uninspiring a normal crop of MPs is. In fact, MPs' qualifications are already changing; some trade unions have been to considerable lengths to alter the profiles of their parliamentary panels, and ten years of changes in Labour's selection procedures have greatly improved the chances of local candidates at the expense of more national figures. In short, feminisation is part of a more general trend to widen the range of skills and qualifications considered suitable for parliamentary candidacy and to extend the range of representation offered by the PLP.

Cultural change in the Party is closely related to changes in representation. Labour's dominant ethos has been well documented. Cynthia Cockburn (1987) has described how the certainties of traditional Labour politics depend upon the opportunity 'to inhabit a culture that brings together the umbrella of masculine identity, of male fraternity: work, working-class allegiance, trade union membership and Labour Party affiliation'. Women do not inhabit this culture; they may well not prefer the ties between the union movement and Labour. When feminists began to join the Party at the end of the 1970s they found a well-established, elaborately ritualised and formalised politics. To be effective individuals needed to learn the rules and to be able to use them. The culture was a barrier to the influence of all new members and it proved especially unpleasant for women who often had little other experience of organised politics. Nor had the Party been particularly hospitable to its long-standing women members. Sarah Perrigo (1996) has written that the Party's attitudes and its accommodation of women scarcely changed between the 1920s and the end of the 1970s. Party women's organisations lacked power and could not easily be used to press issues of interest to women. Change, when it came, was slow and patchy, and even today there are enormous local variations in Labour's woman-friendliness. Traditional attitudes to women are most prevalent in Labour's old heartlands, in the traditional manufacturing areas — in other words, the constituencies where the safe seats are. This pattern means that the battles to implement quotas will take place in precisely the CLPs where resistance to them is likely to be strongest. As one MP who was asked about the chances of Labour nominating more women candidates for winnable seats commented in 1992 'in a region like this there is a very substantial prejudice against women because it's a traditionally very heavy industry area and ... many people take the view that women have a place and it ain't at the meetings that men attend!' This is a view endorsed by a woman candidate who described her experiences at the 1992 conference:

> You come from London and you think things are beginning to improve, and then you go to national conference and you sit next to people who say, 'I'm here because I'm the women's delegate.' And I say, 'there's no such thing as the women's delegate — you've got 400 additional members so you've come as an additional delegate.' And the man has got the votes, and sits with his mates in

the union block and never consults her about how they're going to vote. And on Wednesday, she says to me, 'I've got to go home today,' and I say 'Why?' And she says, 'Well, I can't afford to stay any longer.' I say 'You're entitled to expenses.' She said, 'Oh no, he got all the expenses.' The 'real' delegate, she kept calling him.   (British Candidate Study 1991)

But there is some evidence that feminisation is altering the Party culture. The *Guardian* (2 October 1993) reported an occasion last summer when Tessa Jowell apologised to the Health Select Committee for not being able to make the afternoon meeting because her daughter had insisted on attendance at her twelfth birthday tea. Male colleagues were said to be gracious. The arrival of the women's majority on Sedgemoor council in Somerset has brought a more co-operative, less adversarial style to its debates. Most observers agreed that the presence of the women's majority among CLP delegates in 1993 transformed the atmosphere of the conference.

Assessing the debate

At least six arguments against quotas have surfaced in the debate so far. Opponents say there are not enough good women to fill all these new places. As there is no systematic evidence to back this assertion, its proponents are forced to rely on anecdotes to support their contentions. At the end of her somewhat ill-informed diatribe against quotas in the *Observer* (3 October 1993), Melanie Phillips cited the instance of a male Stoke-on-Trent-North delegate who was banned from attending conference because of the rule which said, having sent a man the previous year, this year's delegate must be a woman. Apparently no woman could be found who was willing to go. This instance is likely only to be a temporary setback. Many of the women delegates at Brighton would never have dreamed of putting themselves forward, had the obligation to send a woman not been there. They responded to the opportunity when it arose. This and experience in other countries suggests a growing number of women will come forward to take places when they are made available to them. I am willing to bet that the next time Stoke on Trent North CLP is required to choose a woman delegate, there will be no shortage of able candidates.

The second argument which surfaces is that women who get into politics because of quotas won't be taken seriously, and that women won't want power which is achieved through such condescending and patronising means. This implicitly repeats the bogus assumption that the women who will benefit will not be as able as the men they will displace. At Brighton there were numerous examples of women taking the floor with the remark 'I'm a quota' as their first, cheerful statement. Not only were they competent, thoughtful and serious about their responsibilities, they also seemed well pleased with their experiences. The third argument is that quotas are a sort of 'fast track' for middle-class, professional women who will push out deserving, working-class men. This fairly typical mobilisation of traditional class rhetoric against women is normally used by middle-class men. It ignores the fact that only by increasing the overall number of women in Parliament will there be any chance of getting a diverse representation of women. The fourth argument is that feminising the Party will put off the unskilled male voters who, it is assumed, will break the well-established trend among British voters to vote according to the Party rather than the sex of the candidate. The reasoning that this group of men is particularly susceptible to sexism fails to explain why so many of them voted for Margaret Thatcher during the 1980s.

The fifth argument is that quotas will generate a backlash. This has some merit. Whenever women get anything they didn't used to have, even when men don't want it, there is some sort of backlash. All-women shortlists and other quotas are aimed at things men do want, so an antipathetic reaction is assured, indeed is already starting. As I write the press are gleefully reporting unpleasantnesses about 'assisted places schemes' after the debacle of the Shadow Cabinet elections returned only three, rather than the expected four, women. There were rumours at conference that Harriet Harman got her spectacular NEC vote from delegates who didn't understand the new voting system; there is considerable evidence that women on the front bench get a consistently worse press than similarly competent men. The National Union of Mineworkers raised the matter of women's quotas with the Equal Opportunities Commission (EOC) in the hope that they are unlawful under the terms of the Sex Discrimination Act. On the EOC's decision that such a case would be unlikely to win at tribunal, opponents of quotas began investigating the possibilities of taking action through the courts. These and other nastinesses abound in politics and they should be defied. The sexism of the press, which delights in them, is no justification for abandoning the battle against sexism in the Party. Moreover, the backlash may have a useful function: the controversy it sparks might actually serve to lengthen and extend debates about equality policy, winning new supporters for a whole range of positive action strategies in general and the promotion of women in particular. In other words, it needn't be the end of the argument.

Lastly, quotas are opposed by people who think they are unfair. This is a more serious argument. It says that in the course of attempts to equalise the number of women in positions of power and influence, men who had a right to those places are displaced even though they themselves may not have been guilty of any unfair discrimination against women. The problem with this contention is the language in which it is expressed. It ignores the structural process by which those men came to acquire their 'right' to be members of the dominant majority. Once that process is acknowledged, the right is exposed for the *privilege* that it is and its suspension is far less controversial.

Positive discrimination is inevitably controversial and quotas seem to raise particularly strong passions. But the long debate that has led to quotas in the Labour Party has done so because measures which stopped short of it, which relied on men to stand down, voluntarily to give up their privileges, failed. Many of the women who now support quotas once opposed them. They were convinced by their experience of women's share of the PLP increasing so slowly that parity was unlikely to arrive before the middle of the next century. Even now, some think the quotas do not go far enough. Many argued for compulsory all-women shortlists for *all* seats. They may have a point. Assuming normal rates of retirement and an average swing to Labour, the new regulations ensure that there will be around sixty-three women in the PLP after the next election, and it will now take four to five elections to bring women up to 50 per cent of the PLP. In other words, the requirement for 50 per cent all-women shortlists will take at least a generation to deliver parity.

There is little doubt that these arguments will run for some time. They will be repeated all over the country as CLPs select their new parliamentary candidates for this and forthcoming elections. They will subside only when the goals have been achieved and secured. Quotas are always a temporary expedient: over time, people will get used to the idea that Labour politicians might be women, and a greater number of women will be inspired to come forward as delegates, branch officers, local councillors and parliamentary candidates. A diverse presence of women will ensure not only that the range of women's issues get on the agenda but that most far-reaching of all, the Party culture will change. When that happens, the quotas can be abandoned.

Notes

The research on which much of this article is based was conducted during the British Candidate Study (BCS), an ESRC funded project (R000-23-1991) which was conducted with the co-operation of the Labour Party. The project was designed and directed jointly with Pippa Norris, who has also provided technical help with and moral support for this article. I am grateful to her and to Jackie Goode for her insightful interview and meeting reports. However, the attitudes and viewpoints expressed here are mine.

References

Cockburn, C. (1987) 'Women, Trade Unions and Political Parties', London: Fabian Research Series, No.349.

Dahlerup, D. (1988) 'From a Small to a Large Minority: Women in Scandinavian Politics', *Scandinavian Political Studies*, 11 (4): 275–298.

Hewitt, P. and Mattinson, D. (1989) 'Women's Votes: The Key to Winning', London: Fabian Research Series No.353.

Lovenduski, J. and Norris, P. (eds) (1993) *Gender and Party Politics*, London: Sage.

Radice, G. (1992) 'Southern Discomfort', London: Fabian Research pamphlet 555.

Chapter Seven

Women's Equality Guarantees and the Conservative Party*

with Rosie Campbell and Sarah Childs

The six-month campaign that culminated in David Cameron's election as leader of the Conservative party in December 2005 was unusual for both the quantity and quality of its rhetoric on women's representation and frequent references to women's issues. In the final stretch of their campaigns, both Davids — Cameron and Davis — made direct appeals to potential women supporters. Both were interviewed on BBC's *Women's Hour* (which may now be a fixture of British electoral politics) talking, amongst other things, about what measures they would introduce to increase the numbers of Conservative women MPs and what their policies on maternity leave would be. Once elected, Cameron returned to the 'woman issue' immediately: just two minutes into his acceptance speech he declared 'nine out of ten Conservative MPs, like me, are white men, we need to change the scandalous under-representation of women in the Conservative party, and we'll do that'. Less than a week later in a major speech in Leeds on 12 December, he set out a five-point positive action plan including a freeze on selection and the adoption of a priority list of aspirant candidates. Conservative held and target seats will be required to select from this list, which will consist of at least 50 per cent women and a 'significant' proportion of black, minority ethnic and disabled candidates, all selected on their merits. A 'progress review' will take place after three months, upon which, if insufficient progress has been made, 'further action' will be taken. The supply of aspirant candidates will be increased by headhunting, part of a professional recruitment programme in which potential applicants will be mentored and guidance will be given to local constituencies. Conservative-held and target seats will hereafter be expected to employ either primaries (either open or closed) or community panels (to include local community stakeholders such as local voluntary groups, head teachers, local business leaders and local police). In February the party announced that seven out of nineteen early selections in winnable seats were women. However, it turned out that these were simply fast track reselections of candidates who stood last time.

Cameron's intention to increase the representation of women at Westminster is welcome. The presence of women in the House of Commons currently depends mainly on the fortunes of the Labour party, which returned 98 of 127 women

---

* 'Women's equality guarantees and the Conservative Party' (with S. Childs and R. Campbell) *Political Quarterly*, 2005, 77(1), pp.18–28.

MPs in 2005, when only seventeen Conservative women were elected. However, Cameron's proposed reforms stop short of the equality guarantees that assure the election of women. Moreover, it is far from clear how the reforms will be implemented. Typically, the Conservative leadership relies upon the cooperation of its constituency parties and is normally not in a position to interfere directly in the selection of parliamentary candidates for particular seats.

Even so, Cameron and at least some of his supporters appear to have experienced a Damascene conversion. Although the MPs Ann Widdecombe and Eric Forth continue to rage against any assertion that the sex of our MPs might matter, there is talk of action 'short of positive discrimination' almost everywhere. This new-found willingness to tackle the under-representation of women is somewhat surprising. The contagion effect (where other parties catch the sex-quota bug once one party has adopted them) found in other party democracies has been little observed in the UK. Officially, both Conservatives and Liberal Democrats are routinely critical of Labours all-women shortlists policy.

Cameron's equality rhetoric reflects successful mobilisation by women's advocates in the Conservative party who have been campaigning for increased women's representation in Parliament and the greater representation of women's interests for the last two electoral cycles. These include, most notably in the parliamentary party, Teresa May, and in the extra-parliamentary party the efforts of women associated with the Women2Win campaign, especially Anne Jenkins. Fiona Hodgson and Pamela Parker, Chairman and President of the Conservative Women's Organisation, respectively, have announced their reluctant support for positive discrimination. At Central Office both Trish Morris and Christina Dykes, who were responsible for candidates under previous party leaders, have promoted increases in the number of women candidates.

Experience in other countries and in the Labour party indicates that the crucial step is to convince male party leaders that feminisation is essential to party modernisation. Cameron's decision to frame his leadership campaign in terms of gender suggests that he has been convinced and arguably reflects his desire to signal a repositioning of the Conservative party. In terms of image, women may be, Margaret Thatcher notwithstanding, emblematic of 'modern compassionate conservatism'. More prosaically, here is an acknowledgement that the Conservative party needs to win back women's votes if it is to win the next election. The surprise is, then, not that finally Conservative leaders are explicitly attempting to cultivate women's support and to feminise their image, but that it has taken them so long.

Historically, Conservative attitudes to women in politics may be described, quite simply, as mixed. On the one hand, an idealisation of the traditional family is a prominent feature of party values and rhetoric. On the other hand, the party needs to mobilise women as voters and as party activists. In other words, despite a view of society that assigns women to domestic or private roles, the party depends on women undertaking public duties. Indeed, for most of the twentieth century women were not only more likely to vote Conservative than men, they were also the majority of the members even if few held major national positions in the party. The puzzle of why Conservative women were for so long willing to settle for so little is under-researched, although it appears that the party's contradictory attitudes towards women is not necessarily a problem. It was, and is, possible for women to combine private and public roles in a party that was (once) good at absorbing and containing differences. Although Conservative women asserted their rights inside the party they operated within the conventions of party behaviour, making sure that disagreements were not visible to outsiders. The sexual politics were normally of a fairly restrained kind. Wary of feminist strategies, Conservative women typically sought the removal of barriers to their participation rather than guarantees that they would be included. Their claims were pursued with care and caution and change came slowly, after everyone was persuaded that it was in the best interests of the party to promote women.

This article explores the pressures that underlay the latest turn to women by the Conservatives. We locate our discussion in a consideration of the problems faced by the Conservative party in winning women's votes and examine the options available in the quest to feminise its parliamentary wing. We argue that the poor representation of women at the parliamentary level is symptomatic of the party's wider problems, in particular its narrowing electoral base and the loss of its traditional advantage among women voters. After describing briefly the current and recent position of women candidates and MPs, we outline the barriers and obstacles to increasing the parliamentary presence of Conservative women and then evaluate the available options for change, and finally assess the likely impact of Cameron's suggested reforms.

How did the Conservatives lose the support of women?

The Conservative party has traditionally relied upon the support of women voters. Studies show that until the mid-1970s women were more likely to vote for the Conservative party than men, after which the traditional gender gap disappeared. If at one time the Conservative party could take its majority among women voters for granted - had it not been for the women's vote there would have been no Conservative governments between 1945 and 1979 -their support has leaked steadily away since the mid-1970s. Recently, Pippa Norris argued that the traditional gender gap has been replaced by a gender generation gap whereby younger women are more likely to vote for the Labour party than younger men (Norris 1999). Her findings are confirmed by MORI data showing that in the 2005 general election, for the first time, more women voted for the Labour party and fewer women voted for the Conservative party than did men, recording an overall gender gap of six percentage points.

Although it will take time to be sure if this is a continuing trend, comparative research suggests that it may well be, for at least two reasons.[1] First, international research on gender and voting behaviour consistently demonstrates that, as women in Western industrialised nations have moved into higher education and the workplace their attitudes have shifted. Previously, women were more likely to assert traditional moral values associated with church and family and to vote for parties on the right, but over time they have moved slightly to the left and now prioritise more left of centre values associated with increased government spending on social services such as health and education. The Conservative party, traditionally the net beneficiaries of women's votes, may now have lost its electoral majority amongst women voters, part of an international trend whereby women's preferences have shifted to the left. This trend is most evident in the United States where more women than men have voted for the Democratic candidate in every presidential election since 1980, a reversal of the traditional relationship whereby women were more likely than men to vote for Republican presidential candidates (Mueller 1988). It may be that Britain will see a similar trend, albeit with a time lag. Indeed, British research confirms that younger women are now slightly more left-leaning than younger men (Inglehart and Norris 2000; Campbell 2004).

In addition, changing attitudes toward equality may account for some of the decline in the Conservative party's support amongst women. Research by Bernadette Hayes established that individuals who espouse feminist values are more likely to vote Labour than Conservative. Campbell has found that younger women are more likely to espouse feminist values than younger men and these younger women are also more likely to vote for the Labour party. It is likely that the under-representation of women amongst Conservative MPs contributes to the perception that the Labour party is more open to feminist concerns and values. The likelihood that women voters are affected by the under-representation of women in Parliament is further underlined by a recent Electoral Commission report that demonstrated that women in constituencies where there is a sitting woman MP are more likely to participate and be interested in politics and are also more likely to feel that government benefits 'people like them' (Norris, Lovenduski and Campbell 2004; Hayes 1997; Campbell 2004; Childs *et al.* 2005).

As well as differences between men and women voters there is evidence of attitudinal differences between Conservative men and women electoral candidates and MPs. Analysis of the 1992, 1997, 2001 and 2005 British Representation Studies, surveys of political elites — specifically of candidates and MPs in successive general elections — provide evidence that on a number of issues women have more feminist attitudes then men in the Conservative political elite.

In the three main political parties, women candidates and MPs have consistently been more likely to approve of equality guarantees (quotas) for women than men. However, Conservative candidates and MPs were the least likely to approve of such measures in each survey. It is notable, too, that in every survey Conservative women MPs and candidates were more likely to approve of quotas than Conservative men, though their approval rates were comparatively low. Over the four surveys conducted since 1992, Labour women respondents' approval of quotas ranged between 62.9 per cent and 83.3 per cent. The proportion of Conservative women who approved was between 8 and 17.9 per cent. Equivalent approvals by men were Labour 45 to 69.9 per cent and Conservative 1.3 to 6.7 per cent. These low figures indicate that the Conservative elite does not yet accept quotas. Similarly, more women candidates and MPs from all parties agree that Parliament should have more women MPs, though these differences tend to be minimal. The largest difference is between Conservative respondents, where significantly more women (93.4 per cent) than men (72.6 per cent) in 2005 thought that Parliament should have many more women MPs.[2]

The current position of women candidates and MPs

Cameron's advocacy of women's representation is more likely to be driven by a calculation that the party's male and masculine image is one of the factors that contributes to its electoral failure. The numbers are instructive. One hundred and twenty-six women currently sit in the 2005 Parliament. Seventy-seven per cent are Labour women. As a proportion of the parliamentary party the Conservatives at 9 per cent in 2005 (the same proportion as in 2001) lag far behind the other parties. By contrast, Labour's women MPs constitute 27.5 per cent of their parliamentary party and in the Liberal Democrats they are 16 per cent. Yet in 2005 the Conservatives selected 118 women, finding more than enough suitable candidates to increase substantially their numbers of women. The problem was they were selected in seats the party had little chance of winning. Why have the Conservatives failed to improve their presence of women in Parliament? To answer this we need to examine how recruitment works and to consider what strategies may be employed to change outcomes.

The rules of the game

The recruitment of parliamentary candidates operates in a political marketplace in which the supply of those who might seek nomination interacts with the demand for particular types of candidates. In this market, demand is shaped by gatekeeper and selector attitudes while supply is determined by candidate motivation, qualification and availability.

In all parties, aspirant candidates must overcome a series of hurdles beginning with meeting eligibility criteria and ending with being chosen by voters. For the most part this process is a party matter, subject to rules, procedures and processes determined internally. Their choice of candidate is then determined by the parties' internal organisation, the nature of their selection processes and their wider beliefs about the role of women and men in public life. If political parties are institutionally sexist-dominated by men in terms of personnel, culture, outcome and practice-this will have a negative impact on the selection of women candidates. In the UK, party candidate selection is the crucial hurdle in political recruitment. Representatives are chosen from a menu offered by the major parties and, despite some selector opinion to the contrary, voters do not penalise women candidates.

Political recruitment is therefore a process that operates under important constraints. *Systemic* factors set the broad context within any country. They are the legal, electoral, party systems and the structure of opportunities (the structure of party competition, the strength of parties and the position of the parties across the ideological spectrum), which combine to affect for example levels of competition for selection as candidates. For Westminster, systemic factors are thought to be important insofar as the 'first past the post' plurality electoral system is widely recognised to be less favourable to the election of women than are proportional systems. The *party context*, including organisation, rules and ideology, directly affects the selection process, sets criteria of eligibility and establishes mechanisms for selection. *Individual* factors such as resources, motivations and the attitudes of gatekeepers (party selectorates) determine who comes forward and how they are treated. Finally, *elections* determine the outcome of the process for the composition of parliaments (Norris and Lovenduski 1995).

Strategic options

There are three strategies available to political parties wishing to increase the numbers of women representatives, and indeed the diversity of their representatives more generally: equality *rhetoric*, equality *promotion* and equality *guarantees*. Equality rhetoric is words-the public support given to the need for more women representatives. Equality promotion refers to activities that increase the numbers of eligible and qualified women who come forward as potential candidates. Examples include special training, financial assistance and the setting of targets. Equality guarantees require an increase in the numbers or proportions of women who are elected. Examples are party quotas, legislative quotas and reserved seats. Each equality strategy impacts differently. Equality rhetoric aims to affect attitudes and beliefs. Equality promotion enhances the resources and motivations of potential candidates and also affects selectorate attitudes. Equality guarantees create an artificial demand (which may also impact positively on supply) (Lovenduski 2005).

The selection practices of all the political parties involve broadly similar stages: of approval, application, nomination, shortlisting and selection. The three strategies operate at different stages of the selection process. Each involves a repertoire of activities that parties have available and use to promote particular types of candidacy.

If, as is increasingly accepted, the problem for the Conservative party (and the other main parties in the UK for that matter) is one of demand rather than supply, then neither equality rhetoric nor equality promotion is likely to have a great effect. Equality rhetoric may encourage greater numbers of women to enter the candidate recruitment pool and equality promotion may ensure that women aspirant candidates are better prepared, trained and resourced. But neither of these is sufficient to *guarantee* that constituencies will select women for party-held or winnable seats. For example, the Labour party and Liberal Democrats used equality promotion in the form of a compulsory minimum of women on their shortlists for the 2001 general election. They increased the supply of potential women candidates, but singularly failed to deliver the election of greater numbers of women MPs. Conservative party rhetoric in advance of the 2001 election similarly had little effect on its own. The problem therefore was one of demand. Selectors did not want women candidates.

The solution therefore is equality guarantees, which operate by creating an artificial demand. The idea behind quotas or reserved seats is to normalise the presence of women, creating a new equilibrium after which guarantees are no longer required to maintain a fair balance between women and men MPs. UK legislation now permits equality guarantees. The Sex Discrimination

(Election Candidates) Act 2002 introduced a new section (42A) to the Sex Discrimination Act. Valid until 2015, the legislation permits but does not prescribe the use of equality guarantees by political parties selecting electoral candidates. This was a change to the *systemic context* of political recruitment, after which it was up to political parties to decide whether to take up the opportunities offered by the new legislation. However, only Labour made use of equality guarantees in advance of the 2005 general election.

The Conservatives did raise their game, however. While they failed to take advantage of the new act, they altered their procedures-partly, they said, to enhance the prospects for women candidates. After the 2001 general election the Conservatives changed their *party context*. Selection still took place at constituency level but some of the rules were altered affecting the approval, application, shortlisting and selection stages of the process. At the approval stage, successful attendance at a Parliamentary Assessment Board (PAB) is the first hurdle that aspirant candidates must pass in order to make it onto the party's approved list. Following consultation with the academic psychologist Jo Silvester, and informed by equal opportunities good practice, the PABs changed their focus from the more gladiatorial activities that they had previously emphasised. Under new procedures, six 'gender neutral' core competencies were assessed:

1. communication skills (listening as well as speech making)
2. intellectual skills (take on board/distil complex information)
3. relating to (different kinds of) people
4. leadership and motivation (enthusing, supporting, enabling)
5. resilience and drive (avoiding arrogance)
6. conviction (to Conservative ideas and commitment to public service)

Once on the approved list, women, especially those selected for target seats, were offered training, some of which was designed especially for women.

At the application stage changes were devised to enhance the diversity of candidates, including the removal of education from CVs to avoid decisions based on attendance at the *'right* school or university'. At the shortlisting stage constituencies were encouraged to undertake their 'paper sift' of applications in London where the process was overseen to ensure there was 'nobody languishing' in the 'no' pile who 'shouldn't be' there. At the selection stage non-party members in local constituencies (recruitment experts, in particular) were invited to participate, although not vote, in the selection process.

More dramatically, the party introduced American-style 'primaries' and the 'city seats initiative' (CSI) strategy. Both of these approaches were efforts by the centre to introduce measures, short of equality guarantees, to encourage the selection of greater numbers of women, black and minority ethnic candidates. In the 'primaries' the selectorate is effectively extended beyond the members of the local association (in open primaries anyone who registered was permitted to participate whereas in closed primaries participation was limited to those who registered as Conservatives). Constituency parties continue to determine the shortlist from which the final selection is made and endorse, through a special general meeting, the final choice. In the 'city seats', part of a wider strategy to revive the party's fortunes in the inner cities, teams of would-be MPs were brought together, with the assistance of party HQ, to campaign citywide. Near to the election individual candidates were 'slotted' into particular seats. Local parties were given the opportunity to reject individual candidates as members of their city team (Childs 2006).

In practice and despite the changes in both the *systemic* and the *party* contexts, the explanation for the relative success of women candidates at the 2005 general election is the standard explanation the type of seats for which they were selected. The majority of women Conservative candidates were not placed in the seats held by the party or thought by party strategists to be winnable. Only fourteen Conservative women were selected for seats that the party held in 2001 and only four for seats winnable with a 5 per cent swing to the party. Women were candidates mainly in seats where the Conservatives were placed third last time, or in seats where the majority achieved by the winning party in 2001 was greater than 10 per cent of the vote. It therefore did not matter that the party selected 50 per cent women candidates for its CSI and primary seats, which were all located in the party's unwinnable constituencies.

Discussion

Cameron's announced reforms of the party's selection procedures stop far short of equality guarantees, an indication of their likely limited impact. In this respect, and despite Cameron's claim that his measures will 'guarantee' the election of more women MPs, it is unclear to us precisely how many more women will be elected. As the plans stand - and unless tighter measures are introduced following the three-monthly review - it is unlikely that *significantly* greater numbers of women will be elected. The Conservatives may manage to double their numbers of women MPs. However, while that would constitute a much-needed increase, it brings them nowhere near a fair proportion of women MPs. In order to get their percentage to near Labour's proportion of 27.5 per cent of the PLP, the Conservatives will need to act quickly to ensure that early selections for safe and winnable seats are secured for women. But the new rules are currently too loosely defined to *guarantee* such an outcome.

Whilst equality guarantees may not be to everyone's taste they work because they require a particular outcome - the selection of more women in party-held and winnable seats. The Conservative party's reluctance to adopt all-women shortlists or other measures such as a finite list of candidates from which local associations must choose their candidates (for example, 150 candidates for 150 vacancies), arguably reflects two dynamics: firstly, the party's reluctance to interfere with local association autonomy in the selection of parliamentary candidates and secondly their understanding of the concept of merit. Protection of local constituency autonomy is undoubtedly a pragmatic policy. The final choice of their candidate by local constituency associations is a longstanding and jealously guarded prerogative. Leaders interfere at their peril.

Nor is the issue of merit a trivial obstacle. The Conservative party's new procedures are couched in the language of merit. Those aspirant candidates who will be selected for the priority list will be selected on 'merit', as Cameron made clear. But other parties have learned that definitions of merit are contextual; they evolve as demands for more equality of representation are made. Thus new definitions of equality and merit have been debated and eventually accepted in the Labour party. The Conservatives have some way to go in this process. They must reflect on whether a system of selection that returns men in over 90 per cent of selections is really meritocratic. Hardly, and leaders know this. They also know that, short of equality guarantees, they cannot deliver significantly more women MPs. Despite the rhetorical flourishes of Cameron's accession, the Conservatives will probably proceed cautiously: party equality advocates believe they cannot yet win the inevitable argument necessary to implement equality guarantees. This is a process. Such arguments are often won only when all the other options have been exhausted. So Cameron's new procedures are likely to disappoint sex equality advocates. In theory they may improve matters, but as currently designed, they leave space for avoidance and subversion. All the evidence is that the Conservatives are not ready for sex equality, that they need more time to get used to the idea.

But time is not on the side of the Conservative resistors. The 'fast track' to women's equal political representation is a worldwide phenomenon - more than ninety countries use equality guarantees. The rationale is that if women's exclusion from politics is the problem then their inclusion is the obvious solution (Dahlerup and Friedenvall 2005). Inevitably, pragmatic considerations play an important role in decisions by male dominated parties to introduce such measures. They may wish to make a claim that they represent women and require quotas as a symbolic means of demonstrating their commitment to meeting that obligation. They may be responding to the claims of party members who have come to see the importance of quotas if change is to occur. They may also adopt quotas for electoral reasons. For example, Carlos Mennen (president of Argentina from 1989 to 1999) supported quotas when he thought he would lose an election if he did not. The extent to which the Conservative party responds positively to Cameron's exhortation and equality promotion - for this is what his measures are - is likely to be influenced not only by electoral imperatives, but also by the party's understanding of equality, and in particular its reconciliation with more modern gender roles.

As the launch of the Women2Win campaign demonstrated, the Conservatives look to be beginning to come to terms with a Britain characterised by rapidly changing gender relations. Demands to increase the numbers of women MPs come not only from those women who want to be MPs, they are supported by women in local associations, in party organisations, and by many male MPs. At the same time, traditional attitudes continue. The grass roots may be less convinced. A recent internal report commissioned by the Conservative Women's Office found some members more influenced by traditional Conservative rather than feminist attitudes to women's roles. It remains to be seen how Cameron's policy reviews will deal with the work-life balance and tensions between business interests and women's maternity leave and pay, for example.

However, if the Conservatives are finally facing up to some of their problems - their three successive electoral defeats, an ageing and declining membership, defunct or inactive associations, and the loss of their ability to absorb difference and dissent - then the time might well be ripe for change. It is in such situations that the rules of the game change. Changes in candidate selection procedures and party organisations typically follow electoral defeats. Although an aged membership in control of decision-making positions may delay change, as defeat follows defeat the pressure to reform becomes overwhelming. Assuming the party is able to rebuild, it will do because it recognises the wider changes in social attitudes that translate into voting behaviour and other kinds of political participation. This process involves choosing among competing accounts of how attitudes and behaviour are reflected in patterns of party support. Thus, demands for modernisation offer opportunities for advocates of women's representation to press their claims which, to be successful, must not only take account of the changing party context but also of developments in the electorate.

Conclusion

The combination of attitude change in the electorate, the apparent gender gap in the 2005 general election and an identifiable group of influential women members of the Conservative party holding feminist values have come together to produce an unprecedented interest amongst the Conservative party's elite in the representation of women in the House of Commons. Although by no means directly analogous, the issue of feminising the party's parliamentary contingent could well be the Conservative party's 'Clause Four moment'. For advocates of women's equal political representation it will be important to track the coming round of selections to determine if the new rhetoric and equality promotion measures deliver sufficient numbers of Conservative women MPs at the next general election.

There is no mystery about the causes of women's under-representation in British politics or what can be done. All the evidence points to 'demand side' rather than 'supply side' factors. The absolute number of women candidates is not really an issue - more than 400 women candidates were selected by the main three political parties for the 2005 general election. The Conservative party's 'woman issue' is how to ensure that more of these women are selected for party-held and winnable seats at the next general election. David Cameron's reforms go some way towards this, but stop short of equality guarantees. The shift of emphasis is, however, significant in the recent history of the Conservative party.

The current debate in the party did not come into being by accident. The achievement of increased women's political representation rarely takes place without a political struggle in which equality advocates must both mobilise and take advantage of the available opportunities. Party women's organisations, feminist movements and women's interest groups have become skilled at demanding quotas to achieve increases in women's political representation. To introduce quotas against severe resistance 'requires that women have already gained some power' (Dahlerup 1998). Conservative women have some power and they have begun to use it. Some of the party's male leadership have accepted much of their analysis. The path they have taken leads straight to equality guarantees. The question is how long it will take them to get there.

Notes

1. Source: MORI Final aggregate analysis from the pooled campaign surveys, 16 May 2005, total N = 17,595; http://www.mori.com
2. http://www.bbk.ac.uk/polsoc/research/brs.php

References

Campbell, R. (2004) 'Gender, ideology and issue preference: is there such a thing as a political women's interest in Britain?', *British Journal of Politics and International Relations*, 6 (1): 20–44.

Childs, S., Lovenduski, J. and Campbell, R. (2005) *Women at the Top*, London: Hansard Society.

Childs, S. (2006) 'Political parties', in P. Dunleavy, R. Heffernan, P. Cowley (eds) *Developments in British Politics 8*, Basingstoke: Palgrave, pp. 56–77.

Dahlerup, D. (1998) 'Using quotas to increase women's political representation', *Women in Politics: Beyond Numbers*, Stockholm: IDEA.

Dahlerup, D. and Friedenvall, L. (2005) 'Quotas as a fast track to equal political representation', *European Journal of Women's Studies*, 7 (1): 26–48.

Hayes, B. (1997) 'Gender, feminism and electoral behaviour in Britain', *Electoral Studies*, 16 (2): 203–16.

Inglehart, R. and Norris, P. (2000) 'The developmental theory of the gender gap: women and men's voting behaviour in global perspective', *International Political Science Review*, 21 (4): 441–463.

Lovenduski, J. (2005) *Feminizing Politics*, Cambridge, Polity.

Mueller, C. (ed.) (1988) *The Politics of the Gender Gap*, vol. 12, Sage Yearbooks in Women's Policy Studies, Beverly Hills: Sage.

Norris, P. (1999) 'Gender: a gender generation gap?', in G. Evans and P. Norris (eds) *Critical Elections: British Parties and Voters in Long-term Perspective*, London: Sage, pp. 148–163.

Norris, P. and Lovenduski, J. (1995) *Political Recruitment: Gender, Race and Class in the British Parliament*, Cambridge: Cambridge University Press.

Perrigo, S. (1996) 'Women and Change in the Labour Party', *Parliamentary Affairs*, 49(1): 116–129.

Chapter Eight

Obstacles to Feminising Politics*

The correction of women's political underrepresentation is work in progress, much of which remains to be done. By 2003 only thirty-nine nation-states had ever selected a woman as prime minister or president. Worldwide, fewer than 10 per cent of cabinet ministers, 20 per cent of lower ranking government ministers and 15 per cent of legislators were women (Inter Parliamentary Union). These low figures are historic highs, achieved after decades of struggle.

Although there is significant regional variation, the underrepresentation of women is a persistent political fact of life in modern states, present across all types of institutional arrangements and cultures. It is one of the few generalisations that it is safe to make about the position of women.

How can such underrepresentation be explained? The explanations are complex; the absence of women from representative offices is the result of a combination of institutional and social factors. The social obstacles are the most familiar. Women experience three main social obstacles to becoming politicians. First, they have fewer of the resources needed to enter politics. Women are poorer than men and are less likely to be employed in occupations that are supportive of political activism. Second, various lifestyle constraints mean women have less time for politics. Family and other caring responsibilities are typically undertaken by women, reducing their time for other activities. Third, the job of politics is coded as male, which inhibits women from seeking political careers and also impedes the recruitment of those who come forward.

Constitutional and legal obstacles have also been important. Democratic states have laws that determine who electors and representatives may be and how representation takes place. Rules about representatives may specify the characteristics that a representative should have. Age, citizenship and residency are frequently specified. Women were barred by law from being representatives in many states until recently. By 2003 only some Middle Eastern states continued with such exclusion. These were Kuwait, Qatar, Saudi Arabia, Oman and the United Arab Emirates. More generally, the type of electoral law a system operates affects its representativeness in various ways and is thought to have an effect on opportunities for women to be elected as representatives. In general, more women are elected under party list proportional representation (PR) systems than under majoritarian electoral systems, although there is considerable variation within each type of system (Norris 2004).

---

* 'Obstacles to Feminizing Politics', Ch. 3, in *Feminizing Politics*, Cambridge, Polity Press, 2005, pp. 45–82. 'Male Dominance Broken' in D. Dahlerup and M. Leyenaar (eds) *Breaking Male Dominance in Old Democracies*, Oxford, Oxford University Press, pp. 72–96.

Although most of the possible explanations turn out to be widespread phenomena, few are universal. Women's political disadvantages are embedded in particular social and institutional arrangements, subject to many different constraints. In this chapter I explore barriers to women's political representation in modern democracies. I use the example of the Westminster system to illustrate my arguments. I examine in detail the barriers to women's presence in the House of Commons and the barriers to their political recruitment in British political parties. I argue that British political institutions are characterised by a culture of traditional masculinity that is a major obstacle to women. I describe the culture and draw on feminist social theory to explain the processes through which it developed. This culture supports institutional sexism in the political system. Although there are some signs of recent change, there is considerable evidence of persisting institutional sexism in the political parties and in the House of Commons.

Sexism is not the only barrier to women's presence at Westminster, where it is comparatively difficult for any recently mobilised groups to gain a foothold. In constitutional terms the UK has a high threshold of representation compared to other representative democracies. The Westminster electoral system is based on single-member constituencies in which the winning candidate needs to secure only a simple majority of the vote, a system known to be associated with low levels of women's representation. Westminster is no longer the only significant site of British political representation. A process of constitutional change has brought new assemblies into being in Scotland, Wales and Northern Ireland. These assemblies are elected on PR systems which, in Scotland and Wales, have facilitated measures to increase the inclusion of women. In Northern Ireland, advocates of women's representation have been less successful, though some progress has been made. The UK system therefore provides a good illustrative example of the impact of various electoral systems on women's representation (*see* chapter 7 [this refers to the original volume]).

Institutional Constraints

The laws that regulate political recruitment are only part of the process, which is also affected by the various institutions to which and through which recruitment takes place. The institutions that affect the level and nature of women's representation include political parties, elected assemblies and various pressure groups and social movements, including feminist movements. As we have seen, feminists have often been ambivalent about claiming political representation. Part of the reason for that ambivalence is an appreciation that political institutions are characterised by priorities, cultures and practices that privilege certain kinds of masculinity. Feminist engagement with politics takes place in an already well-established set of institutions and practices. Its effectiveness conditioned by traditional political practices, including voting, participation in parties and associational life, and by attitudes, beliefs and values that are produced and reproduced in particular settings.

When women began to participate in such settings, even if they were not feminist, they affected how they worked. They were, in the words of Nirmal

Puwar, 'space invaders' who challenged gender norms by their very presence. The institutions and practices apparently adjusted to and absorbed the invaders with little or no relaxation of their sexism. Hence feminists are concerned that the practice of political representation will require women to behave like the men they seek to replace (Puwar 2004: 65). Joan Acker (1992), for example, refers to the occasional biological female who acts like a social man when she writes about women who were in powerful positions prior to the 1990s.

In practice, then, the most difficult obstacle is the deeply embedded culture of masculinity that pervades political institutions. When women become members of a legislature or other representative assembly, they are normally entering a male domain. For a long time Westminster was one of those places where men gathered with other men. Its ways were the ways of the gentlemen's clubs and public schools that were so important in establishing the norms of appropriate male behaviour. Parliament is masculine. I mean this in the sense that it institutionalises the norms of the men who founded it and for so many years inhabited it as a wholly male institution. This is why Westminster for so long boasted a rifle range but not a crèche. No conspiracy was necessary to exclude women; indeed, often the exclusion of women was not even a consideration. Like many institutions of the state, the Westminster culture embodies practices that reward traditional forms of masculinity and disallow traditional forms of femininity.

But it is too simple to state that women in such environments become men. The presence of even one woman in a previously all male arena illuminates its gendered nature and exposes its masculine characteristics. The disruptive effects of the entry of women into this environment are well illustrated by the career of Nancy Astor, the first woman to take her seat in the House of Commons. She experienced enormous resistance to her presence. Her most recent biographer writes of the almost overwhelming effort of courage and will needed to stand up to the hostility — petty, persistent and often vicious — from her colleagues in the House of Commons. The hostility came mostly from her own party. There was an unwritten consensus among the Conservatives, her party, that a female MP was by nature wrong. The idea was to freeze her out, cause the maximum embarrassment and humiliation, and so discourage constituencies from adopting other women candidates. Conservatives that she knew well turned away from her, including her two brothers-in-law. They refused to give her a seat at the corner of the bench, forcing her to climb over men's legs. At first they pretended they could not find a lavatory for her and made her walk to the far end of the building. Before a debate on venereal disease, they put the most graphic photographs they could find in the lobby, hoping to embarrass her. They made speeches that they considered unsuitable for a woman's ears. 'Shortly before she died she told her son David that if ... "I had known how much men would hate it, I would never have dared do it"' (Fox 1998).

When Liberal MP Margaret Wintringham became the second woman to take a seat in the House, she found the feeling of hatred she experienced when she went into the House to be so great that if Nancy Astor was not present in the chamber at the same time, the atmosphere was so unbearable that she had to leave (Fox 1998).

Such resistance is evidence that women representatives, by their very presence, threaten established patterns of behaviour. The institutional masculinity encountered by Astor was of a traditional kind. Historically it was bolstered by a variety of all-male organisations such as public schools, professions and the gentlemen's clubs. In the UK the House of Commons reflects the masculinity of its heyday in the Victorian era.

Why Does the Culture of Traditional Masculinity Persist?

Both gender theory and institutional theory suggest that institutions have considerable capacity to reproduce their cultures. Institutions are able to create and recreate gendered patterns through constantly repeated processes of exclusion. Gender inequalities, whereby some types of masculine behaviour are favoured, are produced and reproduced in political organisations such as legislatures. The underrepresentation of women and their near exclusion from powerful positions is underpinned by a set of practices, discourses and images that are associated with political institutions. For example, in politics leadership is often discussed in terms of military discourses in which war, battle, strength and victory are invoked. Such symbols and images express and reinforce gender divisions. They are embedded in the institution in various ways and may persist long after associated behaviour has become unacceptable in the society outside of the institution.

Institutional Masculinity

The argument that public institutions are characterised by an invisible masculinity draws on the same kinds of argument used by Lister (1997) in her account of the masculinity of citizenship discussed in chapter 2 [this refers to the original volume]. Research on public institutions in the 1980s and 1990s described in detail the way gender is shaped by public as well as private institutions (Bologh 1990; Davies 1994; Hearn 1989; Jones 1993; Savage and Witz 1992). The research shows how the shaping of gender by public institutions privileges certain kinds of masculinity and operates to maintain its dominance during periods of change, implementing a kind of insulation process that is familiar to students of political elites. This phenomenon is well expressed by Celia Davies (1994), who argues that cultural codes of masculinity and femininity shape identity from earliest childhood and are encountered and reencountered in the 'frozen social relations' of institutions. The cultural codes of gendered behaviour do not match exactly the beliefs and behaviour of 'actually existing women and men' — they are cultural codes, hence they are both complicated and idealised, but able to affect women and men. There are numerous competing masculinities and femininities. In real institutions gender biases are not static because gender is relational, that is masculinity and femininity are understood and can be understood only in relation to each other. When one participant in the relationship changes, so must the other. Moreover, the relation of masculinity to femininity, although dominant, is uneasy.

Theories of bureaucracy are a cornerstone of studies of state institutions. Feminists have shown that influential conceptions of bureaucracy are gendered. For example, they have criticised the influential theories of Max Weber about rational bureaucracy, professionalism, leadership and the institutionalisation of authority (Bologh 1990; Ferguson 1984; Jones 1993). Weber's theory of bureaucracy offers a model of how public administration should work. His model maps almost directly onto Lister's male citizen model. It is an ideal type, the main characteristics of which are hierarchy, routine, accountability, regulation, professionalism and impartiality. Feminist critics often elide Weber's descriptions of ideal bureaucracy with practices in 'actually existing bureaucracies'. Whilst unfair to Weber, this does not invalidate their insights into real institutions. They contend that Weber's professional, his rational bureaucrat and his legitimate ruler are the same idealised *man*.

Weber's ideal man is, of course, a construct of a particular idealised masculinity. For example, his ideal public bureaucrat is a rational, impartial, public-minded individual who wishes to make a difference in the world. Such men engage in autonomous action, each behaving rationally in pursuit of individual interest. Relations to each other are aggressive and competitive in a public world of '*hostile strangers*' in which collective action occurs only where power is exercised, where some men dominate everyone else (Bologh 1990). Other men are controlled through fear and loyalty which is institutionalised into hierarchy. Women and femininity are ignored. For example, the significance of women's paid and unpaid work and the dependence of the performance of the rational bureaucrat on domestic labour is unacknowledged or invisible. Love and protection are illusory. Amongst hostile strangers it is possible to accede to codes of femininity only by withdrawing. In the world of the rational bureaucrat, women remain in the private sphere under the protection of men (Bologh 1990; Davies 1994).

The theories of Max Weber and his feminist critics are more complicated than this brief account suggests. Nevertheless, it is clear that feminist accounts of bureaucracy agree that public organisations have institutionalised the predominance of particular masculinities, thereby empowering and advantaging certain men over all (or almost all) women and some men.

Institutional Sexism

Such theoretical claims may be applied to political institutions to illuminate gender biases in personnel, policy and cultures of political organisations, making visible some of the dynamics of gender and politics within organisations. In the terms of this framework, political institutions are gender-biased. Where bias against women and femininity is entrenched, an organisation is institutionally sexist. Institutional sexism is evident when an organisation is dominated by one sex in terms of its personnel, outcome and practices.

Institutional sexism may be a precondition of modern politics. The spread of public organisations was predicated on the existence of male power over women (and some men) in private life and private organisations. Political institutions such as governments, legislatures and political parties were part of the process in which men in organisations set rules of the game that ensured that the qualifications most likely to be held by some men were better valued and led more reliably to power and rewards. The historical association of state formation with physical strength, violence and war and the importance of the soldier to the formation of the modern state are instances of such processes. Diplomatic, colonial and military policy in most states is formed around a conception of masculinity that places a premium on toughness and force. An idealised separation of state and society parallels and supports a division of labour in which the contribution of women has been rendered unimportant or invisible. In short, institutional sexism pervades political life.

Feminist critics of British politics agree that its organisations and structures institutionalise the predominance of particular masculinities and in so doing support the dominance of some men. Such biases in part reflect women's political underrepresentation. Biases are most apparent in the levels of women's presence at each level of organisational hierarchies. The more powerful the position in any organisational hierarchy, the more likely it is to be dominated by men.

Does such imbalance affect policy? Probably. There is considerable evidence that policy-makers have been poorly attuned to women's interests and perspectives. Institutional sexism ensures that public policy reflects the needs of one sex more than the other in some way. Such biases are manifested at the agenda-setting, formulation and implementation stages of the policy process. Examples abound. Throughout the world the paid and unpaid work of women is undervalued, but male institutional advantage enables men to resist government policies for employment and pay equality between women and men. The male-dominated criminal justice systems, charged with treatment of the survivors of sexual violence, repeatedly fail to implement good practice, even where good will is present.

Institutional sexism supports gender hierarchies in which some male preferences are conditioned, favoured and rewarded, often long after changing gender relations have removed their original purpose. Jeff Hearn believes that public organisations are crucial supporters of often outdated, traditional conceptions of masculinity. He argues that a narrow range of acceptable (heterosexual) masculinity was established with the development and spread of public organisations. Their development created a power base for certain kinds of men who sustained that power over generations by increasing the quantity of sites upon which male power could operate. To exercise that power men were required to succeed in public bureaucracies, firms and other rule-bound hierarchical establishments (Hearn 1989).

Here is a syndrome that biases organisations, shapes rules, norms, structures and policies and makes it extremely difficult for most women and many men to perceive and pursue their gender interests. An example in the UK is the declamatory, adversarial style of Westminster debate that favours rhetoric, speechifying, posturing and arcane practice in the House of Commons rather than cooperation, consensus-seeking and real discussion of alternatives. Political practices involving demagoguery, ruthlessness and aggression require qualities that are culturally accepted in men but not women. Low turnover ensures that new MPs are quickly conditioned into these practices. As MPs learn and are distracted by these conventions, their lack of real power and ability to ensure government accountability may become secondary to their ability to function in Parliament. Even where turnover is high, however, there is evidence that the system of institutional socialisation continues to be effective. An example, detailed further in chapter 11 [this refers to the original volume], is the 1997 intake of Labour women who soon found they had to conform to parliamentary rules if they were to be effective. Hence, if it is not possible to show that a political institution is intrinsically male, it can be shown that its arrangements support characteristics associated with certain kinds of masculinity.

In the UK, institutional sexism is apparent both in implicit biases and explicit resistance. In the House of Commons, resistance to women by some men continued throughout the twentieth century, expressed in blatant form by MP John Carlisle who in 1987 told the *Evening Standard*:

> Women are natural bitches. They mistrust other women and have a general sense of insecurity about representing their interests. The day's work here at the House of Commons is more naturally tackled by a man. Once you start giving women special privileges and pushing them forward — and it's the same with ethnic minorities — you give them a false sense that they are equal to the task.
> (Cited in Abdela 1989: 26)

Resistance does not need to be so explicit, although it is surprising how often it is. In the House of Commons itself Teresa Gorman was shaken by the cruelty of some of the MPs: 'Shortly after I got into the House of Commons, Dennis Skinner would shout across the Chamber to me, "Tell us your age! Where's your birth certificate? Here she comes, Harvey Proctor in drag"' (in Abdela 1989: 23). When Joan Ruddock protested in the House about police strip-searching of women at Greenham Common, Conservative MPs opposite shouted '"*Cor*, we'd like to strip search you too"' (Abdela 1989: 26).

There were many reports of such sexism. For example, in 2001 the *Guardian* carried the story of an unnamed Labour woman MP who objected to the routine shouts of 'melons, melons' when she got up to speak. When she complained to the Speaker of the House Betty Boothroyd, she was told that such experiences came with the territory. Boothroyd's advice was to respond by shouting 'chipolatas, chipolatas' the next time it happened (*Guardian*, 11 January 2001). Commenting on the effects of this atmosphere, Clare Short, MP, remarked: 'Just the style of the House of Commons makes you very aware you are a woman ... Even the rituals enforce it. For example, if you make a point of order while a division is on, you have to sit down and put a top hat on' (Abdela 1989: 24).

Its origins and habits make the House of Commons a brutal example of the dominance of a culture of traditional masculinity. But elements of institutional sexism are to be found throughout political life. Sometimes this is a matter of ignoring the constraints on women's lives. Fiona Mackay's study of Scottish councillors exposes the delegitimisation of women's domestic concerns in local political structures. One of her councillors told her:

> They have meetings at 3 o'clock — now why do they start a meeting at three? Now if I say 'It's not fair, you do realise that schools come out at this time and if I am in a meeting, how am I to pick up the kids from school?' they're not in the least bit interested. In fact, that's better, because that means I can't go to the meeting, and if I am not there I'm less likely to be a nuisance to them ... and whenever we have tried to get meetings at night or change times they have said, 'Well you knew what you were coming into when you put your name forward, we all have to make sacrifices and it suits us to come at this time ... so too bad!'
>
> (Mackay 2001: 168)

Political Parties

If parliament is the warehouse of traditional masculinity in British politics, political parties are its major distributors. In the UK the responses of political parties are crucial to the outcome of women's claims for representation. This is not unusual. In the systems of party government that characterise so many democratic states, the work of equalising men's and women's representation must begin in the political parties. However, although most have women members and activists, modern political parties tend to be defined in terms of their relationship to government, traditionally an almost exclusively male activity. According to a recent definition, a political party is 'an institution that (a) seeks influence in a state, often by attempting to occupy positions in government, and (b) usually consists of more than a single interest in the society and so to some degree attempts to aggregate interests' (Ware 1996: 5). Parties vary greatly in their organisation, ideology, size, policies and the extent of their political significance. Some states are built around a single party (China), others feature parties that are active only at election times (Canada) and others are governed by coalitions of numerous parties (Switzerland, Italy).

Parties are crucial gatekeepers to government office, one of the main channels of political mobilisation in a society and a major source of public policy. Although voters choose candidates, they do so only after political parties have limited the options. Electoral systems are matters for government, but candidate selection rules are made inside political parties. Voters express party preferences; hence much of the explanation of the male-dominated profiles of representatives that are so characteristic of modern electoral politics is the result of internal party decisions. It is parties, not voters, that determine the composition of elected assemblies. Moreover, parties often determine who is awarded appointed offices of various kinds, not only at cabinet level but also in state committees and organisations, including women's organisations. For example, in both Chile and France it is party standing, not women's movement experience, that is decisive in determining which women are appointed to the 'state feminist' bodies (Jenson 1990).

The practices and conventions of Parliament are shaped in political parties, where recruitment practices tend to seek to reproduce parliamentary stereotypes. Recent research on women in the British political parties shows them to be institutionally sexist in the sense that they favour certain kinds of masculine behaviour, offer a vision of the world that implicitly accepts the gendered division of labour and resist claims made by women for political power and responsibility. This set of preferences is built into the organisations, rules and procedures of the parties, so that it survives for generation after generation.

The feminisation of political parties is therefore important to the representation of women, whether considered in terms of presence in legislatures and governments or in terms of interests and perspectives. However, for much of their history, political parties have been effective barriers to women's presence in elected office, a pattern well described by Barbara Nelson and Najma Chowdhury (1994). Drawing on evidence from forty-three countries, they reported that women were more likely to get power when political parties were dormant or in disarray during some major regime event. When parties were re-established, women lost ground. Such evidence may tell us why women are typically less likely than men to be members of political parties and why so many women prefer informal and often less effective ad hoc political activity.

Parties vary in their hospitality to women both within and across systems. British political parties are frequently criticised for their excessive 'masculinity'. What is meant here is not so much that they are male organisations, although at leadership levels they generally have been. The argument that the parties are 'masculine' points out how in their different ways the parties have been built around unacknowledged traditional conceptions of gender relations. The argument is analogous to the one made above about traditional legislatures. Thus, although since obtaining the vote women could be members of political parties and their role was often important, they were subordinate. For decades men's and women's roles in parties were ordered by traditional conceptions of masculinity and femininity. The practices were largely accepted, though there were always some resistors among women members.

Party Ideologies

Political parties institutionalise ideas about politics that have gender implications. Party ideologies are the basis of their enduring reputations and, according to many accounts, fundamental to voter and member trust. Parties may change their ideologies, but only slowly and in tune with wider social change. As institutions, they are able to carry ideals forward from one generation to the next. To paraphrase Putnam (1993), institutions are able both to shape political outcomes and to carry attitudes and behaviour into the future because they shape and are shaped by the identities of the men and women who constitute them. That the institutional sexism of the parties is apparently invisible to mainstream analysts of their ideologies and organisations is a major failing. The vast political science of party politics pays little attention to the effects of gender. Yet gender effects are present in various ways in party life and are reflected in both their ideologies and structures. Moreover, recently, major changes in gender relations have begun to impact on political parties. Thus any study of political parties that fails to take account of gender effects will be inadequate.

How then may we determine if a political party is institutionally sexist? First, it is necessary to outline the standard accounts of party culture, then to consider, as best we can, its gendered dimensions in terms of their susceptibility to feminist arguments for equality, using the categories of justice, pragmatic and difference arguments outlined in chapter 2 [this refers to the original volume]. In his characterisation of the ideologies of the major UK parties, Paul Webb describes the Conservative Party ideology as more a matter of 'dispositions' to protect the established social, political and economic order, this to be done by securing and retaining political power. The Conservatives' 'set of dispositions' includes the rejection of ideas of abstract rights and the effectiveness of social engineering, a belief that the very longevity of traditions is evidence of their utility, a belief in common sense — defined as what usually happens — hierarchy, leadership and authority in an organic society that should be able to maintain its balance by being allowed to evolve rather than be reformed. Social reform is justified only when necessary to appease the masses and promote social unity (Webb 2000: 90–2). Within this almost seamless set of ideas there are divisions and differences that feed occasional divisions in the party. There is a persisting faultline between those who emphasise tradition, community and evolution and those who favour individualism, enterprise and markets.

There is little in the Conservatives' 'set of dispositions' to comfort feminists, and almost nothing to suggest policies of political recruitment that will prioritise the equality of women and men MPs. However, this party has until recently received majority support from women voters. Moreover, for many years its organisational rules reserved places for women at all levels of the party hierarchy (Maguire 1998). Organisationally, however, the party members had no means of controlling its leadership as parliamentary wings, central office and branches were separate until the Hague reforms of 1997. In the Conservative Party, only pragmatic arguments for women's representation are likely to have much purchase. Party ideology offers no ideals of egalitarianism or popular participation on which women's advocates could draw to claim equality of representation. The main resource for supporters of women's equality is the party commitment to power. The historic but now fading dependence on women's votes, the need to win elections and, for many younger Conservatives, to modernise the party offer possibilities to make pragmatic arguments for sex equality. However, despite growing pressure from women activists, the Conservatives continue to resist taking special measures to ensure the nomination of women as candidates for safe seats.

The Labour Party, by contrast, has an egalitarian tradition. However, sex equality has not been a party priority. Historically Labour has sought social equality, defined in terms of class. Internal divisions have turned around whether equality is best promoted by fostering growth (not always possible) or by redistribution policies. These arguments were cross-cut by a common prioritisation of class differences. Thus the ideology of the party expressed in its discourse, rhetoric and policies was founded on principles of class equality. Class-based ideology has always been the basis of internal divisions underpinning a constant factionalism in the party. Generally, the divisions were controlled by a dominant alliance of pragmatic parliamentarians and key trade-unionists skilled at operating the party's complex federal structure and system of representation. Claims for other equalities by groups based on gender, race or physical ability were, if regarded at all, secondary to class.

The place of women in this canon was well illustrated by the way they were members of the party. From 1918 women members were integrated through women's sections that had no guaranteed say in decision-making and were cut off from the main party organisation. Although five places for women were reserved on the ruling National Executive Committee (NEC), these were filled by trade unions which selected women whose first priority was their unions' interest, whether or not that interest coincided with the views of party women. Until the 1990s the party was dominated by powerful affiliated unions representing male-dominated heavy industry and manufacturing. The model of the political activist in this party was the male unionised worker; women were defined as wives and mothers, as supporters rather than actors. Their roles were subordinate (Perrigo 1996).

By the 1990s, both changes in the structure of employment and mobilisation by party and trade union women led to some reconsideration of the male activist model. Unions began to court women members, and some party modernisers recognised the need to present a less traditional image. A redefinition of equality occurred that enabled women's advocates to make successful gender-based claims. Labour women were therefore able to demand equality both on pragmatic grounds of vote maximisation and ideas about justice. However, difference arguments tended to work against them as class continued to trump gender in hierarchies of diversity.

Liberal Democrat responses to women's claims for equal representation are in some ways the most puzzling. This is a party that historically (as the Liberal Party) favoured the spread of voting rights and embraced rationality. Such beliefs should make the party susceptible to arguments for sex equality. However, there are really two ideologies in the Liberal Democrat Party — classical liberalism and social liberalism. Classical liberalism was dominant for most of the nineteenth century; social liberalism took root after the 1880s. Both strands of liberalism are influential in today's party. Liberals are profound believers in individualism. While classical liberals believe their obligation to individualism is satisfied by the absence of external restraints, social liberals understand that goals of self-realisation are thwarted by the inequalities of industrial society, hence intervention in the market may be necessary to adjust outcomes.

In terms of ideas, this division almost exactly mirrors party fault lines over special measures to equalise women's representation, such as quotas. Those who oppose quotas argue that they undermine individualism by demeaning women, denying merit and treating men unfairly. Those who favour quotas believe that change is overdue, that only by intervention in the marketplace of political recruitment will a fair gender balance be achieved. What is odd is that the interventionists, who otherwise dominate the party, appear to lack the power to insist on equality of women's representation. This is in part an organisational artefact whereby constitutional change in the party requires a two-thirds majority vote in party conference — a measure designed to ensure consensus on major changes. Ironically, Liberal Democrat advocates of women's equality have available the ideological resources that come with a belief in egalitarianism. But, perhaps because egalitarianism is so central to their belief system, they also have intrinsic objections to special treatment. In the Liberal Democrat Party, ideas of justice are therefore highly contested, their third party electoral status weakens pragmatic arguments and difference arguments appear only to deepen divisions.

Thus aspects of both ideology and organisation are part of the explanations for differences in the way the main British political parties respond to demands for women's political representation. In each party, established sets of ideas are more or less supportive of equality and either favour or oppose intervention. Organisational arrangements reflect divisions that in two of the parties are centred on notions of equality. But claimants for women's equality are latecomers to party politics. Persisting ideological legacies support opposition to their claims and are built into organisations and procedures; they continue to affect attitudes and are capable of impeding women's mobilisation.

There are also some constants. Ideology interacts with tradition in all the parties. Success in internal party politics is to a large extent a matter of making alliances among people who can understand and predict each other's behaviour. Gender difference makes two impediments to such alliances. First, women are the unknown 'other'. In the UK, until fairly recently most of the influential classes were educated in single-sex schools and gained public experience in single-sex organisations. Male public leaders had experience of women only in private life. They were unused to women in public life and had no experience or other basis on which to trust them, no habit of making alliances with them. Thus male insiders were particularly inhibited from playing their part in integrating women into politics. However, second, equalisation strategies were not viable for the ambitious politician who inevitably feared that women might want special treatment which might not be good for him.

Political Recruitment

How does party masculinity map onto representation? In most modern democratic systems, political recruitment is the job of political parties. Voters choose among menus of candidates offered by political parties. Social, constitutional, institutional, cultural and political factors constrain those choices in various ways. It is useful to think about obstacles to equal representation in terms of supply and demand. The process of political recruitment is analogous to a market in which the supply consists of those who wish to be representatives, while those who select them determine demand. Demand is affected by the number of available vacancies, perceptions of voter preferences and the attitudes of selectors. Supply is conditioned by the ambitions and motivations of potential candidates and their perceptions of available opportunities. Both are embedded in institutional cultures that produce meanings of political representation and establish the identities and images of appropriate representatives. Resistance is a demand-side constraint, while resources affect both supply and demand. Supply and demand interact in the process of political recruitment. As demand increases, supply expands and vice versa.

It is well established that British voters do not penalise women candidates. The electorate votes for candidates according to party, not sex. In this configuration, the structures that determine candidate selection are crucial. In each party, special rules and procedures determine how candidates are selected. These have been likened to a ladder of recruitment in which different parts of the party exercise vetoes over candidates at each stage of the ascent (Norris and Lovenduski 1995). The precise rules vary in each party. The process begins with eligibility, determined by electoral law, and proceeds through qualification (party membership and experience are normally required) to aspiration, application, nomination, shortlisting and selection stages. In terms of supply, eligible candidates must decide to be party members and then to qualify through a period of activism. They must then apply to be considered as a candidate. Typically, a small committee draws up a shortlist from which members select their candidate. From the point of application, the dynamics of demand predominate.

Political parties differ from each other and vary over time in terms of how the balance of supply and demand factors affect women. Incumbency effects, whereby most MPs expect to keep their seats through several elections, mean that altering the composition of the House of Commons requires continuous effort. British political parties are reluctant to oust incumbents to make space for incomers. The recruitment process is by its very nature a barrier. It is arduous, expensive and frequently disappointing for both women and men. Most applicants fail.

However, there is considerable evidence that aspiring women candidates experience both direct and indirect unfair sex discrimination in all the political parties. Below, I detail the findings of research conducted during 2001 and 2002 on the experiences of women who wished to be candidates and reproduce some of the interviewee responses.[1] The findings illustrate widespread discrimination against women and institutional sexism in the main British political parties.

The Labour Party

Labour has the most complicated selection procedures. Selection rules are a matter for the party constitution and are intended to be binding on all constituencies. Rules tend to change with each electoral cycle but the basic framework is fairly stable. Nationally, the party maintains a parliamentary panel (list) of approved candidates. Members of this panel are invited to apply for upcoming selections by constituencies which then operate the rest of the procedure. Each constituency consists of various units such as local branches, trade union branches and other affiliated organisations. Each of these units may nominate one candidate to be considered for shortlisting by a general committee.

Prior to the 1999 'Party into Power' organisational reform, women's sections operated at branch level and could make nominations. However, that reform consolidated woman's sections at constituency level, thus reducing the potential for their nominations at branch level because there were fewer women's sections to make nominations.

Selections for the 2001 general election operated as follows. The general committee of the selecting constituency met all nominated candidates and then held a shortlisting meeting. The committee voted on all nominees by single transferable vote. If no sitting MP contested the seat, shortlisting requirements decreed that there should be an equal number of men and women on the shortlist. Shortlisted nominees were then provided with a list of members who were eligible to vote in the final ballot and were entitled to approach those members for support. Voting took place either by postal ballot (applied for in advance) or at a hustings meeting. Often the postal ballot was decisive.

The system of 50/50 men and women on the shortlist of vacant seats replaced the all-women shortlist arrangements of the mid-1990s. It was widely regarded to be a failure. Not only did the 2001 general election return fewer women than in 1997, but also many women thought that the provision was systematically abused. The mechanism was chosen as the least worst option by a Women's Representation Taskforce, which met to make recommendations for selection methods after the 1997 general election. The Taskforce was instructed that all-women shortlists and other quota mechanisms were ruled out for Westminster selections. In practice, the decision may have been worse than nothing, although it did illuminate the continuing resistance to selecting women, and was therefore probably instrumental in the change of policy over quotas after the selection round was completed.

The pitfalls of Labour's 50/50 shortlist policy were all too evident. It became apparent that the device would be used by equality opponents to humiliate and block good women candidates. Labour women were angry and resentful about their selection experiences. They had spent time and money campaigning in seats for which they had been shortlisted. However, at a certain point in the process they came to understand they were not being taken seriously by constituency parties, which had no intention of selecting them. They did not feel that this was because they were not good enough, but because the constituencies had already decided they were going to select a man.

A chap came up and said ... 'I suppose you are one of the women we have got to look at?'

You find yourself on the short-list but again you are there as a token. You sort of build up this false sense of security.

If you put me on the list that still doesn't do me any good. Why should I be going on the list all the time if I am not going to stand a chance?

One woman also claimed that the 50 per cent requirement was open to abuse due to the fact that the final shortlist had to be gender-balanced. She claimed that in some constituencies, the leading men organised to ensure that the places reserved for women went to those with the fewest local nominations (and therefore the lowest chance of winning) in order to narrow the competition for that seat. Similar allegations were made in the preliminary interviews of party officials and activists that I conducted for the British Representation Study, 2001.

> In some constituencies the women who got the most nominations from branches or unions were not shortlisted because … a deal was done to keep the … two women with the most nominations off the shortlist. … So the only two women that got on the shortlist had one nomination each, so they were never going to beat the men. The men organised to keep the best women off.

Since 1992, the Labour Party has made significant efforts to correct both supply and demand side barriers to the selection of women candidates. However, there is considerable internal division over the policy and many local selectorates resist choosing women candidates. Although the Labour Party has a history of attempting to address discrimination, the perception in many 'individual' cases was that good intentions were not followed through. Discrimination, both overt and covert, reportedly took place throughout the selection process. Moreover, ethnic minority women reported discrimination on grounds of race. Both sexism and racism affected selection processes.

After the 2001 general election, when the numbers of Labour women MPs fell, the government changed the law in order to permit political parties to take special measures, such as creating all-women shortlists to ensure the selection of women candidates. The Labour Party immediately took advantage of the legislation. By March 2004, all-women shortlists had been used in sixteen of twenty-six Labour retirement seats. However, the policy was contested in parts of the party. In Blaenu Gwent, South Wales, a group of Labour Party constituency officers resigned in protest when it was designated for an all-women shortlist selection. All four of the available Welsh Labour seats selected women. Although Labour was set to lose seats, the early indicators were that their proportion and possibly their numbers of women MPs would rise.

The Conservative Party

Conservative selection operates differently and in some ways resembles recruitment for professional employment. Instead of selection rules, the party issues guidelines to constituencies that include recommended codes of practice to be followed in the selection of candidates. The codes are not always adhered to but it is difficult to complain because they are not binding. The traditional selection process is a series of hurdles that applicants must clear. Hopeful candidates must first apply to be included on an approved list. Their suitability for the list is determined by central office interviews followed by attendance at a weekend selection meeting, where they are judged by experienced party members and officers and MPs. Approved candidates are then notified of upcoming selections by constituency associations.

The final decision is a constituency matter. The CVs of interested candidates are circulated to a constituency candidate selection committee. This committee chooses up to twenty-five candidates for interview and shortlists between five and seven for interview by the larger Executive Committee of the Constituency Party. Until 2001, the Executive Committee formally met all the candidates on the recommended list then invited them, along with their partners, to a formal interview at which the candidate made a speech and answered questions. The recommended list was then reduced by the Executive Committee to between two and four people who went forward to a Special General Meeting of members of the association. Shortlisted candidates made another speech and answered questions at this, often rather large, final selection meeting. Then attending members voted by secret ballot to choose their candidates.

When I observed selection meetings in the Conservative Party during the 1990s I saw that aspirant candidates thought it was very important to present their partners. Unmarried men brought their women partners and referred to them in their speeches. A number of betrothals were announced during the course of a selection process. Constituencies expected to get two people, the candidate and his wife. This expectation offers a means of affirming traditional gender relations. By presenting their women partners, male candidates affirmed their commitment to heterosexual norms and traditional gender relations. When women presented their male spouses, they challenged such traditions.

Much of the traditional selection system is still in place. However, after 2001 there was a debate among some Conservatives who believed the party should be more open to structural change. Party women's advocates mobilised to claim equality of representation. The point has not been won. The problem appears to be one of demand. Since 2001 party leaders have stated that, despite leadership willingness to change, party selectors have continued to be hostile towards women candidates. Despite formal party support for the Sex Discrimination Electoral Candidates Bill in 2001, all-women shortlists have been ruled out. Under the chairmanship of Teresa May, recruitment procedures were scrutinised and overhauled, but stopped short of a real commitment to select women. The party invited equality recruitment expert Jo Sylvester to redesign their recruitment processes to make them more women-friendly. The job description of an MP was formalised in an effort to draw selector attention to the necessary qualifications and to overcome the problem of repeated unthinking selections of favourite sons. In addition, the Conservatives experimented with new selection methods such as the 'open primaries' held at Warrington South and Reading East in 2004. However, early evidence is that the effects are likely to be limited.

The Conservative women we interviewed were angry about their experiences. They reported many examples of overt discrimination during the 2001 selection round. Selectors failed to observe conventions of equal opportunities, judged women differently from men and were guilty of both sex discrimination and, in some cases, sexual harassment.

> They have no concept of women working. They have no concept of women with children working.

> They always plant this bloody question with a woman to ask it... 'What are you going to do about the children?' I thought if this was a job interview I would tell you to mind your own bloody business.

> One chap told me they looked through all these CVs, they had 200 CVs and they didn't interview one woman in the first round ... he said he turned round to the committee and said 'Don't you think we should have at least a couple of women for a change?' They all looked at him and said it just wasn't an issue for them.

> The male members of the party tend to run a very fine line. Eighty per cent of them don't want you as their MP and 20 per cent of them are actually really nice and really try to help you and a 100 per cent of them want to shag you!

> There is definitely harassment even from people at a very high level. You know, 'Let's go away for the weekend to talk about how I can help you get selected', that kind of thing.

Unlike the Labour Party, Conservatives have a supply problem whereby relatively few women come forward for selection for winnable seats. But the selection experiences of those who do come forward send a message that may well put off potential applicants. To increase its numbers of women MPs, the Conservative Party will need to make changes to its structures and processes. Until recently the Conservatives have not seriously considered how their selection process could be improved to increase the numbers of women selected. Historically, the party defends its selection process (borrowed from British army officer recruitment practices) as 'meritocratic' and has claimed that it 'does not need quotas'.

It is frequently claimed by Conservative Party spokespersons that it is women members who do not want to select women candidates. While there is no reliable systematic evidence that supports this claim, it has been reported so frequently that it has almost become a mantra. In 2001 the Conservatives returned only fourteen women MPs, but ninety two of their candidates were women. Current party practice is to draw attention to equal opportunity policies and to make provision for equal access to candidate training for women and men. In addition the candidate selection team tries to encourage women to come forward for nomination. In short, the Conservatives continue to rely upon weak policies to support women's selection. Yet such strategies were long ago proved by Labour to be ineffective. At the end of 2003 Fawcett research showed that changes in Conservative candidate selection processes made only a slight difference to women's chances of securing nominations. Of 132 seats by then selected, only twenty-seven were women. Only two of eight retirement seats had by that time selected women. Fawcett predicted that if the Conservatives won forty new seats in the next general election, only four would go to women (Fawcett 2003).

The Liberal Democratic Party

For the 2001 general election, the Liberal Democrats also maintained an approved list from which a local candidate selection committee drew applicants by advertising vacancies. Aspirants applied to the committee. Using agreed selection criteria, up to ten candidates were invited for interview and at least three people were shortlisted. For 2001, shortlists of three were required to include at least one man and one woman, and shortlists of five had to have at least two of each sex. Voting on the final selection took place at a hustings meeting attended by party members.

In contrast to other political parties, overt discrimination was not reported to be a significant problem amongst the Liberal Democrats. This could in part be explained by their liberal ethos and their formal commitment to tolerance and equality of opportunity. However, covert discrimination did take place and the party is clearly affected by the self-perpetuating male MP model. The shortlist quota was thought to lead to tokenism and both the rural and urban bases of the party were felt to be a disadvantage. Liberal Democrat women reported experiences of unfair discrimination by selectors.

> I certainly wouldn't have minded being the 'token woman' *[in a safe Liberal Democrat seat]*. But what I objected to was the three weeks' cost of going down there, moving in and doing all this ... when they had already decided quite obviously way, way in advance that there was no way a woman was going to do it, that is what I think is wrong.

> Unless there is masses and masses of women applicants you do tend to get shortlisted anyway. They always assure you politely that they would have shortlisted you anyway and it is not just because you are the 'token woman' ... but they had all decided they were going to back *[a now sitting male MP]*... what really bugs me is that they didn't bother to tell me ... I don't think they ought to make use of people like that.

> If you go into an industrial area, your members will say to you a woman will never manage in this industrial area ... and if you go to the rural areas they will say a woman will never do in a rural area, so really we are condemned.

Some Liberal Democrat women thought that the strong preference for 'local' candidates impeded their chances of selection.

> I think my advice for women would be that if you are going to go for a seat, then make sure you were born there, bred there and lived there all your life.

It's not as easy for women to just up and move everything whereas a lot of men in the party had seen that the selection was going to happen and they moved to the constituency six months before the selection. It's not so easy to do if you're a woman, you're married and you have a family.

The reason they give you is that they think 'that's the candidate *[the successful candidate]* who the wider electorate, not the party members' ... are going to choose because they're local.

In the 2001 round, Liberal Democrat selectors asked women questions that they did not ask men. One candidate realised she had lost when asked what she would do with her children while campaigning. She replied that, if selected, she would of course have them adopted, an ironic comment that was lost on the selection committee. Our interviews uncovered numerous instances of indirect discrimination, suggesting that, despite efforts to the contrary, equality of opportunity is not consistently operated in the Liberal Democrat selection procedures. Moreover, the shortlisting quota, as in the Labour Party, was not only ineffective but also produced many negative consequences. For Labour and Liberal Democrat women the frequent subversion of the intentions behind quotas on shortlists made a mockery of the efforts made by many qualified women to get selected. As well as dealing with defeat, they had to pay the costs of participation in lengthy procedures even though no one had any intention of selecting them.

Measures to increase the selection of women candidates are a continuing issue for the Liberal Democrats. The 2001 party conference rejected a motion to use all-women shortlists in party seats and in target seats. Instead they opted for weaker measures such as the provision of training and support for women candidates. A Gender Balance Task Force was established to direct their efforts. By the end of 2003, forty of the 110 Liberal Democratic candidates already selected were women. Because the Liberal Democrats select their best seats early, this number may portend an improvement, as it is a significant increase on the 22 per cent selected for 2001. Candidate selection is ongoing and it may be that these improvements do not hold up. Moreover, by the end of 2003 only one woman had been selected to fight a party retirement seat but one woman MP announced that she would retire. Even if the early pattern of selecting more women continues, the electoral fortunes of the Liberal Democrats do not promise a massive contribution to an increase in the overall numbers of women MPs (Fawcett 2004).

However, by stepping back from quotas, Liberal Democrats are attempting to demonstrate that in their equality-minded party, such measures are unnecessary to progress towards balanced representation of women and men. It may be that the combination of political will and egalitarian ethos will ensure continued progress to sex equality. However, this will mean an enormous change in the party's selection habits. A struggle is taking place in this party that merits the attention of equality advocates and experts. Many party women are unconvinced by soft measures, hence demands for quotas continue to be raised.

Common Obstacles

In all three parties the barriers to women's selection could be explained by institutional sexism. In addition, becoming a candidate is an expensive process. Women not only have fewer resources with which to cover these costs; they also include additional costs, with fewer sources of support.

> I do have to pay the bills and so certainly I think in seats where, for example, men have been supported by their unions and given time off to go and do that, that is very important.

> The other thing that has to change quite radically is the amount of money that can be spent on campaigning ... some people will be spending £800 on a glossy leaflet whereas I would be spending £11 printing it myself ... you automatically preclude those mothers who are at home who just don't have the money to pay the child care, the petrol, the stationery, the £500 stamps that you have to do to leaflet.

> Men are still paid better than women and a lot of these male candidates were from London ... so they were even more well paid than the average woman. It is a very, very expensive process. Even doing it as cheaply as you possibly can, you are talking thousands of pounds to run a campaign knowing that as a woman you are not going to get there.

> It must be probably one of the few elections in this country where you can actually spend precisely what you want on this. I think that is something that does need looking at.

In all three parties women reported that they were judged on a different basis from men. They reported numerous examples of overt discrimination, ranging from traditional assumptions about their roles to outright and explicit discrimination including sexual harassment. In each party the procedures offer numerous opportunities for the overt expression of selector preferences for white male candidates even where rules explicitly prohibit unfair discrimination. Our interviews uncovered examples of sexual harassment in both the Labour and the Conservative parties. For example, in the Conservative Party:

> *[A Conservative woman going for selection in a safe seat]* was asked ... 'if she got *[the seat]* and was in Westminster during the week, what would her husband do for sex?'

> I was talking to a group of people *[involved in the selection in which I was unsuccessful]* and I was telling a story ... of how I unusually had spent the whole night awake thinking about it ... this chap said to me, he was in his sixties, he looked as though he had parked his Range Rover outside and his wellies were still in the boot, and he said to me 'yes, I lay awake all night

thinking about you too' ... I knew in any other environment I would have said 'how dare he speak to me like that'.

I am not a very PC sort of person but I really do believe that women should not be subjected to that *[sexual harassment]*, they wouldn't get away with it in the workplace nowadays.

The main thing I would do differently next time is to learn how to say 'no' *[to offers of sex]* without making enemies.

Labour appears not to have been much better:

They are absolutely adamant they will not consider a woman ... it was said to me ... 'we do enjoy watching you speak, we always imagine what your knickers are like'. It is that basic. 'We picture you in your underwear when you are speaking.' That is what you are dealing with.

There are small groups within the party who come out with the most outrageous comments. But the very fact that these comments are made and with any regularity ... that they go unchallenged is quite staggering in this day and age.

Sexism and Racism

Institutional sexism was compounded by racism. Minority ethnic women experienced additional problems in both the Labour and Conservative parties. Labour women reported experience of overt racism:

There are people in the local parties and at constituency level who will say they won't have a woman or a black person.

Ordinary party members still have this stereotype that what makes an MP is a white male.

When it comes to selection you have got 51–80-year olds. How can you change the mind of that man? They are probably not dealing with black people a lot. They don't deal with women a lot. They have a perception from fifty years ago that a man is the guy to do the job.

There is a group of people in the party ... who will not want a woman; will not want a black woman.

They also reported problems they attributed to ill-formed policies to contest racism in the party. The ethnic minority women interviewed said that in the same way that women in general were always on shortlists but very rarely got selected for winnable seats, they found it incredibly easy to get on shortlists but they felt they were there merely as 'tokens' without any real chance of getting selected.

They make certain there is a black minority ethnic person on the final shortlist. That has actually worked against us. All the time you find yourself on the shortlist but you are there as a token.

They called all the people who had gone for that seat of ethnic origin and they called us all into this fabulous room in Millbank. They had the press and all these eminent MPs ... and it was all a farce. It was all for one *[male]* individual ... I felt I was totally violated, used, abused, I was so upset afterwards.

It is all lip service. It is saying we want more black and Asian people in. You can't get them in if it is only lip service. You need a mechanism to make it happen.

We are there to make the list look good as black women.

Most of the ethnic minority Conservative women interviewed said they had been extremely reluctant to acknowledge that racism was a factor in their failure to get selected. However, after having been through the selection process many times, this was precisely the conclusion they were coming to.

What they want is a nice, young white boy who they can see marrying their granddaughter.

If they can't see you in their social environment, they don't want to select you.

I've looked at everything else and there isn't another reason. It could be they just don't like me, but then how do you differentiate between they don't like me, and they don't like me because I'm brown?

In both the Labour and Conservative parties, ethnic minority women face additional discrimination. Sex and race discrimination interact in candidate selection processes so that well-qualified women repeatedly fail to be selected. Moreover, a compounded tokenism may ensure that minority ethnic women are shortlisted only to be rejected by selection committees.

Especially in the Labour Party, but also in the Conservative and Liberal Democrat parties there were frequent accusations that procedures were not followed, that advantages were given to some candidates. For Labour and Liberal Democrat women the repeated subversion of the intentions behind quotas on shortlists made a mockery of the efforts made by many qualified women to get selected.

Summary of Obstacles

In all three parties women's selection was found to be impeded by institutional sexism, which in the Labour and Conservative parties was frequently compounded by racism.[2] Barriers to the feminisation of politics are institutionalised into the political organisations in which representation takes place. These barriers can be summarised as amounting to institutional sexism and racism which support particular kinds of white masculinity in political organisations, manifested in its personnel, procedures and policies. In the British case, sexism seems especially well insulated and can be seen to operate in both Parliament and the political parties. It is worth noting that the Victorian ideals of heterosexual masculinity, so prevalent in UK political imagery, is specific to the political culture (though there is evidence that it was exported to the empire). Such traditional attitudes to women's roles take a number of forms and are frequently an impediment to women's representation (Norris 2004). They are most visible on the demand side of political recruitment but may also, as in the case of the Conservative Party, affect supply.

Many of the barriers and obstacles to women were common in all the main parties. Labour, the Liberal Democrats and the Conservatives all reported overt discrimination, the lack of a genuine culture of equal opportunities, greater financial constraints for women than for men, tokenism, 'favourite sons' and the syndrome of the self-perpetuating male stereotype whereby safe constituencies tend to try to reproduce the MP they have always had who may have been selected thirty years previously.

To some extent, barriers are a manifestation within the parties of the disadvantages experienced by women in society at large. Change may follow the entry of new generations of party members. Party members vary by age in their willingness to nominate women candidates. Older party members of both sexes in all parties are reported to hold traditional views of women's roles; hence, they prefer their MP to be a man. But such reactions are compounded by the party cultures that have institutionalised codes of behaviour that make discrimination against women both possible and acceptable.

In addition, the Conservative Party has both supply and demand problems (few of those few women who do come forward are nominated for winnable seats) especially in target seats or seats where a Conservative MP retires. Labour and the Liberal Democrats have demand problems. In all the parties supply and demand interact. Labour's experience shows that as demand increases, women are more likely to come forward.

Under pressure from feminist advocates, all three parties have at various times acknowledged the problem of women's underrepresentation. All three have made attempts to increase the presence of women in Parliament. Their efforts have had varying success. Neither Conservative nor Liberal Democrat women have made much progress at national level. In the Conservative Party especially, efforts by leaders to expand women's representation have met with selector resistance. Leaders continue to be reluctant to impose the kinds of measure that will bring change, claiming that party members would not comply. Liberal Democrats support equality of representation in formal terms but are divided over the means. Advocates of change have been unable to secure support for effective special measures. Labour has had more success but has also been more determined. In 2001 Labour introduced compulsory special measures at the actual point of selection, thus mandating the selection of minimum numbers of women. However, Labour incumbents are protected by their selection policies, which reduces the number of vacancies available to women.

Nevertheless, however tentatively, all three parties have embarked on a long-term change that has the potential to transform their cultures, images and possibly their fortunes. The variations between the parties are large. Whilst the Labour Party has apparently been able to step over its institutional sexism and take the risks of selecting more women by compulsory measures, the other parties are more hesitant. The Liberal Democrats still seem to be ambivalent, while the Conservatives, if they do favour equality, are cautious almost to the point of paralysis. These differences reflect varying obstacles to equality of women's political representation that are explained by party ideology, organisation and leadership. They are also affected by variations in the mobilisation of party women for change, a process discussed in more detail in chapter 5 [this refers to the original volume].

Notes

1. I designed a Fawcett research project that considered the experiences of well-qualified aspirant women candidates who had not been selected for the 2001 general election. In all, sixty-seven women were interviewed for the project, which was conducted with Laura Shepherd Robinson who was then working at Fawcett. Although there was some variation by party, the experience of aspirant women was remarkably similar in all the parties.

   This project was designed to enable aspirant women candidates to speak about their selection experiences. Following the 2001 election, Fawcett conducted focus groups with fifty-one women and telephone interviews with sixteen women from the Labour, Conservative, Liberal Democrat and Plaid Cymru parties between July 2001 and February 2002.

   Interviewees were well-qualified women candidates who had tried but failed to be selected by a safe or winnable parliamentary constituency for their relevant party for the 2001 election. The first nineteen were selected on advice from party activists and further selections were made on a reputational 'snowball' basis. To enable them to speak freely, respondents were seen in party groups and were promised complete confidentiality. The interviews were assessed in the light of the results of the British Representation Study 2001 conducted by Joni Lovenduski and Pippa Norris. *See* the British Representation Study 2001: http://www.pippanorris.com.

2. We were unable to interview ethnic minority women from the Liberal Democratic Party. The Liberal Democratic women we interviewed did not mention race discrimination.

References

Abdela, L. (1989) *Women with X Appeal*, Bristol: MacDonald Optima.

Acker, J. (1992) 'Gendered institutions: from sex roles to gendered institutions', *Contemporary Society*, 21 (5): 565–569.

Bologh, R. (1990) *Love or Greatness: Max Weber and Masculine Thinking: A Feminist Enquiry*, London: Unwin Hyman.

Davies, C. (1994) 'The Masculinity of Organisational Life', paper presented at the Conference on Women and Public Policy, Erasmus, University of Rotterdam.

Fawcett (2003) *Conservative Candidates – Where are the Women?*, London: The Fawcett Society.

Fawcett (2004) *Liberal Democrat Candidates – Where are the Women?*, London: The Fawcett Society.

Ferguson, K. (1984) *The Feminist Case Against Bureaucracy*, Philadelphia: Temple University Press.

Fox, J. (1998) *The Langhorne Sisters*, London: Granta.

Hearn, J. (1989) *The Sexuality of Organisation*, London: Sage.

Jenson, J. (1990) 'Representations of difference: the varieties of French feminism', *New Left Review* 180 (24): 127–160.

Jones, K. (1993) *Compassionate Authority: Democracy and the Representation of Women*, New York: Routledge.

Lister, R. (1997) *Citizenship: Feminist Perspectives*, Basingstoke: Macmillan.

Mackay, F. (2001) *Love and Politics*, London: Continuum.

Maguire, G. E. (1998) *Conservative Women: A History of Women and the Conservative Party, 1874–1997*, Basingstoke: Macmillan.

Nelson, B. and Chowdhury, N. (1994) *Women and Politics Worldwide*, New Haven, CT: Yale University Press.

Norris, P. (2004) *Electoral Engineering*, Cambridge: Cambridge University Press.

Norris, P. and Lovenduski, J. (1995) *Political Recruitment: Gender, Race and Class in the British Parliament*, Cambridge: Cambridge University Press.

Perrigo, S. (1996) 'Women and change in the Labour Party', *Parliamentary Affairs*, 49 (1): 116–129.

Putnam, R, (1993) *Making Democracy Work*, Princeton, NJ: Princeton University Press.

Puwar, N. (2004) 'Thinking about making a difference', *British Journal of Politics and International Relations*, 6 (1): 65–80.

Savage, M. and Witz, A. (eds) (1992) *Gender and Bureaucracy*, Oxford: Blackwell.

Ware, A. (1996) *Political Parties and Party Systems*, Oxford: Oxford University Press.

Webb, P. (2000) *The Modern British Party System*, London: Sage.

Chapter Nine

United Kingdom: Male Dominance Unbroken?*

Introduction

Access to British political institutions is dominated by the political parties. Not only do parties control nomination at all levels of government, they also control appointments to the House of Lords and to the various decision-making agencies, commissions and committees that design, implement, and deliver public policy. This means that effective feminist and other women's movement activism on the issue of women's political representation has been action either within the main political parties or directed at the parties, most often via other established organisations that operate within, or in close association with, the political class, such as trade unions, government agencies, or think tanks.

Compared to other old democracies, especially those from Western Europe, women's representation has remained exceptionally low at Westminster. However, as this chapter will show there are considerable variations among the major political parties as well as between Westminster and the devolved political institutions in Scotland and Wales.

The core argument of this chapter is that internal party politics mobilised by party women explains decisions to increase the position of women in elected office. The critical actors were and are mainly women leaders in different parts of party organisations who have taken advantage of opportunities provided by processes of party modernisation to insert their claim. Party crises and subsequent reforms are an important part of the story, as are changes in gender roles whereby wholescale shifts in attitudes made women's votes available to parties and made voters responsive to women candidates. However, progress was not and is not straightforward. Moreover, such progress as there has been is neither uniform across parties nor fully established in parliament and other legislatures.

This chapter will analyse the history of women's entrance into British politics separately for the two major parties, Labour and Conservatives, as well as the Liberal Democratic Party. It will be shown that even if the sequences of change have been somewhat similar, the trajectories differ greatly, with substantive changes in the Conservative Party emerging two decades after those in the Labour Party. No significant contagion effect can be traced in the British case (Matland and Studlar 1996).

*   'Male Dominance Broken' in D. Dahlerup and M. Leyenaar (eds) *Breaking Male Dominance in Old Democracies*, Oxford, Oxford University Press, pp. 72–96.

Historical Overview

Women over thirty years of age obtained the right to vote and those over twenty-one the right to stand as candidates in 1918, following long and sometimes violent suffrage campaigns. The anomaly between voting and candidate ages was not corrected until women were given the right to vote on the same terms as men in 1928. In the case of Jennie Lee (who was to become a Minister in Harold Wilson's first government), that meant that she was nominated to stand as a parliamentary candidate before she was entitled to vote.

Following the suffrage, although there were numerous campaigns on issues of social policy such as childcare, education and health in which women including many former suffragists were active, there was relatively little mobilisation to ensure that women were nominated for winnable seats. Hence only a handful of women were elected before 1945 and it took until 1997 for women to break through the 10 per cent threshold. Until the 1980s no political party was much interested in the political representation of women. The issue then came firmly onto the agenda for two reasons. First, the nature of party competition changed when the new Social Democratic Party was founded. Second, Women's Liberation Movement feminists entered the Labour Party and mobilised to secure representation. The Social Democratic Party soon merged with the Liberal Party to become the Liberal Democrats, and its interest in the representation of women faded. However the movement of women within the Labour Party grew and began a process that established strict quotas of women throughout the party.

At the various levels of the UK political system we find different institutional configurations and patterns of women's representation. Each reflects specific mobilisations and resistances. There is, therefore, significant variation from Westminster patterns at 'lower' levels of the system. The devolved systems of Scotland and Wales are cases in point. Since its establishment in 1998 the Scottish parliament has been characterised by an unbroken period of there being a large minority of women Members of the Scottish Parliament (MSPs), ranging from 33 per cent to 39 per cent of the total of 129 seats. Wales, meanwhile, has enjoyed gender balance in its assembly, with women members varying from 40 per cent to 50 per cent of the sixty Assembly Members (AMs). It is noteworthy that both devolved legislatures have equality committees but Westminster does not (although one is currently being mooted by Labour women MPs). However, direct comparisons between Wales, Scotland, and Westminster are tricky as the devolved regions have different party systems from that in England and nationalists play an important part in Scotland, which in May 2011 elected a majority of Scottish nationalists. There is very little support for the Conservative Party in either Scotland or Wales. Both legislatures are elected by Mixed Member systems, while Westminster is elected by a plurality first-past-the-post system which is distinctly not proportional. In short the UK features a number of different electoral systems, each of which offers different strategic opportunities for women's advocates and may be associated with a different party system from the Westminster model (Table 9.1).

Table 9.1: Electoral Systems in the UK

System	Type	Where used
Plurality Majority	First Past the Post	House of Commons, Local elections in England and Wales
	Alternative Vote (Supplementary Vote)*	Mayor of London and all other elected mayors in England and Wales where there are more than two candidates
Proportional Representation	Single Transferable Vote	Local and European Parliament elections in Northern Ireland, Northern Ireland Assembly Local elections in Scotland
	Party Block Vote	European Parliament Elections (except Northern Ireland)
Mixed	Mixed Member Proportional	Scottish Parliament, Welsh Assembly, London Assembly

* Supplementary Vote is a variation of the Alternative Vote that differs from it in that the Alternative Vote typically allows for many rounds of counting.

It is difficult to speak of a take-off phase of women's political representation in the UK. Much of the limited progress on women's political representation has been recent and is very much work in progress, as considerable movement has been evident in recent years. In terms of numbers, the match between the plurality systems of Westminster (22 per cent) is a striking vindication of the literature that says majoritarian systems return fewer women, while the proportional systems of the European Parliament (33 per cent), Scotland (36 per cent), Wales (42 per cent), and the London Assembly (32 per cent) are striking examples of the greater capacity of some proportional electoral systems to elect women. (The Northern Ireland figures show that STV, however, does not help as women are 16.8 per cent of the Assembly at Stormont.) Each experienced differences in performance by party, with, in general, Labour performing better than other parties.

Westminster

At Westminster MPs are elected in a first-past-the-post system for which candidacy is controlled by the major parties. Each party has its own nomination procedures but there are clear similarities. The three main parties all maintain approved lists of aspirant candidates and each has a selection procedure that involves shortlisting, that is the selection of a small number of applicants (normally between three and six) by local members and activists from the approved list to go forward to the next round. In recent elections the Conservatives have experimented with primaries partly in order to reduce the power of local members. Generally policies to increase women's representation are based in rules about approved lists and shortlists, but all the major parties are considering the extended use of primaries in future selections. Figure 9.1 shows the development of women's representation at Westminster.

Figure 9.1: Women's Representation in House of Commons, Scottish Parliament and National Assembly for Wales, since 1945

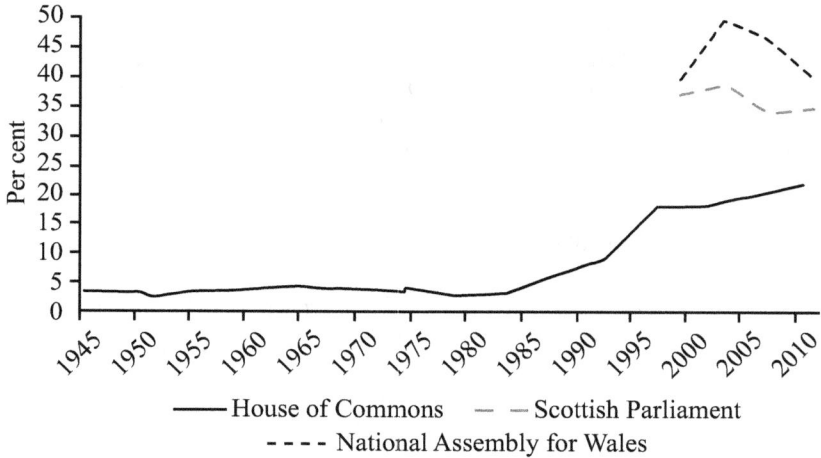

——— House of Commons   — — Scottish Parliament
- - - - National Assembly for Wales

At the general election of May 2010, 143 women, 22 per cent of the total, were elected as Members of Parliament — the highest number ever, with one in five MPs now a woman. Of these MPs, 49 were Conservative; 7 Liberal Democrats; 81 Labour; 1 Green Party; 1 Scottish National Party; 1 Social Democrat and Labour Party; 1 Sinn Fein; 1 Alliance and 1 Independent. Of the three main parties, Labour has the highest proportion of women MPs at 31 per cent; the Conservatives have 16 per cent and the Liberal Democrats 12 per cent. No party has gender balance and only Labour has a significant minority of women. The male monopoly of the House of Commons did not break until 1997 when a small minority of women were elected. Prior to 1997 the percentage of women MPs was below 10 per cent and until 1987 it was below 5 per cent (Figure 9.1).

Figure 9.1 indicates stagnation in all the parties until 1987 when the number of Labour women MPs doubled. The Conservatives 'take-off' came only in 2010, while the Liberal Democrats continue to stagnate. Thus this chapter tells three party stories.

The Labour Party

There are three periods of Labour women's representation at Westminster: male monopoly and small and large minorities of women.

1918–1992: Male monopoly

The Labour Party is a mass-branch party that was founded by trade unions, and cooperative and socialist societies of various kinds, and is based on both federal and individual membership. In practice the structure and ethos of the party were similar to that of the industrial trade unions that dominated it, an ethos that according to Sarah Perrigo (1996) privileged traditional masculinity. The trade unions held much of the power in this configuration and to this day are major funders of the party. For many years individual members in party branches had little power in a highly formalised and ritualised politics that required long apprenticeships, rulebook knowledge, trade-union backing and support, and a variety of probably non-transferable meeting skills. This culture was hostile to incomers and uncomfortable for women who often had little direct experience of organised politics. Cockburn wrote in 1987 about how the certainties of traditional Labour culture depended upon the possibility of 'inhabit[ing] a culture that brings together the umbrella of masculine identity, of male fraternity: work, working class allegiance, trade union membership and Labour Party affiliation' (Cockburn 1987: 25). These three certainties were all to disappear in the coming decades (Lovenduski and Randall 1993; Perrigo 1996). However, as a federation of traditional organisations with limited provision for individual members, the Labour Party provided few direct points of purchase for women who sought to alter its masculinist institutional norms. To be effective, feminist activists had to operate through several different parts of the federation at once. Moreover, the barriers of traditional norms were compounded by the necessity to work through trade unions, many of which did not themselves become gender sensitive until the end of the 1980s. Each organisational sector of the party constituted an organisational barrier. Because the Labour Party was founded to represent the working class via the trade unions, struggles that could not or did not invoke discourses of class inequality were and to some extent still are routinely dismissed (often by middle-class men) as a distraction from the real issues. This phenomenon is all too evident in the struggle to win support for women's representation in elected office.

Prior to 1992 the proportion of Labour women MPs was below 10 per cent and was often less than 5 per cent of the total number of Labour MPs. Women candidates were typically nominated (if at all) for unwinnable seats and their fortunes tended to follow the fortunes of the party. When the party did well the proportion of women MPs rose. A women's organisation was founded in 1906 and admitted to the party in 1909. Until 1997 the women's organisation paralleled the party organisation, with separate sections for each branch and constituency. Its role was to draw attention to problems of special significance to women but its powers were limited, indeed its annual conference could not guarantee agenda status, which was routinely refused at the party conference (Hills 1981: 18).

Although there were reserved seats for women at all levels within the party organisation, the women who filled them were not selected by the women's sections. Instead they were chosen by party leaders and the trade unions, and few women were ever elected to non-reserved seats (Russell 2005). Nevertheless, there were issues on which party women mobilised effectively and signs of change became apparent during the passage of the Equal Pay Act in 1970, which saw considerable mobilisation of women in the trade unions, perhaps because it was possible to frame the issue in terms of class equality.

Around that time a debate ensued about abolishing the women's sections and the reserved seats because they trivialised and marginalised women members. However, arguments were made that without such spaces women would be even more marginalised (Hills 1981).

After the 1970s the number of women candidates increased, rising each year thereafter. But only in the 1980s did there begin an effective mobilisation for women's representation. In 1979 the number of women MPs dropped to eleven and in 1983 it dropped further to ten, precipitating outrage amongst women in the party, who mobilised in various ways. Most observers believe that the rising influence of women was accelerated by the movement of British feminists from the Women's Liberation Movement into the Labour Party in the 1980s as they realised how destructive the Thatcher regime was to women's interests, broadly conceived.

Five developments in the 1980s contributed to changes in the political status of party women. These were the entry of feminists into mainly urban party branches, the rise of local authority women's committees which gave party feminists an additional and high profile political base for most of the decade, the change in the nature of employment and therefore of trade union constituencies, a shift in the demands of party women from requests for integration to demands for representation within and for the party, and the realisation that women voters were put off by the Labour Party (Lovenduski and Randall 1993).

By the early 1980s demands for women's representation were being put on the agenda of party meetings and conferences by feminists who organised inside the party. The party was fractured by serious political divisions that were expressed in continuous factional struggles between the left and the right wings. Claimants such as the Women's Action Campaign and the Campaign for Labour Democracy were strongly associated with the left of the party and it was widely perceived that if met, their demands would strengthen the left. Despite nominal support for the greater representation of women across the party, demands for compulsory targets of women first emerged as a demand from the left (along with such measures as compulsory annual reselection of MPs), framed as part of the demand for internal democracy. Hence the opposition of the right was guaranteed. Demands for affirmative action, and particularly for the inclusion of at least one woman on the shortlist from which constituency parties selected their candidate, were put to each annual party conference from 1982 to the end of the decade. At first they were opposed by the party's National Executive Committee (NEC) and by trade union delegates. Over time, however, the pattern changed. Campaigners organised in party constituencies and also in the trade unions, which in these years were setting up or revitalising women's sections. A crucial element of the eventually successful campaigns was a package of demands to require quotas of women inside party organisations.

1992–1997: Small Minority of Women

In 1992 the number of Labour women MPs nearly doubled from twenty-one to thirty-seven. Shortly thereafter the party adopted a system of quotas of women for its winnable parliamentary seats. After 1992 women gradually became better established in the party. Margaret Thatcher's third electoral victory in 1987 was a landslide and a watershed for the Labour Party, marking a determination to modernise that provided opportunities for advocates of women's representation. Although, with the possible exception of John Smith, leader briefly after 1992, the modernising Labour leaders were not that interested in women's representation and were uneasy about positive action, the process itself was important to women's representation. Change, when it came, was part of a wider overhaul. The subsequent integration of women was in part a product of opportunities provided by restructuring that aimed to make the party electable and which eventually made it responsive to wider social change. Essentially women's advocates were able to influence changes in the rules so they operated more in women's favour. For example, a number of key moments and decisions were especially illuminating of the agency of party women and of the interplay between different parts of the party, such as the establishment of the position of opposition spokesperson on women's rights in 1983, the decision to require that women be represented with at least 40 per cent at all levels of the party in 1989, the 'One Member One Vote' decision in 1993, the adoption of the policy of all-women shortlists in 1993, its subsequent abandonment in 1995 and eventual replacement after 2002, and the struggle to convince the New Labour leadership that women's votes could be available to the party throughout the 1990s.

All-Women Shortlists

Although advocates were excited by the use of quotas in sister parties in the Socialist International (Short 1996), the constituency-based system of election and candidate selection posed considerable tactical and legal problems. The nomination of parliamentary candidates takes place within parties and is jealously guarded by party constituencies who resent any interference from the centre. Each constituency selects only one candidate for Westminster elections, hence increasing the number of women candidates is perceived as a zero-sum game. The quota mechanisms that work in party list or other proportional systems are not suitable here. Therefore a bespoke mechanism to secure women's nomination for winnable seats had to be devised and it proved to be awkward, conspicuous and controversial. All-women shortlists treat the issue of central interference in who the party selects by restricting the pool from which they can select. For it to work some constituencies must agree to select their candidates from a list of women.

It took some time to reach agreement and doing so was something of a process. It began with measures to ensure that a certain number of women were on shortlists (starting with one woman where a woman had been proposed). The results were disappointing and gradually supporters of women's representation began to realise that some compulsion would be necessary. Despite the return of the highest ever proportion of women MPs in the 1992 election, women's advocates were disappointed. Only two of Labour's retiring MPs were replaced by women and most of the newly elected women were in marginal seats, hence electorally vulnerable (Russell 2005: 111).

Moreover, against poll predictions of victory, Labour lost the election, creating an environment of great caution in the party leadership. Advocates drew on new academic and public opinion research to argue that the gender gap in voting and party support had reopened (Stephenson 1998), a claim that was disputed by election specialists but which proved very useful in internal party arguments (Lovenduski 1999). Shadow Women's Minister, Clare Short, consulted specialists on gender politics and polices via a seminar she convened in the House of Commons in the mid-1990s. In addition, in conjunction with the party women's officer Deborah Lincoln and other leading women, activists set up a working group called 'winning words' to gather, analyse, and proselytise among the party leadership data that not only showed that women's votes were available to the party but also made suggestions on how to secure those votes. The group was attended by leading Labour women, including future MP and Minister Patricia Hewitt, pollster Deborah Mattinson, and Liz Lloyd, who was a member of Tony Blair's staff, as well as notables such as the publisher Carmen Cahlil. Most importantly, the group was attended, and its findings utilised, by New Labour pollster Phillip Gould, a friend of Mattinson's. When she succeeded Clare Short as Shadow Women's Minister, Tessa Jowell continued the initiative. By the time of the 1997 election campaign its meetings were attended by Labour women MPs and candidates who would play a part in the governments after 1997 including especially Harriet Harman, Hilary Armstrong and Margaret Hodge, all of whom were prominent members of Labour governments after 1997.

Meanwhile, in 1993, in the wake of a complex set of internal party alliances in which trade union women and women officials supported by party leader John Smith proved decisive (Lovenduski 1997; Russell 2005), the party agreed to the introduction of all-women shortlists in the selections for the coming election. The measure was quickly implemented using a system based around regional meetings of constituency officials (half of whom by now were women) who decided which seats would be all-women shortlists. Once agreed, the new rules remained controversial both inside and outside the party where the press were vituperative in their opposition. *The Daily Mail* ran a 'quota watch' column in which women selected under the rule were ridiculed. Two disgruntled male would-be candidates contested the rule successfully at an industrial tribunal (*Jepson vs. Dyas Eliot* 1995), forcing the party to rescind it. But most selections were in place by then. A record 101 (24 per cent of the total) labour women were elected in the Labour landslide of 1997.

Thus change occurred on several fronts and was a slow process of acquiring and mobilising resources and constructing alliances, especially with women trade unionists, to bring about a succession of changes in party structures and policies on women. What is clear is that the three certainties of masculinity so vividly described by Cockburn in the mid-1980s were already under threat. In 1979, 9.5 million men and 3.9 million women were members of trade unions; by 1992 there were 5.5 million men and 3.6 million women — evidence of a rebalancing of the sexes in a declining Labour movement. In retrospect, the process appears to have been relentless. First women secured guaranteed positions on internal party bodies at all levels, a tactic which was mirrored in the trade unions.[1] Then they used these positions to bring about changes in candidate selection procedures that led to the adoption of quotas and major increases in the selection of women candidates for winnable seats.

Almost Large Minority 1997–2011

Shortly after the 1997 election arrangements were made for devolved assemblies in Scotland and Wales. In Scotland women's advocates demanded equal representation. The demand was effective in the Labour Party which promised to implement it. The subsequent 1999 mixed member proportional elections included quota arrangements that were undoubtedly eased by the absence of any incumbents. The Welsh Assembly comprised 40 per cent women, the Scottish parliament 39 per cent. The positive public reaction undoubtedly softened elite opinion at Westminster. Nevertheless, party leaders mindful of the legal constraints, opted for 50/50 shortlists for the 2001 general election. The policy failed. Only one in five new candidates were women, and the absence of an effective rule to secure their nominations for party and winnable seats was thought by campaigners, experts, and women leaders to be the reason that the number of women in the Parliamentary party fell. By this time almost all of Labour's women MPs and many men were convinced of the need for quotas, arguing that only compulsion would change the gender equilibrium of the party. An important document produced by Meg Russell outlined the legal constraints, at least some of which were a matter of EU employment law (Russell 2000). Legal opinion confirmed that the Amsterdam Treaty removed such constraints and the political leadership agreed to support equality guarantees. A change in the law was promised in the 2001 manifesto. Accordingly the Sex Discrimination Electoral Candidates Act which gave parties the legal right to use positive action in cases of underrepresentation was passed unopposed in 2002. Labour made use of these provisions, and from then on the policy required all-women shortlists in 50 per cent of all seats where an incumbent retired and in 100 per cent of all late retirements. As Table 9.2 shows, the measure was effective. The policy ensured that the proportion of women MPs in the party group rose in the electoral defeat of 2010.[2]

Institutional Rules and Norms

Positions in the party organisation are subject to gender-balance principles that were not only defended but extended to the leadership at the 2011 annual conference. Cabinet membership is by decision of the Prime Minister. Between 1997 and 2010 women constituted about 18–22 per cent of the Cabinet. After the 2010 general election, Ed Miliband's shadow cabinet[3] — following Labour Party rules for periods of opposition and the first government cabinet after an election — was elected by the party and included a quota of six places for women.

Table 9.2: Number of Labour Women Nominated and Elected as MPs on All-Women Shortlists, 1997–2010

	1997	2001	2005	2010[a]
Nominated	38	No all-women shortlists	30	64
Elected	35		23	31

a. According to Sarah Childs (Childs et al. 2010), this compares poorly with previous elections. In 1997 and 2005, 50 per cent of women MPs were selected via All-Women Shortlists, whereas in 2010 only 38 per cent of women MPs were so selected. This reflects both the electoral swing against Labour and the use of AWS in sixteen seats that Labour did not hold in 2005, including two that selected, but did not return, Black and Minority Ethnic women. This is both an inefficient placement of AWS and one which, moreover, renders these individual cases something short of constituting an equality guarantee. The failure to select women in enough of the Party's safest seats — those with whopping 2005 majorities — generated grumblings amongst gender equality grassroots activists and NEC members. Had the NEC designated all seats where MPs stepped down AWS or ensured that women were placed in its safest seats, Labour would have exceeded its target of 40 per cent women MPs in its parliamentary party (and its 'longer' term target of 50 per cent) (Ashe *et al.* 2011).

In fact ten women were appointed (38 per cent). In 2011 the party's annual conference, its supreme decision-making body, voted at Leader Ed Miliband's behest to put membership of the shadow cabinet in the gift of the party leader. Miliband accordingly appointed a new shadow cabinet of twenty-three members including eleven women (48 per cent).

There is some evidence of change in Labour Party norms, though what it has changed into is something of a puzzle. On one hand the Labour Party is the political home of left feminism in the UK. On the other is the history of patriarchal certainty and traditional masculinity. While in 1987 the ethos of the Labour Party in respect of women was unchanged from its foundation (Perrigo 1996), by 2000 changes in the trade unions were affecting the party. The roles of the trade unions are complex; they have been since the early twentieth-century sites of campaigns to improve women's rights and they are historically responsible for huge improvements in women's pay and working conditions. But they resisted demands for the representation of women until they themselves were feminised.

The current provision for selecting women candidates is stronger than it has ever been, despite some evidence of the supply of women candidates running down in the 2010 election (*see* Mullin 2011). Only one woman candidate, Dianne Abbott, stood in the closely fought 2010 Labour leadership election. The other candidates were all Oxford- or Cambridge-educated male '40 somethings' in smart suits. The winner, Ed Miliband, forgot to appeal to women at the start of his campaign, an oversight that was quickly corrected, apparently by his women supporters, but nevertheless was the subject of press comment. However, women and women's issues were prominent in the campaign hustings, and according to some analyses women were responsible for his election. No woman has ever been elected to the leadership of the Labour Party. Two deputy party leaders acted as leader when the position was vacant, Margaret Beckett in the summer of 1994 and Harriet Harman in the summer of 2010. Internally, however, women are a significant presence. The battles described above were fiercely fought and were a major preoccupation of those involved who saw them as a key element of party modernisation. However, the modernising leaders — Kinnock and Blair — were rarely more than rhetorically supportive. Tony Blair was uneasy about positive action because he believed it to be a vote loser. Once convinced it was not, he quietly dropped his opposition (Campbell 2011). When we read the accounts of the major players in the modernisation of the Labour Party — Blair, Brown, Mandelson — there is almost no reference to the struggles over women's representation. They simply were not on the radar of the key players. However, the 2010 leadership contenders all made bids for party women's votes. This may have been the result of younger, more feminist men coming into contention and standing against a (albeit unlikely) women candidate. However, there were good pragmatic reasons for making an appeal to women. The Alternative Vote electoral system for the Labour leadership and deputy leadership is conducted from an electoral college that becomes more unpredictable as the number of contenders increases. Previously, in 2008, Harriet Harman, who was not the favourite, won the deputy leadership against five male candidates in the final round of the count. Knowing that the circumstances and the arithmetic were similar, the six leadership candidates in 2010 studied the 2008 vote very closely and acted accordingly. Women in the party questioned them closely on their policies on women's issues. The candidates ensured that women were prominent in their campaigning teams. In short, there was an evident competitive bid for the women's vote; perhaps a portent that changes in the party's institutional norms are well established.[4]

The Conservatives

1835–2010: Male Monopoly

The 2010 general election more than doubled the number of Conservative women MPs to forty nine, who were 16 per cent of the parliamentary party, up from seventeen women (3.5 per cent) in 2005. Despite their earlier establishment as a party, their continued electoral success, and their long association with women members and voters, the Conservatives have a poor record on women's representation. Effective mobilisation to elect more Conservative women MPs is relatively recent. Yet the Conservative woman has often been described as the party's 'secret weapon' (Campbell 1987).

Historically, the Conservative Party accommodated women. There was provision for their presence at all levels of the party organisation, a principle put in place in 1928 and deviated from only occasionally thereafter. Exceptionally William Hague, the party leader from 1997 to 2001, undertook a party reorganisation in which the Conservative Women's Organisation (CWO) was downgraded, but this ran into some resistance and proved of brief duration.

Women's fortunes improved under David Cameron's leadership, which began in 2005. Cameron understood that a more feminised profile would help the party to shed the 'nasty' image that had been one of its problems following Margaret Thatcher's leadership, which lasted from 1975 to 1992 and included ten years with her as the UK's first and only woman Prime Minister.

Over the years commentators have frequently remarked that Conservative women were the backbone of the party — the loyal volunteers who were at least half the membership, who kept the local branches going, did the daily work of the party, and saw to its image in the community through various social activities (Campbell 1987; Lovenduski *et al.* 1994; Maguire 1998; Childs 2008). But the tradition of activism at local level did not result in parliamentary office for women. Although the CWO included the promotion of women for elected office in its aims, it did not publicly challenge the party's poor record until recently. Indeed there were few such challenges. An exception was Emma Nicholson who was vice-chair of the party in charge of the selection of parliamentary candidates between 1983 and 1987. Nicholson, who later defected to the Liberal Democrats, was vociferous in her advocacy of the need for the party to select more women candidates, and a tireless encourager of women to come forward. In the 1990s Lady Seccombe, the Vice Chairman (sic) in charge of women was well known for her efforts to encourage women to become candidates. The episodic nature of such efforts was symptomatic of a parliamentary party in which women were absent.

When Margaret Thatcher became party leader in 1975 less than 3 per cent of Conservative MPs were women. By the time she left office in 1990 the figure had risen only slightly to 4.5 per cent. During her time in office she never appointed a single elected woman to her cabinet. While women's concerns were not neglected — there was a ministerial group on women's issues from 1986 onwards — no one thought that women needed to lead such policy. Mrs Thatcher was not a supporter of women, not a sister, and certainly not a feminist. Nor were most of her party. The women's brief and women's issues were disdained. Her legacy to Conservative, and indeed all UK, women was symbolic rather than descriptive. This became apparent when John Major succeeded her in December 1990. Major's first cabinet contained no women. This attracted a great deal of media and public criticism, in response to which he added responsibility for women's issues to the portfolio of Angela Rumbold, a Minister at the Home Office. Rumbold shared Thatcher's contempt for the notion of women's presence and made her distaste known, telling the press that the term 'Minister for Women' was their invention. 'Your profession has dumped that on me. My responsibility is prisons' (Lovenduski and Randall 1993: 162). But by this time there were public expectations that at least one cabinet position should go to a woman. After he was returned to office in the 1992 election John Major put two women in his cabinet and continued the 'Minister for Women' assignment until 1997, although it was sometimes held by a man.

While there is some anecdotal evidence of her inspirational effect on young Conservative women, there is no systematic polling evidence to suggest that the symbolic effect of Margaret Thatcher's tenure empowered women in the sense of encouraging them to put themselves forward as candidates. Yet Labour Party private research at the end of the 1980s revealed that the general public were under the mistaken impression that there were more women on the Conservative than the Labour benches. During her fifteen years as party leader and her ten years near the centre of the world stage, her carefully dressed, coiffed, shod, accessorised, and made-up feminine image was broadcast daily, a constant reminder that the head of state was a woman.

In general, Conservative women bought into the argument that party selection was a matter of merit and that in the fullness of time as they became more qualified there would be more women in elected office. That the scales were beginning to fall from at least some eyes was evident in a few public skirmishes over the issue in the 1990s. An example is Fiona Buxton's 1998 Bow Group pamphlet 'Equal Balance' which put the case for increasing the number of women MPs. In her interviews with party women conducted in 1988 she found considerable evidence of sexism, a discrimination that was intertwined with ageism.

Inevitably the CWO began to challenge the party's record. Protest became more evident after 2001 and by 2005 some Conservative women were going public. *Women2Win* was a ginger group established by prominent Conservative women which aimed to press women's representation issues during the 2005 party leadership campaign. It was resolute in its goal to see more Conservative women MPs (Childs 2008: 51–3). At the same time the CWO was experiencing an upsurge of interest and the Conservative Women's Forum was founded. This organisational activity was new; it marked a shift and a new determination to see change. In some respects the change carried echoes of the rumblings in the Labour Party two decades earlier. The party was in crisis, had been voted out of office in 1997, and could not find its way back. It was ripe for modernisation and reform, offering an opportunity to insert claims for women's representation.

When David Cameron was elected leader in 2005, he introduced a range of new candidate selection procedures that were designed to bring new people into the party and into prominence within the party and secure his own support. Cameron's challenge was to turn his ailing and divided party more towards the political centre in order to make it electable. He needed to mobilise constituencies that had been overlooked by previous leaders who were still influential in the party. The push for more women became associated with Cameron's leadership.

After 2005, therefore, the Conservative Party moved on a stage in its strategies to select women, adding equality promotion to its previously rather thin repertoire of ineffective equality rhetoric. The exhortations to nominate more women that were made by Major led to only minimal improvement in women's seat share. Although the party did nominate more women candidates, they did not do so for winnable seats. As late as the 2005 general election 79 per cent of women candidates but only 59 per cent of male candidates stood in unwinnable seats (Childs 2008: Table 3.4).

Under Cameron's leadership the party sought to create an artificial demand for women candidates by manipulating the approved list, by altering the selection criteria to make women's qualifications more plausible and by altering the selectorate to include groups thought to be more favourable to women than constituency members had been. The list strategy was innovative but it nevertheless fell into the same trap as Labour had, in simply requiring that women should be present on the list. The mechanism was known as the 'A' list, a priority list of 100 candidates that included fifty well-qualified women and fifty well-qualified men. Party seats with vacancies were expected to select from this list, an expectation that was further guided by 50/50 shortlist requirements. It was thought that, faced with qualified women, selectors who were by this time versed in equal opportunities selection methods would select them. In addition primaries (both open and closed) were introduced where larger selectorates made decisions. According to Ashe et al. 2011, primaries were thought to be less likely to work against women. But the Conservative Party failed to go the whole way to all-women shortlists or other forms of equality guarantees. It may never do so. The equality promotion rules were a source of considerable tension in the party, which understood very well that Cameron expected the procedures to select Cameronites. Hence 'A'-list candidates were criticised as unqualified, and it was argued the women had replaced better-qualified men (Ashe *et al.* 2011: 467). Moreover, selection rules were circumvented or ignored in eighty-nine constituencies which selected a local rather than a priority list candidate. This is possible under Conservative selection rules where an exceptional local candidate was available. Some 86 per cent of these exceptional local candidates were men (Cowley and Childs 2011). Here a discursive strategy of resistance was adopted by opponents to Cameron's policies. A false competition between A-list women and local men was created in order to disguise opposition to women per se (Ashe *et al.* 2011: 467). The A list was shut down in 2007 in response to protests about it. At this time it was thought that most selections had already taken place and such work as could be done was complete. However, the parliamentary expenses scandal of 2009 led to a large number of late retirements leaving vacant seats for which women could have been nominated. Indeed, Cameron told the Speakers' Conference on Parliamentary Representation in 2010 that through special rules for late selections (parties normally use by-election rules for such selections) he would implement all-women shortlists. He did not do so (Ashe *et al.* 2011). However, women and men on the priority list fared well, and women also did well in the primaries in comparison to their success at both selection and election in the rest of the party (Ashe *et al.* 2011: 469–70).

Institutional Norms

The tradition of loyalty and unity in the Conservative Party made it difficult for researchers to identify the activities of women's advocates. Only after the end of the twentieth century was internal dissent made public. In *The Iron Ladies* (1987) author Bea Campbell argued, mainly using anecdotal evidence, that there was a duality in Conservative attitudes to women, whereby on the one hand they stood for the values of the traditional and domestic women's roles, while on the other they relied on powerful and independent women who organised the party's work. This argument seemed more intuitively obvious then when Margaret Thatcher was at the height of her powers. Thereafter women's fortunes were limited, and various studies showed considerable sexism in the party. Women who attempted to become candidates understood very well the obstacles they faced. Fawcett research conducted by the author and Laura Shepherd-Robinson in 2001 and 2002 found much the same complaints about sexism that Buxton revealed after the previous election (Shepherd-Robinson and Lovenduski 2002).

2010–2015: Small Minority of Women

The House of Commons elected in 2010 included a large number (49) of new entrants, many of whom were women. Only three were appointed to cabinet positions, including Baroness Warsi from the House of Lords, the first Conservative woman cabinet minister from a minority ethnic group. Early activity on women's policy issues included a successful effort to block the Liberal Democrat demand to rescind anonymity provision for rape victims. However, other policy initiatives removed rights and benefits in ways that affected women more than men. Under its red tape initiative the government considered the repeal of the Equality Act of 2010, which enshrines a number of equality promotion measures aimed at women. LIFE, a prominent anti-choice group, was appointed to the Government's Sexual Health Forum, while the pro-choice British Pregnancy Advisory Service was excluded.

Although in 2010 a record number of Conservative women were elected, there is plenty of evidence that the party has not yet adapted to a more woman-friendly culture. David Cameron's treatment of Maria Eagle, MP, when he told her to 'calm down dear' after she questioned his arguments in Prime Minister's Questions in May 2011 attracted widespread press condemnation. Similarly, when Kenneth Clark, Minister for Justice, opined that certain forms of rape were not serious there was an outcry. Both felt obliged to apologise and did so publicly. Cameron and Clark survived; they had their defenders.

It is difficult to draw firm conclusions about the future for Conservative Party women. On the one hand they are better mobilised to claim representation than ever before. On the other hand their current fortunes are tied to Cameron's leadership which is not based on deep party support. Nor does it depend much on his attitudes to women. At the time of writing it is not difficult to imagine a Conservative retreat on women. Nor can we be confident that the traditional institutional norms of the party are being replaced. The party has not agreed to guarantee women's presence in parliament and government and it retreated from the relatively weak forms of positive action of Cameron's A-list strategy. Further retreat is not impossible, as the Liberal Democrat experience shows.

The Liberal Democrats

The Liberal Democrats were founded in a merger of the old Liberal Party and the shortlived Social Democratic Party in 1988. Despite an early and long association of Liberal Party women with feminist claims, and innovative action by the Social Democratic Party component, the Liberal Democrats do not do well when it comes to the election of women MPs. They face more obstacles than Labour or the Conservatives, having no safe seats and fewer resources (Evans 2008). But there are other problems. In common with the Labour and Conservative Parties, internal women's advocacy organisations operate in a context of left–right divisions. Another factor is the party obsession with obtaining state power. Although they are in some respects women friendly and ideologically predisposed in favour of equality goals, they seem unable to take effective action. The bi-annual policy making conference has repeatedly rejected calls for effective measures to support increased women's political representation. To be fair, it is also disadvantaged by the electoral system which means that its share of seats is significantly less, proportional to its vote share, than other parties. In such a context selectorates tend to play safe and this means nominating male candidates. Since 1988 the party complement of women MPs has fluctuated around the male monopoly/small minority of women borderline. While women constituted 10 per cent of MPs in 1992, the figure dropped below 10 per cent in 1997 and 2001, rebounded to 16 per cent in 2005, and dropped to 12 per cent in 2010.

Historically women liberals were caught between their support for suffrage and their party loyalty (Evans 2011). Today they are similarly torn on the issue of women's political representation. In 2001 the party rejected the use of all-women shortlists and, for Westminster elections, it has relied on the dual list strategy of aiming to bring women onto its regionally based approved lists of candidates and requiring that selection shortlists are gender balanced (Evans 2008; Ashe et al. 2011). However, the party does have internal quotas requiring that the memberships of all internal party bodies are comprised of at least 30 per cent women, and it has used equality guarantees in the past in the form of 'zipping' in the 1999 European Parliament elections.

There is deep division in the party over the use of equality guarantees. All-women shortlists for Westminster selections were rejected by the 2001 conference. Opponents to quotas mounted fierce objections to the measure in a bitter debate. They were supported by young women Liberal Democrats dressed in skimpy pink t-shirts bearing the slogan 'I am not a token woman'. In 2002 the t-shirts were back as the party voted to rescind its use of zipping in European elections (Lovenduski 2005; Evans 2008). Thus, one of the key internal battles about increasing the number of women candidates was lost only a few years after it appeared to have been won. Although there is some support within the party for all-women shortlists, the internal women's organisations are cautious to the point of timidity about it.

There are three organisations to promote women. The Women Liberal Democrats is the main party women's organisation. It aims to facilitate women's presence and draw attention to their concerns throughout the party. The Campaign for Gender Balance was established in 2001, charged by the Federal Executive Committee with achieving a target of 40 per cent of women in the party's parliamentary group. A Diversity and Equality group specifically supports women and minority ethnic candidates. In parliament there is a women and equality spokesperson, and Liberal Democrat MP, Lynne Featherstone, was incoming Undersecretary of State for Women and Equalities was appointed Equalities Minister in the 2010 coalition cabinet.

As a party which historically (as the Liberal Party) favoured the spread of voting rights and embraced rationality, the Liberal Democrat responses to women's claims for representation are something of a puzzle, one that is partly explained by a split between classical and social liberals who are ideologically divided over social intervention (Lovenduski 2005). The party culture may also be an obstacle. Evans (2008) found evidence of sexism in selection processes and reports of a real difference between party members and the public to which the party appeals. Evans holds that potential Liberal Democrat voters are broadly supportive of equal representation for women, but not so the activists. She found evidence of institutional sexism in attitudes to candidates. Candidates were reportedly expected to conform to certain male stereotypes of a politician, a perception that selectors were looking for 'ballsy women' and sometimes plain sexist abuse. *'I'm not voting for you, you're a bloody woman'* (Evans 2008: 599).

Recent studies of the promotion of women in the Liberal Democrats indicate progress depends on a small number of critical actors, a few advocates who keep the issue to the foreground.

'Other Parties'

Normally a number of smaller parties elect MPs to the House of Commons (27 in 2010), almost all of which are for Northern Irish, Scottish or Welsh constituencies. However, in 2010 the Green Party elected their leader, Caroline Lucas, as the first ever Green Westminster MP. Lucas won Brighton Pavilion, an English constituency. A former MEP, Lucas is known for her support for women's equality and the party itself is relatively hospitable to women, who are prominent among its activists and elected representatives. Thus, in 2011, 10 of 23 Green Party councillors in Brighton were women, as were 5 of 15 on Norwich City Council, 1 of 2 London Assembly members, and 1 of 2 UK MEPS.

On Parties and Policies

While some scholarly attention has been given to the internal sources of party policies on women's political representation in the UK, relatively little attention has been paid to party policies on women's concerns or issues.

In 2004 the Fawcett Society, the lead NGO on women's political rights in the UK, published a list of criteria for assessing party manifesto pledges on and to women. These were used by Sarah Childs to analyse party promises to women in 2005, and later to examine Conservative manifesto pledges between 1992 and 2005. Finally, she did a comparative study of party manifestos in the 2010 elections (Childs 2005, 2008; Childs *et al*. 2010; Campbell and Childs 2010). Her accounts track both change and continuity, and similarity and difference in the ways that the major UK parties constitute their electorates and treat women.

Such efforts to identify and attract women voters mark a post-war high point in party addresses to women voters. The manifesto analyses give a good indication of how the parties regard their potential to attract the support of women voters. Their silences are as interesting as their contents. For example, one of the most important and effective Labour Party policies in terms of equal pay was the Minimum Wage Act but the policy was not 'marketed' in terms of its impact on women. Similarly, public expenditure cuts following the 2008 financial crisis impacted much more on women than men, but no party promised to protect women from this disadvantage (Annesley 2010; Stephenson and Harrison 2011; Women's Budget Group 2012).

Here we are dealing with considerable complexity. In their reanalysis of the results of the RNG's policy data, McBride and Mazur (2010) found that women's movements fared better in terms of policy outcomes when certain configurations of left-party power, women in parliament, and women's movements were present (although none of these components were either necessary or sufficient to a feminist outcome). In the UK, clear changes are evident in political representation policy. The main party of the left has so far returned more women to parliament and some of those women have acted for women, a finding that concurs with developments elsewhere (Lovenduski and Guadagnini 2010). It is possible to trace changes in representation policy in the Labour Party through to government and to policy changes such as the Sex Discrimination (Candidates) Act of 2002.

Women as Leaders

To summarise, historically women have not been well represented in leadership positions (*see* Table 9.3). The UK has had only one woman Prime Minister, and two women have acted as Labour Party leaders for short periods. One woman, Betty Boothroyd, has been Speaker of the House of Commons. Until the early 1990s women were not routinely appointed to the Cabinet. Between 1997 and 2010 there were from four to six women in the Cabinet, and by the end of that period women had held the powerful and prestigious positions of Home Secretary and Foreign Secretary. Moreover, there were women junior ministers in most of the departments of state, and therefore in the pool of eligibles for high office. However, no woman has yet been appointed Chancellor of the Exchequer.

The 2010 government saw a reduction in the number of women MPs who were appointed to the Cabinet and in women junior ministers, but Prime Minister David Cameron promised he would appoint 'more' women to key positions, though it

Table 9.3: Women and Men in the UK Political Leadership

Position	Period 1 1945–1997	Period 2 1997–2010	2011
MPs	3–9% women	18–22% women	22% women
Party Leader (Main parties)	25 men 1 woman acting leader	12 men 1 woman acting leader	3 men
Speaker of the Lower House	7 men 1 woman	1 woman 2 men	0
Chairs of parliamentary committees[a]	0	1 woman	14% women
Cabinet[b] Minister	9 women, 451 men	19 women, 73 men	17% women
Prime Minister	1 woman, 11 men	0	0

a. Departmental select committees only. Considerable reform of parliamentary committees took place in 1979 when departmental select committees were established.
b. Estimate counting the number of appointments of women and men, hence each cabinet minister is counted again for each 'new' cabinet, i.e. those formed after an election or change of prime minister. Assumes a cabinet membership of twenty-three, but many cabinets include ministers 'in attendance' who are not part of the cabinet payroll. The estimates do not take account of reshuffles in which a further two appointments of women were made in period 1, six in period 2 and one in 2011.

remains to be seen how he will select them as the pool of eligible women from the coalition parties in parliament is relatively small.

Conclusions

The short conclusion to be drawn from comparing the strategies of the three parties to increase women's representation is that only equality guarantees in the form of all-women shortlists deliver substantial progress. There are striking similarities of resistances in each party and equally striking evidence that parties failed to learn from each other and did not read the writing on the wall. Each began by selecting more women but only for unwinnable seats. As protests were raised, each then attempted to meet demand for increases by using weak strategies, that is by introducing requirements to increase the proportion of women on both approved lists and shortlists but not selected candidates. Each of the three main parties went through a similar sequence of events, but different trajectories, and today they still have remarkably different levels of representation for women. Women candidates' success rates in the two large parties are still considerably lower than those of male candidates (Table 9.4).

Another commonality was that local party members used their autonomy to resist the imposition of non-local candidates, which, when such local candidates nearly always turned out to be men, many observers thought was designed to disguise their resistance to women candidates. At various times in all the parties policies were circumvented, sometimes by refusal to use the list, sometimes by nominating less qualified women candidates who had no chance of winning through. Also illustrated is the lack of cross-party cooperation by elected women, unsurprising perhaps in a country that historically has rarely had coalition governments. This is a reflection of the deeply entrenched party tribalism whereby party loyalty is the 'gold standard' of political behaviour, especially in the two larger parties (Wright 2009). There is no tradition of trust across party boundaries and party discipline, often termed party loyalty, is a paramount principle. As recently as 2011 Labour women MPs declined to participate in a cross-party parliamentary group, believing it would operate to the benefit of other parties and to the detriment of Labour. The group was finally established in 2012.

Party differences are embedded in histories and cultures that impact differently on their attitudes to equality strategies. Whilst no party denies that equality is a desirable goal, they differ in their hospitality to equality strategies. Thus all parties first adopted equality rhetoric and later equality promotion, but only the Labour Party embraced equality guarantees (Lovenduski 2005). Labour's strategy stems not only from mobilisations by party women but also from its historical commitments to political equality. Its discourses and practices are, albeit after struggle, amenable to claims for equality of representation. The Conservative Party on the other hand has historically been pragmatic, adopting equality discourses late and largely for electoral reasons. Finally the Liberal Democrats balance both positions making it almost impossible to sustain a coherent strategy to promote the descriptive representation of women.

While male dominance may have been broken and one party has crossed the threshold of a large minority of women, voters and the press continue to visualise and represent politics as a male activity. Despite the best efforts of campaigners, there is no widespread public movement for parity of women's representation. While the majority of the population regard claims for women's equality as legitimate, opinion poll evidence indicates that many think such change has gone

Table 9.4: Election Rates of Women Candidates in 2010 by Party

	Conservatives	Labour	Lib Dem
No. of women candidates	149	191	134
No. of women elected	48	81	7
Percentage of women elected	24%	30%	12%
No. of men candidates	481	439	495
No. of men elected	257	177	50
No. of men elected	53%	40%	10%
Differences between per cent of elected women and men	-29%	-10%	2%

far enough and there remains a substantial minority who wish to preserve women's traditional roles while others believe that equality of representation is inevitable and nothing needs to be done to accelerate it. The quotas policy adopted by Labour is not popular; it finds little support from a public that does not like politicians and in which women continue to be much less interested in politics than are men.

Thus British women remain dependent on political parties for their political representation. The fortunes of women in terms of both presence and policy in all the assemblies, parliaments, and councils are party dependent and party support is essential. The long and painful march of women has taken place as parties themselves have declined. While there may be opportunities for feminist takeover of hollowed-out organisations, as advocates of the shrinking institutions hypothesis argue, such a victory may well prove pyrrhic if political recruitment becomes fragmented and candidate centred and breaks free of party control.

Notes

1. Throughout the process party and affiliated trade union women were key actors. As well as those already mentioned Joyce Gould, Jo Richardson, Janet Armstrong, Frances Morrell, and Vicky Phillips were joined by trade union women including Angela Eagle, Maureen Rooney, Bernadette Hillon, Margaret Prosser, and Anne Gibson. Their work attracted some support from senior male party officials including especially Larry Whitty and Peter Coleman.

2. The date beyond which an MP retirement is deemed late is normally decided by the National Executive Committee of the party which then takes over the management of the nominations from the constituency party and imposes a shortlist from which the candidate must be selected.

3. The shadow cabinet is the cabinet of the main opposition party.

4. Ed Miliband was a protégé of Harman's and the components of his victory in the last round of the count were remarkably similar to hers.

References

Annesley, C. (2010) 'Gender, Politics and Policy Change: The Case of Welfare Reform under New Labour', *Government and Opposition*, 45 (1): 50–72.

Ashe, J., Campbell, R., Childs, S., and Evans, E. (2011) '"Stand By Your Man": Women's Political Recruitment at the 2010 UK General Election', *British Politics*, 5 (4): 455–80.

Buxton, F. (1998) *Equal Balance: Electing More Women MPs for the Conservative Party*, London: The Bow Group.

Campbell, A. (2011) *Diaries*, Kindle Edition.

Campbell, B. (1987) *The Iron Ladies*, London: Virago.

Campbell, R. and Childs, S. (2010) '"Wags", "Wives" and "Mothers"...But What About Women Politicians?', *Parliamentary Affairs*, 63 (4): 760–77.

Childs, S. (2005) 'Feminising British Politics: Sex and Gender in the 2005 General Election', in A. Geddes and J. Tonge (eds) *Britain Decides: The UK General Election 2005*, Basingstoke: Palgrave Macmillan, pp. 150–167.

Childs, S. (2008), *Women and British Party Politics*, London: Routledge.

Childs, S., Webb, P., and Marthaler, S. (2010) 'Constituting and Substantively Representing Women: Applying New Approaches to a UK Case', *Politics and Gender*, 6: 199–223.

Cockburn, C. (1987) 'Women, Trade Unions and Political Parties', Fabian Research Series 349, London: The Fabian Society.

Cowley, P. and Childs, S. (2011) 'The Politics of Local Presence: Is there a Case for Descriptive Representation?', *Political Studies*, 59 (1): 1–19.

Evans, E. (2008) 'Supply or Demand? Women Candidates and Liberal Democrats', *British Journal of Politics and International Relations*, 10 (4): 590–606.

Evans, E. (2011) *Gender and the Liberal Democrats: Representing Women*, Manchester: Manchester University Press.

Hills, J. (1981) 'Britain', in J. Lovenduski and J. Hills (eds) *The Politics of the Second Electorate*, London: Routledge, pp. 8–32.

Lovenduski, J. (1997) 'Gender Politics: A Breakthrough for Women?', *Parliamentary Affairs*, 50 (4): 708–19.

Lovenduski, J. (1999) 'Sexing Political Behaviour in Britain', in S. Walby (ed.) *New Agendas for Women*, London and Basingstoke: Macmillan, pp. 190–209.

Lovenduski, J. (2005) *Feminizing Politics*, Cambridge: Polity Press.

Lovenduski, J. and Randall, V. (1993) *Contemporary Feminist Politics*, Oxford: Oxford University Press.

Lovenduski, J., Norris, P., and Burness, C. (1994) 'The Party and Women', in A. Seldon and S. Ball (eds) *Conservative Century: The Conservative Party Since 1900*, Oxford: Oxford University Press, pp. 611–635.

Lovenduski, J. and Guadagnini, M. (2010) 'Political Representation', in D. E. McBride and A. Mazur (eds) *The Politics of State Feminism*, Philadelphia: Temple University Press, pp. 164–192.

McBride, D. E. and Mazur, A. (eds) (2010) *The Politics of State Feminism: Innovation in Comparative Research*, Philadelphia: Temple University Press.

Maguire, G. E. (1998) *Conservative Women: A History of Women and the Conservative Party 1874–1997*, London and Basingstoke: Palgrave Macmillan.

Matland, R. E. and Studlar, D. T. (1996) 'The Contagion of Women Candidates in Single Member and Multi-Member Districts', *Journal of Politics*, 58: 707–33.

Mullin, C. (2011) *A Walk-On Part: Diaries 1994–1999*, Kindle Edition.

Perrigo, S. (1996) 'Women and Change in the Labour Party', *Parliamentary Affairs*, 49 (1): 116–29.

Russell, M. (2000) *Women's Representation in UK Politics: What Can Be Done Within the Law*, London: The Constitution Unit, UCL.

Russell, M. (2005) *Building New Labour*, London and Basingstoke: Palgrave Macmillan.

Shepherd-Robinson, L. and Lovenduski, J. (2002) *Women and Candidate Selection in British Political Parties*, London: The Fawcett Society.

Short, C. (1996) 'Women and The Labour Party', *Parliamentary Affairs*, 49 (1): 17–25.

Stephenson, M. A. (1998) *The Glass Trapdoor: Women, Politics and the Media during the 1997 General Election*, London: Fawcett Society.

Stephenson, M. A. and Harrison, J. (2011) 'Unravelling Equality? A Human Rights and Equality Impact Assessment of the Public Spending Cuts on Women in Coventry', University of Warwick and Coventry Women's Voices, available at http://www2.warwick.ac.uk/fac/soc/law/research/centres/chrp/publications/unravelling_equality_full.pdf (accessed 13 April 2015).

Women's Budget Group (2012), available at: http://wbg.org.uk/ (accessed 13 April 2015).

Wright, T. (2009) 'Doing Politics Differently', *Political Quarterly*, 80 (3): 319–28.

PART 3

GENDER AND PUBLIC POLICY

Chapter Ten

The New Politics of Abortion*

with Joyce Outshoorn

Most Western democracies liberalised their abortion politics during the 1960s and 1970s. The process involved and the political circumstances in which new policies emerged were often very similar, although the content of the new laws varied considerably. In general the political systems did not welcome the abortion issue. Those which were organised around socio-economic cleavages were ill suited to cope with abortion politics. Neither did those countries whose major institutions expressed cultural cleavages fare well.

From the mid-1960s onwards liberal, medical, social welfare and feminist pressures impacted upon religious, natalist and traditionalist concerns to produce abortion law reform movements prepared to use a range of strategies in order to achieve their objectives. These movements began from different starting points. In Europe and in the United States restrictive laws had been passed during the nineteenth or the early twentieth centuries. Some of these laws had been moderated by the mid-1950s. In Scandinavia, for example, a limited availability of abortion was acceptable to popular feelings as a result of a long process of legitimation. There, further reform met with relatively little resistance. Elsewhere attempts to liberalise abortion laws generated widespread public debates and complex political conflicts, as in Great Britain, the Netherlands, France, Italy and the USA. In Ireland the issue led to a constitutional amendment prohibiting abortion law reform. In Belgium the political system avoided action, neither altering existing statutes nor enacting new laws on the issue.

In West European politics abortion is unusual in that it cuts across the dominant socio-economic or Left–Right dimension of party politics. Parties in such systems rarely developed a specific stance on abortion before it arose as a political issue. Discomfited, they find the abortion issue difficult to link to their main corpus of doctrine. Confessional parties too have their problems with the matter. Doctrinal indicators notwithstanding, political expediency has led religious parties to the prioritisation of economic matters. The constraints of coalition building, as well as purely electoral considerations, dispose them to downplay their stands on abortion. Only when religious parties are essential to the formation of government are they in a position to follow their doctrinal inclinations on abortion policy.

The cross-cutting nature of the abortion controversy may have consequences not only for the way in which the issue is perceived but also for the political

---

* 'Abortion and the Political System' (with J. Outshoorn), in J. Lovenduski and J. Outshoorn (eds) *The New Politics of Abortion*, London, Sage, 1986, pp. 1–4.

system itself. In multi-party systems conflict over abortion policy has led to additional conflicts in coalition formation. This has been the case in Belgium, the Netherlands, Italy and Norway. In general, politicians have been reluctant to press the issue. The exceptions are the leaders of both the major Irish confessional parties (who compete for Catholic support) and the leaders of the small parties of the European religious right.

Three major strategies have characterised political responses: abstinence, postponement and de-politicisation. Abstinence occurs where governments, parties and leaders refrain from taking a stand. Postponement is less straightforward. Ostensibly simply a delaying tactic, it may also result from a perception that reform groups will be unable to sustain mobilisation. De-politicisation may take a number of forms. Most commonly, abortion is redefined as a technical issue enabling politicians to pass responsibility to experts. Few governments have been able to sustain strategies of abstinence or postponement for long. De-politicisation offers greater flexibility but depends both on the complicity of the designated experts and on the government's capacity to maintain its definition of the issue. However, as medical practitioners and courts have indicated their preference for clear guidelines from the state, de-politicisation strategies have become less feasible.

But the major challenge has been over the way in which the issue is defined. The criminalisation of abortion during the nineteenth century had made it a penal matter. Church interest added a moral dimension. In some countries it became a medical matter and in most it developed into a polarised political and philosophical issue, a matter of competing notions of rights. More than many other issues, abortion has been subject to continuous redefinition.

Redefinition first occurred in the early 1960s when both medical practitioners and liberal reformers sought a restricted legalisation in many countries. At this stage it was considered that demand for the termination of pregnancies would be limited to a few special cases. Essentially, leave was sought to perform abortions in the event of particular pathologies: psychiatric, medical and, more rarely, social indicators were to be used. The aim here was to prevent 'deserving cases' from having to seek backstreet abortions. It was widely agreed that this was best achieved by providing legal, medical terminations. These arguments were accepted and reform was achieved early in Scandinavia, Great Britain and some US states.

The first reforms left the matter very much in the hands of the experts, a pattern which prevailed until feminism re-emerged as a political force in the late 1960s and 1970s. Precipitating incidents such as the Bobigny trial in France, the White amendment in Britain and Dolle Mina demonstrations in the Netherlands focused feminist attention on the issue. The result was in many cases, a further redefinition. The right of women to decide whether to have an abortion became an issue. Seen from such a perspective abortion restrictions were instruments of social control and experts were the agents of that control. It was redefinition of this kind which finally undermined government de-politicisation strategies.

Meanwhile, those who opposed the extension of abortion rights stressed what they regarded as the moral dimensions of the issue, eventually redefining abortion in terms of the rights of the unborn. In this they have had considerable support from the churches, particularly the Roman Catholic church. Church activity was most apparent where the religious dimension was organised into politics. In such cases a traditional social institution came to be opposed by a social movement espousing modern values.

The redefinitions of the issue offered by both the women's movement and the groups opposing legalisation had the effect of making abortion a matter on which the public felt competent to judge. This widened discussion, considerably enlarging both the scope and terrain of conflict. Once this point was arrived at, mass mobilisation became possible. A whole range of groups became active on the issue and many new groups emerged. In several countries (the Netherlands, Italy, Norway) social movement organisations prevailed, while in Britain and to a lesser extent West Germany, traditional interest group politics predominated.

In all countries except Sweden debate over abortion policy was virulent, divisive and protracted. As the dispute gained momentum governments were forced to deal with it. But in most cases when the matter came before the legislature a 'free vote' was allowed, even where, as in France and West Germany, the legislation was government-sponsored. Only in the Netherlands and Norway were parliamentarians expected to toe a liberalising party line and there only because of special circumstances. In the USA, Congress was not involved in the resolution of the issue which was decided in the courts. A national referendum forced the issue on the Italian Chamber of Deputies, while in Britain and Belgium private members' bills brought the matter before the legislature.

Religious variables had a considerable effect upon the mode of resolution. In predominantly Roman Catholic countries the issue was resolved, if at all, in a formal and legalistic manner with practice often bearing little resemblance to statute. In Protestant countries more of a coincidence between law and policy could be observed.

In all of the countries considered in this volume [this refers to the original volume] the effects of abortion legislation have in many respects been marginal. The most important variable in the availability of abortion to a particular population of women is not the law, but the independent existence of a network of good medical facilities organised either by the state or the private sector. Sweden and the USA supply a useful contrast on this point. Both countries have liberal policies. In Sweden the scrupulous provision of adequate facilities makes access to abortion a reality for women. In the USA, on the other hand, access to abortion is often severely restricted. There free access to abortion is merely an abstract principle for many women. Such examples show that implementation is as important an issue as legalisation. In many countries abortion policy is of the 'posturing' variety, often subject to the vagaries of the political climate.

The various pressures which surround abortion policy are ongoing ones and in none of the countries discussed below may the issue be said to be resolved.

Groups on both sides remain vigilant and developments in medical technology may lead yet again to redefinition. And redefinition, as we have seen, has been the main strategy for placing abortion on the political agenda. Its capacity for being redefined may therefore be sufficient to ensure that the abortion issue continues to challenge established political arrangements.

Chapter Eleven

Sexing London: The Gender Mix of Urban Policy Actors*

with Stefania Abrar and Helen Margetts

This article investigates the gender mix of policy-making elites and networks across London. First, we use the concept of a 'gender system' to explore what is distinctive about the gender mix of the environment within which policy making in London takes place — the relationship between gender and the local state, economy and culture. Second, we investigate the extent to which local authority decision-making structures are 'gendered,' thereby identifying some key characteristics of London's gender system. Change in the gender mix of these structures is a vital indicator of change in the system as a whole. Third, we consider the extent to which there exists an autonomous women's movement in London, another defining characteristic of any gender system. We examine the resources of the pressure groups, educational groups, charities, umbrella groups and national organisations that endeavour to influence policy and service provision directly affecting women. And fourth, we look at some specific urban issues and examine both the extent to which the gender mix of policy actors in these areas differs from the more generalised view and the impact of such differences on policy making. In this way, by taking several 'views' of the gender mix of policy actors, we obtain a more detailed understanding of London's complex gender system than has previously been available.

Before proceeding with our analysis, it is necessary to define the term gender, a word which is often used interchangeably with sex but which in feminist scholarship has become loaded and complex. Notably, many feminists now insist on a distinction between sex, defined as a biological marker, and gender, defined as the social consequence of sexual identity. In other words, the term gender is used to capture the way relations between the sexes are produced and institutionalised. In this article we define gender as the social construction of biological sex.

Gender Systems

Some authors have claimed to establish the ways in which the political, economic, and familial systems of cities combine to produce gender inequality

* 'Sexing London: the gender mix of urban policy actors' (with S. Abrar and H. Margetts), *International Political Science Review*, 1998, 19(2), pp. 147–171.

(Appleton 1995). This inequality may be captured within the notion of a city's 'gender system:' what Connell (1987) calls a 'gender regime.'[1] Such systems or regimes are considered to vary with urban form. Different cities have distinctive relationships between their political, economic and familial systems which affect prevailing ideologies of how men and women should act, think and feel, the availability of cultural and behavioural alternatives to those ideologies, men's and women's access to social positions and control of resources, and the relationships between men and women (Appleton 1995). In addition, different areas within a city can display different constituent elements of their gender system; Appleton claims that higher density and more heterogeneous central cities produce a different gender regime than do the suburbs.

Each gender system has three main dimensions: its distribution of the resources that constitute power, its division of labour, and its structure of emotional attachments. As Appleton puts it, 'the city must be conceptualised as the nexus of three basic institutions, the state, the economy and the family.' In local authorities, as in the central state, the structure of power includes the system of political representation, the public bureaucracy, informal networks, systems of coordination, and other structures that parallel the public bureaucracy. Each of these may have contradictory gendered aspects. Systems of political representation in British local authorities have been male-dominated, but, insofar as feminists have mobilised in political parties, they are responsive to demands for women's representation made through the parties. The public bureaucracy of local authority officials is a gendered hierarchy in which men have traditionally held senior positions. However, the concentration of women in middle and lower levels of the hierarchy is a potential site of organisation for change. At more senior levels the predominance of women in certain professions is another source of change. Once women have access to the public bureaucracy, for example through their preponderance in the white-collar work force, then 'rational' principles of bureaucracy may be mobilised to eliminate organisational barriers to women — for example through the development of more extensive equal opportunities programs of recruitment, promotion and training. Public sector trade unions organised at both levels began demanding equal opportunities staffing policies during the 1980s. Such policies both insist on 'merit' criteria for advancement and, by offering access to the requisite qualification and certification, produce a growing pool of recruitable and promotable women. However, such achievements may be subverted by other aspects of gender regimes. Informal networks may survive the implementation of formal sex equality policy, leaving important barriers to women's advancement. Less is known about the possible effects of gender patterning of emotional attachments (but *see* Stivers 1993; Bologh 1991; Ferguson 1984). These are important components of organisational cultures and may comprise either resources or disadvantages for women.

Feminists have attached great importance to the distinction between the public and private spheres. Any gender system is rooted simultaneously in both spheres. The private sphere is premised on a strongly gendered division of labour (unpaid work) inside the home and women's dependence on the income of individual men. Its main site is the traditional family in which heterosexuality, parenthood, and marriage are hegemonic (Appleton 1995: 47). The public sphere, on the other hand, is characterised by the replacement of women's dependence on individual men with greater dependence on the state for income (either through employment or benefits) and lesser emotional interdependence with men. Paid work tends to be segregated vertically and horizontally by sex. Such work has become more central to women's lives in contemporary society and has inevitably created strains in the private sphere. Hegemonies of traditional familialism have been challenged as alternative visions of men's and women's lives develop. Struggle over gender relations becomes a more common feature of the 'public' realm and may form into demands for a more women-directed public policy. Therefore, establishing the nature of a city's gender system must include empirical research into relationships within and between the city's public and private realms.

Accordingly, London's gender system may be explored by examining the gender dimensions of state, economy and family. Relationships between public and private realms may be gauged through an analysis of demographic composition, in terms of the proportion of families which contain dual wage-earning partnerships of men and women or consist of women who live in households without a male wage-earner.

Gender, Demography and Employment

London attracts and keeps women. It has a slightly higher percentage of women (51.2 per cent) than England and Wales as a whole (51 per cent). While the female majority in the rest of the country is accounted for in the age groups over 50, in London the age–sex pattern is rather different, with majorities of women at earlier ages, notably ages 20–24 and over 40. In central boroughs the female majority occurs at ages 15–24, 40–49 and all ages over 65. In the rest of inner London the female majority is at ages 25–29 (50.4 per cent compared to 48.7 per cent in England and Wales). This pattern has been attributed to the combined pulls of employment and educational opportunities particularly in Central London. Yet, having moved to London, women are less likely to leave it in their thirties and forties, a phenomenon that requires explanation. Such explanation is probably connected to employment opportunities, but is also likely to be a function of the provision of various kinds of services and a reflection of family and life cycle patterns (census data reported by London Research Centre 1995). London has a racially diverse population compared with the rest of the country; thus 25 per cent of women in inner London are non-white compared with 5 per cent in Great Britain as a whole.

Although London's population increased during the fifteen years up to 1993 (the last year covered by our statistics), employment has decreased, with the loss of 460, 000 jobs. Part-time (normally women's) jobs increased, as did self-employment (traditionally men but increasingly women). One-third of employed

London women work part-time, in contrast with the national proportion of 45 per cent. About 25 per cent of London's self-employed are women — 7.8 per cent of the women's work force. London has a largely service-based economy with 84 per cent of its work force in the service industries; the national average is 72 per cent. One in five London employees has a managerial occupation. Patterns of vertical and occupational sectoralisation by sex are well established. Employment data in Table 11.1 indicate that London women were clustered in distribution and catering, banking and finance, and other services which account for over 83 per cent of all women's employment. The comparable figure for Great Britain is 79 per cent. A fluctuating rise in self-employment in London since 1981 is marked by a steady increase in self-employment for women, which is apparently increasing structurally, unrelated to economic cycles, but possibly related to the

Table 11.1: Distribution of Women's Employment by Industrial Sector, Greater London and Great Britain, Including Self-Employment (%)

Industrial Sector	Greater London (%)	Great Britain (%)
Agriculture, Forestry, Fishery, Energy and Water, Housing	1.7	3.3
Manufacturing	7.9	12.2
Construction	1.4	1.5
Distribution and Catering	19.8	24.5
Transport	4.6	3.2
Banking and Finance	21.4	13.3
Other Services	41.9	41.2
Outside UK/Unknown	1.2	0.7
TOTAL N	127 750	1 032 722

Source: Calculated from data supplied by the London Research Centre from 1991 census data (10% sample)

contracting out of local authority functions. Long-term unemployment trends are worse in London than in the country as a whole (*see* Table 11.2). Men are more than twice as likely as women to be unemployed.

However, the unemployment data may conceal some involuntary part-time employment, as women are four times as likely as men to take part-time jobs. One-third of employed women but less than 9 per cent of men in London work

Table 11.2: Unemployment Rates by Sex (February 1995)

	Total (%)	Male (%)	Female (%)
Inner London	16.5	22.1	9.5
Outer London	9.2	12.1	5.3
London	11.5	15.8	6.9
ROSE	6.7	8.9	3.8
Great Britain	8.9	11.9	4.9

Source: London Research Board (ROSE – Rest of South East)

part-time. London pay rates are higher than the national average for both men and women.

Of Londoners in full-time employment, men earned an average of £434.40 per week and women earned £308.60, compared to £341.50 and £243.00 nationally. Such figures are partly accounted for by a concentration of higher paid non-manual jobs in London and higher average levels of qualification of the London workforce. The difference between men's and women's earnings is largely explained by reference to the effects of different occupational status and sector of men's and women's employment.

Gender and the Family

Much of women's employment is in caring services either in the public or private sector. This division of labour is also part of a hierarchy in which women's work is less valued, less visible, and lower paid than men's. In this respect the public sphere replicates the division of labour in the traditional (private) family, understood in feminist theory as the 'primary site for enacting gender and thereby maintaining patriarchy' (Appleton 1995). The traditional heterosexual family of male breadwinner (father/husband), wife/mother, and dependent children is a declining phenomenon in Britain; 25 per cent of all households in 1993 followed this pattern, down from 38 per cent in 1961 (Church 1995). Although family and gender roles continue to be developed around its powerful and pervasive image, the decline of such traditional families is a well-established, long-standing trend. London is at the forefront of this trend. In 1993, 32 per cent of households in London consisted of adults living alone compared to a national average of 27 per cent. About 5.5 per cent of Inner London households were single parent, of which the vast majority, 94 per cent, were female led. Only 34 per cent of Inner London households include one male and one female adult, compared to 49 per cent in England and Wales. More than twice as many London households consist of three or more adults (1.3 per cent) as in England and Wales as a whole (0.5 per cent). In Inner London 32 per cent of females and 35 per cent of males are married; 5.2 per cent of males and 6.9 per cent of females are divorced. The comparable national figures are 47 per cent of males are married, 45 per cent of females are married, 4.3 per cent of males are divorced, and 5.5 per cent of females are divorced. These mixed patterns of variation from the national averages in family statistics indicate the presence of a diverse range of domestic arrangements. They do not, however, mean that Londoners produce fewer children. Fertility rates in London are higher than in the rest of the population. Crude birth rates in 1993 were 16.2 (per 1000 residents) in Inner London, 15.1 in Greater London, and 12.9 in England and Wales. Twenty-nine per cent of live births in Greater London took place outside of marriage; the equivalent figure for England and Wales was 33 per cent.

Gender and the Metropolitan State

London's political system has changed dramatically in the last ten years. From 1963 until 1985, London was run by a single strategic authority, the Greater London Council (GLC), while the delivery of services was run by thirty-three local councils covering geographical sections of the capital. In 1985, the GLC was dismantled by central government and authority devolved to the thirty-three local authorities. Similarly, the Inner London Education Authority (ILEA) that used to control education policy across London was broken up in 1990 and responsibility also devolved to the boroughs. Since that time, a variety of boards, committees, and offices have been created to deal with some London-wide issues, creating a pluralistic and confusing collection of policy-making bodies. Thus, in the post-GLC era, different strategic issue areas exhibit distinctive policy-making arrangements. The 1990s have seen the creation of some more general central bodies with authority over London as a whole, including the Government Office for London, the London Pride Partnership, and a Cabinet Committee for London, the relative responsibilities of which remain unclear.

A second, more recent, change to London's political system has been a succession of centrally directed management initiatives across central and local government, an extreme version of public management change introduced to varying degrees throughout OECD countries throughout the 1980s and 1990s, summarily described as the 'New Public Management.' At the local level, borough councils have been mandated to subject successively larger parts of their work to competitive tender, through the Compulsory Competitive Tendering (CCT) initiative. Even where in-house teams of local authority employees have been successful in winning such contracts, they are compelled to organise themselves in semi-autonomous units known as 'Direct Service Organisations' (DSOs), which are less subject to central control than the traditional arrangements for public service provision.

Here we want to explore the extent to which the resultant policy-making arrangements are gendered, thereby establishing the nature of London's gender system. The reform of London governance after 1986 included two characteristics that are known to be significant to gender systems. First, decentralisation led to a proliferation of authority sites, especially at local and neighbourhood levels. These more numerous, often less hierarchical structures, are thought to be more accessible to women, who are more local in their political interests than men. Mainly because of domestic circumstances, but also because of provision for transport and other urban planning decisions, women are more confined to activities in their immediate localities than are men. Second, we must consider the possibility that 'new public management' changes have not been gender neutral; the removal of large sections of local authority work to the private sector, at a greater organisational distance from central control, might have undermined sex equality strategies introduced during the early 1980s.

Politically, London is a major base of British feminism for three reasons. First, the second wave of feminism in the 1970s and the 1980s was a largely urban phenomenon in Britain and London was one of its main sites of activity and organisation. Second, the GLC, ILEA, and many London boroughs offered institutional bases for feminists who became administrators and local politicians, later forming a pool from which some elites were recruited in the 1990s. Third, as the political and cultural capital, London is home to the headquarters of a large number of national organisations and agencies with an interest in the promotion of sex equality. Feminism rapidly became an acknowledged presence in London and feminists were relatively well placed to take advantage of opportunities offered by radical reform and the restructuring of formerly centralised, hierarchical administratively coordinated structures of power which have shifted, with mixed effects on women's status and on gender relations.

New non-statutory policies to promote the interests and welfare of women were introduced to local authorities during the 1980s, generally promoted by the introduction of women's committees or other similar bodies which Brownhill and Halford (1990) call 'women's initiatives' in local government. Lewisham was the first initiative, a 'Women's Rights Working Party' in 1978; after 1981 the first women's committees were established and by 1988 there were sixty-four such initiatives across the country, with a geographical concentration in Greater London, amounting to 23 per cent of the national total. By the early 1980s the GLC, ILEA, and most London boroughs had adopted some kind of sex equality strategy and had established committees or subcommittees with responsibilities for women's rights both in the authority itself and in the locality. Two-thirds of Inner London and one-third of Outer London boroughs set up initiatives. Over half of all full committees in the country were in London and, with respect to budgets and staffing numbers, London initiatives did well in comparison with the rest of the country (Brownhill and Halford 1990: 399). Half of the initiatives in London had grants budgets ranging from £1500 to £268,000 per year; Camden, one of the earliest to establish a women's committee, had a grants budget which reached a peak of £869,000 in 1987/88. All had an officer support unit of two or more staff and one had twenty-three permanent staff. Such committees had the broad aim of exploring the gender implications of council policies and authority practices (thereby in one place or another addressing almost every conceivable issue). Only a few committees were able to establish such a long reach, generally women's initiatives concentrated on issues relating to the local authority's role as an employer and on influencing the delivery of remedies for domestic violence at local level (Abrar 1996). In general, women's committees were more feminist and more radical than equal opportunities committees and the most extensive programmes were devised in authorities with both types of committees.[2]

It was not women councillors *per se* who were responsible for such initiatives: 'it is rather *feminist* councillors who are the prime movers of change' (Brownhill and Halford 1990). Feminist councillors were almost exclusively associated with the Labour Party. And feminist officers were appointed to posts in the newly created women's units, providing evidence of 'femocrat' type arrangements at the local level similar to that prevalent at the central level in Australia (Watson 1990; Eisenstein 1985) but persistently absent from the central level in the UK (Watson 1995).

The drive to institutionalise sex equality concerns into English local authorities slowed significantly by the end of the 1980s. Their political support had always been weak. Although established by Labour-controlled councils, women's committees rarely had the unanimous support of Labour groups (Lovenduski and Randall 1993: chap. 5). By the beginning of the 1990s Labour was distinctly unenthusiastic about women's initiatives, due to the reputation for being excessively discriminatory in favour of women that some equal opportunities units had developed in the press during the 1980s, notably in Islington and Lambeth. Regardless of whether such reputations were deserved, the units were undoubtedly the subject of repeated controversy. Non-feminist councillors resented the use of public funds to resource women's interest groups, arguing that such groups were not representative of the community as a whole. There were other disagreements amongst feminists over the use of state funds at all. And local government cutbacks of the late 1980s allowed previously quiescent councillors openly to oppose women's committees on grounds of financial prudence. By 1994 only two women's committees remained in London boroughs, their functions either lost or subsumed in a much diluted form into the terms of reference of equal opportunities committees with responsibility for race, disability, class, etc.

A second threat to sex equality strategies has been the radical changes to public management of public service provision, noted earlier. There is evidence that CCT at the local level has generated what the Equal Opportunities Commission (EOC) calls a 'contract culture,' in which it is easier for hours or jobs to be cut and terms and conditions of service to be altered. Across all services there has been increased use of part-time workers on short hours. Such changes seem to have affected women more than men and previous differences in men's and women's pay have been exacerbated. Many female part-time jobs have been lost in areas where men's have increased, while in other jobs hours and pay have been reduced.[3]

When work is contracted out to private sector providers, the only way that a local authority can guard sex equality in working conditions or influence the way that the staff carrying out the work are recruited, promoted, or paid would be by specifying that the successful tenderer must operate an equal opportunities policy. However, they are prevented by law from making such stipulations. Equal opportunities are designated 'non- commercial' matters in the Local Government Act of 1988 and restrictions are placed on their inclusion in the CCT process. In general the implementation of equal opportunities policies in local authorities has traditionally rested with equal opportunities units and the EOC found that the majority of equal opportunities officers did not initially participate in the CCT process. A combination of the legislative framework for CCT, failure to understand the CCT process, and the structure of local authorities accounted for this lack of involvement. These factors have combined to produce a situation where CCT officers responsible for the tendering process have usually not sought the involvement of equal opportunities officers; likewise, equal opportunities units have often chosen not to be involved in CCT. As a result, the EOC concluded that equal opportunities were accorded 'no significance' in the preparation of contracts. For those contracts awarded to private sector contractors, sex equality in public services provision becomes reliant on the equal opportunities policies of the contract providers. Initial findings by the EOC suggested that local public service-providing contractors tended to have equal opportunities statements but little commitment and they did not monitor employment. Evidence from interviews carried out since the EOC report was published in 1995 suggests that some equal opportunities units are starting to become involved in contract specification by pressing for the 'quality conditions' clause to be included in contracts. This clause allows contract managers to insist upon a workforce that contains the same gender mix as the client group in some areas where the sex of service providers is deemed to affect the quality of service. But this exception to the restrictions applies only to areas where the client group is largely women.

With respect to in-house providers, central personnel departments and equal opportunities units have far less influence over DSOs than they had over the more homogeneous local authority workforces of the past. As one official put it, 'departments do not want a central unit overseeing their work, they would rather just do it themselves.' Incentives for DSOs to introduce equal opportunities policies are small; better working conditions entail expenditure which can jeopardise an in-house bid and equal opportunities policies are often viewed as an expensive luxury when failure to win a bid means extensive job loss. The EOC found that in only two out of thirty-nine local authorities studies were equality targets set and progress of the DSOs regularly monitored (EOC 1995). In local authorities where all in-house bids have been successful, it can be possible to re-establish the authority of equal opportunities policies; Coyle (1995) describes one such inner London authority which successfully employed such a strategy. But overall, it seems that the implementation of CCT has occasioned a distinct step backwards from the policies implemented by local authorities during the 1980s. As one official put it, CCT represented a barricading in of remaining male hierarchies, whereby men formed a higher proportion of the elite that were left when lower layers have disappeared.

Nevertheless, women's committees left an important institutional residue. There is evidence to suggest that the sex equality units introduced during the 1980s did to some extent achieve their objectives, although there was and is a wide variation across boroughs. The committees were instrumental in establishing sex equality policies in a large number of local authorities (Stone 1988; Edwards 1989).

They share the credit for the reputation of local authorities in the 1980s, as 'model equal opportunities employers' (Lovenduski 1989) and were credited with being women-friendly employers during the 1990s (Coyle 1995). However, this inheritance was not secure. Monitoring the acid test of equality policy was often poor and inconsistent, programmes were under threat, and core funding was repeatedly slashed. In the mid-1990s equal opportunities was a delicate area, an easy target for anti-'political correctness' campaigns. By that time, its advocates had learned new ways of dressing and disguising their initiatives, for example in one (Conservative) borough the positive action training for women in management was changed to 'personal awareness development' in order (in the words of the senior training manager) 'to keep the show on the road.'

To summarise, London's gender system features a small but significant establishment of feminism in the reorganised local state, a replacement of male by female employment and several kinds of shifts away from the traditional family. This pattern supports Appleton's account of changing gender relations in some central cities. It is reasonable to surmise that London offers alternatives to traditional ideologies about how men and women should act. Extensive subcultures of unmarried people and individual-based life styles offer a significant counterweight to familism as the ideology of adulthood (Appleton 1995: 47). Thriving feminist and gay communities reinforce social trends which are destructive of private patriarchy and offer a social and political base for groups likely to contest it.

Gender and London Governance

Movement from private to public bases of patriarchy in London was not inevitable. Feminist political pressure and organisation have affected institutions and policies. From the early 1980s London feminists sought to increase the representation of women using a mix of formal and informal strategies to promote women, and especially feminists, into elite positions in the local state. In the remainder of this article we assess the effects of these strategies in some detail. First, we describe local authority employment patterns, examining variations in local authority structures that are not revealed by the discussion of formal change provided above. After the break-up of the GLC and the removal of formal authority from the centre to the boroughs, differences were reinforced, fragmenting the gender system. Second, we look at the influence of those interest groups and voluntary organisations which direct their activities specifically towards women-centred policies; what we loosely term the 'women's movement' of London. Third, we examine the London-wide policy-making arrangements for two strategic issue areas, homelessness and hospital reorganisation, to illustrate the relationships between policy outcomes and the gender mix of policy actors.

Gender Mix of the Local State

Table 11.3 shows that while women's presence in the very highest levels of local bureaucracies is extremely low, the higher incidence of women's committees,

Table 11.3: Women Departmental Directors, England and Wales, 1993

Women Directors	London	County	MDCs	Other	Total
Total no.	32	47	73	296	448
Percentage of total that are women:					
Chief executives	13	2	3	2	3
Finance	0	0	0	1	1
Education	22	13	7	n/a	12
Housing	3	n/a	0	4	3
Social services	22	9	4	n/a	9
Economic	6	4	3	4	4

Source: Tickell and Peck (1995)

equal opportunities committees, and sex equality strategies in London government may have had an effect. London compares well with the rest of the country in terms of women's presence at the highest levels of the executive. But Table 11.3 also demonstrates strong sectoral differences, showing finance and housing administration to be areas where women's participation at the most senior levels is especially low.

In terms of gender representation in elected members of councils, London also compares well with the rest of the country. Table 11.4 shows how the percentage of council members of women has changed over the twenty years between 1974 and 1994.

Tables 11.5 and 11.6 display data concerning the gender mix of legislative and executive elites of seven London boroughs, using the database from the Metropolitan Governance and Community Study (MGCS). Legislative elites consist of committee chairs and vice-chairs, plus the leader and deputy leader of the opposition parties; executive elites consist of directors, deputy directors, and head officers. The tables also show 'media reputational' scores for the elites; that is, the names of actors were entered into the FT Profile[4] database for the year 1992–93 and a count made of all articles mentioning the actor for the period. Thus, the scores give an approximation of the amount of media coverage an actor received, but must be used with caution as such scores do not indicate whether the publicity was good or bad.

Tables 11.5 and 11.6 indicate that the highest levels of local government executives are partly feminised, more so than the legislatures. Table 11.5 shows men's and women's shares of the executive elite for all seven boroughs, indicating a wide variation across the boroughs. While five authorities have

Table 11.4: Members of Council Across Eight London Boroughs, 1974–94

	Council Members 1992: Elected Members		Committee Chairs	Council Members 1974: Elected Members	
	% women	total N	% women	% women	total N
Westminster	35	60	29	19	70
Wandsworth	34	61	44	21	70
Islington	33	52	25	21	70
Lambeth	30	64	25	14	70
Tower Hamlets	28	50	20	17	70
Croydon	27	70	0	17	70
Barking	21	48	8	22	54
Hillingdon	13	69	17	13	70

Source: Municipal Yearbook and data provided by local authority information offices

Table 11.5: Executive Elites Across Seven Boroughs, 1992–93

	Female				Male	
	No.	%	Profile Score	Average Profile Score	Profile Score	Average Profile Score
Tower Hamlets	4	33	4	1	9	1
Lambeth	2	29	2	1	10	2
Islington	4	19	4	1	8	1
Hillingdon	1	9	2	2	9	1
Westminster	1	9	0	0	16	2
Wandsworth	1	7	0	0	8	1
Croydon	1	5	0	0	2	0

Source: MGCS Database
Note: Executive Elites include Chief Executives, Directorate Heads and Head Officers

Table 11.6: Total Executive and Legislative Policy Elites Across Seven Boroughs, 1992–93

	Female				Male	
	No.	%	Profile Score	Average Profile Score	Profile Score	Average Profile Score
Westminster	22	31	67	3.0	496	9.9
Wandsworth	23	29	12	0.5	679	12.1
Lambeth	23	29	47	2.0	147	2.7
Islington	21	28	35	1.7	166	3.0
Tower Hamlets	15	25	7	0.5	60	1.3
Croydon	21	23	1	0.0	37	0.5
Hillingdon	10	12	2	0.2	64	0.9

Source: MGCS Database
Note: Executive Elites include Directors and Deputy Directors. Legislative Elites include Council Leader and Deputy Leader, Committee Chairs and Deputy Chairs and Leader and Deputy Leader of the Opposition Parties

less than 10 per cent of directors and head officers who are female, for three the percentage is considerably more respectable and Tower Hamlets heads the table with 33 per cent. The tables show that where there are women at the highest level, there is little difference between the amount of press coverage they receive in comparison with men. However, it should be noted that, in general, executive officers of local authorities receive very little publicity in the national press. Notably, the highest profile female executive officers have been appointed to take over local authorities that have undergone a period of crisis; the acting and permanent chief executives of the beleaguered Lambeth Council in the 1990s were both women; the eventual permanent Chief Executive, Heather Rabbats, had previously been appointed by Merton Council to carry out extensive reform.

Table 11.6 shows the complete legislative and executive elite, by sex for the seven London boroughs, showing all legislative members, directors and deputy directors. Women's share of elite positions in six of the seven boroughs clusters around the 25 per cent level, with Hillingdon markedly lower. The reputational data also demonstrates a gender bias, with the average profile score for female elite members consistently lower than that for men, an illustration of how even where women have made it to the highest echelons of London governance, their stock of the reputational resource remains lower than that of their male counterparts.

Although the above tables show the seven authorities exhibit a bias in favour of men at elite levels, there are pockets of high status women both across and within local authorities. Such phenomena may be explained by organisational change either in a locality or a functional area. Two related examples illustrate this point: Tower Hamlets and the reorganisation of the Inner London Education Authority (ILEA). Tower Hamlets appears at the top of Table 11.5, which shows the executive elites of the seven boroughs. In addition, a considerable number of women have made it to the rung just below the top level in this authority. By 1994, of all the London Authorities, Tower Hamlets had the greatest number of female chief officers and the largest percentage of female councillors. Interviews with officials revealed interesting differences in the working environment since the onset of this phenomenon, corroborating existing evidence that when a critical mass of women is present in an organisation, real change occurs. The acting chief executive commented:

> It is a joy I think to work in an organisation that has such a strong female led culture. In fact I often say that Tower Hamlets is a borough run by women … there is a deputy leader of the council and two of the main service chairs are women. The principal of the local Tower Hamlets college is a woman and so is the chief executive of the Training and Enterprise Council who we work with very closely. And just generally, wherever Tower Hamlets appears, wherever we go to meetings you can always be sure to meet lots of senior women.

Tower Hamlets reflects what appears to be a more general rule, that women have been most successful in penetrating senior or higher levels after some organisational rupture or the implementation of some unorthodox organisational arrangement. Such change followed the Liberal period of rule between 1986 and 1994. Under Liberal rule Tower Hamlets was broken up into fiercely autonomous neighbourhoods. Reorganisation removed the power of directorate heads. Real authority was given to Neighbourhood Chiefs, who were, bar one, all women. When the Liberals lost power, the powerful Neighbourhood fiefdoms were dismantled and the former advisors were confirmed as directors of the new departments.

Another example of this phenomenon is the break-up of ILEA, an organisational fissure which created the opportunity to appoint female Chief Education Officers. Women from a variety of backgrounds, but significantly from the teaching profession, were appointed to a number of these new posts. Once there, they acted as catalysts for other female appointments across the country. The reorganisation of ILEA created thirty-two new education CEOs. The expansion increased the number of women CEOs overnight; there were eighteen female Chief Education Officers by 1992. It was easier for politicians to appoint women as there were no male-dominated bureaucratic structures in place to resist the placement of women in leadership positions. The new appointees set up their own departments and structures from scratch: 'There was nobody to resent me being brought in over and above them because there was nobody here. I was appointed, then I had to set the authority up.' It is notable that the ILEA culture had also prepared the ground for the acceptance of women into senior positions in London; there were strong feminist currents within the organisation; many schools were headed by women. As one interviewee remarked, 'I can really remember in ILEA, for a period of time, white men really felt under pressure. They really thought that if they went for a job they would not get it.'

Other variations in women's occupation of senior roles are attributable to sector. Women have been much less successful at gaining elite positions in some functional areas than others (*see* Table 11.3). For example, there were only two female chief finance officers in London in 1993. Interviewees described the London Society of Treasurers as the 'male and masonic network of finance officers,' comparing its behaviour and attitudes to 'the competitiveness and pack mentality of young male professionals in the treasury department of the GLC.' The same is true of SOLACE, the group for Chief Executives. The lack of women at the highest levels means that professional elite networks tend to be almost exclusively male. In housing, a less male-dominated area, some male directors have a long-standing clique and do not share information with newcomers, 'especially if they are women.' Similarly, the main professional network for education, the Society for Education Officers, was described as 'a longstanding bastion of chauvinism.'

Inevitably, elite women began to construct their own networks. The higher presence of women in the education area allowed one female director to set up a Conference of Chief Education Officers as an alternative network, comprising all Chief Education Officers but able to secure greater representation for women on its executive board. One female acting Chief Executive belongs to an action group, a subset of Chief Executives, and this subset works in a different way, with a facilitator, meeting quarterly, with some part of the day to be taken up in considering a management case study or some piece of management theory for discussion. The Women in Local Government Network was set up to help 'shift the focus from survival to success' (*Municipal Review and AMA News*, June 1991), after a meeting in Greenwich in January 1988 for senior women managers in local authorities to discuss issues of common concern. Membership is open to any woman working in a local authority or related organisation who feels herself to be in a position to influence decision-making and bring about change. Most of the members work in London and the South East; time and travel restraints mean that it is more practicable for several regional networks to develop. Self-organisation by women as they work their way into and up through local elites has been an important factor in the feminisation of London governance. The feminisation of London elites has been a matter of organisation and opportunity, a combination of political mobilisation and the creation of a supply of able women. As we have shown, change was facilitated by institutional restructuring and political opportunity; gradually a supply of 'qualified' women was developed who were appointable to elite positions. But demand factors have also been important, particularly where old institutions and politics failed. In such circumstances women normally have the advantage of bearing no responsibility for previous errors.

The Women's Movement in London

In addition to the gender mix of policy-making elites, a gender system may be influenced by the extent to which an autonomous women's movement exists in the city. The presence of groups which exist entirely to promote issues concerning women, to deliver services to women, or to campaign for policy change that specifically affects women will tend to influence the extent to which gender struggles take place in the public realm. We use the phrase 'women's movement' loosely to incorporate all those voluntary organisations and pressure groups that fall into the following categories. First, groups whose membership is restricted to women. Second, those groups whose client group is largely female. Using this classification, it is possible to identify a constellation of gender-specific organisations which endeavour to influence policy making and service-delivery in London. Some of these groups are the headquarters of national organisations (such as the National Council of Women of Great Britain) which are based in London by virtue of it being the capital; in this sense London is the epicentre of whatever autonomous women's movement exists in Britain. It makes no sense, in London, to distinguish between national and local groups. Women's groups tend to undertake a wide range of functions, carrying out campaigning and lobbying activities as well as service provision and maintaining memberships. Therefore many national groups that are based in London play a distinctive role within the capital in addition to their national activities.

Most of London women's movement activity takes place across an archipelago of different functional and sectoral areas. There are a large number of groups related to family and welfare and another subset centred around health. The women's units of the political parties at borough level and sections of some trade unions, especially those related to education, are extremely active. Sector-specific groups are organised around the institutions they intend to influence. There are church-based groups, for example, such as the Mother's Union. There are groups attached to various professions, such as Women in Banking, the Women Engineers Society, and the Medical Women's Federation. There are what might be described as 'second wave' feminist groups, such as rape crisis groups and Women's Aid. There is a more diffuse network of women working in sex equality (the 'equal ops' network) based around local authorities, private firms, the professions, and the women's sections of trade unions. In addition to national and metro-level groups, there are a large number of organisations operating at the micro-local level, such as those offering consciousness-raising, assertiveness training, self-help, or women-only gyms or sports clubs. Finally there are international groups such as the European Union funded 'European Network of Women,' which has a London branch.

The above groups are linked loosely together by membership in a variety of umbrella organisations, for example, the National Alliance of Women's Organisations and the Standing Conference of Women's Organisations and the Women's National Commission (a government advisory body). Another such organisation is the Fawcett Society, a direct descendant of the women's suffrage movement which has a unique status as a membership and campaigning organisation concerned with all women-specific political issues. The Society acts as a facilitator, identifying sector specific groups for especial lobbying causes and organising the lobbying effort across London. Thus, for example, the Fawcett Society brought the Lewisham Older Women's Project, the Women's Institute, and various single issue organisations together to lobby on pensions. They initiated the Child Benefit Coalition which brings together, *inter alia*, the Maternity Alliance and the Mothers Union. Thus a central aim of the Fawcett Society is to coordinate the lobbying effort, rather than to gain publicity for itself.

For various reasons it is increasingly hard in the 1990s to talk of *the* London Women's Movement as a single entity. In part, fragmentation came during the 1980s with the growing of subdivisions of the feminist movements. The effects of the rise of Black feminism, identified as a cause of the fragmentation of the Women's Movement in the 1980s, were especially severe in inner London, where the percentage of black women (25 per cent) is much higher than the percentage in Great Britain as a whole (5 per cent). Also, in London there was an early and high concentration of groups such as Camden Black Sisters, Southall Black Sisters, and the Brixton Black Women's group. In the list of fifteen women's groups funded by the London Borough Grants Committee in 1993, seven related to ethnic groups.

London's women's groups, in comparison with the London 'pressure group world,' are notable for their lack of three out of the four resources considered by Dowding (1991, 1996) to contribute to actors' bargaining capacity when seeking power: authority, reputation, money, and information/expertise. The principal organisation with authority and a brief to consider women's position in Britain as a whole is the government funded quango, the EOC, but the EOC is based in Manchester and maintains only a small publicity office in London. Most of those organisations falling into our classification of the London women's movement operate outside the boundaries of the state and few possess any statutory authority at all. The principal exception is the Women's National Commission, which has authority in its role as an advisory committee to the government and is co-headed by a government minister but receives limited funding and remarkably little publicity. Before 1994, the Equal Opportunities Division of the Cabinet Office had central controlling powers over equal opportunities across central government departments, but in 1994 after the delegation of pay and personnel procedures announced in the White Paper *Taking Forward Continuity and Change*, such authority was devolved to departments and the division's role subsequently consisted of monitoring and guidance. The only other organisations with statutory authority are the equal opportunities division of the Department for Education and Employment and equal opportunities units of local authorities, but as the previous section illustrated, such authority is declining in the 1990s. With respect to money, women's groups exist on extremely small budgets and staff allowances, relying heavily on volunteers. Of the 250 organisations identified in 1992–93, only ten had more than ten staff.

With respect to reputation, the activities of women's groups receive low levels of press coverage in comparison with other organisations. Table 11.7, showing the number of articles mentioning both London and the name of the organisation in the year July 1992 to July 1993, indicates just how little press attention women's pressure groups receive. The lack of attention is especially notable given that such reputation as women's groups do receive is probably concentrated in London. Most publicity is good publicity, although sardonic accounts of recent women's networking activities are clearly negative. While men's elite networks are taken for granted, the press respond to accounts of women's networking organisations with comments like 'women don't socialise anymore, they network,' the *Independent's* response to the organisation 'Network,' which exists to maintain a forum in which successful women can develop professional and social contacts and has a membership of 800 senior women mangers. Many groups lie dormant in the eyes of the media for many years, receiving publicity only when their issue hits the national agenda, for example, organisations campaigning to retain current legislation on abortion. Women's groups show remarkable ability to organise, seemingly from nowhere, when the need arises. Such an ability is neatly evidenced by the high level of publicity received by the Movement for the Ordination of Women and Women Against the Ordination of Women, which both came to prominence when the ordination of women came under heavy discussion during 1992–93. Table 11.7 is equally interesting for those organisations that do not appear in it. There are around 250 gender-specific organisations in London, affiliated to the Women's National Alliance or listed by the Women's National Commission, that received no publicity at all, and another ninety that received between zero and eight mentions. Important organisations with statutory authority such as the Sex Equality Branch of the Department of Employment, gain no mention at all. The Women's Unit of the National Health Service, much plaudited by the publicity of Opportunity 2000, received only five.

The exception to the rule that any publicity is good publicity is provided by the experiences of local equal opportunities units, especially Islington, whose Women's Equality Unit received a barrage of bad publicity during the late 1980s and early 1990s. Stories of 'lesbian gym mats' constantly recur[5] ('journalists are lazy,' as one interviewee put it), meaning that the Unit must keep looking for 'banana skins' and has to make an effort to keep the Unit out of the press rather than seeking publicity, a reversal of the normal public relations role. Staff of the Unit try, however, to continue with their normal work in the face of such publicity:

> There are certain issues that I would be more careful now about how we write about them, but I am kept a bit more radical than I am by people around me which is good and members want to be on the whole. They do not want to run away from the key issues, we have to remind ourselves that a lot of the time quite establishment groups do way out issues and no one says anything about it. It's just when a local authority does them they get laughed at.

Table 11.7: Reputational View of Women's Groups, July 1992 to July 1993

Group Name	Profile Score	Group Name	Profile Score
Refuge	43	Bereavement Care (CRUSE)	13
Royal College of Nursing	74	British Pregnancy Advisory Service	13
Opportunity 2000	40	Parents at Work	12
Church Army	34	Women's Environmental Network	12
Family Planning Association	33	Hackney Council Women's Unit	11
Suzy Lamplugh Trust	31	London Women's Centre	11
Foundation for Study of Infant Deaths	27	Maternity Alliance	11
Girl Guides Association	27	National Childbirth Trust	11
NUCPS (Women's Section)	27	Spare Rib	11
National Council for One Parent Families	19	Morden Women's Group	10
Royal College of Midwives	18	Pre-School Playgroups' Association	10
Southall Black Sisters	18	REUNITE	10
Women in Management	18	Carers' National Association	9
Relate (National Marriage Guidance)	17	National Federation Women's Institutes	9
Brook Advisory Centres	15	Emily's List UK	8
Mothers Union	15	Fawcett Society	8
Movement for the Ordination of Women	15	Girls' Brigade	8
Working Mothers Association	15	Women Against Pit Closures	8
300 Group	14	Women Against Rape	8
Women Against Ordination of Women	14		

Note: The table shows all organisations scoring 8 or more. Excluded from this table are more general charities and trade unions which, although affiliated to women's umbrella organisations, are not gender specific.

In contrast to authority, reputation and money, feminist groups do possess information and expertise, often gathered over a long period of time, which is called upon in times of crisis within male-dominated elites. Central groups perform vital networking activities, drawing resources together for specific campaign issues and carrying out consistent but low-profile activity over a sustained period of time. An example of such a strategy where specifically feminist groups have had an influence on a crucial policy area is domestic violence, where in localised areas, such as Islington, loss of legitimacy by the traditionally dominant policy-making body, the Metropolitan Police, created a perceived need for feminist expertise and information regarding strategies for dealing with domestic violence (Lovenduski and Randall 1993; Abrar 1996). Feminists operating both inside and outside the boundaries of the state appear to have acted as an advocacy coalition (Sabatier and Jenkins-Smith 1993), affecting policies in specific locations and at particular periods of time. Although possessing few resources, such groups (particularly when they carry out some kind of service delivery function, as for domestic violence) tend to develop a sustainable professionalised base which in turn plays a campaigning role when necessary.

Finally, such resources that women's organisations do possess are concentrated on key areas, with even those organisations with different primary objectives still devoting some effort to particular issues, such as sex equality and domestic violence. Of one hundred organisations coded along key characteristics under the Gender and New Urban Governance project, 58 per cent made some attempt to deal with sex equality and 23 per cent were concerned in some way with overcoming domestic violence. Thus, it seems that the constellation of women's groups, although lacking in resources, acts as a funnel of activity, bringing in such resources that do exist from all directions, and concentrating them upon areas of priority.

Gender and Urban Policies

To what extent do alternative visions of women's and men's roles characterise policy making in London? This question is best answered through an account of two major urban policy issues of the early 1990s: homelessness and hospital reorganisation. For these issues we raise two questions concerning gender. First, is (or should) the policy be 'gender sensitive'; is the client group predominantly female (such as issues concerning childcare) or wholly female (such as women's health)? Second, are the officials and professionals working in the policy area biased towards either sex and/or influenced by feminist ideas?

Homelessness

The extent to which metropolitan issues are perceived as gendered varies greatly across issues. The gender dimensions of some issues may remain latent for some time, emerging only when organisations or individuals intervene to make them explicit, for example, homelessness. Homelessness offers an interesting example of how gender dimensions of urban policy may become explicit when divisions of gender and divisions of organisations occur along the same fault lines. Homelessness, as a problem, is perceived as almost wholly male. Media attention focuses on homeless men, while the dangers specific to women of living on the streets, often in equally bleak situations, keep them out of sight and the limelight. Yet homelessness is a gendered issue, not least because women with children have particular housing needs and rights. Women become homeless for a variety of reasons which may be qualitatively different to those of men. Women's homelessness is often the result of domestic violence, sexual abuse and, most notably, low income. Women are consequently more dependent on the provision of adequate public sector housing. Although the 1977 Homeless Persons Act imposed a duty on local authorities to house women with children, single women, even those who have experienced violence, are not priority categories. Women's homelessness is frequently referred to as the 'hidden problem' (Dibblin 1990; Sexty 1990). Although agencies report equal numbers of women and men making enquiries (in fact, housing aid centres in the London area say that 70 per cent of their initial enquiries come from young women, Dibblin 1990), fewer women than men are visibly homeless. This difference is partly due to safety considerations, which prevent women choosing the streets as an option; hostel provision for women is considerably less than that available for men. One study showed that less than one in eight bedspaces in London hostels were women-only hostels, a calculation that included women's refuges (Eardley 1989; quoted in Sexty 1990). Many of the spaces available are in mixed hostels, which women find stressful and unsafe — women are vulnerable to sexual harassment and abuse (Sexty 1990: 53).

The latent gendered characteristics of homelessness became manifest because of the presence of women in some of the organisations with responsibility for the issue. However, a feminisation (and feminist predominance) of the voluntary sector dealing with homelessness was not reflected by similar feminisation of the housing sector public bureaucracy. During the 1980s, the voluntary sector was able to press women's claims, but in the tougher climate of the 1990s masculine bias in local authority housing departments proved to be a decisive barrier to the servicing of women's interests. All British local authorities have a statutory duty to house women with children, defined as homeless under the 1985 Housing Act. Women's need in the housing sector was perceived as an issue during the 1980s and women's issues were prominent at the 1987 conference for International Year of Shelter. Various client groups in the housing area have high proportions of women, such as low income earners, single parents and the elderly. Differential access to housing has been a widespread concern. For example, Shelter produced numerous publications up to 1990 detailing women's particular lack of access to housing. The National Federation of Housing Associations also held an annual conference on the issue.

Interest was stimulated partly by a number of feminists operating in decision-making capacities in the voluntary sector. The comparatively high commitment to equal opportunities in the voluntary sector and a number of posts devoted to women's issues attracted a number of overt feminists. Sheila McKechnie

(Director of Shelter) and June McKerrow (Director of Stonham and trustee for Shelter), for example, are both feminists, the former with a long history in the women's liberation movement networks. By contrast to the housing officers in local authorities, all interviewed in the homelessness voluntary sector were feminists. Moreover, the major feminist actors had informal feminist networks. Organisations in the voluntary sector, for example Centrepoint and Shelter, have good representation of women at all levels, after dramatically improving the representativeness of their workforce in the 1980s through the implementation of equal opportunities in recruitment. Being a woman became a positive advantage. The predominance of women in the voluntary sector together with the rapid growth of the sector itself means that there are few traditionally male networks.

The large number of women in senior positions in voluntary homelessness organisations does not extend throughout the housing sector to housing associations or local authority housing departments. In housing associations, although 63 per cent of the staff are women, only 24 per cent of senior posts are occupied by women. In local authorities there are few female housing directors (*see* Table 11.3). In contrast to the voluntary sector, these elite networks are male dominated. Both housing directors of local authorities and heads of housing associations have well-established male social and professional networks. For example, for the chief executives of housing associations: 'We have a Chief Executives' Conference, all the Chief Executives from all the housing associations come once a year. You have never seen so many grey suits in your life. You can't organise a disco afterwards because there are so many men!'

Thus organisationally the policy elite of housing and homelessness consists of two groups, with the housing workers predominantly male, the homelessness workers predominantly female. The gender mix reinforces an existing bifurcation, in which housing workers are paid more and the homelessness people regarded as junior partners. 'There is a matey, sort of Housing Association director network, you weren't allowed to belong to it if you worked for a homelessness agency.' Such a distinction originates from the 1980s: 'Housing associations adopted some of the attitudes of the local authorities in the 1980s and said what were we to do, what were we doing, who were these little voluntary groups that buzzed around talking to Cabinet Ministers. Clearly for anyone earning £80,000 that was their job.' The 'little voluntary groups' such as Shelter and Centrepoint are now massive organisations with large budgets and more statutory authority than previously, but the distinction remains, reinforced by gender differences.

In the early 1990s, as budget cuts hit the whole housing/homelessness sector, there was a decline in interest in women as a specific client group by the homelessness agencies. There was a recognition that central government was not receptive to lobbying for sectional groups. After 1990, the idea that single mothers, who as single parents had priority in terms of local authority housing, were 'parasites on the state' gained currency in the tabloid press and among Tory politicians. Even feminists such as Sheila McKechnie felt that in a climate where housing for all groups was declining, arguing about the particular merits of one group over another was counterproductive and missing the point: 'They got into this syndrome of the feminist hierarchies, you know, lesbian and single parent, disabled, preferably black, you know, and I actually stood up and thought the roof was going to fall in on me, and said "I am fed up with listening to you lot — it is a bit like shifting the chairs around on the *Titanic*. The bloody *Titanic* is sinking, when will you get your brains round how power actually works".'

Funding for homelessness in London received a boost in 1992 through the Rough Sleepers Initiative, a government-funded scheme which initially ran for three years from 1990 to 1993 at a cost of £96 million and was extended subsequently for another three years with another £86 million funding. Although the initiative provided a strong thrust towards dealing with the highly visible problem of rough sleepers, it involved a move from core funding to project funding that affected women's initiatives adversely. The Rough Sleepers Initiative excluded voluntary sector actors who were not London-centred or sought to provide long-term accommodation. Special needs housing associations, such as Stonham, were hit by the withdrawal of core funding in the form of Deficit Grants and Special Needs streams. They therefore set up an alternative network to the Rough Sleepers Initiative called 'CITRA.' Other members were Women's Aid, Homes for Homeless People, and Scottish Homes. The reduction in funding for the special needs lobby impacted badly on women, particularly on refuge funding for victims of domestic violence. Despite the increasing reputation of the domestic violence problem during the late 1980s, the government was able to reduce rather than increase funds directed towards housing problems in this area. The Rough Sleepers Initiative provided major benefits to the crisis relief agencies dealing with visible homelessness, but rough sleepers are largely a male phenomenon. Due to issues of personal safety and the close connection of prostitution with women's street homelessness, women were less likely to be on the streets and therefore to benefit from this money. Thus the policy indirectly discriminated against homeless women whose circumstances may have been similar to men's except that they did not choose to live on the streets. For these reasons, some feminists campaigned against the initiative: Louise Casey and Julia Unwin were vocal feminists who were heavily involved in the Homeless Network, which worked on the campaign against the Rough Sleepers Initiative. However, it is also evident that when funding was received via the Rough Sleepers Initiative, staff in voluntary organisations tried to be sensitive to women's needs in the ways in which it was spent. For example, disparities in temporary hostel provisions for men and women in London were redressed through the Rough Sleepers Initiative.

Voluntary sector organisations campaigning on homelessness take up women's issues when they see them as pertinent. Lobbying specifically on women's homelessness and housing needs largely disappeared in the 1990s, until the White Paper proposal for revised housing duties for local authorities in 1995. The London Housing Unit considered gender in their response, recognising that women and domestic violence victims stood to lose out. Earlier in the year, proposals to put single mothers in hostels were blocked by Centrepoint, primarily by demonstrating to civil servants that this policy would be a more expensive option than the current benefits system. The media have continued to focus on men on the streets, although the voluntary homelessness organisations have made some recent efforts to alter that perception, for example, in August 1995 the *Big Issue* and various organisations ran a 'What Women Want' campaign.

Hospital Reorganisation

The reorganisation of London's hospital services is another policy issue area which appears initially to be 'gender neutral.' This reorganisation was heralded by the publication of the Tomlinson Report in 1992, which worked on the premiss that London had a disproportionate number of beds in comparison with the rest of the country. The report advocated the closure of several major London hospitals and a reorganisation of many key services among the remaining institutions. Of all the 329 press articles which mentioned the Tomlinson Report in 1992 to 1993, none mentioned specifically women-centred or gendered issues. But in reality, there are many gender-demarcated strands running through the issue. The Tomlinson recommendations represented a continuation of the policy to move provision away from hospitals and on to general practitioners, resulting in an overall reduction in the number of hospital beds. This shift was promoted as beneficial to women; by far the larger proportion of users of GPs' services are women. But many commentators believed that the apparent expansion in funding of general practitioners was illusory; such services had been severely underfunded before. Reorganisation of primary health care provision in conjunction with the closure of alternative services at hospital level affects women as the main users of health services, both for themselves and their children. The closure of hospitals such as St. Bartholemews meant that women, often non-car owners, were travelling further for emergency services. The Queen Elizabeth Hospital for Children was one of the hospitals targeted under the Tomlinson Report and the Elizabeth Garrett Anderson Hospital in Bloomsbury, London's last hospital for women, was also targeted, the last battle of a twenty-year war to keep the hospital open reportedly saved only by the personal intervention of the Queen with Margaret Thatcher in the 1980s. Women's health is an area with a women-only client group, with a large number of reasonably high profile national groups operating from London (especially relating to pregnancy; *see* Table 11.7). The size of the NHS and the sex composition of health service workers is a policy issue in itself, with the NHS as a whole employing over one million people, of whom around 76 per cent are women, the biggest employer of women in Western Europe (Coyle 1995: 30). Women make up 90 per cent of nurses and midwives, 74 per cent of ancillary staff, 84 per cent of clerical and administrative grades, and 88 per cent of Professions Allied to Medicine *(ibid.*: 31). Women are underrepresented in management and at senior levels of the profession; men hold more than a third of nursing officer posts. The nursing profession consists of around 80 per cent women. However, the top jobs are performed by around 80 per cent men.

Yet, groups lobbying specifically on women's issues did not feature in the press coverage of the Tomlinson Report between July 1992 and July 1993. Women's health groups seem to focus on medical techniques and women's health rather than service provision; for example, they are concerned about cancer treatment and diagnosis techniques rather than the length of time spent waiting for cancer treatment. Family health service delivery is locally organised with little lobbying activity, which is left to the national groups. There are exceptions, organisations that show concern about service provision, but they tend to be fragmented. The World Health Organisation tries to establish a network of 'Health for All' groups across authorities, which works across sectors and across agencies to promote health in a given locality. One such example is the Islington Healthy 2000 group, with five staff, funding from Islington Council and Health Authorities, and the addressing of inequality issues within health as one of its four key objectives. Together with Islington Women's Equality Unit and the local Community Health Council, Health 2000 forms a Women's Health Forum which tries to bring some women-specific issues to the attention of policy makers. For example, when the Elizabeth Garrett Anderson Hospital was targeted for closure, and the new service proposed by University College Hospital was to deal with maternity and pregnancy termination in the same unit, they pointed out that this combination would be extremely unhelpful for some women. Such groups exist to varying degrees throughout London, although not all relate specifically to a local authority area. Camden has a similar arrangement to Islington and the two units work closely together, as they share some health resources. In other authorities different strategies are pursued; Tower Hamlets has a Health Strategy Group, for example. Such groups vary widely in their funding and other resources, so variation in their activities (and the extent to which women's health is a priority) varies greatly across localities.

Thus, there appear to be few centres of feminist advocacy operating in the health service, and no focus on women's health or gynaecological issues within the campaign against Tomlinson. Hospital reorganisation remains an ungendered issue in the eyes of most commentators. The invisibility of women's issues in this campaign may result from the way women-initiated change operates in a deeply segregated environment. The health service is divided into professionalised groups with no core beliefs in common: nurses, health service managers, and doctors, with loyalties to such groups providing primary incentives. After hospital reorganisation, the health service was further fragmented by a patchwork of divisive loyalties. In this environment employees are influenced both by professional groups (doctors, nurses, health service managers) and by organisational loyalties to hospitals under threat from the Tomlinson Report. Health service reform increased such divisions. London hospital reorganisation took place at a time of dramatic management change throughout the health service, with the introduction of an internal market and purchaser/provider splits. Hospitals previously under the control of District Health Authorities were to be allowed to bid for independent status as NHS trusts in order to become separately managed providers of health care services, distinct from and sometimes in competition with other hospital trusts and the Health Authorities. Thus trusts operate in competition with each other, inhibiting consensual working habits built up in the past. Such change has affected women more than men, as they were heavier users of consensual networks operating across organisations and professional groups.

Summary and Conclusions

Analysis of London's 'gender system' has revealed a diverse set of activities across the city, with a wide range of organisations working on behalf of women and great variation in the extent to which implementing agencies are 'gendered.' The demographic composition of the city indicates that alternative visions of gender roles may be available in London to a greater extent than in the rest of the country. This change, however, has not dramatically balanced the gender mix of the local state. Concurrent changes in London's political system mean that women's participation at the top of local authority employment structures varies greatly across boroughs. Previously women's presence at the top was uniformly low. The high concentration of women in some areas (notably Tower Hamlets) is due as much, if not more, to specific political events than to sustained sex equality strategies of London's governing institutions. Although sex equality policies at the borough level during the 1980s had some effect, such policies were weakened by public management change, before many women broke through to the higher echelons of local authorities. Other factors influence the extent to which gender battles are fought in the public realm. The success that has been achieved by a fragmented London women's movement relied upon the possession of information and expertise rather than the other three resources of authority, reputation, and money, all of which are at low levels throughout the women's pressure group world. Nevertheless, there is evidence that the constellation of women's groups provides a sustainable base for feminist activity.

It seems that women and particularly feminists can influence policy, but the degree of influence varies by locality, organisational context, and issue. To return to the three questions about the gendering of policy raised earlier, in each of our issue areas there are good reasons to expect that policy should be gender-sensitive. In housing and homelessness there are important gender differences between client groups. Hospital reorganisation affected London's men and women differently; moreover, health service staff and employees were mainly women. Domestic violence overwhelmingly involves abuse of women, who often become particularly reluctant to engage male professionals in police and housing departments. The influence of feminist ideas in combatting male gender biases has been patchy. While domestic violence is normally now understood in a gendered way, gender issues in hospital reorganisation appear to remain latent. Homelessness was more likely to be understood in a gendered way, but this was not consistent.

In attempting to identify the relationship between the gender mix of policy actors and the extent to which women influence policy, we have established that organisational context is an important intermediary variable. There are no examples of radical transformation of an issue area through feminist advocacy. Rather, feminist success in highlighting the gender dimensions of a policy resulted from activity sustained over a long period of time and change has been localised, patchy and gradual. And such change depended crucially both on pre-existing organisational patterns characterising an issue area and the extent to which feminist activity could become part of these patterns. There is evidence of a relationship between the gender mix of organisations and the gendering of policy issues, with sustained feminist activity over time producing policy change.

Thus each urban policy issue demonstrates a different dimension of feminist intervention. Hospital reorganisation took place within a fragmented environment that was not conducive to the formation of an advocacy coalition arguing for women-centred policy change. The issue illustrates an absence of effective intervention and remains ungendered. By contrast, homelessness was more likely to be understood in a gendered way, partly as a result of the higher proportion of women operating in the sector. Here, too, fragmentation proved important; the importing of explicit feminist ideas was patchy, fragmented by the existing division of the housing and homelessness sectors and difficult to sustain. At the other end of the spectrum, perceived entirely in gendered terms, was domestic violence policy. Here, feminists operated in and across state boundaries to influence policy on domestic violence, changing the operational strategies of even such a male-dominated hierarchical organisation as the Metropolitan Police and forming an advocacy coalition of explicit concentrated feminist activity over a sustained period of time and with considerable success. In the last few years, in specific areas there was some measure of change, as male-dominated hierarchies of domestic violence policy suffered a crisis of legitimacy in the 1980s and acknowledged the need for feminist information and expertise.

Notes

1. Appleton (1995) uses the term gender 'regime'. In this article, however, we require a descriptive rather than normative term and therefore use 'system' to avoid the problem of the regime concept as a descriptive label identified by Stoker (1995:57), whereby 'regime terminology is used but a regime analysis not really provided'.

2. Edwards (1989), Halford (1998), Bagihole (1994) and Lovenduski and Randall (1993) all make this point.

3. The Northern Irish Equal Opportunities Office was so alarmed at the effect of CCT on women's employment that in 1996 it called for emergency suspension of CCT.

4. FT Profile is an online computer system, marketed by the *Financial Times*, containing the full text of a wide range of newspapers and periodicals. All data here were obtained using the file UKNEWS, which contains all UK broadsheet newspapers and the *Evening Standard.* Data are available for one to ten years, depending upon the newspaper, and are updated daily.

5. This story recurred in 1996; *see Evening Standard,* 23 May 1996.

References

Abrar, S. (1996) 'Feminist Intervention and Local Domestic Violence Policy', *Parliamentary Affairs*, 49 (1): 191–205.

Appleton, L. (1995) 'The Gender Regimes of American Cities', in J. A. Garber and R. S. Turner (eds) *Gender in Urban Research*, London: Sage, pp. 44–59.

Bagihole, B. (1994) *Women, Work and Equal Opportunity*, Avebury: Avebury Press.

Bologh, R. (1991) *Love or Greatness: Max Weber and Masculine Thinking — A Feminist Enquiry*, London: Unwin–Hyman.

Brownhill, S. and Halford, S. (1990) 'Understanding Women's Involvement in Local Politics: How Useful is a Formal/Informal Dichotomy?', *Political Geography Quarterly*, 9 (4): 397–414.

Church, J. (1995) *Social Trends*, London: HMSO.

Connell, W. (1987) *Gender and Power: Society, the Person and Sexual Politics*, Cambridge: Polity Press.

Coyle, A. (1995) 'Women and Organisational Change', Equal Opportunities Commission, Discussion Series.

Dibblin, J. (1990) 'Wherever I Lay My Hat: Young Women and Homelessness', Shelter, London.

Dowding, K. (1991) *Rational Choice and Political Power*, Aldershot: Edward Elgar.

Dowding, K. (1996) *Power*, London: Macmillan.

Eardley, T. (1989) 'Move-on Housing: the Permanent Needs of Residents of Hostels and Special Needs Housing Projects in London', National Federation of Housing Associations, London.

Edwards, J. (1989) 'Women's Committees: A Model for Good Local Government', *Policy and Politics*, 17 (3): 221–226.

Eisenstein, H. (1985) *Gender Shock: Practising Feminism on Two Continents*, Sydney: Allen and Unwin.

Equal Opportunities Commission (EOC) (1995) 'The Gender Impact of CCT in Local Government', Equal Opportunities Commission, Manchester.

Ferguson, K. (1984) *The Feminist Case Against Bureaucracy*, Philadelphia: Temple University Press.

Halford, S. (1988) 'Women's initiatives in local government ... where do they come from and where are they going?', *Policy and Politics'*, 16 (4): 251–260. (doi:10.1332/030557388782454957).

London Research Centre (1995) *London '95*.

Lovenduski, J. (1989) 'Implementing Equal Opportunities in the 1980s: An Overview', *Public Administration*, 67 (1): 7–18.

Lovenduski, J. and Randall, V. (1993) *Contemporary Feminist Politics*, Oxford: Oxford University Press.

Sabatier, P. and Jenkins-Smith, H. C. (eds) (1993) *Policy Change and Learning: An Advocacy Coalition Approach*, Boulder, CO: Westview Press.

Sexty, C. (1990) 'Women Losing Out', Shelter, London.

Stivers, C. (1993) *Gender Images in Public Administration*, London: Sage.

Stoker, G. (1995) 'Regime Theory and Urban Politics', in D. Judge, G. Stoker and H. Wolman (eds) *Theories of Urban Politics*, London: Sage, pp. 54–71.

Stone, J. (1988) *Equal Opportunities in Local Government*, Equal Opportunities Commission, London: HMSO.

Tickell, A. and Peck, J. (1995) 'The Return of the Manchester Men: Men's Words and Men's Deeds in the Remaking of the Local State', Business Elites and Urban Politics Working Paper, no. 4, Manchester: University of Manchester.

Watson, S. (ed.) (1990) *Playing the State*, London: Verso.

Watson, S. (1995) 'Producing the Right Sort of Chap: The Senior Civil Service as an Exclusionary Culture', *Policy and Politics*, 22 (3): 211–222.

Acknowledgements. This article is based on research from the Gender and New Urban Governance (GNUG) project which was conducted at the London School of Economics, ESRC award number L131125304901. This research was carried out by Stefania Abrar who was the Research Assistant for GNUG and produced several of the insights developed here. We would like to thank Patrick Dunleavy, Dilys Hill, Alan Ware, and Michael Goldsmith for valuable comments on an earlier draft and all the anonymous interviewees who generously contributed time to the project.

Chapter Twelve

Feminism, Violence, and Men*

BRITISH women report a fear of violence three times as great as men, yet official statistics show that the risk of violent crime is higher for men (NALGWC 1990). This is often interpreted as evidence that women are oversensitive to crime and have unfounded fears; it contributes to women's vulnerable image. But if we take into account the spectrum of abuse that women receive and how often the violence is committed by people who are known to their victim, and thus goes unreported, women's fear may well be a legitimate response in a society in which male violence is often unchallenged and frequently condoned.

When the demand for freedom from male sexual violence split the British WLM in 1978, it was entangled with the debate about separatism. Arguments about women's right to determine their sexuality and about whether feminists should interact with established (male) power structures were conflated with arguments about the relationship between maleness and violence. At the heart of the split, was a division over whether violence is a universal attribute of men which is crucial to their domination of women, or whether that violence was, like the domination of women by men, an effect, albeit a complex and mediated one, of capitalist society. Feminist analyses of the significance of male violence to women range from Sheila Jeffreys's view that the former was the case, to those Socialist feminists who took the latter view. On issues of male violence, the strength of feeling that attends the split in feminism waxes and wanes, but the disagreement continues. Over the years, the arguments on each side have become more sophisticated, more nuanced, more knowing, and, at the level of theory, the positions have become more entrenched.

At the level of practice, there was an apparent division of labour between feminists in the years immediately following the split. Revolutionary and Radical feminists concentrated an increasing amount of their energies on issues that were defined in terms of male sexual violence. Domestic violence and, later, rape and pornography were the focus of their activity and thought. Socialist feminists were preoccupied with other issues, namely, their work in the Labour Party, in the trade unions, and around the miners' strike of 1984–5. In some localities this amounted to no more than a difference of emphasis, whilst in others activities were quite sharply separated. Many feminists engaged in a range of campaigns that were determined as much by what was an issue in their locality as by theoretical disputes between feminist intellectuals. Despite a growing interest in psychoanalytic thought during the 1980s, which brought Socialist feminists into

*   Selection from 'Feminism, Violence and Men' in J. Lovenduski and V. Randall (eds) *Contemporary Feminist Politics*, Oxford, Oxford University Press, 1993, pp. 305–351.

debates about sexuality and sexual difference and into a resulting coincidence of preoccupations, the two sides did not come any closer together. It is fair to say that, for most of the decade, Radical feminism had the political initiative in the task of theorising male sexual violence. Only at the end of the 1980s, when large-scale campaigns to censor pornography began to gather strength and influence throughout the movement, did many Socialist feminists begin to think and argue and, most importantly, to organise politically about masculinity and its connections with sexual violence.[1]

To the extent that feminists wished to win the hearts and minds of ordinary British women, to the extent that the feminist project develops through a process of gaining political support for its definitions and issues, Socialist feminists were at a disadvantage. Policies to control violence were popular; issues about male sexual violence struck a responsive chord in the many women who have first-hand experience of it. Thus, the problem of male sexual violence was successfully maintained on the feminist agenda of the 1980s by Radical feminists. But Socialists were suspicious of these initiatives, not least because such policies were easily hijacked by law and order lobbies, they could easily become part of the arsenal of the extreme Right. An important feature of debate at the beginning of the 1990s, therefore, is the extent to which co-operation with the political Right is possible or wise.

Understanding male sexual violence draws on key dimensions of feminist thought. It involves conceptualising the relationship of sexuality to power. Because policy-making institutions and agencies of law enforcement are implicated, it raises issues about the state and how to relate to it. Because women experience violence in different circumstances and in different ways, it raises questions about the differences between women, and requires a thoroughgoing critique of tendencies towards universalism and essentialism in Radical feminist thought. In this chapter we shall look in detail at four of the issues which feminists have defined in terms of male sexual violence: wife battery or 'domestic' violence, rape, sexual harassment, and pornography. A fifth issue — child sexual abuse — was dealt with in Chapter 8 [this refers to the original volume]. Of the five issues under scrutiny, four would not be on the political agenda had feminists not become interested in them.

We describe two different kinds of politics here. The first is an issue-based politics in which, although definitions were contested, basic agreement among feminists was rapidly established. The issues of domestic violence, rape, and sexual harassment have generated a politics that focuses on the practical work of institution-building, resource allocation, and networking as solutions were sought to important problems. But the politics of pornography continues to be a politics of contested definitions in which feminists compete with each other and with other established political actors to determine the nature of the issue. The accounts that follow are accounts of feminists identifying problems, struggling to establish feminist definitions of these problems, and devising solutions for them. The various demonstrations, campaigns, lobbies, organisations, arguments, strategies, theories, and other interventions that are included are examples of feminist practice at the grass roots of politics and in a number of state arenas.

Domestic Violence, Feminism, and the Women's Refuge Movement

Women's Aid is unusual in contemporary feminism in that it has sustained an organisation at national level since 1975. In virtually all other cases, autonomous feminist organisation is local, community-based, with communication a matter of informal networking. Women's Aid's organisational continuity is possible because the federation is extremely loosely constructed, and local organisations have considerable autonomy. Members have identified clear advantages in having a national office which is able to act as an information exchange and to lobby national government.

The women's refuge movement was very much an initiative of the WLM of the 1970s. The problem of male violence to women in the home became an early concern of the second wave of feminism. The sheer scale of domestic assault shocked the women who became interested in the issue. Knowledge about male violence to their partners grew as women shared experiences in consciousness-raising groups, and the first refuges were established either in women's centres or by squatting in suitable property. Erin Pizzey's refuge at Chiswick (actually the second refuge to be set up in London) received widespread publicity in the national media, and the issue of 'wife abuse' found its way on to the political agenda. By 1977 there were nearly 200 refuges in the United Kingdom. In 1990 there were almost that many in England alone. After considerable discussion at the WLM conference in Manchester in 1975, a national co-ordinating body, the National Women's Aid Federation, was established. This was a federation of refuges which accepted five basic working principles and demands. These aims illustrate the dual concern of Women's Aid: to offer a service to battered women, and to campaign for policies to protect women. They also embody feminist principles of self-help, a 'woman-centred' understanding of domestic violence, and a feminist understanding of the social structure. The aims are:

1. To provide temporary refuge on request for battered women and their children.
2. To encourage these women to determine their own futures and to help them achieve this, whether it involves returning home or starting a new life elsewhere.
3. To recognise and care for the educational and emotional needs of the children involved.
4. To offer support and after-care to any women and children who have left the refuge.
5. To educate and inform the public, the police, the courts, the social services, and other authorities with respect to the battering of women, mindful of the fact that this is a result of the general position of women in our society (Stedward 1987: 217–18).

The title was deliberately chosen to avoid a reference to the domestic battery of women, a term that was disliked because it did not suggest the social construction of domestic violence to women. At the end of the 1970s the organisation divided into Welsh, Scottish, English, and Irish federations, all of which maintain communication with each other.[2] The English federation (WAFE) was the most disunited of the national organisations, and its failure to agree on a constitution resulted in the loss of state funding for some years during the 1980s, although this was finally restored. The Welsh federation celebrated ten years of existence in 1988, by which time refuges were open in every Welsh valley. Scottish Women's Aid (SWA) was established with funding from the Scottish Office in 1976 and the opening of its Edinburgh office. The Dundee office was opened in 1981. All the federations survive on a base of state funding, making up the shortfall with money from donations and charitable foundations. Not all women's refuges belong to Women's Aid; some are autonomous because they disagree with some of its aims and practices, others are local authority initiatives which do not run open-door policies. However, the majority of refuges in 1990 are affiliated to Women's Aid, and most of those which are not receive information mailings from the federations. In other words, they are a part of the network.

The political history of Women's Aid shows both the contradictions and the more general dilemmas of feminist politics. It illustrates the continuity and expansion of certain issues and networks, the growing but always ambivalent engagement with the state, and the accompanying risks of 'incorporation'. On the one hand, there is evidence of the growth and establishment of feminist expertise and increased political dexterity. On the other hand, there are clear signs of the strains of providing a service that protects women, but is true to feminist principles; that insists that society take responsibility for the consequences of its gendered power structure, but empowers the women whom it seeks to help.

Initially, refuge workers concentrated on achieving recognition of the problem and on organising provision for battered women according to feminist principles. A parliamentary select committee on violence in marriage reported in 1975 and firmly established violence against women at home as a social rather than an individual problem. Continued campaigning ensured that public knowledge of the issue grew. The 1977 Homeless Persons Act required local authorities to rehouse women at risk of violence. The need to rehouse the women who came to the refuge, and to make provision for their children, meant that women's refuge groups tended to focus their day-to-day political activity on local authorities, because they had the relevant statutory powers.

To find and develop feminist ways of working was a central concern of the refuge movement. Its feminist principles challenged common assumptions about domestic violence. Its ways of organisation are drawn directly from the WLM. A high value is placed on non-hierarchical, democratic functioning in which conflict is dealt with collectively, and distinctions between helper and helped are overturned. Most refuges employ paid workers and rely on volunteers. As the years have passed, an increasing number of the paid workers and the volunteers are women who once lived in the refuge. Women who come to refuges are encouraged to take part in its collective management. This has been an important part of their empowerment. The 'management structure' of the refuges has been evolved to avoid hierarchy.

An emphasis on co-counselling, discussion, and collective agreement underlines an interchangeability of helper and helped that is a very important part of feminist political practice. Such ways of working were developed as a challenge to the existing hierarchical structures of the contemporary Welfare State. Feminist refuges were formed with the explicit aim of providing an alternative political practice to that of the state. Although Women's Aid refuges are cheaper to run than local authority hostels and other homeless provision, the absence of 'client' status for refuge dwellers has often offended local authority professionals. Local authorities are challenged in other ways: refuges often begin as squats in local authority property. Open-door policies mean that refuges may violate council regulations about crowding and sanitation. Collective working principles mean that refuge administration is difficult for local officials to comprehend. There is therefore a predictable desire by local authorities to try to take more control over refuges. Such interference may range from insisting on particular kinds of administrative structure to the establishment of local authority hostels which run refuges on traditional welfare bureaucratic lines. These initiatives are on the increase. They amount to an effort by welfare professionals to neutralise the political challenge of Women's Aid feminism. Ultimately, they will probably fail, although they may destroy the refuge movement in the process. Women's Aid argues that it provides the best service for women, and that no alternative construction of service and empowerment will be effective.

Feminism is the key resource of the refuge movement. The participatory structures and therapeutic perspectives that it supplies foster confidence in women, and help them to lead the lives that they want to lead. Paying attention to the reality of women's lives has enabled feminist refuge workers to build up an expertise which involves social-structural explanations of domestic violence and is translatable into policies to protect women. This translation is an important part of the story of the women's movement in Britain. It is a significant instance of the impact of feminism on policy. But, before we can elaborate this point, we need to describe the changing nature of the feminism of the refuge movement.

Difference: Race and the Refuge Movement

All recent feminist politics are in some measure conditioned by the debates about sexuality and violence that we have described above. Within that framework, two objects of feminist debate in the 1980s are important here: the first is the different experiences of different groups of women, and the second is the problem of engaging the state. As we recounted in Chapter 3 [this refers to the original volume], the meaning of difference has been most extensively explored around gender, race, class, and sexuality. Each of these has been important in the refuge movement, but race has probably been the most significant. The issue of race surfaced at about the same time as the divisions about the causes of sexual violence. Black women felt that their circumstances were not taken into account, that demands for women's protection and safety were white women's demands which took no account of the impact of racism on the black community. Black women coming to refuges were often met by racism. Racism also meant that black women were under considerable pressure not to accuse black men of violence; such charges were regarded as treacherous in the black communities. Women from Asian backgrounds were under additional pressure because of the threat of deportation if they sought state aid or if they did not stay with their spouses for at least one year after entering the country. Restrictive immigration laws result in women staying with abusive spouses in order to avoid deportation.

Amina Mama has described the perspective of black women who were involved in the black community struggles in the late 1970s. Those struggles focused on police violence, a perennial problem in the black communities. This experience meant that it took 'a long time to address a reality in which black women are more likely to be assaulted by their male partner than to be attacked by racists' (Mama 1989, 1990: 11). The matter was brought to a head in Women's Aid as more black and working-class women used the refuges. Racism poisoned relations in many refuges, promoting guilt and irritation amongst white women and righteous anger on the part of black women. What was needed was open discussion, but this was not always easy or even possible.

Black women's groups established refuges during the 1980s, and several black women's groups developed strategies for working around the issue of domestic violence. Their initiatives appeared throughout the country, encountering different degrees of local authority support and different kinds of community response. In Scotland there were uproar in the black communities when aid for black women was started: 'It was seen as a shame to the community.' Amina Mama believed that neither feminist theories nor black rhetoric about women being traitors when they called in the police and divided up black families can capture the reality that she found in her research on women of Asian, African, and Caribbean backgrounds in London. She argues that 'the community should be challenging violent men not calling women who try to escape them traitors. The beating and maiming of women in the home is what is destroying black family life' (Mama 1989).

This point is well substantiated by the experience of Southall Black Sisters. Gita Sahgal has described the pressures on black women to keep silent about their experiences of male violence. The engagement of the issue of domestic violence by Southall Black Sisters broke an important silence in their community. Not only did they challenge the right of male leaders to speak for them, but black feminists also implicitly challenged the 'heroic' tradition of antiracism. These challenges took the form of a number of campaigns in support of justice for women murdered by their spouses and for women gaoled for fighting violence with violence. Speaking out in this manner raised acute dilemmas for women, who were pilloried as traitors to their communities' fights against racism (Sahgal 1989).

The pressure for silence is strong and deep-rooted. When the first Asian women's refuges were set up, they were often not intended as a challenge to community values. An account of the Brent Asian Women's Refuge showed how, in the first few months, workers saw their duty as helping women to go back to their husbands. They understood how the role of the woman in her community made her the moral mainstay of her family, the bearer of its honour, its *izzat*. Transgression would corrupt the honour of the family and, indeed, of the whole community. The wife and mother were responsible for the behaviour of husband and children; if they beat her, it was her fault for not changing them. All women found it difficult to leave home, but for Asian women there was the added burden of maintaining the *izzat* of the family. Feminists soon became established in the refuge at Brent, but their antiracism and sensitivity to local values prevented them from publicising their experiences.[3]

The complexities of the problem of racism for feminists are apparent here. In everyday practice, feminists have to address both their own racism and the racism of the larger society. Antiracism has sometimes taken the form of forgiving instances of the sexual violence by black men by regarding it as an understandable effect of racism. Here is a situation in which the only way forward is a painful identification and exploration of the experiences of different women. That progression must be led by black women, and it has been. By the early 1990s considerable experience had been gained of addressing racism in the refuges. Discussion was more readily undertaken, black women numbered prominently amongst refuge volunteers and workers, and black women's groups were well established in Women's Aid. This does not mean that the problem was solved; rather, that it was acknowledged and was being worked on.

The Refuge Movement and the State: Local Authority Policy

The reality for women who experience violence at home is that, if they are to escape it, they must be in a position to relinquish their dependence on men. In practice, it is the woman who must leave her home, and for most women this means poverty and homelessness. Although local authorities have statutory obligations to rehouse women with children who are at risk of violence, in practice they are often reluctant providers, and they make it extremely difficult for women to claim their entitlements. Refuges support women as they make their way through this process. To provide the relevant expertise, feminists in the refuge movement must engage the state. The same applies when refuge workers seek police protection, government funding and change in public policy.

This is another instance of the dilemma that feminists face when they encounter public institutions. Fear of incorporation or of the loss of autonomy is central to this dilemma. The range of feminist responses to it is wide. At one end of the spectrum is the liberal view that citizenship requires such activity; at the other is a radical separatist view that no such engagement is ever justified. The work of Women's Aid places it at the sharp edge of this difficulty. On the one hand, it is committed to the protection of women; it provides a service for which the backing of the state is required. On the other hand, Women's Aid is committed to feminist principles of autonomy and self-help and to mounting a continuing challenge to the gendered power structures of society.

This is not a problem that is exclusive to feminist initiatives. Many groups in Britain operate both insider and outsider strategies, depending upon which aspect of their political identity is in play. Such 'thresholder' groups, as political scientists call them, are uneasily situated in their policy communities, but they are nevertheless capable of considerable policy success (Stedward 1987: 211–12). Insider strategies became increasingly important during the 1980s, when the refuge movement played a growing role in local and national policy communities which were concerned about policy towards domestic violence. This work took a variety of forms, and was probably most sustained in the areas of law enforcement, housing, and social security. At government level, WAFE participated in working parties, presented evidence on legal reform, and made representations to the Home Office, the Law Commission, and the Department of the Environment.[4] In the regions, the most sustained interactions were with police authorities and in local authority multi-agency forums set up to deal with sexual violence.

The Refuge Movement and the State: The Police

It is difficult to see how the refuge movement might avoid taking up issues of law-enforcement policy. From the days of the first refuges, issues about policing have been prominent. These were often dealt with locally. The Home Office took no interest in the work of the refuge movement when it first began, and the inclusion of the police and the criminal justice system within the domestic violence policy community was not envisaged. By the beginning of the 1990s, however, the Home Office was publicly concerned about the issue of domestic violence in general, and about the role of the police in particular. In the provinces, Nottingham, Manchester, West Yorkshire and Newcastle police forces, amongst others, initiated contacts with refuge workers.

There are several aspects of the role of the police in protecting women from domestic violence which have been identified as important. These include the seriousness with which police treat the issue, and the degree and the kind of protection that they provide; their knowledge about domestic violence as a syndrome; the way in which they relate to feminist refuges; the problem of police racism; and the widespread perception that the police themselves number prominently amongst abusers of women. For a considerable period of time, the police tended to underestimate the violence of men and the need for police assistance by women and by refuges operated by women. The Domestic Violence Act of 1976 enabled courts to attach a power of arrest to injunctions restraining abusive men, but this power was not often used. Injunctions that do not include the power of arrest are widely regarded as ineffective when it comes to restraining violent men, although they have a value in 'entitling' women to rehousing.

Nor were the police much motivated by professional imperatives to prioritise domestic violence. Women who were beaten by their partners were notoriously reluctant to give evidence, and because these crimes were not likely to lead to convictions, individual police constables regarded such complaints as a waste of their time. Moreover, complaints about inadequate policing proved ineffective and sometimes counter-productive. SWA found that some women who complained about the policing they received were later charged with wasting police time when they requested assistance. Feminists were often philosophical about such treatment, taking the view that the police are no better than the society they serve, and that they reflect uncritically a social endorsement of domestic violence as well as racist perspectives on the protection of black women. The experience of the refuges made it clear that policing practice and ideology was not compatible with the needs of the women who experience domestic violence.

But even the most sexist institutions have the capacity to change. By the beginning of the 1990s there were some indications that the policing of male violence to women would be reformed. There were several reasons for this. First, and possibly most importantly, public attitudes towards the police were changing, becoming less trustful and more critical. Secondly, the Thatcher government sustained its support partly through an emphasis on law and order, increasing public expectations of personal safety. Thirdly, the women's movement was successful in bringing the issue of domestic violence on to the political agenda and keeping it there. The fourth development was the appearance of child sexual abuse on the public agenda after 1986.

A series of Home Office memos to police forces between 1983 and 1990 instructed them to take domestic violence more seriously. These memos were given considerable press publicity. Home Office guidance was issued to police forces in England and Wales in 1983. In 1986 the Home Office issued a circular reminding police of their powers under the 1984 Police and Criminal Evidence Act. A report the same year by the Metropolitan Police working party on domestic violence (attended by the Home Office) made extensive suggestions on training, referrals to refuges, and advice and information for women. This was followed up by a report from the London Strategic Policy Unit on police treatment of violence to women in the capitol. Police everywhere have been enjoined to take the problem more seriously; the Metropolitan Police has been ordered to do so. It is now a requirement that domestic violence complaints are fully recorded, and police receive training about domestic violence (Hague et al. 1989). In 1991 the Home Office instructed police forces to set up data banks of women at risk.

The result is mixed, not least because of variations in the police forces themselves. Police forces are organised regionally in Britain, and they are jealous of their independence. Discretion is wide, and practice varies from locality to locality. Moreover, the police on the beat have considerable autonomy. Consequently, the policing of domestic violence now varies from very good practice in a few localities to dreadful (in other words, no change) in others. There are forty-two police domestic violence units in London, but few or none in some of the large provincial cities. Many police officers now accept that domestic violence is as serious a crime as stranger assault, and the tendency to encourage reconciliation as the stock response appears to have declined.

The Refuge Movement and the State: Co-option or Co-operation?

These changes are not uniformly welcomed by feminists. Adjustments in police priorities to take on elements of the feminist agenda may augur a loss of feminist control over the issue. The same problem is raised when feminists co-operate with the government at local and national levels. During the three Thatcher governments, the context of this co-operation was a series of social policy initiatives that consistently eroded the provisions which make it possible for women to leave violent men. Reductions in publicly owned housing stocks through the sale of council houses reduced the possibilities of being able to offer adequate accommodation for homeless women and their children. Changes in benefit payments reduced the rents that were paid for women in refuges. Cuts in local authority funding led to reductions in funding for refuges. The result was that refuge workers had to spend increasing amounts of time on trying to make ends meet, and bottlenecks occurred as refuges filled but no permanent housing was available for women to move into. Average stays in refuges increased, and it is believed that many women returned to violent relationships rather than endure long periods of living in a refuge. In 1990 WAFE estimated the provision of refuges to be one per 60,000 of the population, nowhere near the one per 10,000 of population that had been recommended by the parliamentary select committee on violence in marriage in 1975.

Yet housing authority co-operation is essential to the refuge movement. The powerlessness that women experience when dealing with the authorities that have to be mobilised when they try to leave home is often overwhelming. The very negative experience of black women when leaving violent men has been extensively described by Amina Mama. Her London-based study showed that it took as long as three years for women to be rehoused. Women were passed from one department to another, with little right or power to resist encroaching webs of coercive and punitive state interventions (Mama 1989: 11). This is described here in words that vividly express the strength required to cope with bureaucratic obstructiveness:

> Once they've made the enquiries, they're supposed to send you a paper called Section 64, which says they consider you homeless and will rehouse you. It took them six months to send me that paper. This paper is like a passport to lots of other things. You need it to feel secure, and they know you need it. Without it, you can't convince any other borough or anywhere else that you have registered. It took six months and in the meantime I had to keep phoning, going down there. When I rang up they used to tell me to stop bothering them, that they would send the paper. Nothing arrived, so I went down there in person, and I was told not to make any enquiries until I hear from them. I rang again and he put the receiver down on me. (Mama 1989: 11)

Meanwhile, welfare professionals and local officials continued to seek control of the policies. Once they became aware of the radical nature of the feminist critique and of its implications for client–professional status, notably at a DHSS conference in 1981 (Stedward 1987), welfare professionals and experts became very wary of close association and developed arms-length strategies. The state employs professional carers who, although often radical as individuals, are impelled by the demands of professionalism to separate the status of client and carer. Inevitably, professional carers have an interest in imposing their own definitions of, and solutions to, violence to women in the home, and they develop strategies to do this. For example, local authorities have established their own women's refuges in Birmingham, London, Manchester, and other British cities. As with the police, these initiatives are often couched in feminist rhetoric and show sensitivity to many aspects of feminist analysis. Official refuges offer safety, but they do not encourage residents to become involved in the running of the refuge. They are not founded on an ethos of empowering women. The irony here is that although the refuge movement made the problem visible, unleashing a huge demand to which it offered a solution, that solution was a radical one that was unacceptable to many members of the policy community. The anti-authoritarian ethos of feminist self-help strategies is not compatible with the goals of the New Right, and its implied autonomy offends the welfare professionals and local officials. During the 1980s there was an increase in such tensions. Because the government wanted to reduce the powers of the state by devolving responsibilities to the community in the form of the voluntary agencies, the refuge movement was able to gain financial support from the state. This enabled refuge collectives to assert feminist values. In other words, as the form of the state changed, space was created for feminist interventions. But the welfare bureaucracy was bound to contest the erosion of its authority. The resulting political struggle is at the heart of disagreements between feminist Women's Aid workers and welfare professionals.

Another way in which the refuge movement intervenes in the state is by monitoring policy, making representations to relevant bodies, and campaigning for policy changes. This activity is very much the responsibility of the federations, whose roles and skills are different to those of the local groups. Refuge workers and volunteers developed counselling and therapeutic skills which were not transferable to the campaigning and administrative tasks that turn their expertise into policy. Women's Aid policy development initiatives met with some success. The Home Office has taken an increasing interest not only in the area of policing, as we have seen above, but in the area of domestic violence generally. Following the publication of Home Office Working Paper 107, a review of the literature on domestic violence, the ministerial group on women's issues met in July 1989 to examine the issue of domestic violence. WAFE submitted a report to the group, and will monitor the progress of the initiatives that the group suggested: a review of civil law, guidance to chief officers of police, a project on the education of domestic violence offenders, and the development of good practice guidelines for health and social service staff.[5]

At the beginning of the 1990s the problem of violence to women in the home is visible and large; 25 per cent of all violent crime in Britain is domestic assault on women; over 1,000 women telephone the London police each week with complaints of domestic violence. The refuge movement is the primary agency for helping battered women. In any one year, about 12,000 women and 21,000 children experience refuge life. Feminists have placed domestic violence on the political agenda. Women's Aid has fought its corner and continues to emphasise the unique service that is offered by the refuge movement. The underlying principle that women's needs are best met by involving women in meeting those needs continues to be central to its work. Inevitably, Women's Aid (and the rest of the feminist refuge movement) oscillates uncomfortably between its insider and outsider statuses and strategies. Like other voluntary organisations concerned with welfare, Women's Aid is part of the welfare system. Every time its expertise is used by official bodies, every time it is included in an inter-agency forum, control of the issue becomes open to other contenders. Whatever the ambivalences about engaging the state, the problem and its solution are, in all important respects, political. And this is well recognised in the movement. Refuge workers are certain in their affirmation that creating space where women can talk and deal with their problems collectively in an empowering way is political work. Bringing an issue out from the private sphere, making it visible, and offering a social diagnosis and a public solution is the essence of feminist politics.

Rape

Working on the issue of domestic violence made feminists increasingly aware that, in practice, women have more to fear from men whom they know than from violent strangers. The way in which this perception was dealt with and understood in the movement led to the split between those second-wave feminists who came to believe that male sexuality was inherently violent and those who did not. Action over rape was widespread by the end of the 1970s as feminists organised in a number of British cities. Groups such as Women against Rape (WAR) and Feminists against Sexual Terrorism (FAST) organised 'Take back the Night' marches from July 1977 onwards, when the first of these marches took place in Edinburgh. An important part of the context of this organisation was the 'ripper' murders that took place in the north of England. These murders and attempted murders received widespread publicity in the national media and had a particularly important effect on feminism in Leeds and Bradford. On 27 November 1980, ten days after the death of Jacqueline Hill (one of the victims), 500 women attended a conference on sexual violence in Leeds. The conference brought together women who had been organising around issues of sexual violence. They were linked in a new campaign, Women against Violence against Women (WAVAW), which planned campaigns to combat male violence and asserted every woman's right to defend herself against it.

Actions included the occupation of the *Sun* newspaper offices to protest at the use of rape stories for titillation, the formation of local anti-pornography groups which leafleted family newsagents for stocking pornography, demonstrations outside cinemas showing 'Dressed to Kill', smashing the windows of strip clubs, putting glue in the locks of sex shops, etc. In Leeds a woman drove her car through the front of a sex shop. Women were angry about the failure to solve the 'ripper' murders, angry that the 'solution' was, in effect, a curfew for women, angry that the media coverage of rape seemed to have titillation as its objective. Susan Brownmiller's book *Against our Will*, published in Britain in 1975, became very influential. This book presented an enormous amount of information about rape, much of which was drawn from 'speak-outs' by United States feminists who had been raped. It demonstrated the shocking prevalence of the crime. Brownmiller argued that rape was the means by which all men kept all women in a state of fear, and that such fear was the basis of male oppression. It was a powerful message, one that was difficult to dismiss when so many women had experience of sexual coercion. Gradually, the belief that rape and wife-beating were the product of men's essentially violent natures gained support. The connections that revolutionary feminists made between male sexual violence and women's subordination led them to the view that all instances of sexual coercion (including pornography and sexual harassment) were forms of rape.

The issue developed in this way partly because of rage (Segal 1987: ch. 3). As the prevalence of male violence became more apparent, anger became more widespread. Reactions from the police, the media, the courts, the police, doctors, and other (mainly male) professionals exacerbated this anger by treating the issue with contempt. There is considerable evidence that the press used the 'soft pornography' of rape-case reporting to boost sales and circulation (*see* Soothill *et al.* 1991). The reasonable and easily understood argument that crimes of sexual violence form a continuum, reflecting women's social subordination, was treated with derision by male opinion leaders, who wrote sneering articles which claimed that feminists were confusing courtship and seduction with rape.

Part of the source of women's anger was surprise. There is a huge and contradictory mythology that surrounds rape, and women born before 1970 were brought up in thrall to that contradictory mythology. We were led to understand that rape was a rare event, that *normal* men aimed to protect women from violence, that only women are raped, that rape was normally the act of strangers, that women lie about being raped to conceal their promiscuity — so much so that a woman claiming to have been raped should be disbelieved as a matter of course. We knew that women were only raped if they wanted to be, and that only psychopaths raped, but that male sexual desire was so uncontrollable that they could be driven to rape by our inappropriate behaviour. Feminist research exposes all of these myths and shows how they protect male aggressors (Segal 1987: ch. 3). Feminists offered two — opposed — explanations of rape. The first, and most widely publicised, is the Radical feminist view that the cause of rape (and other sexual violence) is male sexuality itself (Brownmiller 1975). The basis of this explanation is the widespread incidence of male sexual violence to women, the considerable effect that the fear of sexual violence has on women's lives, and the notoriously unsympathetic attitudes of the mainly male officials who treat rape victims. This makes for a fairly simple politics: the problem is male sexuality, especially as expressed in heterosexuality. The solution is political lesbianism.

Lynne Segal is perhaps the most consistent advocate of the other explanation, which is that the problem is not maleness, but masculinity. Her work draws attention to the large number of men who do not coerce women, and she has attempted to explain the construction of masculinity in contemporary society in an effort to show that male sexual violence is about gender and roles rather than essential biological characteristics (Segal 1990b). This is a feminist version of the nature–nurture argument, and it is likely to continue for some time yet. Its implications for feminism have been profound, both in organisational and theoretical terms. But the effect has been different in different parts of the country. Divisions in London are deep, continuing, and bitter, but feminists in Leeds are able to work around their differences. Feminists there stress the importance of the 'ripper' murders and the subsequent investigations as something that had a compelling local effect. Nevertheless, a split did occur in Leeds between revolutionary and Socialist feminists. One feminist recalls early discussions about male sexual violence:

> we seemed to get a lot of opposition from particularly Socialist Feminists at even raising it ... they were saying 'well you're making women feel frightened, and it's not as bad as this' ... I suppose it was because it was saying that all men are potential rapists ... rather than saying it was a class issue 'cos it obviously isn't ... if you've got the money you can get a taxi but you can still be raped ...

And race, too, became an issue in Leeds. Black community leaders have long argued that rape charges are one more opportunity for racist police to set them up. The black communities resented the Take back the Night marches through Chapeltown: black feminists repeatedly raised such issues in the women's movement. Some white feminists found the charges of racism difficult to understand. Why, they argued, were left-wing marches through ghetto areas regarded as demonstrations of racial solidarity, but feminists marches (which, after all, were expressions of solidarity amongst women) were regarded as instances of racism? Divisions eased, not least because some of the points that the Radical feminists made about male violence were partly accepted in Leeds. A lot of women were controlled by the 'ripper' murders: they gave up jobs and evening classes, women students left university and returned to homes in other parts of the country after Jacqueline Hill was killed. Their lives were altered. And some men took advantage of women's fears:

> Local youths were jumping out of shrubs saying 'I'm the ripper' not funny, terrifying ... Women were getting 'helpful' lifts from male colleagues who would then try it on in the car. Or under the guise of helpfulness, coming to collect their partners after classes, immediately after, so she could not go for a drink with her friends. Made to think that you need men's protection all the time.

Under these circumstances, women shared taxis, organised lifts for each other, and lent each other their guard dogs. Instead of a siege mentality, there was the development of a sense of collective strength, a sense of a shared experience, which continues to affect the attitudes of Leeds feminists to this day, however divided they might otherwise be.

Rape Crisis

Feminist action about rape involved more than collective protection. Apart from the direct action of marches and demonstrations mentioned above, there were two other main strands of activity: the rape crisis groups, which offered telephone counselling on rape crisis lines, and feminist research on the nature, causes, and solutions to rape.

The appearance of rape crisis groups was very much a local phenomenon which occurred more or less spontaneously in different parts of the country. Although the groups are networked, in that members of their support groups attend conferences on sexual violence and are generally active in the sexual violence policy communities, there is no formal organisation to link them. The links are shared feminist networks and commitments. The first rape crisis centre[6] opened in London in March 1976, and others appeared over the next several months and years in Leeds, Tyneside, Manchester, Edinburgh, Bristol, Newcastle, Nottingham, and elsewhere. The centres were influenced by the practices of feminists from the USA, where such centres appeared at the beginning of the 1970s. A group of about forty women began to meet in London in the early 1970s because they wanted to do something about rape. One group set up London Rape Crisis, and this became the London rape crisis group (LRG). A similar period of preparation before the opening of a rape crisis centre was a feature in other regions. In Birmingham the rape crisis group began meeting in 1979, but it was two years before they had a crisis line for calls. LRG took about 150 calls in the first year; by 1978 about twenty-five new callers telephoned each week. Over the years there was a shift from talking about old rapes, never reported, to detailing new ones as knowledge about the line spread and recourse to it increased. By the early 1990s LRG was taking about 100 counselling calls per week, and on a Saturday night the line is permanently in use as one call after another comes in.[7]

The organisation consists of a support group, a telephone line and arrangements to cover calls. LRG runs a twenty-four-hour service, which it regards as an essential feature of its work. The collective operates on three levels: as a sustaining developing collective, as providers of a service, and as a campaigning group. The themes of feminist political action are very apparent here. Decision is by discussion. Organisation is kept to the barest minimum, and the collective takes care to support its members as well as rape survivors. Over time, LRG and other rape crisis groups have established their expertise on rape survival, and they have become involved both in the policy community and in public debate and discussion about policy.

Rape counselling has not developed in the same way as other feminist group-based service provision, because the use of the telephone makes the service an individual one. Telephone counselling has enormous advantages for the rape survivor. It is anonymous, the caller is in control — she can hang up or ring back as she wishes. It is also confidential in a way that a drop-in centre can never be. Counselling is central to the work of rape crisis lines. The pioneer group in London was very careful to seek training from other organisations with relevant experience, including the Samaritans, sympathetic GPs, other counsellors, and psychologists. And whilst callers were encouraged to join consciousness-raising groups, it was decided not to offer 'survivor groups' to the women who telephoned. Counsellor stress was less of a problem than might have been envisaged. Because the process was strengthening for the callers, it was also strengthening for the counsellors; and internal support groups worked hard on supporting each other.

Funding came from charitable foundations, local authorities, and the DHSS (because the twenty-four-hour line was a national service). It was important to the collective that it was not entirely state-funded. The fact that the funding came from a range of groups made its acquisition more time-consuming, but it gave greater flexibility. However, the straitened financial climate of the 1990s meant that local authority funding became more important. In 1991 the London Borough Grants Scheme considered withdrawing LRG funding in favour of other rape crisis initiatives. LRG was able to argue that their woman-centred approach, their twenty-four hour-line, and guarantee of confidentiality were unique in London, and funding was maintained. Like other rape crisis groups, LRG is autonomous, and contacts with other such groups are mainly informal. Many people imagine that because LRG is in London, it must be a national headquarters, a misconception that causes resentment from provincial groups, and makes LRG a focus for foreign visitors, journalists, and much of the publicity that the movement receives. The decision not to have a national organisation was taken at the end of the 1970s, and although the idea of a national co-ordinating structure was raised at various conferences on sexual violence in the intervening years, there appears to be no real sense that such an agency would be of value. Members of the group see no reason why there should be a consistent policy between centres, and they are unwilling to devote precious time to the arduous tasks of formal networking. Such strategies are regarded as forms of male power-building which are inappropriate to feminist service provision. Their charitable status prevented LRG from overt support of WAVAW, but ideas are exchanged through groups such as FAST and through bilateral exchanges with groups in other British centres. Other ways of networking include conferences about sexual violence, which are often organised by local authorities and local multi-agency committees which have been established by council women's committees to treat the range of crimes of sexual violence.

During the 1970s, feminist activists in WAR stressed the uniqueness of the rape issue, resisting attempts to combine strategies and policies on other forms of male violence as potentially deradicalising. However, the view that all sexual coercion is a form of rape gained acceptance during the 1980s. The formation of the Incest Survivors' Group in 1981 was as a result of knowledge obtained through rape crisis work and was a rationalisation of effort rather than a division of principle. Since rape crisis groups have been in operation, there has been a shift of emphasis from a focus on rape to sexual violence more generally. This is partly a result of what has been learned by listening to survivors, and partly a reflection of the course of debates amongst feminists. Rape crisis workers are themselves often rape survivors, and their direct and indirect experience of male violence seems to predispose them towards essentialist explanations of sexual crime. There is a widespread belief that sexual violence is the ultimate expression of male dominance: that it is men who cause rape. A member of a rape crisis support group in Leeds told us:

> There is a lot of tinkering away at the edges of the problem as if rape is caused by bad street lighting … I mean bad street lighting may aid the rapist in his endeavours but it is not the cause. And its like we do away with the bad street lighting and we change the design of flats and that and everything will be all right … but the cause of the problem is untouched and women become more and more controlled.

Feminist direct action on rape continues. In July 1990 WAR protestors caused a sitting of the Court of Appeal to be suspended when they called for the judge, Lord Justice Watkins, to be sacked for his decision the previous week to clear a policeman of raping a teenage girl in his panda car (*The Independent* 10 July 1990). In 1991 Take back the Night marches took place in a number of cities. In many respects, the feminist construction of work on rape is similar to the work developed in the women's refuge movement. The stress is on empowering women, on listening to and believing what they say, and on developing expertise as a result. The use of the word 'survivor' rather than 'victim' is a deliberate strategy of empowerment, product of the perception that casting women as victims underlines their subordination.

Rape and the State: The Law, Rape Trials, and the Police

On 14 December 1991 the *Independent* carried reports of two trials. In one, a woman who strangled her husband and dumped his dismembered body in a nearby cornfield after eight years of violence and humiliation was placed on two years' probation. In another, two boys were freed by a judge who accepted that their rape of a 15-year-old victim was a childish prank. The juxtaposition of these two cases is interesting and raises a number of points about the way in which the law takes circumstances into account when it treats crimes of violence. What strikes us about the two cases is their obvious inconsistency. In the first case, the sitting judge took male sexual violence so seriously that only a token punishment was required for the serious crime of a brutal murder. In the second case, a different judge ruled that the sexual violence meted out to a young woman was trivial — a 'prank'. The decisions reflected the differing concerns of the two judges rather than a coherent legal position. There are many such decisions in cases of sexual violence that we might have cited here. They remind us that at the beginning of the 1990s the law about violence between men and women is in some disarray, reflecting confusion as attitudes change more quickly than judicial personnel.

Feminist work about rape and domestic violence has been instrumental in creating some of this confusion. It has challenged dominant views of the way in which power is constructed in gender relations. This effect has been complicated by divisions between feminists about the appropriateness of intervention in different state arenas. Currently, there is at least an implicit feminist acceptance that it is not possible to work on the issue of rape without taking account of the role of law and the problems of policing. The most radical and separatist of feminist positions implicitly supports the policing of the dangerous group. And police forces themselves may facilitate service provision. Rape crisis groups normally try to persuade statutory agencies to refer women rape survivors to their helpline. This involves contact and negotiation. Local government is important, at least as a source of funding. Local authority social services also sometimes provide links between rape crisis groups and the police.

Feminist attempts to understand and influence the law have been of three kinds. First, feminist lawyers, criminologists, and sociologists have made intellectual critiques of the gendered bias of rape law, and especially of the conduct of rape trials. Secondly, feminist activists have campaigned for reforms in the law and in the conventions of rape trials. Thirdly, feminists have worked with the police in some areas to alter police practice in respect of rape complaints.

Feminists have several objections to the way in which rape trials are conducted. Rape is normally a matter of criminal law. The requirements of proof are that the evidence of the raped woman must be collaborated. In court, the woman is a witness to the crime, subject to cross-examination, but not protected by any defence. Because there is rarely any collaborative evidence, because there are rarely any other witnesses, the trial will turn on the issue of consent. The accused will claim consent, and the defence will use almost any means to undermine the woman's assertions that she did not consent.[8] Her sexual history will often be regarded as relevant evidence, and there is a strong tendency to disbelieve her account. Part of the reason for this lies in the nature of criminal trials, but much of it is to do with the way in which male and female sexuality and consent is understood by the important (normally male) actors in the trial. The trial is offensive in other ways as well, and many feminists believe that the legal process itself is a sexual violation.

Carol Smart is prominent amongst feminists who have criticised the conduct of rape trials (Smart 1989). She offers what is basically a discourse analysis of such trials, an effort to reveal the mechanisms by which the law misunderstands accounts of rape. Her argument is built around a view of sexuality which says that male and female heterosexualities are differently constructed and understood, and that this is magnified in the rape trial. The dominant view of sexuality is a phallocentric construction which emphasises the pleasures of penetration and intercourse. The context of the trial is a belief that rape must be pleasurable for women because it involves penetration. Actors in the trial share an understanding that female sexuality is problematic, that it is capricious or whimsical. The core of the trial is the woman's 'no'. This 'no' is automatically undermined by the culture of phallocentrism and is overlaid with contradictory meanings. As a result, her evidence may not be credited. The following remarks were made by Judge David Wild in December 1982: 'Women who say no do not always mean no. It is not just a question of saying no. It is a question of how she says it, how she shows and makes it clear. If she doesn't want it she only has to keep her legs shut and there would be marks of force being used.'

Not only is the context in which a raped woman must prove her non-consent one that infantises her (she does not mean what she says), it also humiliates her. *Her* sexual history is relevant to the question of rape, but *his* is not. In practice, consent is assumed, and a raped woman may have to provide evidence of considerable force for her to be believed. One of the most important difficulties arises when a woman agrees to a certain amount of intimacy, but not intercourse. Smart points out that the rapist will argue a continuum, that she consented to be with him, therefore ... if she submits rather than risk violence, her credibility is undermined. The issue of 'promiscuity' is also relevant. Many men believe that if a woman consents to one man, she has somehow consented to all men. A verdict of innocence for the accused is also a verdict of sexual complicity on the part of the victim. In this way, the phallocentric view of women's capriciousness is confirmed (Smart 1989: 33–4).

Proving non-consent is not the only difficulty experienced by raped women during the trials. It is well known that trial and pre-trial events in the police station are found to be profoundly disturbing by many women who have been assaulted. MacKinnon has argued that women do not want to pursue charges of rape because the evidence that they have to give in court becomes a pornographic vignette in which the naming of the body parts is almost a sexual act. The public may gaze on this performance and re-enact her violation in their imaginations (MacKinnon 1987). The woman must name parts of her body, use words which are heavily encoded with sexual meaning. As Sue Lees has observed, it is *her* intimate garments which are handed around, not *his* (Lees 1989). Prosecution rebuttals of the woman's claim that she did not consent, together with prevailing attitudes which associate sex and violence, obstruct the distinction that a jury must make between rape and seduction. The judicial view is often that a degree of violence is taken for granted; that quite a lot of violence is necessary to overcome genuine non-consent. Moreover, there are racist presumptions that a white woman would only have intercourse with a black man if she were forced to, and that black women are sexually more available. In Carol Smart's analysis, the rape trial is the particular legal expression of the dominant culture, and she is pessimistic about the possibilities for reform. She finds it problematic that reforms might make the trial tolerable enough to be endured, without any guarantee that its phallocentric assumptions have been altered. Like many feminists, she is uneasy about making alliances with agencies of law enforcement.

During the 1970s there were feminist-inspired reforms to prevent disclosure of the names of raped women in the press and to restrict the use of their sexual histories as evidence. The public nature of the humiliation was therefore modified, although trial judges are notoriously lenient in allowing details of the sexual past of raped women. The high degree of independence of the British judiciary makes it difficult to control their prejudices, so feminists have gradually sought ways of protecting raped women in court. Rape crisis workers attend trials with survivors in order to provide psychological support. Efforts have been made to reorganise courts so that rape survivors do not share waiting-rooms with their rapists. But many critics believe that more fundamental change is necessary.

There have been two important sets of proposals. One is that raped women should have an advocate in court to protect their interests. This system has been tried in Denmark and it might be worth trying in Britain. Danish police are required to inform all raped women of their right to free legal representation, which may begin from the moment of police questioning. Advocates may interrupt if questioning is improper, and ask questions, which are recorded, if important issues have not been covered. They have access to all statements, including the defendant's, although this may not be revealed to the raped woman. They cannot cross-examine, but they can object to defence questions, particularly those relating to the woman's sexual history. This reform was rejected by the male-dominated Criminal Law Revision Committee, an advisory group of senior jurists, who deemed it unnecessary in 1984. The advisory group thought that if witnesses were represented in rape cases, it would be difficult to refuse such represention in other kinds of cases (Temkin 1987). Another suggestion has been to use expert witnesses to educate juries about rape trauma syndrome; this would enable them to understand such behaviour as delayed reporting, continuous crying, etc. on the part of raped witnesses. An obstacle to this reform is that the British judiciary is especially hostile to the expertise of the 'psy' professions. And, as Carol Smart points out, such a reform would not requalify women's accounts; rather, it would empower 'experts' to speak for them (Smart 1989).

Any demand by feminists to reform the conventions of rape trials will be resisted by one of the most powerful, independent, and unrepresentative sections of the British élite (*see* Chapter 5 [this refers to the original volume]). It may be, therefore, that reform of the law itself offers a more promising strategy. For example, feminist campaigns in the 1980s to reform the law on rape in marriage appeared to have met with success by 1991. Early in 1991 the Law Commission reported its deliberations on the law on rape in marriage. Its recommendations were that such rape be criminalised. The report reviewed the history of the legal immunity of Englishmen from prosecution for raping their wives. It dates from a 1736 opinion given by a Chief Justice Hale, who asserted that: 'By their mutual matrimonial consent and contract the wife hath given herself up in this kind to her husband, which she cannot retract.' No authority was cited for this statement, but it became the accepted legal wisdom incorporated into common law and assumed in the 1976 Sexual Offences Act. The Law Commission made its case on the basis that modern marriage is a partnership of equals; rape is non-consensual sexual intercourse, and women are entitled to refuse to have sexual intercourse on any particular occasion. The Law Commission considered and rejected all the objections normally raised to the criminalisation of rape in marriage as irrelevant to the fact that rape is a crime.[9]

The Law Commission's statement might best be seen as one of intent, a sign that attitudes are changing, rather than that rape in marriage will be prevented by legal change. It is likely that such a law will prove impossibly difficult to implement as evidential problems become apparent. Nevertheless, such a change is to be welcomed as an authoritative statement of social values and principles. Even if it does not bring immediate change in sexual behaviour, it adds to the resources that an individual woman may use when seeking her rights.

Our third example of feminist-state interaction on the issue of rape concerns the police. This is political work, similar in many respects to the political work undertaken by the women's refuge movement, and its examination reveals many of the same difficulties, although there are some differences. Two differences between rape crisis and women's refuge work are that the police appear to be more interested in the issue of rape, and that rape crisis groups appear to feel less able to co-operate with local police forces than many refuge workers do. Otherwise, the parallels are striking. For example, the struggle over definitions is central. Feminist control over the definition of rape and its solution is one of the issues. As police attitudes to rape begin to change, they have a tendency to seek to control the way in which it is processed. Feminist success in altering definitions of the issue has led not to the acceptance of feminist principles, but to their modification and incorporation by an institution with its own imperatives. This is progress, and it is progress in a feminist direction, but it is also part of a political struggle in which feminists risk incorporation and must become ever more skilled in order to fight their corner successfully. Another similarity between the rape crisis and the women's refuge movement is that, in addition to the skills of campaigning and administration, the skills of counselling and support are acquired. Thus (and this is the third similarity), what rape crisis has to offer is its expertise, the knowledge that it has gained about raped women in the course of its work. The police want (for whatever reasons) women to report rape, and they want to prosecute rapists. Rape crisis workers know why women are reluctant to report such crimes, and what may help to change that.

For most of the 1980s, LRG had a remarkably unsatisfactory relationship with the police. During its first ten years of operation, the police thought that LRG dissuaded women from reporting rapes, and group members say that the Metropolitan Police obstructed negotiations to co-operate by demanding such things as the names and addresses of all the women working there. They say that the police issued a memo to its officers telling them not to co-operate with LRG.[10]

LRG learned about police attitudes from the women who came to them: 'At the beginning we just didn't know. We discovered all kinds of appalling things like women being left with no clothes, being driven home with only a blanket around them, being taken around the streets immediately after the rape to look for the rapist … we were wary of developing a relationship with the police because of these things. We didn't want to be associated with that kind of treatment of raped women.'[11]

Other rape crisis groups had different attitudes and different experiences. Feminists became involved in police training, and local authority women's committees in Leeds and Norwich instituted committees in which rape crisis workers, Women's Aid workers, police, and welfare professionals concerned about violence to women regularly take part.

By the middle of the 1980s there were signs that the police were becoming more sensitive. Undoubtedly, the exposure of their practices by feminist action was part of the reason for this. And public outrage followed a television documentary by Roger Graef which was broadcast on national television in early 1982. The programme showed the hostile and brutal way in which the police treated a raped woman, who attempted to make a complaint to the Thames Valley police. In 1985 Metropolitan Police Superintendent Ian Blair wrote a book called *Investigating Rape.* This was a catalyst for revamping police procedures. In the same year the Metropolitan Police set up a working party on policing and rape. Blair has been at the forefront of the police drive to facilitate rape complaints by London women.[12] Following the working party's recommendations, the force organised four special rape suites in which to interview raped women. Women police officers were recruited and trained about rape trauma, women police surgeons were recruited, raped women were given a night to recover before their statements were taken, and better and more sensitive advice was given about the risks of pregnancy and venereal disease. The Home Office put pressure on other police forces to follow suit.

The differences between police and feminists remain. At the beginning of the 1990s, LRG members were sceptical about accounts of changes in police practice which were receiving widespread publicity. In reality, there were very few rape suites in operation, and for most women things had not really changed. For example, the Sexual Assault Referral Centre at St Mary's Hospital in Manchester, which is widely cited by the police as a model of provision, is rejected by feminists, who see the initiative as a 'medicalisation of rape' and who are not involved in the centre, which is staffed by paid professionals. The fear is that feminist words and phrases have been incorporated into a professional rhetoric about rape, but that the empowering politics to underpin those words is absent (Scott and Dickens, 1989).

Similar objections are raised to Home Office initiatives to fund the training of counsellors on victim support schemes for rape survivors. This was regarded by rape crisis group members as a way of providing alternatives to rape crisis lines. And feminists are concerned that the medicalisation of rape empowers medical professionals rather than rape survivors. It is a process whereby medical professionals try to establish themselves as the only appropriate definers and treaters of rape trauma. Such developments inevitably affect feminist capacities to deliver services, and must therefore inform their political strategies. As always, the struggle over definitions is crucial. The usurpation of rape by other experts may result in cuts in the funding of feminist initiatives and in the loss of the empowering element of feminist initiatives in rape counselling. 'The previously dominant definition of rape as an issue of crime and punishment left the field free for feminists to define the response of the woman who had been raped; because no one else was interested' (Scott and Dickens 1989: 191).

Rape crisis group members are not the only feminists in the policy networks. Local authority women's committees have looked for ways of providing support to women survivors of rape. NALGWC recommends that local authorities provide funding for rape crisis ventures, and that they facilitate liaison between the police and the voluntary sector. Progress has been made in some localities, including the provision of better facilities for the examination of rape survivors, liaison over training, and the encouragement of the police to inform raped women about rape crisis centres. Amongst the most important types of local authority initiatives in the 1980s and 1990s are the conferences on violence; these bring together the policy community and often lead to the establishment of continuing liaison groups. For example, the Crimes against Women conferences held in Leeds in the mid-1980s set the agenda for negotiations between feminists and the police which led to the establishment of the Leeds rape suite. Such conferences have been repeated all over the country. These are promising initiatives which may ensure the continuation of rape crisis group activity and feminist input into public responses to rape.

The problems facing feminists in reforming the law and the law enforcement of rape are enormous. Any demand concerned with sexuality risks being transposed into the language and policy of the moral purity campaigns (the relevance of this to the anti-pornography campaigns is discussed below) (Smart 1989). There appears to be an intractable contradiction between the need to give due weight to a raped woman's complaint and the need to maintain the presumption of the innocence of the accused in rape cases. This means that reform of the trial procedure may be an ethical and political minefield. On the one hand, it is vital to establish that women's experience is valid, but, on the other hand, the requirement that guilt be proved is a major resource which we would not want to see eroded. Rapists have been protected over the years by the mythology of rape, especially by the presumption that accusations of rape are more likely to be false than is the case for other crimes. It is the mythology, and the cultural phallocentrism that supports it, which has to go, rather than the need to prove that the accused is guilty.

Although the path across this minefield has not yet been cleared, much has been accomplished. A major shift in the understanding of rape is apparent amongst some policy-makers. Rape is less likely to be conceived of now as stranger attack, and more likely to be reported; it has been shown that rape accusations are no more likely to be false than any other accusations. The struggle about issue definitions and control makes their work difficult for feminists, but it is also a sign of success, an indicator that the issue of rape is on the political agenda.

Sexual Harassment

Sexual harassment at work is another issue that is part of the spectrum of male sexual violence, but it has generated a rather different kind of feminist politics from the other issues in this chapter. Because it is a 'workplace' issue with important equal opportunities implications, we seriously considered placing our main discussion of sexual harassment in Chapter 6 [this refers to the original volume].

But there are good reasons for including it here. Typically, instances of sexual harassment are evidence of the way in which men use sexuality to control women, and, as such, they are important to feminist explorations of sexual coercion. It has been recognised as a problem by feminists since the 1970s, and was raised in their discussions about the sources and meanings of male sexual violence. Sexual harassment includes a large area of behaviour ranging from verbal to physical abuse and rape. It is a salacious issue which often gets a lot of press coverage, but which was not recognised as an appropriate matter of concern in Britain until the early 1980s. It is a vexed issue for workplace managers and negotiators. Behaviour that most women would define as harassment is often considered to be harmless fun by many men. The problem is to gain acceptance of the perspectives that women may have of the issue. Once again, definition is very important.

Women against Sexual Harassment (WASH) was formed in 1984 and is the main feminist group campaigning on the issue. WASH defines sexual harassment as behaviour of a sexual nature which is unwelcome and unreciprocated and which might threaten job security and create a stressful or intimidating environment. The behaviour may include comments, looks, jokes, suggestions, pin-ups, and physical contact ranging from touching to pinching and rape. It is a widespread practice. A TUCRIC survey commissioned by the EOC found that, in 1983, 60 per cent of the women interviewed had been sexually harassed at work, most of them on more than one occasion (EOC 1987: 2–6).

Perhaps because it is harassment in the 'public' rather than in the 'private' sphere, it has engaged different policy networks from other debates about sexual violence. Because it is a workplace problem, both the trade unions and the equal opportunities policy communities have developed strategies to deal with it. In the trade-union movement, it was the women members of NALGO in Liverpool who took the lead. The local equal opportunities working party initiated discussion in 1981. Nationally, NALGO put out a statement in 1981 entitled 'Sexual Harassment is a Union Issue', and NATFHE, prompted by its women's rights panel, followed with 'Fighting Sexual Harassment at Work: An Issue for NATFHE' in 1982. During the 1980s other trade unions took up the issue, which was consistently endorsed by the TUC after 1983. Sarah Boston attributes this to the increasing presence of women in the unions during the 1970s and 1980s. The efforts that unions made to attract more women workers and to negotiate benefits for them were clearly a factor (Boston 1987: ch. 12).

The EOC was also interested in the issue of sexual harassment by the early 1980s. Complaints and queries started around 1984, after which they came in at an increasing rate, but there was no statutory provision against such harassment. Characteristically, the EOC watched for an appropriate legal opportunity. The opportunity came in 1986, when the Scottish Court of Session found that sexual harassment constituted sex discrimination in *Porcelli* v. *Strathclyde Regional Council.* In giving judgment, Lord Emslie said: 'Sexual harassment is a particularly degrading unacceptable form of treatment which it must have been the intention of Parliament to restrain.' This decision was strengthened when the Court of Appeal ruled in *DeSouza* v. *The Automobile Association,* confirmed in

1986, that employers are liable for acts of discrimination by their employees. That the courts and tribunals will take the issue seriously is evident in the rising levels of compensation that were being awarded by tribunals at the end of the decade.[13]

Most feminists who write about sexual harassment are clear that it is about power. It is primarily a demonstration and assertion of male power which serves to 'keep women in an inferior position. Treating women as sexual beings rather than working people undermines them and helps prevent them being treated as workers on the same terms as men' (Tysoe 1982). Perceptions of feminist involvement in this issue vary. Melissa Benn wrote in 1985 that, despite its importance, she was able to find little enthusiasm for campaigns about sexual harassment. In 1988 she repeated this assertion in the *Guardian,* commenting that the sexual harassment issue had never really ignited or mobilised feminists. This is partly attributable to the fact that it is a quite technical campaign, but also, she suggests, it is because the sexual harassment campaign did not really come out of the autonomous women's movement. Rather, she categorises it as an initiative by individual women within mixed, but male-dominated, organisations such as trade unions. Melissa Benn is very critical of the campaign, arguing that sexual harassment does not affect all women in the same way, and that those who are active on the issue show little awareness of the importance of racism. Other commentators see it differently. Sarah Boston (1987) details the activities of both black and white women trade-unionists in her account of women's organisation in British trade unions during the 1980s. Vicky Seddon's account takes a rather different line. She regards the questioning of male sexual power at work and on the street as an obvious development of the WLM (Seddon 1983: 20–4). In this sense, the politicisation of the issue of sexual harassment did come from the autonomous women's movement.

Anti-Pornography Campaigns and the Pornography Debates

Pornography is another issue that has been processed in 'established' political channels. But feminist activity in this area is different again from other issues that are defined in terms of male sexual violence. Divisions among feminists about pornography are severe, and the argument about definitions is a continuing feature of the politics of pornography. There has been feminist interest in the issue since the early 1970s, but activity took off during the 1980s, when new campaigns about pornography attracted increasing popular support. But popular support for their campaigns has not established feminist definitions of the issue in the minds of the public, in the view of 'informed opinion', or amongst policy-makers. This is partly because many other groups have an interest in making pornography a political issue. But that is not the only obstacle. Definitions of the pornography issue are also contested within feminism, where there is disagreement about the causes, nature, effects, and responses to pornographic representations and their marketing. The most influential views are those that stress the violent associations of pornography. The very fact that we discuss the issue here, in a chapter about sex, violence, and institutions, is a recognition of the effect of feminist interpretations of pornography which have emphasised its violent and coercive dimensions. But some feminists would argue that the connections between violence and pornography are beside the point, part of another issue. They maintain that once the two issues of pornography and violence are separated, the futility and, indeed, the danger of censorship as a solution become apparent. But such arguments have not prevailed. The acceptability of censorship has provoked divisions between liberals and New Right both amongst feminists and in the wider political arena. Pornography therefore presents a complex pattern of politics in which different groups of feminists have allied with groups on the Right, the Left, and in the centre of the political spectrum. It is almost impossible to isolate the arguments and debates from the context in which they take place. Moreover, the absence of agreement about definitions, and the controversial nature of censorship as a proposed solution, set a framework in which feminist interventions might best be characterised as struggles over definitions. Our account of pornography therefore includes a considerable amount of background detail and an extensive discussion of different efforts by feminists to understand the nature of pornography and the discourse in which it is embedded.

Contemporary feminist debates about pornography really began in the USA, where the issue trundled along for some years before it took off with the publication of Andrea Dworkin's *Pornography: Men Possessing Women* in 1979, which was published in Britain in 1981. Pornography is an issue which emphasises many of the divisions between feminists. It also taps the ambivalence of women who find positions on one or the other side of these divisions difficult to sustain in the face of contradictory experiences and emotions. As we write, the debate is in full flow. It is a debate that has both popular and intellectual manifestations, and it is often bitter and sectarian. It is difficult to predict which views will prevail either in the women's movement or in British society generally.

It is possible to distinguish three kinds of problems in making policy about pornography: problems of response, problems of meaning, and problems of strategy. Each of these affects and is affected by each of the others. The main problem of response is the extreme difficulty of trying to understand and analyse pornography from feminist perspectives. Feelings of anger, arousal, despair — sometimes all of these at once — are frequently reported. If feminists are to be true to their principles of empowering women, then each type of response must be confronted and understood. Problems of meaning include difficulties and disagreements about definitions, the nature of evidence, and literal effects. Feminists disagree both about appropriate definitions of pornography and about whether the construction of such a definition is an appropriate endeavour. This overlaps with disagreement about whether pornography may be identified by the specific images that it offers, or whether it is the context of the images and their offering which gives sexual images a degrading character. There is also an important argument about whether pornography causes rape and other sexual violence, or whether it simply represents it and elicits a response only at the level of fantasy.

There are two problems about strategy: one is what to do about pornography, and the other is what sort of alliances should be made to obtain a preferred solution.

Should feminists ally with the Right to promote bans or licensing restrictions on pornography? Is it appropriate to increase state powers over the production of images and their display? Is it appropriate to seek protection from the state at all? In engaging the issue of pornography, feminists find themselves caught up in debates about censorship and state power that have been hotly and bitterly contested for some years.

Most feminists agree that pornography eroticises power and domination. The domination of women by men is the mainstay of most pornography. This (for a variety of reasons) arouses both men and women, which leads to the assumption that, in sex, domination by men and submission by women must be natural. If it is natural in sex (which is natural), it must also be natural in other parts of social life. There is also agreement that violent or sadistic pornography, which shows women and/or children as raped, mutilated, murdered, etc., is objectionable. However, the meaning of violent pornography, and its importance, are matters of disagreement. During the 1980s two basic views of pornography were developed by feminists. Beverly Brown (quoted in Smart 1989: ch. 6) called them the 'pornography as violence' position and the 'pornography as representation' position. Revolutionary and Radical feminists take the former view, arguing that pornography is society's most significant means of subordinating women and that violent pornography reveals men's true sexuality.

Other feminists disagree. A group of Socialist feminist intellectuals is prominent in advancing the 'pornography as representation' position, citing feminist work on images and representation and its meaning and effects. Drawing on work by Ros Coward (1987), Annette Kuhn (1985), and others, the argument is that pornography is a 'regime of representation'. The representations show bodies, usually naked, in a sexualised way, or people involved in the sex act, according to certain conventions which are interpreted by society as pornographic. On this interpretation, nothing is intrinsically pornographic. Rather, there are codes of interpretation which we learn and apply. These are conditioned by context and circumstance. There is a growing body of scholarship which demonstrates that there is a pornographic 'genre' attached to the way in which women are portrayed. This pornographic genre is widespread. Many of the poses, expressions, juxtapositions of bodies, arrangements of clothes, even the vulnerability of the posed model — common devices in the advertising that makes use of images of women — may be shown to conform to this regime of representation. The codes of pornography are fragmentation, submission, and availability, and these are apparent everywhere. The display of women's breasts in the daily newspapers, the arrangement of women's submissive bodies around motor cars, etc., is evidence that pornographic representation is now openly encoded. Both pornographers and advertisers promote a repertoire of images that promise certain kinds of pleasure. When a viewer is invited to desire a particular object, this is often done by making it appear available, submissive, and compliant. It is there to please. 'The object (whether a woman or a car) is ready and able to do anything, go anywhere you please. Any possible assertion of autonomy (i.e. saying no, breaking down) is excluded.'

It is this reduction to the level of commodities, the signification of women as having no autonomy, which constitutes the offensiveness (Coward 1987). To summarise: pornography is only one source of degrading images of powerless, submissive women. The political implications of the 'pornography as representation' position are twofold. First, nothing will be gained by banning pornography when so many other representations of women encode the same meanings; and, secondly, there is no reason why pornography should degrade women; it is possible to construct a non-sexist pornography, a feminist-inspired erotica.

That such an erotica is possible is denied by many Radical feminists, who are much more concerned about the association between violence and pornography, a concern which shows itself in two ways. First, their writing often concentrates on specific items of violent pornography rather than considering its full variety and its context. Secondly, at the heart of their political analysis is the contention that pornography is one of the main causes of male sexual violence. Indeed, some British Radical feminists accept unreservedly that pornography is the main cause of women's subordination.

The debate is difficult to assess, not least because it tends not to be conducted at the same intellectual level, over the same issues, or on the same political terrain. It is unusual to find the protagonists answering each other's arguments. More usual is a crossfire of parallel accusations which leaves each side convinced that their case is irrefutable. Matters are made more complicated by the fact that, as we described in Chapter 4 [this refers to the original volume], this is a three-sided debate for feminists. There were three main feminist campaigning groups at the end of 1991: Campaign against Pornography (CAP), Campaign against Pornography and Censorship (CAPC), and Feminists against Censorship (FAC). As their names imply, much of the debate was about censorship.

The Political Context of the Pornography Debates

In order to provide an adequate contextualisation of the feminist pornography debates, it is necessary to provide two brief background sketches. The first is an outline of the various positions in long-standing debates about censorship in Britain; the second is an account of the MacKinnon/Dworkin ordinance which many feminists in the USA have tried to incorporate into American law.

In Britain, feminist debates about pornography intersect — and therefore compete for attention and influence — with two well-entrenched positions on censorship: that of the liberal establishment and that of the moral Right. As is the case with feminist views, each position is a continuum, each contains contradictions and ambiguities. There is not enough space to explore all of this here, so we offer only a brief and somewhat simplified outline. Carol Smart wrote what, in our view, remains the best feminist-inspired summary accounts of the two positions (Smart 1989: ch. 6). She inferred the liberal establishment view from the 1979 report of the Williams Committee on Obscenity and Film Censorship. The strategy of the Williams Committee was to treat sexual matters as matters of individual taste, preference, and concern. The committee was not interested in the wider questions of sexual power and dominance. Their definition of pornography identified two components: intention to arouse sexually, and the explicit representation of sexual material. This two-part definition was constructed in order to protect 'art' from legal interference, and the individual from unwanted encounters with pornography. The idea was that such a definition would offer objective measurable criteria for classifying material as pornographic, and then the display of such material could be controlled. Both components needed to be present for the matter to be classified as pornographic. In practice, however, the two-part definition collapses into one, as only explicitness can be 'objectively' measured. Intention is always contentious, and, argues Smart, actual arousal may only be presumed. In practice, therefore, both will be read off from explicitness.

The Williams Committee did not find the evidence that pornography led to violence convincing, and therefore it did not think that censorship was necessary. Its general view was that censorship should be kept to the minimum possible level. The moral Right, on the other hand, faces no such difficulties. It is pro-censorship, and seeks the widest possible ambit of control. Its strategy is to expand the definition of pornography. In the context of British law, custom, and practice, such a strategy is fairly straightforward. The tendency has been to restrict the publication of materials deemed to be 'obscene' or 'indecent'. Both terms have working legal definitions: if an object or representation is obscene, it is likely to deprave. The general public are not regarded as uniformly depravable, and policy about obscene material normally restricts its scope to those likely to come into contact with it. 'Indecent' is a more flexible term, defined in the 'Clapham omnibus' tradition. It consists of 'anything', said Lord Denning in 1976, 'which an ordinary decent man or woman would find to be shocking, disgusting or revolting'. Leaders of the moral Right such as Lord Longford, Mary Whitehouse, and Winston Churchill have sought to substitute the wider notion of indecency for the more restricted notion of obscenity. They have had some success. The Indecent Displays Act of 1981 prohibits public display of materials which would be offensive to the general public. For example, pornographic magazines may not be kept at or below eye-level in newsagents. The moral Right believes that pornography is harmful and that it consists mainly of representations of sex. Their views would not preclude the banning of all representations of sex, including sex education materials. The moral Right tend to be sexual conservatives, and the liberal establishment tend to be sexual libertarians, a division that informs their views about censorship.

To understand the debates amongst United States feminists that became so influential in Britain during the 1980s and 1990s, it is important to start with the campaigns initiated by Andrea Dworkin and Catherine MacKinnon. City councils in the USA can pass local legislation as they wish. Such laws, called ordinances, must be constitutional, but otherwise they are unrestricted. Dworkin and MacKinnon inaugurated a new phase in the United States anti-pornography campaigns when they drafted an ordinance that was submitted to Minneapolis City Council in 1983. The ordinance enabled women to take pornographers to court on the grounds that pornography discriminated against women, denying them the equality to which they were legally entitled. The draft ordinance generated considerable controversy, as the city council considered its implications in a set of widely publicised hearings in which evidence was given by women who had been harmed by pornography, by academics, lawyers, and jurists. Minneapolis decided not to pass the ordinance; it was later passed by the Indianapolis City Council, but it was declared unconstitutional by the Supreme Court. Briefs (evidence) were presented to the court by opposing groups of feminists. Feminists who opposed the ordinance called themselves the Feminists Anti-Censorship Task Force (FACT). The signatories of the FACT brief were mainly feminist intellectuals and artists, including a few men. The censorship and pornography debate among American feminists is a very bitter one which shows no signs of subsiding. The point of the Dworkin/MacKinnon ordinance (or the Minneapolis ordinance, as it is sometimes called) is, its sponsors argue, that it categorises pornography as a 'discriminatory practice based on sex which denies women equality in society'. It offers six alternative definitions of pornography which specify that it is images that are violent in various ways, that the images depict male domination of women and that they are degrading to women, and that they show women enjoying their degradation. Such images encourage men to believe that women enjoy violent and degrading sexual treatment, and the supporters of the ordinance assert that pornography is behind male sexual violence and that it is the chief cause of the domination of women by men.

The strategic thinking behind the ordinance is that it is the women who have been discriminated against, rather than law-enforcement officers, who may decide to take cases to court. This ostensibly avoids the problem of increasing the powers of state censors. Cases may be brought against producers or sellers of pornographic material which meets any of the six definitions. FACT disagrees with the analysis that pornography is central to male domination, and it does not think that it is appropriate to use the law to restrict speech and images. There are also disputes between the two camps about every possible point of detail and strategy. The significance of this debate to Britain lies in the general issue of whether it is appropriate to use the law to restrict images and in specific proposals to adapt the ordinance for British legislation.

During the 1970s few British feminists would have sought to increase state censorship as a solution to the problem of pornography. At that time, the state was regarded as an important site of patriarchy, and the obscenity laws were seen as obstacles to women's efforts to control their fertility. Gradually, however, critiques of pornography were built around the idea that it constituted the root of the male aggression and violence which were regarded as the basis for male domination (Segal 1990a). As a result, feminists became prominent actors in the different initiatives on pornography during the 1980s. These ranged from direct action and protest demonstrations of various kinds, to parliamentary tactics, to carefully elaborated theoretical arguments in academic journals and feminist publications. By the end of 1991 all three of the campaigns that were competing for feminist support were well established. They comprised the largest feminist mobilisation since the pro-choice campaigns of the late 1970s and early 1980s. They were remarkable in that, as in the USA, a public and bitterly contested dispute took place between feminists.

What were the issues and points of difference? In answering this question, it is important to understand that support for, and opposition to, censorship was only one part of a dispute that ranged over the whole terrain of feminist politics and that brought into sharp relief many of the divisions which had been present in the movement since the end of the 1970s. A careful sift through the many statements, leaflets, pronouncements, speeches, polemics, and reasoned arguments produced by feminists yields no fewer than ten main contested issues. These may be posed as a series of questions.

1. How should pornography be defined? In particular, is it a matter of content — that is, the image itself — that makes a representation pornographic, or is it a matter of context?
2. Does pornography cause male sexual violence?
3. Is pornography the mainstay of the male dominance of women?
4. Should there be state censorship of pornography?
5. May women be empowered by particular kinds of anti-censorship laws?
6. Why has pornography depicting sexual violence become so widespread?
7. Is it ever appropriate for feminists to ally with the anti-feminist Right?
8. Is a feminist erotica possible (or worth having)?
9. Is it the right time to make restrictive laws which necessarily increase the powers of the state?
10. Is anti-pornography campaigning an appropriate activity for feminists at a time when there are so many important things to campaign about?

These questions reveal many of the feminist concerns of the 1980s. There are elements of commitment to the development of empowering strategies, questions about appropriate attitudes to the state, issues arising from different conceptions about the nature of (male and female) sexuality. Difference is also an issue, not only because pornographic representations often draw on the cultural eroticisation of images of black women, but also because imperatives of class and race are important in forcing women to work in the sex industries and because the politics of sexual difference informs feminist responses to pornography. An important element in the campaigns about censorship has been the experience of Section 28 of the 1988 Local Government Bill, which has become Section 2*a* of the 1988 Local Government Act. This clause restrains local authorities from 'promoting' homosexuality. It was introduced after widespread homophobia about a library book called *Jenny Lives with Eric and Martin*, an educational children's book produced to show that gay men can be parents too, and live as a family. The book was made available under parental control in libraries in Haringey. This was not the only influence. As we outlined in Chapter 3 [this refers to the original volume], the issue of sado-masochism became a hot potato in the British gay communities in the mid-1980s. The one and only issue of a lesbian sex magazine called QUIM was banned from Sisterwrite and Gays the Word bookshops (*see* Chapter 3 [of the original volume]). The meaning of fantasy and the nature of lesbian sexual arousal became part of the debate about pornography and censorship.

The terms of the debates between the opposing camps are sometimes reasoned and careful, but more often polemical and bitter. On occasion, they are simply vicious. Sheila Jeffreys asserts in her essay in the *Feminism and Censorship* collection edited by Chester and Dickey that what motivates anti-censorship feminists is not their convictions but their ambitions, their desire to climb career ladders and thus avoid offending the powerful liberal establishment figures who control such ladders. Anti-censorship feminists have been accused of being in alliance with the pornographers, whilst pro-censorship feminists are accused of being against sex. Elizabeth Wilson has remarked that the danger of focusing campaigns on the sexually explicit and on literal effects is that connections between pornography and other degrading images of women are ignored, and the contradictory uses to which the imagery is put goes unremarked (Wilson 1989). Speech, words, and images are simply speech, words, and images. What matters is behaviour, and laws already exist to prohibit the violent behaviour that is objected to by pro-censorship feminists. FAC warns against relying on the state not to misuse its powers, and points out that the increasing strength of the right makes the 1990s a very bad time to call for any increases in state power.

In practice, the feminist pornography campaigns involve different sorts of people with different preoccupations. CAP and CAPC are led mainly by people who have some experience of sexual violence, either in their work or as victims, and they campaign mainly on the basis of information and evidence about sexual violence. The material that they oppose and analyse is offensive, involving strong, violent images which they describe in their debates. The fact that this evidence is episodic, and that the evidence of literal effects is often anecdotal, is often obscured by the sheer power of the images and the strength of the popular emotional response to them. FAC, on the other hand, is led by academics, intellectuals, and artists, some of who are directly involved in the production of feminist erotica. They abhor the violent and degrading images of much pornography, but they are concerned to protect 'art' and to explore sexual imagery and representations. The result is that the two groups often do not address the same issues. What is taking place is not so much a debate as the telling of a set of parallel accounts by feminists who are separately engaged in working out their positions on the pornography issue. Their accounts will have to become a debate if feminists are to achieve any unity on the issue.

Conclusions: Feminism and Male Violence

Our discussion shows that despite a significant cross-fertilisation of feminist views about different aspects of male sexual violence, and despite considerable co-operation in particular campaigns, there are still many important disagreements over these issues. For over twenty years, concerns about male violence have been interwoven with other significant feminist issues. They were argued about and discussed in an atmosphere that was often uncomfortable, sometimes mistrustful and hostile, as British feminists became aware of the importance of the issues that divide them.

Some of the divisions have eased. By the early 1990s, as the arguments about racial difference and racism which were so bitterly fought during the 1980s begin to recede, black feminists were beginning to note the similarities between their circumstances and those of white women. For example, in a discussion of the violence of the 1985 Brixton riots, Anna Hearne argued that the sadism and racism of the British should not obscure the sexism of black men to black women, two of whom were raped during the riot by black youths. She complains that, too often, fear of racism led white women on the Left to keep silent about violence in the black communities. It is wrong, she wrote, for white women to corrupt their reasons for fighting racism with the idea that racial oppression excuses the sexual violence of the black male. Only when black women speak out against the violence that they received within their communities will things improve for black women (Hearne 1986: 9-14). By 1991, when we interviewed black feminists working in refuges, such implicit comparisons between black and white women were being made explicit.

Race was not the only 'difference' issue to feature in feminist work about male violence. Division about sexuality also persisted, this time expressed as a problem of how to understand male sexual behaviour. This disagreement continues to be sharp. Margaret Hunt recently pointed out in *Feminist Review* that a clear analogy could be drawn between the contemporary moral Right and past social purity movements. She found a striking parallel between the sexual views of the women in the nineteenth-century social purity movement and those expressed by the contemporary Radical feminist Sheila Jeffreys. She expressed concern that in allying with the moral Right, Radical feminists were ignoring the lesson of the past — that conservatives normally co-opt feminists, rather than the other way around. Jeffreys and her supporters continued to blame sexual libertarians for the growth of male sexual violence (*see* Jeffreys 1990, for a recent restatement of this position). The implication of Jeffreys's arguments is that there is a correct feminist sexual practice, one in which only certain kinds of sex are acceptable. This was apparent in the Radical feminists' widespread rejection of attempts to produce a feminist erotica. Such rejections, and their accompanying calls for censorship, were rejections of difference and variety, the product of a notion, often unarticulated, of an essential female nature. From that notion, there was a relatively straight path to strategies of intolerance and control. In a climate of sexual panic such as that generated by the AIDS crisis, the consequences of such intolerance may be catastrophic (Hunt 1990).

Socialist feminists were quick to criticise any feminist alliance with the political Right. They were especially mindful of the fact that feminist campaigners did not have the power to secure their definitions and priorities through the processes of law-making and law enforcement. They drew attention to the parallels between the social purity campaigns of the last century and the new anti-pornography campaigns. Such campaigns were always dangerous, because there could be no guarantee — indeed, there was little likelihood — that censorship or social purity policies would be implemented by officials who are sympathetic to feminist values. It was not feminists who controlled the levers of state power (Betterton 1985). Too often, Radical feminists appeared to be unaware of such dangers. Indeed, they sometimes appeared to believe the very opposite. For example, Sheila Jeffreys attributed an unrealistically large measure of political power to feminism when she asserted that it was the insecurities felt by men in the face of newly powerful women which made them crave images that assert male dominance and female submission — in other words, that the growth in the market for violent pornographic representations was an indicator of a dimunition of male power (Jeffreys 1990).

Jeffreys's contention seems to us to be a somewhat optimistic and overly simple formulation. The feminist achievement in the politics of sexual coercion is a reformulation of the problem. Although much has been accomplished, this work is far from complete. Feminists have defined problems in terms of male violence, because it was possible to marshall a huge body of evidence which showed that this was a reasonable way of understanding the problems. That was a necessary beginning. Now the plausibility of such definitions should be examined and, if it is false, exposed. For feminists to do this, it will be necessary to look closely and courageously at evidence and ideas about maleness and the construction of masculinity and feminity, and the structures of thought which support that evidence and those ideas. Such exploration should be constrained neither by essentialist assumptions about sexual characteristics nor by gloomy prognostications about the political uses to which feminist work might be put.

We also take issue with the view that feminists are too weak politically to risk placing the pornography issue on the public agenda. The weakness of this argument — that feminists have insufficient power to risk imposing their preferred policy solutions — lies in its implicit assumption that feminist ambition should be commensurate with feminist political power. We dispute this understanding of political power. Although we are not convinced of the case for censorship, we do not agree that the reason for its avoidance lies in asymmetric power relations. That would mean giving up the battle before it is joined, that ignores the power of ideas to alter political outcomes. The project to understand sexual coercion has its own (compulsive) dynamic, and the task now is to make further explorations of the significance of images and representations to constructions of identity and sexuality, whilst at the same time developing the practical policies that feminism has initiated. If the campaigns in favour of censorship are dangerous, and we believe that they probably are, then what will alter their focus is the open debate and the development of new understandings which come from a continuous exploration and contestation of dominant meanings of particular phenomena. The politics of the movements to alter the political treatment of domestic violence, rape, and sexual harassment are all proof that such a strategy, whilst difficult, is possible and productive.

Notes

1. Accounts of the movement by Rowbotham and Coote and Pattullo which were published in 1990 barely mentioned the issue. Lynne Segal's books (1987, 1990b) were amongst the first in Britain to offer analyses and critiques of feminist preoccupations with male sexual violence.
2. For lists of refuges and other information, *see* WAFE, *Women's Aid into the 1990s: Annual Report, 1989–90* (Bristol 1990); SWA, *Scottish Women's Aid: Annual Report, 1989–90* (Edinburgh 1990); WWA, *Welsh Women's Aid: Annual Report, 1989–90* (Cardiff 1990).
3. Muneeza Inam, 'Opening Doors', in Southall Black Sisters, *Against the Grain*.
4. *See* WAFE, *Women's Aid into the 1990s*.
5. WAFE, *Women's Aid into the 1990s*.
6. The term 'rape crisis centre' normally refers to rape crisis lines. Experience and fear of attack by hostile men and the importance of survivor anonymity meant that 'drop-in' centres were not really feasible.
7. For a full account, *see* Liz Kelly's interview with Romi Bowen and Bernadette Manning in *Trouble and Strife*, 10 (Spring 1987). This is the source of most of our account of LRG.
8. The question of consent in rape trials is avoided only if the man says it is a case of mistaken identity, e.g. that he was somewhere else at the time.
9. 'Law Commission on Rape and Marriage', *Spare Rib*, Mar. 1991.
10. *See* Liz Kelly, *Trouble and Strife,* 10 (1987).
11. *See* Liz Kelly, *Trouble and Strife*, 54 (1987).
12. *See* Ian Blair's letter to the *Guardian*, 20 Dec. 1990.
13. For a good review of the implications of early cases, *see* 'Sexual Harassment at Work' (1987).

References

Benn, M. (1985) 'Isn't Sexual Harassment Really about Masculinity?', *Spare Rib*, 156: 6–8.
Betterton, R. (1985) 'How Do Women Look? The Female Nude in the Work of Suzanne Valedon', *Feminist Review*, 19: 3–24.
Boston, S. (1987) *Women Workers and the Trade Unions*, London: Lawrence and Wishart.
Brownmiller, S. (1975) *Against our Will*, Harmondsworth: Penguin.
Coward, R. (1987) 'Sexual Violence and Sexuality', in Feminist Review (ed.) *Sexual Violence: A Reader*, London: Virago, pp. 307–325.

Hague, G. Harwin, N., McKinn, K., Rubens J. and Taylor, M. (1989) 'Women's Aid: Policing Male Violence in the Home', in C. Dunhill (ed.) *The Boys in Blue*, London: Virago, pp. 89–91.

Hearne, A. J. (1986) 'Racism, Rape and Riots', *Trouble and Strife*, 9: 9–14. 89–91

Hunt, M. (1990) 'The De-Eroticization of Women's Liberation: Social Purity Movements and the Revolutionary Feminism of Sheila Jeffreys', *Feminist Review*, 34: 23–46.

Jeffreys, S. (1990) *Anticlimax*, London: The Women's Press.

Kuhn, A. (1985) *The Power of the Image*, London: Routledge and Kegan Paul.

Lees, S. (1989) 'Blaming the Victim', *New Statesman and Society*, 1 December.

MacKinnon, C. (1987) *Feminism Unmodified: Discourses on Life and Law*, Cambridge, Mass.: Harvard University Press.

Mama, A. (1989) 'Violence against Black Women: Gender, Race and State Responses', *Feminist Review*, 28: 16–55,

Mama, A. (1990) 'A Hidden Struggle', *Spare Rib*, 209: 8–11.

NALGWC, (1990) *Responding with Authority: Local Authority Initiatives to Counter Violence against Women*, Manchester: Pankhurst Press.

Sahgal, G. (1989) 'Fundamentalism and the Multiculturalist Fallacy', in Southall Black Sisters, *Against the Grain: Southall Black Sisters, 1979–1989*, Southall: Southall Black Sisters.

Scott, S. and Dickens, A. (1989) 'Police and the Professionalisation of Rape', in C. Dunhill (ed.), *The Boys in Blue, pp. 190–191.*

Seddon, V. (1983) 'Keeping Women in their Place', *Marxism Today*, 27 (7): 20–24.

Segal, L. (1987) *Is the Future Female?*, London: Virago.

Segal, L. (1990a) 'Pornography and Violence: What the Experts Really Say', *Feminist Review*, 36: 29–41.

Segal, L. (1990b) *Slow Motion: Changing Masculinities, Changing Men*, London: Virago.

'Sexual Harassment at Work'. *Industrial Relations Review and Report,* 384 (20 January 1987): 2–6.

Smart, C. (1989) *Feminism and the Power of Law*, London: Routledge and Kegan Paul.

Soothill, K., Walby, S., and Bagguley, P. (1991) 'Judges, the Media and Rape', *Journal of Law and Society*, 17 (2): 211–33.

Stedward, G. (1987) 'Entry into the System: A Case Study of Women in Scotland', in J. Richardson and G. Jordan (eds) *Government and Pressure Groups in Britain*, Oxford: Clarendon, pp. 217–18.

Temkin, J. (1987) *Rape and the Legal Process*, London: Sweet and Maxwell.

Tysoe, M. (1982) 'The Sexual Harassers', *New Society*, 4 Nov.

Wilson, E. (1989) 'Against Feminist Fundamentalism', *New Statesman*, 23 June.

Chapter Thirteen

Feminist Ideas and Domestic Violence Policy Change*

with Stefania Abrar and Helen Margetts

The extent of influence of feminist ideas and efforts on domestic violence policy has been the subject of some contention. For example Hanmer, Radford and Stanko (1989) argue that by 1989 it appeared that '... the police and caring professions have responded ... to feminist criticisms of the 1970s, but have done so in a way which has completely negated feminist definitions, politics, research and provision of support services'. In their view the wide and radical aims of feminist advocates to shift official thinking about domestic violence and to insert feminist practices into policy have not been met. Institutional analyses of the development of domestic violence policy since the early 1970s would, with their emphasis on formal policy making roles tend to concur with this statement. However, if an approach that focuses on the impact of ideas on policy change is used, a different picture emerges; one of feminist driven change. The advocacy coalition framework is such an approach. Using the belief systems of public officials and policy advocates as its starting point, policy oriented learning as its motor of change and policy change as its measure of success the advocacy coalition framework is a pluralist approach to public policy analysis, with a built-in recognition that policy is carried out by a huge and complex array of networked actors.

The advocacy coalition model was developed in the USA and the available evidence from other polyarchies suggests that it will have most utility for policy areas that exhibit pluralistic characteristics (Parsons 1995: 201). Domestic violence policy is just such an area, complicated by the involvement of actors at different levels of the political system who have different priorities, constraints and traditions including professional values and organisational cultures. These include national and local political elites, national and local officials, regional authorities including the health services and the police, experts and activists. At local level policy delivery is typically the provenance of several agencies. Complex institutional patterns of activity are made more opaque by the nature of domestic violence that is also termed as violence or abuse by known men and spouse abuse.[1] The part played by feminist ideas and the belief systems of relevant officials is central to the policy. Treatment of domestic violence involves a constant struggle to traverse boundaries of public and private, bringing into play a concern with

---

*   'Feminist ideas and domestic policy change' (with S. Abrar and H. Margetts), *Political Studies*, 2000, 48(2), pp. 239–262.

gender relations that has not traditionally informed the study of public policy. The 'radical' feminist policy advocates, who brought the issue into the public sphere and keep it there, have been unwilling to compromise on their understanding of the causes of, and solutions to, the problem. Action-oriented feminist experts are and have been particularly interested in understanding violence at home in a women-centred way, a preoccupation that is reflected in reports, books, public statements and projects.

Feminist scholarship offers a further reason to adopt the framework. Feminists have noted significant similarities and interconnections between feminist action inside and outside the state. Brownhill and Halford (1990) insist that in practice 'people are constantly meeting, consulting or working jointly and resources may constantly change hands'. Eisenstein (1985) and Stetson and Mazur (1995) observe that feminist advocacy functions most effectively where it has a beachhead in the policy making and implementation institutions. Ideally this takes the form of women's policy machinery, that is agencies with responsibility for sex equality, but also useful are feminist individuals in strategic positions in the important institutions. In her discourse based study of feminist accounts of the state Watson (1990) reminds us that it would be wrong to assume that institutional political agendas are monolithic and uniform. Within any institution a range of sympathies will exist and feminist policy advocates have been skilful at exploiting them. Such observations combine to suggest that a policy approach that is sensitive to ideas and belief systems and tracks the policy influence of opposing advocacy coalitions operating across the boundaries of the state will be the most useful in describing policies where feminist coalitions have endeavoured to influence public policy. We argue that such a lens is provided by Paul Sabatier's advocacy coalition framework, 'a descriptive framework outlining what to consider when examining policy change'. Capable of dealing with mess, the framework is a sensible tool for use in an area of research that is currently at the stage of systematic (thick) description of its object. It uses the concept of belief system as 'the template on which change is measured, both with respect to the beliefs of different coalitions and the actual content of public policy' (Sabatier and Jenkins-Smith 1993: 55). In this paper we apply the framework to the making of domestic violence policy in two British localities from the 1970s to the mid-1990s. The case studies demonstrate that by 1995 a significant and effective feminist advocacy apparatus was located around the issue of domestic violence, that considerable feminist influence had been at work and that an identifiable 'traditionalist' opposing coalition was located at various levels of government.

This paper is in four parts. First, we summarise the advocacy coalition framework as a lens for viewing public policy. Second, we give an account of domestic violence policy in Britain, outlining the roles of two opposing coalitions — feminists and traditionalists. We argue that the concerted nature of the feminist 'advocacy coalition' creates an opposing coalition from the diffuse assortment of state actors involved in domestic violence policy making and implementation, a coalition that favours the status quo and is resistant to feminist approaches. Third, we illustrate our points with a detailed exploration of policy change in two localities. Finally, we offer a concluding assessment of the relative influence of the feminist advocacy coalition on domestic violence policy.

The Advocacy Coalition Framework

The advocacy coalition framework is a theory of policy change and learning. As described by Sabatier and Jenkins-Smith in 1993 it requires a perspective of at least ten years, a focus on policy subsystems, an intergovernmental dimension and the conceptualisation of public policy as both analogous to and based upon a belief system capable of establishing value priorities and causal assumptions. The elements of this framework seem especially pertinent to domestic violence policy. For example, the long time span is important because changes in domestic violence policy have taken place only after sustained effort by activists over a significant period of time. Sabatier and Jenkins-Smith argue that for any policy problem (termed policy sub-system), the actors involved in dealing with the problem can be aggregated into a number of advocacy coalitions who 'share a set of normative and causal beliefs and who often act in concert'(Sabatier and Jenkins-Smith 1993: 23). Not everyone in a policy subsystem will 'belong to' an advocacy coalition or share its belief system. There will almost certainly be a category of actors termed 'policy brokers' whose dominant concerns are with keeping the level of political conflict within acceptable limits and reaching some 'reasonable solution', for example civil servants. In any subsystem there may also be advocates who do not belong to a coalition, for example, researchers who have skills to offer, but no particular policy stance. By contrast the coalition will consist of those who prioritise policies that arise from their belief system. In Sabatier's analysis, belief systems are not homogenous, but stratified and hierarchical, building upon previous arguments that beliefs are important and complex yet structured dimensions of policy making (Majone 1989; Putnam 1976). They include what Sabatier terms deep core beliefs, policy core beliefs and secondary aspects. Deep core beliefs are normative and ontological axioms such as beliefs about human nature, the value and priority of freedom, security, power, health. Policy core beliefs are policy propositions such as whether to use market mechanisms or government action to produce policy. Secondary aspects are institutional decisions about policy. Deep core beliefs are hypothesised to be stable and virtually impossible to change from within the subsystem; they are susceptible only to major external influences. Policy core beliefs are difficult to change and secondary aspects are amenable to change under certain circumstances.[2]

In addition to the timeframe, the most important components of the framework for our purposes are its taxonomy of belief systems and its assertion that it is belief systems that drive and constrain policy change which will arise from competition between opposing advocacy coalitions located within and around state institutions. The model has obvious application to the analysis of feminist ideas on domestic violence policy because it incorporates the notion of long-term interests, it is driven by beliefs and learning and it can be adapted to explain feminist engagements with state institutions, for example with the police, with women's policy agencies and with individual feminists located in various government institutions. It enables the identification of the part played by feminist core beliefs about the causes and nature of domestic violence and demonstrates the unchanging nature of such beliefs among feminist advocates and, in specific localities and time periods, their role in bringing about policy change. We will suggest that in the case of domestic violence, the traditionalist coalition was prepared, under pressure, to change its policy core beliefs, probably in order to maintain its deep core beliefs. Under the circumstances we describe, policy core beliefs will change because of the importance of deep core beliefs, an observation that may have important implications for the application of the framework.

Domestic Violence Policy

New knowledge about domestic violence was part of the outcome of the consciousness raising groups that characterised the 1970s women's liberation movement. The resurgence of feminism created a climate of public opinion that was receptive to thinking about the problems of women who wished to escape violence. British feminist interest in male violence to women and children in the home and family is long-standing. Nineteenth-century feminists were concerned about 'spouse abuse' which they thought was largely the product of male alcoholism, hence the slogan 'marry only men who have taken the pledge'. In the 1970s the issue was taken up again by feminists who gathered information on violence at home and became involved in successive campaigns about this issue. According to most accounts this was the issue that split British feminism at the end of the 1970s. At that time British feminist movements were often characterised as divided into two broad wings, socialist feminists who (to simplify) believed male violence to women was the product of capitalist structures and institutions and radical feminists who argued that it was in men's nature to mistreat women. Over time the argument became more sophisticated and divisions blurred, but socialist feminists never accepted the essentialist analysis of domestic violence and radical feminists never quite abandoned it. Versions of this nature–nurture dispute continue to underpin debates in feminism. Parallelling their theoretical disagreement was a functional division of labour in which the main feminist actors on issues of male violence were radical feminists. Other feminists, while supportive of campaigns and action research tended to concentrate their activities in other areas.

From the 1970s onwards a coalition of feminists, including local and national experts and activists involving traditional and new feminist women's organisations, sought to alter legislation and practice on domestic violence. The advocates consisted of a diverse and informal coalition of activists involving new feminist groups such as the Women's Aid Federation, Rights of Women, Justice for Women, Southall Black Sisters, the Zero Tolerance campaigns and Women Against Violence Against Women as well as the long established groups that are included in the Women's National Commission. Strategies included lobbying, campaigns, research, reports, the establishment of alternative institutions and cultural production such as novels, plays, television documentaries and films. A particularly relevant development was the growth of the women's studies movement providing a means of amassing, assessing and communicating knowledge and beliefs about domestic violence to successive generations of activists. Such knowledge constituted a substantial part of the technical information that was used by feminist advocates.

The Advocacy Coalitions

Feminists

In this array of actors the outlines of two advocacy coalitions of the kind envisaged by Sabatier can be detected: feminists and traditionalists. The feminist advocacy coalition consists of municipal feminists, radical feminist groups, the feminist sections of the women's movement, academics and experts, individual feminists located in relevant agencies, the political parties, local councils, Parliament, the civil service and central government. Although it is possible to conceptualise it as a national coalition, its strength and effectiveness varies significantly by locality. As the framework predicts, the feminist advocates' belief system is deep rooted. The coalition is constructed around individuals who share a deep core belief about the patriarchal nature of gender relations and the empowering, women-centred approaches necessary to solve the problem of domestic violence. It is a core belief of feminist advocates that the distinction between public and private life denies protection to women. Personal security and bodily integrity is systematically more likely to be denied to women than to men. Women are vulnerable not only in public but also at home. Their lack of safety has profound effects on their quality of life and affects their rights and capacities as citizens. Crucial to the radical feminist belief system is the view that the problem is caused by men who, as a group, benefit from violence to women. Women's fear of violence and lack of security underpin the male dominance of gender relations. Radical feminists point to the considerable incidence of organised and deliberate abuse of women and children and argue that the great scale of the problem means that its cause is located not in individual male traits but in crucial aspects of maleness. Policy core beliefs follow logically. Solutions, they argue, must be women-centred, and must address fundamental institutions such as the family and heterosexuality (Kelly 1999). Although short-term measures are useful and necessary to address current victimisation, long-term and radical strategies are needed to eliminate male violence to women. Such strategy must be empowering, giving women both autonomy and safety without turning them into victims or prisoners. Empowerment in this context means that treatment must enable women to become confident enough to break away from or change violent relationships. Emotional and psychological support are needed as well as economic support. In other words women are the experts and the best judge of when to leave. Violent men should be made to leave the family home in order to render it safe for family members. All women who flee violence should have a place to go. Women who say they are fleeing violence should have absolute rights to financial, housing and other support and should receive the support of women who have had similar experiences. They should not have to deal with men. The appropriate policies will be multi-faceted, wide ranging, will engage many areas of policy making and face to face provision should be offered only by women. They will crosscut established functional divisions of government and require huge efforts of co-ordination. Feminist academics and researchers play an important role in the coalition:

> ... we have managed to survive as an explicitly feminist research unit ... to stand almost in the middle of a triangle between academia, the statutory sector and the voluntary sector ... have connections, input, networking and I think we are very much seen by individuals and organisations as a point that you go to if you need information, if you want to find out other groups doing certain things... We are always connected up to various networks of women ... are actually physically doing research with them ... or working in a local authority context ...[3]

The feminist core theoretical stance has not shifted, despite the passage of time. The belief system is the foundation of feminist advocacy about the issue of domestic violence(see Table 13.1).

From the early 1970s the focus of the feminist advocacy coalition expanded and by the 1990s it explicitly sought to influence housing and social service departments, the criminal justice community, the health services, politicians and other decision makers, experts and general public opinion. That bundle of policy makers had apparently little in common but was united by a 'status quo' approach to the treatment of domestic violence which in some central government cases resulted in a refusal to recognise the policy area at all.

Traditionalists

The particular nature of the feminist coalition has had the effect of defining another coalition, characterised principally by its resistance to prioritising the domestic violence issues, and sometimes by its opposition to the feminist coalition. This coalition may be thought of as the traditionalists. Traditionalists have a core belief system centred on patriarchal notions of sex roles; the chastisement of wives[4] was legally supported until the nineteenth century and rape within marriage was only recognised as a crime in the 1990s (see Table 13.1). Whilst the legal rights of men to beat their wives has been formally removed, the values that support it remain deeply embedded in the culture. There is a considerable residue from the days of legal sanction and public approval of wife beating. Punch and Judy shows, epigrams, popular songs and doggerel of various kinds reflect its sanction. 'Many people know and use the expression 'rule of thumb' in their everyday conversation. What they may not realise is that one origin of the expression derives from the right of a man to beat his wife with a stick, provided it was no thicker than his thumb' (Malos and Hague 1993: 35).

Table 13.1: Domestic Violence Policy Beliefs of Feminist Coalition and Traditionalist Coalition — Deep Core, Policy Core and Secondary Aspect

Belief system	Feminist Advocacy Coalition 1975–1995	Traditionalist Coalition 1975
Deep core	Public private distinction denies protection to women. Male violence reflects unequal power relationships. Right to personal security and bodily integrity more likely to be denied to women than men. Violent behaviour is in male nature. Men benefit from male violence to women. Home and family are places of potential danger.	Family life is a private matter. Families are important. Home and family are safe.
Policy core	Violence to women is a political matter. Most violence to women is by known men. Solution must empower women — Refuges provide emotional support, renew self-confidence. Women only delivery of policy — sufferers of domestic violence should not have to deal with men. Survivors of violence and feminists are experts. All women must have somewhere to go — open door policy is essential. Women have right to go where they please.	Violence to women is normally stranger assault. DV is a private matter. DV should be treated differently to stranger assault. DV 'not police work'. DV not a matter for criminal law. There is no such thing as 'DV policy'. Families should be reconciled. Professionals — social services, police, health workers are the experts. Professionals deliver policy. Professionals determine need. Violent behaviour is individually learned. Men 'protect' families from violence. Men are not to blame — DV attacks often warranted or provoked. Families should stay together. Women should stay at home and off the streets if they want to be safe.
Secondary aspects (decisions)	Refuges run by residents. DV should have crime status and response priority. Feminists should staff DV units. Women centred multi-agency policy is remedy. Survivors decide when to leave, return home. Resources should be specially targeted to survivors. (e.g. Women's Aid)	Complaints not recorded. Complaints not treated. Long response time. Formal non-arrest policies. No referral to other agencies. Lighter sentences and lower fines than stranger assault. Independent corroboration of homelessness is necessary to get benefit. Resources should be allocated through mainstream providers. (e.g. Victim Support)

De facto tolerance of violence to women was masked by a core belief in the sanctity of family life. In evidence to the 1975 Parliamentary Select Committee on Domestic Violence, the Association of Chief Police Officers expressed the view that '... we are, after all, dealing with persons "bound in marriage", and it is important, for a host of reasons, to maintain the unity of the spouses. ... Every effort should be made to reunite the family' (Smith 1989: 42). The professional values of the police, government officials in housing, social services, the judiciary and so on are major determinants of policy core beliefs. The professionals make the dominant definitions of issues and problems. Such definitions determine what requires explanation, treatment and remedy and where responsibility rests. Police, medical staff, government officials, social service professionals and other public officials may be identified as part of the traditionalist coalition. In the 1970s their policy core beliefs included the views that domestic violence was a private matter and should be treated differently to 'stranger assault'. It was not regarded as appropriate work for the police, nor was it an appropriate matter for criminal law. Then appropriate policy was a matter exclusively for the professionals who were the experts, not for feminists who were unreliable extremists, nor for survivors who may have acted unreasonably in leaving their partners. The traditionalist coalition although dominant was diffuse and therefore susceptible to intervention by the more coherent, more highly motivated feminist coalition, particularly during a period of changing attitudes and widespread institutional reform.

In this configuration the feminist coalition sought to get the value of feminist approaches and expertise recognised, for example by the police or central government personnel. Only then would they have their desired influence on policy. That is feminist policy success could occur only where the opposing coalition's policy core belief system was modified, a situation identified by Sabatier as difficult but not impossible to achieve.

The policy subsystem and policy change

An examination of the development of domestic violence policy between the 1970s and 1990s shows evidence of significant policy change. There is no single public organisation with responsibility for domestic violence policy; responsibility spreads across a wide range of agencies spanning central and local tiers of government and public, private and quasi-governmental sectors. At national level, Parliament, the Home Office, the DHSS, the cabinet sub-committee on women's issues, the shadow Women's Minister and various legislators considered and/ or made policy on domestic violence. These agencies are under pressure from nationally mobilised campaigns, experts and professionals. At the local level, policy on domestic violence is delivered by the criminal justice system, housing authorities, social services, the health service and the voluntary sector. Statutory authorities have considerable discretion in this area which allows widely varying local policies.[5]

Women's mobilisation on the issue of domestic violence led to innovative policies clearly grounded in feminist core belief systems, highlighted by the development of refuges. To escape violence at home women need safe alternative accommodation, a need that was met by the establishment of safe houses or refuges. The first refuge was set up in 1971 and by 1975 there was a national network of refuges run on women-centred principles. The refuges aimed to offer personal security to women escaping violence and to enable them to look after their children and to decide on their own future. To find and develop feminist ways of working was a central concern of the refuge movement, which was committed to the management of the refuges by the residents rather than by public officials. Many refuges were staffed by feminist activists; others were managed by voluntary organisations. Their funding was provided by a combination of central and local government and public and private sectors. Linking with local agencies was acknowledged to be essential from the start. To be effective, the activists had to establish relationships with local police forces in order to ensure that women needing their services were referred to the refuges. From that baseline, policy developed during the 1980s, with different patterns of change and engagement with public officials in different localities. Feminist principles were a challenge to the local housing and social service officials, hence uneasy working relations with local authority professionals characterised the early years (Lovenduski and Randall 1993). More difficult were relations with the police whose values and culture made them especially unsympathetic to intervention in domestic disputes, even where serious assaults occurred. A related problem was the reluctance of the judiciary to accept women's evidence, to make convictions in this area.

At national level, the central government department with prime responsibility for domestic violence policy is the Home Office which has varied in its interest in and prioritisation of the problem. As well as drafting legislation the Home Office oversees the police, funds research on crime, is responsible for immigration policy (which is especially important in relation to violence in ethnic minority and migrant communities) and funds projects and parts of the voluntary sector. The Department of the Environment is responsible for housing policy and the DHSS for the benefits on which women's escape from violence may depend, but although the resources allocated by these two departments are crucial to good policy, the Home Office has been the dominant department. After 1989 it recognised the functional overlap that remedy in this area involves by financing multi-agency initiatives, but it did not make long-term funding available (Abrar 1996). Home Office policy early in the 1990s was contradictory. It funded numerous small-scale initiatives under its Safer Cities Programmes and by 1995 it had funded eleven multi-agency projects on domestic violence. However, after 1991 support for feminist, women-only groups such as Rape Crisis and Women's Aid declined while finance for Victim Support, a mainstream, mixed sex organisation increased. This caused considerable anxiety in the feminist community where there was a feeling that the work of Victim Support filtered funds away from the provision of direct emergency services and marginalised the views of the women who needed them.

Police policy on domestic and sexual violence has been one of the prime sites of feminist contestation of the definition of crime. Police are major actors in this area of policy and domestic violence is potentially an important part of police work. Evidence to the Select Committee in 1975 indicated that between one quarter and one third of all calls to the police concerned 'domestic occurrences' (Malos and Hague 1993: 40). Prior to the 1980s police forces treated domestic violence as a private family affair and left women without legal recourse or protection. But the 1980s crisis in British policing made some forces more responsive to feminist demands for policy change. Discourses of 'new community policing', considerable vocal critique from women and the desire to project an image of the police as protectors of women and children led to a turn about in police responses to violence against women. Force orders in 1985 and Home Office guidelines concerning violence against women in 1986 and 1990 began to meet some of the criticisms from feminists working on violence to women. Good practice ideas about inner city crime, sexual violence and domestic assault were imported from North America where costly class action suits brought by feminists were compelling police to treat domestic violence as a crime and were incentives to police co-operation with feminists to develop women-centred responses to domestic violence. By the late 1980s British policing policy on sexual and domestic violence had changed, it was both officially acknowledged and treated as a crime. The first police domestic violence unit was set up in London in 1987. By 1989 further units were established in West Yorkshire, Manchester and Birmingham. These units were staffed largely by female officers. Variations in police practice have, however, been widely noted. Local police forces have considerable discretion and interpret policy and guidelines in different ways. The attitudes of individual Chief Constables are particularly important to the exercise of discretion. A 1990 Home Office Circular recommended that specialist units be set up to deal with domestic violence and provide follow up services and support for survivors. The circular emphasised that the primary concern of police officers should be the safety of women and children and the arrest of the violent man.

Also crucial to policy delivery are local authorities, especially housing officials and social services. Local authorities act as gatekeepers for housing waiting list applicants, as landlords to tenants experiencing domestic violence, as a general source of housing advice and have clear responsibilities in the provision of housing for women escaping violence in the home. The Homeless Persons Act 1977 and the Housing Act 1985 required local authorities to secure accommodation for unintentionally homeless persons in priority need. According to this provision women experiencing domestic violence, particularly those accompanied by their children could be given priority eligibility for housing. Case law further refined the duty to secure 'permanent' housing and the Women's Aid federation successfully lobbied to get those living in temporary accommodation such as hostels or refuges defined as homeless.

Local authorities also determine whether refuges are adequately funded, whether they can remain open and whether their open door policy is a practical reality. Practice varies widely by authority. Some local authorities lead well-funded and managed multi-agency responses whilst others deny domestic violence is a problem in their community. A few have developed good practice guidelines together with training, information and education campaigns. Most have produced a leaflet on how to get help. Our research indicates that the most 'feminist' and most developed policies are multi-agency initiatives with a number of officers in dedicated posts. Although such initiatives occurred almost exclusively in Labour controlled areas, many Labour authorities had only minimal policies, suggesting that partisan explanations could offer relatively little illumination of varying practices. However surveys in the 1990s showed wide variations amongst local authorities (Malos and Hague 1993), overall lack of written policy (Bull 1993) and virtually non-existent provision for unmarried women experiencing domestic violence.

The definition of domestic violence itself was a major point of disagreement between the coalitions and a cause of local variation. Some authorities adopted a women centred definition, accepting the statements of women leaving violent partners as evidence of priority need, whilst many, possibly most, required women to take out injunctions as a condition of receiving permanent rehousing (Bull 1993). Pressure on housing stock due to the 1988 Right to Buy legislation and increasingly limited allocations of social housing led many local authorities to adopt narrow interpretations of the homelessness legislation and to restrained use of their discretion in domestic violence cases. In this climate a House of Lords decision in 1995 (R v London Borough of Brent, *ex parte* Awua) reinterpreted a local authority's duty to mean securing 'suitable' accommodation rather than 'suitable permanent accommodation'. The Housing Act 1996 amended this position slightly by stipulating a temporary — two year — duty to rehouse. The 1996 act removed domestic violence as an indication of a priority need category and called into question the homelessness status of women in refuges. Most importantly it increased the discretion of local authorities. These elements of the Act are regarded as legislative expressions of the Conservative demonisation of lone parents after Peter Lilley's 1992 speech attacking teenage mothers for, amongst other things, bearing children in order to jump housing queues. Our interviews indicated that the 'pro family' ideology of the Conservative right in the early 1990s was so extensive that no policy that could be seen to assist marriage breakdown would be encouraged by central government, even where the breakdown was caused by criminal assault in the home.

Policy Change in Two Localities 1975–1995

The large constellation of actors, both governmental and feminist, involved in domestic violence policy suggests that there will be variations in policy as it operates on the ground, both by locality and over time. The relative influences of the two coalitions cannot be analysed without looking at particular localities and particular time periods. Accordingly we analyse policy in two localities: a provincial city, Radicalton and an inner London borough, Progressiveham. The authorities differ in their structure, culture, feminist presence and the way they implemented local government reform between 1979 and 1995. Radicalton is a provincial Metropolitan authority under Labour control throughout the period of Conservative local government reform. Although some streamlining had taken place, there was comparatively little structural change in its institutions by the time our fieldwork was completed. Radicalton set up a council women's committee in 1981 following local feminist activism that had been strong since the 1970s. Progressiveham was a modern, recently decentralised Labour led council with a national reputation for initiatives to promote changes in gender relations. A women's committee was set up there in 1981 but, unlike Radicalton, this council was not influenced by a local, autonomous feminist movement. Policy change occurred in both authorities, but to differing extents.

Policy Change in Radicalton

Radicalton offers an example of policy change in the local authority and in the police. Change was driven by a strong coalition of feminist policy advocates. Radicalton at the end of the 1970s became the site of substantial feminist mobilisation around issues of male sexual violence, activity that was strengthened by a widely publicised series of brutal sex murders in the area. Locally the murders became a psychological landmark that drew a wide spectrum of women into political action. Angered by police advice to stay home as a means of ensuring their safety, women gathered in widely publicised 'reclaim the night' marches. In addition a local campaign was organised to secure the release of two Radicalton women imprisoned for killing their drunken and abusive father in self defence. The atmosphere was alive with women's anger and issues of male sexual violence to women were at the forefront of local preoccupations. Thus, when the council women's committee was established in 1981, feminist community representatives prioritised the issue of male sexual violence to women. The council sponsored conferences on sexual violence and feminists on the committee gained access to the police via the council police committee. This enabled the women's committee to work on the 'no crime' status which domestic violence then had with the police. The chair of the women's committee described the initial meeting with the police as 'staggering ... we all came out thinking "good god". The bit ... that always sticks in my memory was the Chief Inspector sitting there saying, "you see, the man in the street is not interested in domestic violence". And we said our concern is the woman in the street and she is.'

Feminist researchers and academics played a central role in demonstrating the legitimacy of their concerns about domestic violence in Radicalton. These experts were well established in national feminist circles and their arguments and research were central to national debates. They were also linked into local networks, working alongside community activists to collect information on the incidence of sexual violence against women. One influential feminist academic was particularly important. She had been there a long time and ran a popular and influential women's studies course on gender and violence. She educated a group of women who have stayed on in Radicalton and play a part in local feminist policy advocacy.

Important to later developments was the continuing access of feminists to the police which over a number of years included action to shift attitudes, via training, the exchange of expert information and research. In the 1980s the force underwent a serious legitimacy crisis due to race problems, the miners' strike and media exposés of the police treatment of rape victims which led to the introduction of rape suites in police stations. In Radicalton rumours were going around that the reason police could not catch the serial sex murder was that he '… was a policeman, he had to be a policeman because why else couldn't they catch him? Or it had to be somebody the police were protecting, perhaps he was a special', evidence of a negative reputation that was damaging to police work. In this atmosphere a catalyst came when a man who had murdered his partner was released on bail leading to a local campaign that further embarrassed the police who had already suffered a loss of legitimacy over their repeated failures to solve the serial murders and more generally to provide safety for local women.

Meanwhile feminist advocates began to realise that in order for arrest to become an answer to domestic violence, other parts of the criminal justice community such as the courts, the probation services and the Crown Prosecution Service would have to be brought on board. Bowing to public pressure the police allowed feminist researchers, funded by the local council, to investigate the force's responses to domestic violence. The recommendations of the research were that the police should not only treat domestic violence as a crime but should also participate in multi-agency co-operation over domestic violence. The recommendations were strongly supported by the Chief Constable who persuaded local constabularies (meeting in police forums) to accept his endorsement of the research. This personal backing symbolised a new commitment by the police to multi-agency co-operation and, most importantly, their recognition that the police alone could not remedy domestic violence. The feminist experts were then commissioned to evaluate the ensuing projects.

The first step was the establishment of an inter-agency working party on domestic violence chaired by the chair of the women's committee and including the police, representatives from local authority departments and the voluntary sector. Members of the inter-agency working group were also able to lobby inside their own agencies. The role of the local council women's committee was crucial, first in establishing a dialogue between agencies and feminists and later in establishing the Radicalton Inter Agency Project (IAP). The chair of the women's committee at the time of the project's inception had been a student on the women's studies programme taught by one of the experts who led the research on the policing of domestic violence. Soon she secured funding from the three council committees most directly involved with women who experienced domestic violence (Housing, Social Services and Equal Opportunities) for a full-time worker to develop interagency work. A co-ordinator was appointed who had wide experience of the domestic violence issues and of the voluntary sector. By that time the local profile of domestic violence was such that securing funding was easy. The establishment grew.

The IAP is a local example of an early effort to produce 'joined up' policy. Its aim was to develop women-centred policy in the agencies that deal with women experiencing domestic violence. Because the project was undertaken during local government reorganisation and restructuring, part of its work is to deal with the confusion and uncertainty generated by the devolution of power to local agencies. For example, influence in the local education department was held up by difficulties about how equal opportunities work would be funded in schools with local management. Once funding arrangements were clarified the IAP was able to link domestic violence work to child protection policies. In the health service the reorganisation of budgetary structures in purchaser provider relationships made it difficult for the IAP to identify the part of the service it needed to influence. According to the co-ordinator

> we did not know who we wanted, we did not know who we were supposed to have, did we want a policy worker from community mental health or someone who is interested in purchasing services? ... or from Accident and Emergency? It was a nightmare.

There were three elements to the work of the IAP: an interagency forum, a comprehensive domestic violence training scheme and the development of good practice guidelines with agencies through such devices as the Good Practice Pilot Project. The IAP aimed to change attitudes and beliefs by training all relevant workers and establishing special education health and court based projects in the area. Training over the years has, according to one of the feminist experts, become 'one of the most challenging programmes that I have ever seen in this country and our trainers are incredibly politicised and the whole structure that has been developed around the trainers is excellent. So on that level we have moved on aeons, light years into creating a very feminist base and centre for debate, discussion and growth.'

The IAP did not confine work to its participating departments; it targeted relevant agencies and attempted to ensure their participation in meeting its goals, working at several levels of its target agencies. For example where policy was not yet formulated, it worked at front line service delivery level as a means of changing practice. In Accident and Emergency services for example one IAP worker spent time in the hospitals to 'get to know senior ... nurses and actually spend time that way, it was about winning their trust and through that actually starting to develop the work'.

Micro policy change was an important part of IAP strategy. In the 'Good Practice' project, multi-agency approaches were followed with intensive community development schemes. The IAP co-ordinator worked to get the agreement of staff in all relevant agencies in one part of the city to be trained by the project. The cumulative impact of the training and community development in a small geographic area has had significant results in awareness of women's possibilities for autonomy and self-determination. Notably

... there is a difference in this part of the city of [Radicalton] in terms of people's understanding, in terms of the workers' understanding. It is interesting, what a number of women are doing who have been on the programme, who I have spoken to, are saying that it has made them reassess the nature of their relationships, their heterosexual relationships and it has made them rethink whether or not they are involved in a violent relationship. There are women who are saying 'my husband is not violent, he does not hit me, it is not about that, but I am starting to understand much more about the ways in which I am controlled and the ways in which I do not have the freedom to choose to do what I want to do'.

It is possible to identify some of the officials at the local level in Radicalton as what Sabatier calls 'policy brokers', strategically placed to form linkages between coalition advocates. Personnel with access to other organisations were deliberately placed on steering groups and committees. For example, one member of the interagency project's steering group was the women's officer from social services with close access to the departmental management team, useful in overcoming past problems with accessing social services and probation offices. Many interviewees stressed the importance of incorporating within feminist networks people at sufficiently high levels to give women's committees access across the policy-making structure.

Changes of personnel due to local government restructuring had advantages and disadvantages. On the one hand turnover may have made IAP goals more difficult to achieve. Since the main aim of IAP work was to educate professionals on domestic violence issues, a frequent turnover of staff was highly disruptive. New staff often arrived with traditionalist belief systems. An IAP worker commented 'We have just constantly had to go back over the same ground, constantly getting the same stuff about should we not be talking about violence to adults here, shouldn't we be talking about men who are abused, should we not be talking about elderly men?' On the other hand, turnover also had the advantage that obstructive individuals eventually left. For example, the restructuring of the Crown Prosecution Service meant that an unsympathetic Chief Prosecutor was replaced by two younger prosecutors anxious to make the service more accountable and open to the public.

The growing strength of the IAP was emblematic of changes in the participating departments. Scrutiny of such changes indicates the strategic significance of different components of the feminist advocacy coalition. In housing, for example, change resulted both from the presence of senior women in the department who were committed to improving domestic violence policy and the acceptance of domestic violence as a legitimate policy area by women politicians. The catalyst appears to have been lobbying by senior women (one of whom had been a founder member of the IAP) in the department for the establishment of a women's officer post. The advocates were backed by the women's committee itself. Women's Aid and the local Asian women's refuge had long been funded by the authority, hence officials were well aware of domestic violence issues. When the women's officer was appointed, the male director of the housing department immediately placed her in charge of drafting a domestic violence policy and an allocations policy. Her policy covered all housing provision and incorporated Women's Aid good practice guidelines for a women-centred policy privileging women's word as proof of violence rather than demanding legal and criminal proof. Also incorporated was the DOE Code of Guidance on the 1985 Housing Act. Initially the chair of the council Housing Committee blocked the policy, but when the chair was replaced, the housing director took the policy to the committee again, via the tenancy subcommittee which, as a smaller committee, allowed for a more sympathetic reading and the possibility of informed discussion. Agreement in the subcommittee meant that the policy appeared as a minuted note on the Housing Committee agenda where it could be agreed with little debate. To the surprise of the officers in charge of presenting the new policy, the document was met with enthusiasm:

> The liberal democrat started by saying 'excellent document, very clear, very easy to understand, should have had it years ago'. I thought 'I am dreaming.' Then Conservative councillor [x], a woman, said, 'I used to work in a refuge years ago, excellent, it is a clear policy'. I am thinking 'no way.' The Labour councillors just looked gobsmacked ... and that was it. They said it was really good and they were supportive. It was accepted at the next housing committee meeting and went out with a circular from the director as policy to be implemented.

The training has produced results, producing political change across a wide range of local agencies (Abrar 1996: 196). The project co-ordinator reported in 1995 that she was beginning to see the results of five years' work:

> just the other day there was a criminal prosecution that was taken forward and the CPS prosecutor was absolutely brilliant. Apparently, the magistrate who was there gave this man eighty hours of community service, which is, I think, unheard of in domestic violence cases, and a fine. We think he is one of the magistrates that have been brought through our training programme. The different agencies are actually starting to support each other, it is wonderful.

Although more intermittent, policy oriented learning also took place in the police. New policies introduced after the research included training on intervention for domestic violence, the development of management information systems to collect statistics and produce annual surveys and reports on domestic violence in the area. Special units staffed by women police officers were established to deal with domestic violence and child protection and became repositories of expertise on violence against women. Evaluation research indicated that women calling on the police to assist them in dealing with domestic violence began to get a sympathetic response.

Our research suggests that the ability of local feminists to challenge police practice fluctuates over time; the attitudes of Chief Constables are central in determining policy priorities. Turnover at this level first brought in a sympathetic Chief Constable who was very interested in domestic violence policing and committed to the IAP. His replacement showed no interest in the issue and feminist advocates felt they had lost influence. One policy setback was the dilution of the specialist domestic violence units in the early 1990s. In line with police 'equal opportunities policies' and because the units were seen in the police as a backdoor through which women were entering the CID, the units were changed to mixed sex staffing despite objections by the IAP. And when the new units proved less effective at dealing with domestic violence the IAP felt that it had no influence: '... there's resistance ... basically we have lost the police in terms of domestic violence ...'. By 1995 the units were named 'Sexual Abuse and Child Protection Units' and one half of a 'vulnerable persons post' was allocated for domestic violence victimisation cases. The Chief Constable was overt in his resistance. According to the IAP coordinator 'he said we are going to treat all victims of crime in the same way, they are all going to get appropriate treatment and there is not going to be any priority for victims of interpersonal crime ...'. However, other organisational changes in the police mitigated the setback. Devolution after 1994 moved considerable decision making away from Chief Constables to Divisional Commanders and the IAP was able to locate a sympathetic Divisional Commander who has spent two days on one of their training programmes and has agreed for them to train probationers and their trainers in one Radicalton police division.

By the mid-1990s the Inter Agency Project was one of the most comprehensive and successful in the country. Located partly in the voluntary sector and partly in the local authority it was able to obtain funding from a variety of sources and to be autonomous while having political backing from the local authority. Funding for eleven workers was secured, with the Home Office making the lead contribution of 25 per cent of the projects total funding. The Inter Agency Project also received money for short-term action projects and central government section 11 money (for the employment of black workers).

The IAP enabled networking in Radicalton, in the interagency project itself and within and between other organisations and institutions. Over time, awareness of domestic violence has grown throughout the area. According to a departmental women's officer:

> The profile that the issue has got in the city now, it is almost like, in the department we have done policy ... a lot of workers in the department have gone through interagency training, there is a tremendous kind of network around that. I have represented the department on the service planning team for women experiencing violence within the community care process, so again that has fed into the network in terms of the health authority and good practice there.

The advocacy coalition is maintained and continued partly by a core of key women who are present in multiple networks.

Policy Change in Progressiveham

Although less substantial than in Radicalton, policy change in Progressiveham was also evident. Feminist initiatives received considerable councillor support, but effects on Housing and Social Services were more limited in this very decentralised borough. As in Radicalton policy oriented learning in the police took place, but it was more restricted. The Progressiveham feminist advocacy coalition had less of a local grass roots base and was more concentrated in authority agencies than was the case in Radicalton. It had more often relied upon the initiatives of a few strategically situated individuals. Individual women police officers in the locality were helpful as were some high profile local feminist councillors. A local university employed feminist experts on sexual violence who contributed to policy change. Through such contact and through participation in national networks, Progressiveham feminists were integrated into the advocacy coalition, and directly linked with the Radicalton project including cross representation on multi agency steering committees.

As in Radicalton the role of the council women's committee backed by a women's unit was central to policy oriented learning and change. The Progressiveham women's committee prioritised women's safety issues from its foundation in 1981, but few of the initiatives taken in the early 1980s survived until the later part of the decade. There was no active borough based women's movement pressuring the council to take the lead on domestic violence policy and co-ordination. Rather progress in the borough was the by-product of increasing pressure on the Metropolitan police by feminists in the Greater London Council, in various London-wide pressure groups and in the media to offer more effective policing of domestic violence. This led most notably to the Metropolitan Police Force Order in 1987 and a commitment to the establishment of Domestic Violence Units in police stations across the city. Pioneering multi-agency work by Radicalton attracted the attention of local advocates who were effective in persuading Progressiveham to adopt the multi-agency approach.

At council level the women's committee acted to raise the reputation of the problem. A survey of domestic violence in the area showing that a high percentage of local women experienced domestic violence shocked councillors, but did not at first lead to change. The establishment of the women's unit in 1988 enabled pressure to develop. A report was produced detailing inconsistency in council provision for women experiencing domestic violence. However, the Director of Housing and Social Services, whose department was targeted by the report, was unsympathetic and able to ignore its recommendation for the appointment of staff with responsibility for the issue. In 1990 a local female police officer encouraged the women's unit to revive a domestic violence working party that had existed in the early 1980s. Further action came in 1991 with the establishment of a Home Office Safer Cities project that enabled the women's unit to secure temporary funding for a Domestic Violence Coordinator post based in the unit. The post was filled by a worker with a background in Women's Aid who linked the women's unit to voluntary sector expertise.

Full funding for the post was provided by the council two years later. Council support resulted from a combination of factors. The rising profile of domestic violence nationally was important, but so was the work of the coordinator who was particularly effective. A further incentive was the presence in the borough of a high prestige Home Office funded action research project, Domestic Violence Matters, which lasted for three years and was located in one of the borough's police stations. The project was developed with collaboration by London-based feminist academics, the Progressiveham police and the Safer Cities coordinator for the borough.

The role of the co-ordinator was to develop good practice and policy, provide training and facilitate the borough-wide domestic violence working party established by the council in 1990. In her dealings with external agencies she sought to influence policy through training and guidelines to front line service deliverers to whom she has access via the working party which appears to be the nexus of inter departmental work. The women's unit also secured representation on the Safer [Progressiveham] Strategy Group, a multi-agency group of senior decision makers, but we did not find evidence of policy change there.

By 1990 links with the criminal justice community were established. These were developed in 1991 by Domestic Violence Matters. The project had a co-operative relationship with the women's unit, but relationships with the police were not straightforward. The local police were regarded as difficult by feminist advocates who worked in the Domestic Violence Matters unit. The advocates reported a continuing reluctance by the police to record domestic violence as a crime or to adopt procedures to deal with repeat victimisation. Domestic Violence Matters was an intervention project in which a unit of experienced domestic violence professionals were located in two Progressiveham police stations to undertake crisis work with survivors. When Home Office funding ended, the police maintained only token levels of staffing in the units. During the course of the project, although there was some appreciation of the unit's role in reducing the burden of work in the station, it was also seen by police as interfering 'with something that is not our business.' 'Lesbians ... probably as trouble makers who are a load of ugly feminists who should be shot at dawn, quite frankly.' Unit staff reported that their civilian status made them outsiders, unable to integrate with police cultures. 'We do not fit in with their culture and what we do is tip toe around them, bend over backwards, swallow our tongues, we are very diplomatic, we sacrifice what potentially might be a great pleasure in telling them exactly what we think of them, just for good relations, they do not do it, they have no notion of subtlety ... we do not call it training because that would antagonise them, you cannot tell them anything they do not know...'

Thus feminist advocates doubted the success of the project. However, it was evaluated by a nationally respected feminist researcher and expert who regarded its significance rather differently.[6] Domestic Violence Matters was intended to be proactive, offering assistance to women in all domestic violence situations. It also aimed to produce cultural change in the police. The evaluator thought that the project was trying to do two very large and opposing things: change police culture and prioritise women. Her analysis is that it inevitably prioritised women and that three years was far too short a time to change police culture. Moreover, by separating strategic from practical work in its structure, Domestic Violence Matters limited the policy change that could occur. The project became a political football within the police and within the council. Nevertheless, in their day to day work, project workers were creating a climate of change by raising issues and keeping staff in other agencies involved. Its effects were significant and the evaluator thought it a positive outcome when the project secured external funding and carried on with two workers.

In both localities policy oriented learning was evident in the council, in key departments of the authority and to a lesser, but nonetheless significant extent in the police and health services. Both established multi-agency structures to treat problems of domestic violence. These involved multi-agency, professionalised fora that facilitated policy oriented learning across coalitions in Radicalton but not in Progressiveham where the feminist advocacy coalition was weaker. The case studies suggest that the Home Office, the Metropolitan Police and the Police Authority in which Radicalton is located may have experienced policy oriented learning.

We have demonstrated that, in the mid-1990s, there was a significant and effective feminist advocacy apparatus located around the issue of domestic violence, including national and local organisation, a set of publicly funded policy development projects, an extensive and widely accepted expertise, knowledge and literature and a well integrated network of policy minded feminist advocates. Evidence of policy change included new laws, official circulars, guidelines and practices in a variety of state and professional agencies. Although not fully accepted anywhere, there were few relevant arenas in which the radical feminist definition of the problem and its solution had not gained some ground. There is evidence that a feminist advocacy coalition existed and was effective.

Discussion and Conclusions

The story of domestic violence policy shows how a network of radical feminists can influence policy in organisations as traditional, conservative and hierarchical as the police, albeit only in some localities and at specific periods of time. Such a development is a proud testament to the role of ideas and beliefs in policy change in unlikely circumstances. The advocacy coalition framework would not have predicted this adjustment of core policy beliefs, but has proved useful in highlighting the conditions that facilitated change.

Our research supports Sabatier's assertion that the probability of policy-oriented learning across belief systems of different coalitions is likely to be increased through the presence of a professionalised forum. The feminist coalition in the field of domestic violence consists of a distinctive mix of experts, practitioners, interest group activists and academics operating on a national as well as a local basis. As one academic observed:

> ... the practitioner conferences, those are in the main the ones we prioritise, that we get asked to speak at, it is much more important to me to go to some domestic violence forum conference or Zero Tolerance conference than to the BSA for example, because those are the people who can make a difference in women's and children's lives, and do make differences, often negative differences so we are in contact often with policy makers at that level. ... we want to do research that is useful. It is not for its own sake, it is to contribute to debate to policy and practice development ... it matters enormously to me to have women from groups that are providing a service, tell me the things that I write, they find really helpful and that they have used it to discuss something.

This unusual relationship between the academic and practitioner community has had the effect of professionalising the policy area, which may have helped to reduce conflict as well as to strengthen links among members of the coalition, thereby reducing the number of different belief systems in the policy subsystem.

Sabatier's framework stresses the importance of policy brokers in achieving learning across advocacy coalitions. By identifying some of the actors in domestic violence policy as such policy brokers, we can start to explain why feminist advocates have an important role even where circumstances are inauspicious. In central government, as one official put it, 'women who work in ... [a department] ... who every now and again will be moles, off the record will tell you what is going on in the internal debates with ministers, what the current line is, it is very important information for women on the outside to have, because it means you can think about strategy, think about targeting particular issues more or less ...'. At the local level in Radicalton policy brokers were strategically placed; steering groups and committees incorporated personnel with access to other organisations. Committees provide the crucial links to other organisations.

But the policy instruments allow considerable agency discretion and this translates into widely varying local practices, raising questions about how to explain local differences. Change was more extensive in Radicalton which had a well established IAP and a well funded and co-ordinated domestic violence policy sector. Resistance from the police remained significant, but a good deal of change was apparent and there was evidence of repeated interactions between feminist advocates and the police. Interaction was initially facilitated through factors external to the policy sub-system — the perceived loss of legitimacy of the police in dealing with violence toward women, which allowed feminist expertise a new legitimacy. But once interaction began, and such actors as the police became used to dealing with feminist activists, then one of the policy core beliefs of the traditionalist coalition — resistance to feminism and women's centred approaches — became more likely to break down. As a result Radicalton's policies could be sustained when national government financial support was withdrawn. In Progressiveham policy change was apparent, but it was less secure. Interagency work was not so well funded and contact with the police was more variable, insufficient for accumulation effects to kick in. Some of the features of Progressiveham might be explained as London effects. The absence of a borough level feminist movement reduced the prospects for the development of feminist advocacy and the restricted competence of borough government by comparison to metropolitan government limited the reach of local components of the advocacy coalition and increased the dependence of policy change on national initiatives. Nevertheless Progressiveham, like Radicalton, was able to find local funding to replace national Safer Cities funding of a domestic violence coordinator. Moreover, the local police station continued their Domestic Violence Matters unit, albeit on a reduced basis.

The key concepts of the advocacy coalition framework, policy oriented learning, coalitions built around belief systems and the nature of policy change, are useful in analysing the domestic violence policy change we have described. The policy sub-system includes pressure groups, civil servants, politicians, professionals and experts working via conferences, campaigns and debates, statutes, laws and policy directives of various kinds. An advocacy coalition of feminists inside and outside the government has functioned for at least twenty years. It would be difficult to argue that the coalition was 'in power' in the policy sub-system but, allowing for local variations, it was influential. It had an impact on different levels of government and a variety of local agencies and organisations, largely without deviating from its members' deep core and policy core beliefs that domestic violence is caused by patriarchy and must be treated by women-centred, empowering approaches. The traditionalist coalition on the other hand altered its policy core beliefs but maintained its deep core beliefs. (Table 13.2)

Our case studies indicate that one partial explanation of policy change is that an accumulation effect of interactions between local policy actors and the feminist advocacy coalition on domestic violence affected the belief systems of officials, influencing some of them to accept feminist definitions of the problem and its solutions. By the mid-1990s both Radicalton and Progressiveham had experienced considerable policy change. Change in these and other localities reflected and probably contributed to wider changes in the policy subsystem, most notably alterations in policy core and secondary aspects of traditionalist belief systems (Table 13.2). Arguably the changes in traditionalists' policy core beliefs resulted from their need to keep faith with their deep core beliefs. In order to maintain a patriarchal deep core belief in the traditional family, in order to 'save' the family, it was necessary to alter policy core beliefs and therefore policy. Feminists were able to insert their views into this process. Such an explanation also shows why feminists found no discernible change in the deep core beliefs of traditionalists.

Table 13.2: Domestic Violence Policy Beliefs of Traditionalists 1975 and 1995

Belief system	Traditionalists 1975	Traditionalists 1995
Deep core	Family life is a private matter. Families are important. Home and family are safe.	Family life is a private matter. Families are important. Home and family are safe.
Policy core	Violence to women is normally stranger assault. DV is a private matter. DV should be treated differently to stranger assault. DV 'not police work'. DV not a matter for criminal law. Families should be reconciled. Professionals — social services, police, health workers are the experts. Professionals deliver policy. Professionals determine need. Violent behaviour is individually learned. Men 'protect' families from violence. Men are not to blame — DV attacks often warranted/provoked. Women should stay home and off the streets if they want to be safe.	Home and family must be protected and policed. Feminists are also experts. Public policy is needed on domestic violence. Domestic violence is a crime. Women decide when to leave violent men. Women are needed to deliver DV policy.
Secondary aspects	Complaints not recorded. Complaints not treated. Long response time. Formal non-arrest policies. No referral to other agencies. Lighter sentences and lower fines than stranger assault. Independent corroboration of homelessness is necessary to get benefit. Resources should be allocated through mainstream providers. (e.g. Victim Support).	Arrest policy. 'Normal' fines and sentences. Complaints treated and recorded. Multi agency approach. Evaluation by feminist experts. Training by feminist experts. Government funding of projects. Regular police / refuge contact. Housing rights for survivors (until 1996).

The focus in this article has been on the involvement of the feminist advocacy coalition in domestic violence policy making and the role played by belief systems. We are aware that the changing role of the less coherent and self-conscious traditionalist coalition in the policy area should be given more detailed consideration. Resistance to feminist proposals appears to come partly from a set of beliefs about gender relations that is deeply embedded in the dominant culture, partly from professional values that lead to 'ownership' of the policy, and partly from the beliefs of senior national politicians far removed from this area of policy making. These elements at times compete. In part the traditionalist coalition is defined by its resistance to the feminist coalition. In part the influence of the feminist coalition in some localities and time periods might be explained by its superior motivation and strong belief system. A further possible explanation is that the deep core beliefs of traditionalists required them to alter their policy core beliefs. It may be that it is in the nature of deep core beliefs that they will lead to changes instead of stability in policy core beliefs, an outcome that has implications for the advocacy coalition framework. This article has concentrated on understanding the feminist advocacy coalition. Understanding the opposing coalition would involve identifying and detailing the exact nature of opposition to women-centred policies — a valuable exercise for future feminist research.

Notes

This article is based on research from the Gender and New Urban Governance (GNUG) project which was funded by the ESRC Local Government Programme, award number L1311250304901. The article was written on the basis of research undertaken by Stephania Abrar. We are grateful to Adam Smith for his comments on an earlier version of this paper and to the very useful comments made by the other contributors to this volume. We are also grateful to Patrick Dunleavy for discussions of and insights into this topic during the course of the GNUG project.

Notes

1. Some experts object to the use of the term domestic violence when what is really meant is violence to women. Domestic violence is violence in the home and family and may affect any family or household member. Here we use the term in its everyday usage and mean violence to women.
2. The advocacy coalition framework allows a large number of actors to be clustered together in a policy subsystem. In practice both advocates and brokers have an interest in sub-system maintenance and differences between them are part of a continuum. (Sabatier and Jenkins-Smith 1993: 27) The dynamic of change is policy-oriented learning which includes the incorporation of technical information and the development of strategies to influence public policy. A distinction is made between learning within and learning across coalitions. The former is relatively unproblematic. However, productive debate is relatively unlikely to occur across coalitions because it may lead to the alteration of policy core aspects of a coalition's belief system.

Once established, policy is unlikely to be revised so long as the coalition that instituted it remains dominant in the subsystem.

3. Expert interview. The GNUG project conducted over 100 interviews with experts and advocates between 1993 and 1995. By agreement with respondents interviews have been anonymised. Unless otherwise indicated quotations are drawn from interview transcripts.

4. The law allowing the chastisement of wives in Britain was repealed in 1829.

5. External instability has characterised the development of domestic violence policy which has taken place over a period of enormous changes both in the patterns of women's lives and in the structure and management of local government. Local government changes led to high levels of staff turnover, unpredictable budgets, changed and reduced statutory functions for local agencies, privatisation of traditional public functions etc. Change in London's political system has been particularly dramatic since 1985. Until then London was run by a single strategic authority, the Greater London Council (GLC), while the delivery of services was the responsibility of thirty-three local councils covering the capital. In 1985 central government abolished the GLC and devolved its authority to the thirty-three local authorities. Since that time a variety of boards, committees, and offices has been created to deal with London wide issues whilst the boroughs have had to deliver services in their areas while experiencing major restructuring. The rest of British local government has also experienced restructuring which has taken the form of a succession of centrally directed management initiatives in which decentralisation, downsizing, job losses, the introduction of purchaser provider splits, privatization and severe budget cuts and loss of areas of autonomy have been characteristic features. These changes greatly affected the framework in which domestic violence policy is made and delivered. As well as changes in urban institutions, agencies are also affected by policy changes on a central level, for example, reforms of the probation service, changes in housing legislation, changing spending priorities. In Radicalton 'right to buy' policy had less impact on women's access to social housing than in many other localities. Where suitable housing stock has been depleted, the council has arrangements with local housing associations to choose tenants for 75 per cent of their housing in exchange for rights to build on local authority land.

6. No name given in order to preserve the anonymity of Progressiveham.

References

Abrar, S. (1996) 'Feminist intervention and local domestic violence policy', *Parliamentary Affairs*, 49: 191–205.

Brownhill, S. and Halford, S. (1990) 'Understanding women's involvement in local politics', *Political Geography Quarterly*, 9 (4): 396–414.

Bull, J. (1993) *Housing Consequence of Relationship Breakdown*, Department of the Environment, London: HMSO, 1993.

Eisenstein, H. (1985) *Gender Shock: Practising Feminism on Two Continents*, Sydney: Allen and Unwin.

Kelly, L. (1999) 'Violence Against Women: a Policy of Neglect or a Neglect of Policy', in S.Walby (ed.) *New Agendas for Women*, Basingstoke: Macmillan, pp. 119–147.

Lovenduski, J. and Randall, V. (1993) *Contemporary Feminist Politics*, Oxford: Oxford University Press.

Majone, G. (1989) *Evidence, Argument and Persuasion in the Policy Process*, New Haven, CT: Yale University Press.

Malos, E. and Hague, G. (1993) *Refuges and the Movement Against Domestic Violence*, Cheltenham: New Clarion Press.

Parsons, W. (1995) *Public Policy: An Introduction to the Theory and Practice of Policy Analysis*, Cheltenham: Edward Elgar.

Putnam, R. (1976) *The Comparative Study of Political Elites*, Englewood Cliffs: Prentice-Hall.

Sabatier, P. and Jenkins-Smith, H. (1993) *Policy Change and Learning*, Oxford: Westview.

Smith, L. (1989) *Domestic Violence: A Review of the Literature, Home Office Research Study 107*, London: HMSO.

Stetson, D. and Mazur, A. (1995) *Comparative State Feminism*, London: Sage.

Watson, S. (1990) *Playing the State*, London: Verso.

PART 4

GENDERING THE POLITICAL SCIENCE
AGENDA

Chapter Fourteen

Toward the Emasculation of Political Science: The Impact of Feminism*

The arguments which follow are centred on two related contentions. These are: firstly, that mainstream Political Science itself is not what it ought to be or what it could be or even what it used to be; and secondly, that so long as Feminist Political Science continues to situate itself within this mainstream it will fail to realise its potential.

No-one would deny that the long-standing dissociation of Political Scientists from the female half of the population has distorted the discipline. But this failure is, I would argue, best regarded as one of many symptoms of a fundamental failure by the vast majority of Political Scientists to come to terms with our object of study. It need not have been this way. Political Science has a thoroughly honourable history. It has been multi-disciplinary in construction, modest in its assumptions, wide-ranging in its preoccupations and radical in its outlook. These origins should have led to a relatively untroubled union between a developed and confident Political Science on the one hand, and a radical, innovative Feminist Scholarship on the other. Instead, in what is one of the minor tragedies of contemporary scholarship, an absorption of a rather constrained branch of women's studies by a one-dimensional academic discipline has taken place.

Determining the causes of such an unnecessary and unfortunate development is far from simple and it is probably impossible to supply a complete explanation. It is possible, however, to identify a number of key elements in the process. Post World War Two developments in the study of politics have combined to produce a dominant form of Political Science which has lost touch with the resources inherent in its manifold origins. Whilst techniques are still regularly borrowed from cognate disciplines, related theoretical developments are not scrutinised. Additionally, there has been a growing American dominance of the discipline of Political Science. In contrast to a greater European concern with moral philosophy, the American study of politics has stressed '… instruments and practices of popular government. It (is) an applied discipline, an exercise in pragmatism …' (Apter 1977: 16).

Indeed, the American Political Science Association was founded in 1904 largely as a way to collect facts. It was Americans 'more than any other,… (who) … made Political Science into a practical discipline and the preferred style was always empirical' (Apter 1977: 29).

*   'Toward the Emasculation of Political Science', in D. Spender (ed.), *Men's Studies Modified: The impact of feminism on the academic disciplines*, Oxford, Pergamon, 1981, pp. 83–98.

And today Americans dominate the discipline in terms of numbers: 70 per cent (McKenzie 1970), 28,000 of 30,000 (Apter 1977), in terms of output, and in terms of access to funding (McKenzie 1967). The impact of this quantitative dominance becomes a qualitative one when it is remembered that the study of politics is not simply an intellectual pre-occupation, it is also a profession with a coherent hierarchical structure within which dominance by a particular kind of scholarship is likely to lead to increasing dominance by that kind of scholarship. Finally, these developments have been combined with a general erosion of the traditional integration of applied politics specialists and the more explicitly normative political philosophers and theorists.

It is these three developments which have, in my view, been crucial in both impeding the development of a Feminist Political Science and in limiting the effect of feminist scholarship, or indeed, of any theoretically demanding and radical scholarship, on the manner in which politics is normally studied. These assertions are central to the arguments of this chapter and they determine the structure of the essay which follows. Thus the first section of this essay will cover a brief and admittedly somewhat simplified examination of how an originally fruitful internal tension[1] amongst professional students of politics has resulted in the ossification of the discipline. This will be followed by an outline of the sexist biases in Political Science practice and such modifications as have ensued in response to feminist criticism. Finally, attention will be given to the potential feminist challenge to the manner in which Political Science has constructed its object and some concluding comments on the likely impact of this challenge will be offered.

The Construction of the Study of Politics: The Emergence of a Positivist[2] Discipline

Political Science is said to have properly begun with Aristotle's investigation of some 158 Constitutions in a search for the 'best' method of government (Aristotle 1962). In his study of *The Politics,* the moral philosopher's pursuit of the good society was combined with the applied researcher's investigation of extant and recorded political arrangements. Origins such as these involve both normative preoccupations and a commitment to objective description, a dualism which has continued to be a feature of the study of politics. Until recently this dualism had never taken the form of a simple bipolarity, rather there existed an uneasy synthesis in which vulnerability to criticism was balanced by an ability to absorb the content of the critique. The argument here is a straightforward one: the object of study, politics, has an active element, and is in fact epiphenomenal — it cannot exist independently of social and economic forces. Thus, so long as society and economy continue to alter, politics will alter. It follows therefore that the Political Science of each generation will develop in response to events in the political arena, and the location of the political arena itself will vary with changing definitions of what is political. Until recently this has been largely a process of expansion. The concerns of Political Science have tended to increase exponentially and theoretical reflection at each stage has been unable to encompass all of what has gone before.

Hence, divided as we are, Political Scientists have long experienced difficulty in producing a comprehensive definition of our subject. Efforts by the most eminent practitioners to produce such a definition (Apter 1977; Blondel 1976; McKenzie 1970; Easton 1965a, 1965b, 1968) have had to take into account not only the changes in the object of study, but also the duality of the subject and have thus had some difficulty in locating Political Science squarely in the social sciences. It has been argued that a case might be made for its status as a bridge between the humanities and the social sciences, (McKenzie 1970) the reasoning being that the study of politics is as much an art based on scholars' intuitions and abilities as it is a science based on the skills of established methods of enquiry. The existence of these two characteristics has been responsible for friction within the discipline which has caused divisions between both the different schools and the different generations of specialists. This has been exacerbated by two important post-war developments: the growth and eventual dominance of the applied side of the subject and increasing specialisation which has cut Political Science off from the humanities and the other social sciences. The connectedness of the two parts of Political Science has inevitably been eroded at the same time as routes via which possible reconnecting theoretical innovations could enter have been blocked. Nevertheless, the traditional duality continues to be present, albeit in a less fruitful form and Political Science remains without a generally agreed definition, which is acceptable to all of the profession. The boundaries of the range of proper objects of study are more or less permanently in dispute and scholars have found it impossible to outline a single distinctive, unifying epistemological basis.

Critics of contemporary Political Science (usually sociologists) suggest that it is at best a form of enlightened journalism which fails to achieve its very modest aims. Such critics would also hold that a strong normative element has meshed with a pseudoscientific attempt at objectivity which has tended to make the academic study of politics status quo orientated and uncritically reflective of prevailing belief systems. Whilst these sallies may sometimes be richly deserved, they fail to take account of the vast range of the subject. Although the 'Science' in the appellation may be limiting, the 'Political' is a clear invitation to expansion. Failure on the part of many students of politics to take up this invitation has been of crucial significance to feminist scholarship as this academic and intellectual self-limitation has, as much as conscious and subconscious sexism, impeded the emergence of a Feminist Political Science.

The absence of a commonly agreed definition of Political Science obviously poses certain problems for a critique of this nature. After all, one needs to be able to recognise the object of criticism. There is, however, clear evidence that identification difficulties are surmountable. There are, in most nations, institutions which employ persons (normally men) as Political Scientists. Indeed, outside of the USA there are very few ways in which it is possible to be a Political Scientist if one is not a member of a research or educational institution of some kind. These Political Scientists have managed to arrange themselves into the normally accepted educational hierarchies, to form national and international associations, to publish academic journals, to write scholarly articles, books and papers, to transmit a common body of agreed knowledge to undergraduates and graduate students, to generate proposals and receive funding for research. They may be observed meeting regularly at national and international conferences, conventions and seminars to discuss their work. Even if this entire edifice were the result of a monumental confidence trick, it would still be necessary for co-conspirators to know how to identify each other and to select recruits to continue the conspiracy into future generations. The crucial point here is that Political Science has become a profession with a recognised set of professional interests. The relative health and elaborate nature of the structure of this profession is an indication that the lack of a definition has not been particularly debilitating problem. Indeed, it might be argued that such a deficiency has been a positive advantage.

Clearly, Political Science is not without an agreed object and the lack of a definition as such may well arise from the polymorphous nature of politics itself. To the extent that there is an intellectual unity amongst political scientists it is to be found in an inchoate commonality of preoccupation with the component elements of political life. The locus of the commonality varies nationally and the process of defining the area of what is political has itself been a constituent preoccupation. Within the postulated commonality there has been a clear bi-furcation of approach which became subject to particular imbalance in the 1950s and early 1960s, the time of the subject's greatest growth.[3]

The argument which follows would normally be a complex one, developed via a painstaking exposition of the major works of influential proponents of the two main types of approaches which have been present in the development of Political Science. Space constraints do not allow this here and documentation is in any case available elsewhere.[4] Hence, the exposition which follows is limited to the arguments of two widely cited and talented representative scholars of the period whose work illustrates the two sides of the bi-furcation.

Making a case which underlines the interdisciplinary spirit and philosophical origins of the subject's development, Sheldon Wolin has argued that the process of defining the object of political study has been little different from that which has taken place in other fields of enquiry.

> No-one... would seriously contend ... that the fields of physics or chemistry have always existed in a self-evident determinate form waiting only to be discovered by a Galileo or Lavoisier ...   (Wolin 1961: 4)

Similarly, Political Science has been a product of the interplay of its practitioners rather than a set of truths or laws discovered by them. The field is, and always has been,

> ...a created one. The designation of certain activities and arrangements as political the characteristic way that we think about them and the concepts we employ to communicate our observations and reactions — *none of these are written into the nature of things* but are ... (an accruing) ... legacy ...   (Wolin 1961: 5 my emphasis)

In other words, Political Science is a construct of Political Scientists. It is a convention.[5]

The other side of the bi-furcation is illustrated by David Easton who makes extremely strong claims for the potential of Political Science as objective, discoverable truth. Stressing its empirical preoccupations, Easton recognised the social construction of Political Science and the first section of his essay on the subject for the 1968 edition of the *International Encyclopaedia of the Social Sciences*[6] is an account of the development of this construction. In Easton's very influential view:

> Two widely differing sets of criteria have emerged in the last hundred years or so, for differentiating political life from all other aspects of society and thereby for isolating the subject-matter of Political Science   (Easton 1968: 283).

These two sets of criteria have been (1) institutional, which Easton caustically suggests has 'not very profoundly' defined government institutions or the state as proper objects of study; and (2) functional, which has concentrated on the study of power or decision-making, emphasising the active or behavioural dimension of politics. Easton's sympathies are clearly with proponents of the second set of criteria which he sees as having developed largely out of dissatisfaction with the first.[7]

However, political power and political decisions must still be distinguished from all other types of power and decisions, a problem which Easton reckons should be solved by applying the criteria generated by the use of the Eastonian model of the political system. Widespread acceptance of this model has been (he modestly asserts) the breakthrough which, combined with major advances in techniques of data collection and analysis, finally released Political Science 'from its *synthetic* past' (my emphasis) and thrust it forward into its more appropriate concern of discovering a theoretical consensus (Easton 1968: 297). In effect, truth only awaited the diligence of Eastonian researchers for its discovery.

On the face of it, Easton and Wolin are often saying similar things. The divergence to be found in their perspectives is at root, an epistemological one. Whilst both recognise the social construction of Political Science, Wolin confronts and accepts this as a characteristic of any information which has the status of knowledge. Easton, on the other hand, regards this social construction as a passing phase, as the *synthetic* false start of a discipline which with the assistance of his insights, has finally been offered a route to truth.

As with division at other levels of understanding, epistemological duality is a perennial characteristic of Political Science. Unfortunately, critical appreciation of the implications of this is not characteristic. Whilst Wolin's philosophical study of the nature of political enquiry shows an acute sensitivity to the implications of his own epistemological predilections, Easton appears to be unaware that he has any. Throughout a long period of positivist ascendency this rather important difference went largely unexamined within the discipline. Such an oversight becomes particularly striking when it is considered that neighbouring disciplines of Philosophy, Sociology, and Linguistics have regularly subjected their methodologies to fundamental criticism. Tragically, this oversight became critical failure for Political Science leading to a virtual termination of its classical marriage between moral philosophy and empirical research.

Easton and Wolin were writing in the ten-year period immediately before second-wave feminism had become politically visible, by which time Easton's views were representative of the mainstream preoccupations of the profession. Political Science, particularly American Political Science, became more and more concerned with studying what politicians regarded as political (Apter 1977: 28) with an increasing number of research efforts being Government commissioned. As Apter argues, the

> management of government business led political scientists to emphasise *pragmatic common sense* and search out alternatives that would work ... . (1977: 29, my emphasis)

What this effectively meant was that

'After WWII ... political science professionals embraced the behavioural approach to the discipline ...' (Apter 1977: 29) and

> The once conventional political science curriculum-political theory, comparative government, public administration, constitutional law, international politics, state and local government — has been drastically altered. New titles: legislative behaviour, political modernisation, political socialisation, political psychology have moved to center stage. (Apter 1977: 30)

Political Scientists such as Dahl (1956, 1961, 1963, 1971), Almond and Verba (1963), Davies (1964), Deutsch (1963), and Lipset (1960) produced regular studies of the various aspects of the disposal of or relations to public power by various institutions and groups of individuals. Although Easton's political systems model, and the variations on it developed by his contemporaries[8] has yet to deliver its promised theoretical unity, these types of initiatives traced the grid which was to be mapped out by today's generation of Political Scientists. It has been their work and the work of their students which has dominated the literature for a generation. Whilst few of these 'pioneers' were so immodest in their claims as Easton, their influence in defining the object, range and research priorities of Political Science is inescapable. Thus, in a very real sense, it has been the research methods and models of the first full post-war generation of professional Political Scientists with which Feminist Political Science has had to contend (*see* below). Instead of inheriting the eccentric, self-consciously constructed discipline of Wolin, Feminist Political Science has inherited the de-constructed version proselytised by Easton and other American positivists. That this was the case has a considerable effect on the directions taken in the new studies of women and politics and it is appropriate that our attention should now be turned to the emergence of these studies.

Sexist Bias in the Study of Politics

The framework accepted for the study of politics during the late 1950s and early 1960s was clearly inadequate for a feminist, or indeed any other radical perspective. Whilst any radical critic of a socially constructed discipline must contend with the cultural biases such a construction contains; the dominance of Political Science by scholars who had not developed the habit of systematically engaging even rudimentary theories of knowledge compounded the problem enormously. There is, of course, no doubt that Political Science has been sexist. Not only did it exclude women from its concerns, it also excluded them from membership in the profession (Converse and Converse 1971; Lovenduski and Evans 1979).

The complication here is that there never was any way that the modern study of politics could fail to be sexist. Its empirical concerns have been almost exclusively those of the exercise of public power, aspects of political elites and aspects of the institutions of government. Such studies are bound to exclude women, largely because women usually do not dispose of public power, belong to political elites or hold influential positions in government institutions. Nor, until fairly recently, have issues of concern to women exercised those who do dispose of public power, belong to political elites, or hold influential positions in government institutions. In an increasingly positivistic discipline, no-one thought to question this. The only enquiries in which political woman was scrutinised were empirical studies of the various components of political participation and, predictably these studies contained numerous examples of sexist bias.

Such examples have been well documented. Bourque and Grossholtz (1974) examined several widely used and cited texts[9] for the way in which data on the participation of women was handled and checked later material to see if Political Scientists had come to see the error of their ways. (They had not). They found four by no means mutually exclusive categories of distortion in common use.

The first, FUDGING THE FOOTNOTES, comprised 'those statements of female political characteristics, attitudes or behaviour which are not substantiated in the manual cited or in the source'.   (Bourque and Grossholtz
1974: 229)

Such misuse of the data was normally a matter of removing the 'qualifications and careful language of the original study'. The second category, THE ASSUMPTION OF MALE DOMINANCE, comprised 'pervasive expectations about sex differences in politics', resulting in failure to question male preponderance in political office and leading to the assumption of male dominance in the family for evidence from which to draw conclusions about actual sex differences in politics. Bourque and Grossholtz's third category, the acceptance of MASCULINITY AS IDEAL POLITICAL BEHAVIOUR, exposes the use of 'unexplained and unexamined assumptions that those stereotyped characteristics held up as the masculine ideal (e.g. aggressiveness, competitiveness, pragmatism, etc.) are the norms of political behaviour as well'. (1974: 229)

This distortion is most frequently found in discussions of explicit political behaviour (e.g. candidate preference, issue preference and saliency, etc.). The final category, COMMITMENT TO THE ETERNAL FEMININE, explains feminine political behaviour as a direct product of women's domestic role. Based on society's reliance upon the services of women in the social realm, the distortion involves 'an assumption that women's present weak political position is necessary and functional ...'. (1974: 229)

This results in the implication that the limited participation of women is to be tolerated in order to ensure that 'we have wives and mothers to preserve the race' (1974: 229).

Besides explicit sexist bias, the most striking feature of pre-feminist political science research on women has been how little of it there was. Although gender was normally a background variable in research involving social surveys and data on women was regularly collected, it was rare for a study to concern itself seriously with the political behaviour of women. The outstanding exception to this was the IPSA[10]/UNESCO study undertaken under the direction of Maurice Duverger in 1952 and 1953 and published in 1955 as *The Political Role of Women*. Working in somewhat debilitating conditions of time and money constraints, Duverger's team undertook a comparative investigation of the political behaviour of women in France, West Germany, Norway and Yugoslavia. The investigators aimed to cover the part played by women in elections and in political leadership. Initially, they experienced considerable difficulty in acquiring the necessary data, which Duverger attributed to a degree of disinterest due to the fact that

The political scientists and most of the organisations invited to supply information often tended to regard its purpose as a secondary one, of no intrinsic importance. This ... was accompanied by ... the reserve shown, at the outset, by certain women's associations of importance.   (Duverger 1955: 8)

These obstacles, combined with the above mentioned time and money constraints, meant that the data on which the report was based were often inadequate, a fact acknowledged by Duverger. Nevertheless, the study was an important one, not the least because it investigated feminine political behaviour during a period now regarded as a patriarchal apogee. Additionally, the research plan and report pretty well anticipated the range of questions which were to be raised by future research on women. Finally, many of Duverger's conclusions came, albeit indirectly, to constitute the assumptions about women and politics which are today being challenged by feminists.[11]

The report's analysis of election data indicated that there were more women than men non-voters, but that this difference was small and varied considerably by type of election, size of community, age group, occupational category and marital status. Duverger held that the variations indicated that such slight overall sex differences as could be detected were likely to be diminishing ones. The study indicated that actual voting differences between men and women were also small and revealed a strong tendency for husbands and wives to vote in the same way. The most important sex difference was seen to be a greater tendency on the part of women to vote for parties of the centre-right when that option was available. This difference was held to be important because conservative victories in elections immediately prior to the study had been gained at the margins and therefore could not have been obtained without the 'extra' women's vote (Duverger 1955: 72). More speculative was a comment suggesting that women voters might have been more likely to be swayed by candidate personalities than issues. On this point Duverger is to be credited with pointing out that German women had been less likely than German men to vote for the National Socialists during the 1930s (Duverger 1955: 71).

In contrast to the electoral surveys, data on political leadership indicated an enormous discrepancy in the representation of women. Few women held electoral office anywhere and these numbers decreased dramatically as the hierarchy of office was ascended. Duverger held that this phenomenon was not solely due to the hostility of the electorate toward women, but was 'primarily due to the fact that few women stand as candidates' (Duverger 1955: 77). This was duly investigated and causes included both feminine 'self-selection' and discrimination against women candidates by men. Even if women did manage the hurdles of qualification, candidacy and election, their impact in assemblies was minimal, characterised by three essential features: (1) Women seldom appeared in the role of political leaders; (2) spoke less than men in debates; (3) concerned themselves largely with issue areas such as health, family policy, children, and women's rights (Duverger 1955: 95); that is, they were seldom to be found in the political 'mainsteam'. Similar patterns were present in public administration posts, and women's participation in the political parties was characterised by an analogous falloff.

Women's membership in the political parties was small and their role in party executives even smaller. Investigation of national variations showed the highest feminine party participation to be in the 'Christian Parties', followed by the Communist and Socialist parties. Liberal and Radical parties contained the smallest numbers of women participants.

All of these tendencies are by now common knowledge (some would argue cultural myth), but Duverger was the first to attempt such a systematic investigation.

Interestingly, Duverger's research was extremely sensitive to possibilities of sexism and sex discrimination as causal factors, and his explanation for the relative absence of women from political life is a lucid one. He points out that there has 'always been extremely keen competition for political leadership' and that in circumstances of intense rivalry

To give a post to a woman is to deprive a man of it, and in these circumstances, the posts given to women are cut down to the minimum required for propaganda purposes ... The mechanism at work here is ... the same as that which makes it difficult for younger men to get into politics and to bring new blood into political leadership, *but the unity of the older generation is less solid than that of the male sex or, more exactly, it is not founded on the same psychological and social substructure.* (Duverger 1955: 125, my emphasis)

Although this point is mitigated a few paragraphs later by the comment that

men's opposition to the participation of women in political life would not have succeeded so well if it had come against vigorous resistance from women. There can be no doubt that women are less interested in politics than men. (Duverger 1955: 126)

This was still a remarkable statement to make in the early 1950s.

A careful reading of *The Political Role of Women* shows that Duverger had all the necessary clues for an understanding of women's political behaviour as well as the sensitivity and intuition to use many of them. Additionally, he seemed sympathetic to the plight of women political aspirants. However, he was ultimately incapable of taking the necessary extra step which involved questioning the basis of the definition of what is political as an alternative to pointing to women's inadequacies when faced with what was commonly accepted by men as political. That this was the case may well be due to the fact that he was a political scientist as it is to his sex or the time at which the study was done.

Despite its faults, the IPSA/UNESCO study was in many respects a pioneering one and an outstanding piece of preliminary research in its own right. Nevertheless, the response over the next fifteen years was a resounding silence. Indeed, there is little indication that the study was actually read by students of political participation during the late 1950s and 1960s (Milbrath 1965; McCloskey 1968; Lane 1959; Lipset 1960). Scrutiny of the bibliographies of these myth-originating works confirms a suspicion that the stereotype of a-political woman has more to do with the processes ascribed by Bourque and Grossholtz than it does to a reading of some solid, if sometimes mistaken, research on the subject. The lack of impact of Duverger's study is more than likely to be due to the American dominance of the discipline (*see* Apter 1977; McKenzie 1970) and their well-documented ethno-centricity — the report, after all, did not concern itself with American women (*see* MacIntyre 1971). Another factor which may be of relevance here is that the Duverger study appeared at about the same time as positivism was beginning to dominate the profession.

To the relatively limited extent that Political Scientists in the ensuing fifteen years gave attention to the phenomenon of low levels of feminine political participation, their explanations tended to rest upon psychological assumptions. Women were said to be more traditionalist and right-wing, to be temperamentally unsuited to masculine styles of political activity, to unquestioningly adopt their husbands' political allegiances, to be more swayed by candidates than issues, to be more moralistic, more emotional and less politically aware and interested than men. Possibly stemming from the isolation of the housewife role, such attitudes were explained by references to a low feminine sense of political efficacy (Milbrath 1965; Campbell *et al.* 1960; Lane 1959). But these explanations were often inconsistently supported or not supported at all by such data as was available (Goot and Reid 1975). Standard explanations of low feminine participation relied therefore on women's insufficient socialisation into their civic duty or on 'insufficient masculinisation' (Currell 1974; Jaquette 1974). And Evans (1980) has pointed out that whilst women's preferences for the conservative and the traditional 'merely posit a sex difference in political attitudes …' the other assertions 'imply that women are less competent than men as citizens'.

Competence is, of course, a normative concept and the problem is not as simple as that. But sexism was endemic in the Political Science of the period under discussion. Goot and Reid (1975) argue that the few Political Scientists who did turn their (passing) attention to feminine political participation apparently viewed the under-representation of women in political life with a certain amount of equanimity, if not outright approval. Dahl (1956: 74) and Sartori (1956: 230–77) saw no diminution in the claim of democracy made by states which withheld the vote from women altogether. Other researchers limited their more intensive data analyses to male respondents (Abrams 1966; Lane 1962). Davies (1964: 137) felt comfortable in asserting that 'Politics is a game, in one simple sense for middle-aged men'. Whilst the limiting tendencies to scientism is the behavioural era combined with an attendant commitment to 'value free' social science could in part account for a failure to explain properly, and sometimes even notice an evident disenfranchisement of half of the world's citizens; these same tendencies often did not prevent sexist attitudes from being substituted for analysis. Admittedly, few went so far as Robert Lane, who wrote

> That working girls and career women and women who insistently serve the community, and women with extra-curricula interests of an absorbing kind are often borrowing their time and attention and capacity for relaxed play and love from their children to whom it rightfully belongs. As Kardiner points out, the rise in juvenile delinquency (and, he says homosexuality) is partly to be attributed to the feminist movement and what it did to the American mother. (1959: 355)

To be fair to Political Science, Lane's comments are unusually blatant and sex roles were never more than a passing concern for these scholars.

Towards a Feminist Political Science?

In most of the relevant disciplines it was only with the development of a feminist consciousness amongst academic women that the study of women was seriously engaged. In Political Science this response was late in coming and tended to correspond with political developments within professional associations. In the USA, articles and papers on women and politics only began to be a regular feature of academic journals and conferences after protests by the Women's Caucus of the

American Political Science Association; and it was only after 1970 that full length books on women and politics began to appear.

Until very recently, most of the new research on women and politics was situated squarely within mainstream political science; this despite a tendency to interdisciplinarity in feminist scholarship generally. The narrow base of the early studies of women and politics may well have been due to the peculiar isolation of Political Science from the other disciplines; and this was probably aggravated by the structure of academic careers. A continuing dominance of traditional single-discipline based departments may have meant that there is a perceived career penalty attached to multi-disciplinary scholarship. This consideration, combined with the fact that full-time women's studies posts are still relatively scarce, could well have been an inhibiting factor in the development of a feminist study of politics.

Whatever the causes, the main contribution of feminism to political studies has been limited to the areas of reinforcement of existing method and the exposure of sexist myths. A major initial concern was with identifying and publicising sexist bias in the standard literature on political participation, political socialisation and voting behaviour (Goot and Reid 1975; Bourque and Grossholtz 1974). This was a necessary task, but not one likely to involve a fundamental challenge to the discipline. Similarly, studies involving the collection of new research material (Kirkpatrick 1974; Currell 1974), whilst innovative in terms of devising methods to acquire a non-sexist data base, remained well within the acceptable limits of positivist Political Science. The point here is not that the above-mentioned studies were not worthy and necessary, this patently is not the case. Rather, the question is one of why these studies were not accompanied or succeeded by a number of works of critical theory which challenge the manner in which Political Studies has constructed its object of study.

It seems likely that this is an area in which the influence of the positivists of the 1950s and 1960s has been extremely important. The models and methods constructed in that era are the ones in which most of us were trained and remain important elements of undergraduate and graduate courses. Moving from combatting the sexist application of these approaches to a position of challenging their foundations will be a crucial step for feminist political scholarship. Unfortunately it is not an obvious one. The continuing dominance of American scholarship over the applied side of the discipline has its effect here. This dominance should be seen not only in conjunction with the strong positivistic tendencies discussed in the first section of this essay, but also in conjunction with a strong national reluctance to engage materialist philosophy, socialist thought or radical theory. When all of these elements are taken into account it becomes fair to suggest that certain important tensions conducive to the construction of a radical critique are not present amongst most of the Political Science profession. Hence the kind of critical feminist scholarship which has informed debates within Sociology and Social Psychology does not appear to have obtained access to Political Science. Additionally, the lack of a tradition of searching self-criticism within the profession has impeded the internal development of habits of thought conducive to a feminist challenge.

Thus one is forced ultimately to face the question of whether there is a Feminist Political Science to assess. Following Reuben (1978) one may state that there does exist a growing body of 'research by and/or about women', but this is, as Reuben points out, not necessarily synonymous with feminist scholarship. However, this research is undoubtedly generated by feminist goals. It is ideological in the sense that it has been motivated by a clear commitment to combat sexist bias in the way the discipline views feminine political behaviour. Lately too, studies of political issues thrown up by the women's movement have become more common; but this may be explained by the fact that the political success of 'second wave' feminism has now been sufficient for such issues to loom large enough to be on the policy agenda, forcing a pragmatic profession to take notice.

All in all, the feminist initiative in the study of politics has been a cautious and not entirely successful one, largely corresponding to the early stages of feminist scholarship outlined by Sherif (1978). Women are today more studied, but mainly by women and few of these women hold prestigious chairs or other important positions in the hierarchy of the profession. Whilst most major new political behaviour research includes sex differences as a major concern (Verba et al. 1979), such efforts as there have been to combat sexist perspectives in undergraduate politics literature appear so far to have been unsuccessful (WCPS Quarterly 1979: 6). The work completed so far has been confined to a very narrow area of study and a great deal of effort has been expended towards the explosion of sexist myths which have arisen from observations of often minute political differences between men and women. In areas where political differences between the sexes are large, research has tended to be concentrated on what insights might be gleaned from the study of the few women who are there (Kirkpatrick 1974; Tolchin and Tolchin 1974). The somewhat larger questions relating to the many women who are not there are only beginning to receive attention.

In the USA, the CAWP[12] has undertaken a major project involving using educational institutions in a programme of training women for public office. Research proposals have recently been submitted in the UK for a study of dropout rates amongst women candidates for electoral office. There have also been a number of studies produced which have as their avowed aim the object of comparing the political behaviour of women with women rather than the more usual comparisons of women with men (Kirkpatrick 1979; Iglitzin and Ross 1976; Wulff 1979). Whilst at a very early stage, developments such as these might be the first indications of a turn from an 'exposé of biases in the discipline' to 'defining new areas for study that will explicate the biases and lead to new scholarship' (Sherif 1978: 220), that, is, they may represent a turn toward the development of a genuinely feminist Political Science.

The way in which Political Science reacts to such a turn will depend upon four factors: (1) openness and responsiveness; (2) developments in the object; (3) on internal professional political developments; and to a certain extent on (4) the quality of the new scholarship itself. Taking each of these in their turn — firstly, there is theoretically no reason why Political Science should not be open to what will inevitably be interdisciplinary research iniatives. The study of politics is, as has been argued above, a convention … an evolved and agreed construct and that construct is an interdisciplinary one (*see* Blondel 1976). Indeed, in many ways, the early development of the academic study of politics bears marked similarities to the perspectives Sherif[13] has suggested for feminist scholarship. Secondly, the impact of developments in the object will depend largely upon the performance of women politicians. There are indications of cause for optimism in this regard, and evidence from recent European elections suggests that at least the Duverger 'Minimum representation of women necessary for propaganda purposes' has been raised. Thirdly, there is also cause for optimism about internal professional political developments. Organisation by women to promote both women and feminist scholarship is at the time of writing taking place in many of the national associations and the Sex Roles and Politics Group of the International Political Science Association appears to be well subscribed.

The fourth factor, the quality of the scholarship, is a more difficult element to assess as said scholarship is in its infancy. Certainly there are likely to be problems in that for a feminist Political Science to come into being, current definitions of political and public must be expanded and attention must be given to factors traditionally regarded as belonging to the private sphere. Tools for such analysis are being forged within other areas of feminist scholarship, however, and may be found particularly in the literature generated by the Capitalism-Patriarchy debate (*see* especially Kuhn and Wolpe 1978). So far this debate has not been engaged by Political Scientists, however, and there are reasons for being concerned that it won't be. Certainly the theoretical propensities of the profession have been such that this and similar debates could pass unnoticed by all but a peripheral few. Indeed, if a route into Political Science for discussions of a radical feminist nature is found, it is likely to be through the success the women's movement itself has in politicising new issues, the study of which will require the development of new analytical frameworks.

Statements about possible future developments must therefore be hedged with uncertainty. Too many of the important variables are outside of our control. Whilst new research techniques and theoretical perspectives are necessary, this necessity does not automatically mean they will be developed. It is also a fact that a situation of contracting finance for scholarly pursuits is likely to worsen, causing increasing competition in which less well-established feminist scholars may be pushed out. Whilst much in the way of socio-political research may be undertaken on little or no funding, sooner or later, expensive data collection is going to be necessary and the prospects for the required funding look bleak.

At the time of writing, feminists seeking to establish the study of women as a legitimate concern for Political Science have gained a toehold. Our concerns have, not surprisingly, been shaped by our training and this training has been predominantly in the scientism of Easton and Almond rather than in the theoretical and normative tradition of Aristotle. Hence our concentration has been on the adjustment of spurious analysis within an existing construct. We have concentrated on removing culturally determined, often implicit sexist assumptions from existing models. In other words, our efforts have been directed at generating a revised standard version of the political science of women, instead of at the development of a radical, altogether innovative feminist Political Science. We have done this because it was the obvious thing to do and only now that the task is nearing completion has it become apparent that for our work to mean anything at all, it must be seen as preliminary to a confrontation with and a challenge to the way in which knowledge has come to be constructed in the Political Science profession. The success of such an endeavour is not assured. The alacrity with which those employed in the study of politics have abandoned or ghettoised an honourable and traditional strand of critical theory has been outlined above and closely argued elsewhere.[14] Nevertheless, that strand has been responsible for much of what has been attractive and compelling about Political Science, and the imperatives of both feminist scholarship and the study of politics demand its restoration.

Notes

1. A particularly lucid discussion of this tension is to be found in J. Blondel (1976).

2. 'Positivist' and 'Positivism' are used throughout this essay as terms referring to the so-called 'scientific' strands of empiricism.

3. This raises the interesting question of why such developments took place in that period of history. Discussion of this is beyond the scope of the essay but the author plans to take it up in a future article of the development of the Political Science profession.

4. *See* works by McKenzie (1967, 1970), Apter (1977), Wolin (1961), Blondel (1976).

5. I am grateful to Jean Hardy of the Department of Government, Brunel University for pointing out the relevance of this insight.

6. In terms of its claim for the utility of systems analysis and its views of the development of Political Science, the IESS essay is representative of the views expressed by Easton in his major works.

7. Noteworthy here is Easton's de-facto exclusion of any philosophical components from his conceptualisation of Political Science.

8. For examples of these variations *see* the *Contemporary Political Theory* series edited by David Easton for Prentice-Hall, and the Little, Brown series in *Comparative Politics* edited by G. Almond, J. Coleman and L. Pye.

9. Including: Greenstein, (1965); Hess and Torney (1967); Dawson and Prewitt (1969); Merriam and Gosnell (1969); Campbell (1960); Almond and Verba (1963); Lane (1959); Hunter (1953); Dahl (1961); Presthus (1964).

10. International Political Science Association.

11. Ironically, Duverger may well have been a victim of a certain amount of 'footnote fudging'. His conclusions are very carefully worded and their

speculative character acknowledged. A careful reading of his report reveals considerable sensitivity to the dangers of sexist interpretation of the data.

12. Center for the American Women and Politics, Eagleton Institute, Rutgers University, New Brunswick, New Jersey.

13. Sherif's view is that the development of an interdisciplinary feminist scholarship will involve the refining of 'the art of judicious borrowing of both information and techniques from the various disciplines concerned with a problem, then to coordinate them, recognising their differing levels and units of analysis ...' (1978: 223).

14. *See* especially Carol Pateman (1970).

References

Abrams, M. (1966) 'Social Trends and Electoral Behaviour', in R. Rose (ed.), *Studies in British Politics*, London: MacMillan, pp.55–67.

Almond, G. A. and Verba, S. (1963) *The Civic Culture*, Boston: Little, Brown and Company.

Apter, D. E. (1977) *Introduction to Political Analysis*, Cambridge, Mass.: Winthrop.

Aristotle (1962) *The Politics*, Middlesex: Penguin (T. A. Sinclair Trans.).

Blondel, J. (1976) *Thinking Politically*, Middlesex: Penguin.

Bourque, S. C. and Grossholtz, J. (1974) 'Politics an Unnatural Practice: Political Science Looks at Female Participation', *Politics and Society*, 4 (2): 225–266.

Campbell, A., Converse, P. E., Miller, W. E., and Stokes, D. E. (1960) *The American Voter*, New York: John Wiley.

Converse, P. E and Converse, J. M. (1971) 'The Status of Women as Students and Professionals in Political Science', *PS: Political Science and Politics*, 4 (3): 328–348.

Currell, M. E. (1974) *Political Woman*, London: Croom Helm.

Dahl, R. A. (1956) *A Preface to Democratic Theory*, Chicago: Chicago University Press.

Dahl, R. A. (1961) *Who Governs*, New Haven, CT: Yale University Press.

Davies, A. F. (1964) *Australian Democracy*, 2nd edition, Melbourne: Longmans, Green.

Dawson, R. E. and Prewitt, K. (1969) *Political Socialisation*, Boston: Little, Brown and Co.

Deutsch, K. W. (1963) *The Nerves of Government: Models of Political Communication and Control*, New York: Free Press.

Duverger, M. (1955) *The Political Role of Women*, UNESCO.

Easton, D. (1953) *The Political System: An Inquiry into the State of Political Science*, New York: Knopf.

Easton, D. (1965a) *A Framework for Political Analysis*, New Jersey: Englewood Cliffs, Prentice-Hall.

Easton, D. (1965b) *A Systems Analysis of Political Life*, New York: Wiley.

Easton, D. (1968) 'Political Science', *International Encyclopaedia of the Social Sciences*, 12: 282–298.

Evans, J. (1980) 'Attitudes to Women in American Political Science', *Government and Opposition*, 15 (1): 101–114.

Goot, M. and Reid, E. (1975) *Women and Voting Studies: Mindless Matrons or Sexist Scientism?*, Sage Professional Papers in Comparative Political Sociology.

Greenstein, F. I. (1965) *Children and Politics*, New Haven, CT: Yale University Press.

Hess, R. D. and Torney, J. V. (1967) *The Development of Political Attitudes of Children,* Chicago: Aldine.

Hunter, F. (1953) *Community Power Structure*, North Carolina: University of North Carolina Press.

Iglitzin, L. B. and Ross, R. A. (1976) *Women in the World: A Comparative Study*, Santa Barbara: Clio Press.

Jaquette, J. (Ed.) (1974) *Women in Politics*, New York: John Wiley and Sons.

Kirkpatrick, J. (1974) *Political Woman*, New York: Basic Books.

Kuhn, A. and Wolpe, A. M. (1978) *Feminism and Materialism*, London: Routledge and Kegan Paul.

Lane, R. E. (1959) *Political Life*, Glencoe: Free Press.

Lane, R. E. (1962) *Political Ideology*, Glencoe: Free Press.

Lane, R. E. and Sears, D. O. (1964) *Public Opinion*, Englewood Cliffs: Prentice-Hall.

Lipset, S.M. (1960) *Political Man: The Social Bases of Politics*, London: Heinemann.

Lovenduski, J. and Evans, J. (1979) 'Women as Academic Staff and As Students in Political Studies', Paper presented to 1979 Political Studies Conference, Sheffield, April.

McCloskey, H. (1968) 'Political Participation', in D. L. Sills (ed.) *International Encyclopedia of the Social Sciences, Vol. 12*, New York: MacMillan, pp. 252–253.

MacIntyre, A. (1971) 'Is a Science of Comparative Politics Possible?', in A. MacIntyre *Against the Self Images of the Age*, London: Duckworth, pp. 260–279.

McKenzie, W. J. M. (1967) *Politics and the Social Sciences*, Middlesex: Penguin.

McKenzie, W. J. M. (1970) *The Study of Political Science Today*, London: MacMillan.

Merriam, C. E. and Gosnell, H. (1969) *Non-Voting: Causes and Methods of Control*, Chicago: University of Chicago Press.

Milbrath, L. (1965) *Political Participation*, Chicago: Rand McNally.

Pateman, C. (1970) *Participation and Democratic Theory*, Cambridge: Cambridge University Press.

Presthus, R. (1964) *Men at the Top*, New York: Oxford University Press.

Reuben, E. (1978) 'In Defiance of the Evidence: Notes on Feminist Scholarship', *Women's Studies, International Quarterly*, 1 (3): 215–218.

Sartori, G. (1956) *Democratic Theory*, New York: Praeger.

Sherif, C. W. (1978) 'Climbing Disciplinary Walls and Learning How to Borrow', *Women's Studies, International Quarterly*, 1 (3): 219–224.

Tolchin, S. and Tolchin, M. (1974) *Clout: Woman, Power and Politics*, New York: Coward, McCann and Geoghegan.

Verba, S., Nie, N. H., and Kim, J. (1979) *Participation and Political Equality*, Cambridge: Cambridge University Press.

Wolin, S. (1961) *Politics and Vision*, London: George Allen and Unwin.

WCPS (*Women's Caucus for Political Science Quarterly*) (1979) 'Scholarly Treatment of Women in Political Science Texts Subjects of Study', May, 6.

Wulff, C. (1979) 'Women Activists in the British Constituency Labour Parties', European Consortium for Political Research, April.

Chapter Fifteen

Gendering Research in Political Science

Introduction

Feminist studies of women and politics have the objective to correct previous biases in the mainstream of political science. Early critiques of the masculine biases (Bourque and Grossholtz 1974; Jaquette 1974; Boals 1975; Goot and Reid 1975; Sapiro 1979) were accompanied by excavations of lacunae, neglect and sexism in Western political theory (Okin 1979; Elshtain 1981; Eisenstein 1981). These were succeeded by analyses of the reasons for the discipline's failure to deal with women as political beings and by systematic expositions of the ways in which political science and political theory were implicated in the exclusion of women from the public sphere (Evans 1980; Lovenduski 1981; Sapiro 1981; Acklesberg and Diamond 1987; Jones and Jonasdottir 1988; Pateman 1989). This literature is notable for the extent of its critique. The criticisms of empirical political science showed a special concern with the neglect of women by traditional behavioural approaches, which, it was claimed, described a stereotype of women's political roles. Feminists outlined a research agenda that would challenge that stereotype by contesting both the way politics was practiced and the manner in which it was understood. This project had an explicit normative dimension; it sought to assist the production of a world in which women were present in a full range of political roles.

These large ambitions were inevitably limited by resource constraints and the need at first to concentrate on the exploration of women's political behaviour at elite and citizen levels. The huge expenses incurred in the administration of purpose-designed, large-scale surveys prevented many scholars from making full investigations of women's political behaviour. Instead they were limited to what could be learned from the reanalysis of data sets in which sex had been a largely unexplored background variable (Jaquette 1974; Goot and Reid 1975; Bourque and Grossholtz 1974). New research into behaviour and attitudes tended to be based on small and sometimes unrepresentative data sets at local or state (US) levels (Githens 1983). Progress reports referred to this as the 'add women and stir' phase of studying women and politics. In fact, practitioners were well aware of the theoretical and methodological limitations of their work and the radical implications of feminism for the study of politics.

How to overcome those limitations became a central preoccupation in developing a feminist political science. Essential to the project was the elimination of the 'bad science' of exaggerating and misconstruing differences between women and men, assuming a male political universe, and using data without their original accompanying qualifications. In addition, feminist political scientists were troubled by the distortions in mainstream behavioural political science arising from an epistemology that separated facts from values and privileged so-called value-free factual accounts (Elshtain 1979; Nelson 1989). The effect of concern only with putative facts was to allow behavioural political science to factor women out of consideration as political subjects. An overemphasis on measurable political behaviour prevented recognition of 'not only the...exclusion of women from what is traditionally political, but also the inclusion of politics in what women have traditionally done' (Nelson 1989: 21; quoted in Carroll and Zerilli 1993). Families, communities, voluntary groups all went largely unresearched as constitutive of political life. Inevitably the feminist study of politics sought to expand the definition of politics, strengthening other challenges to central concerns with electoral behaviour and elite participation while examining differences in men's and women's political behaviour. Discussion of the significance of the public/private split and the confinement of women to the private realm was an important challenge to narrow definitions of politics (Elshtain 1981; Landes 1988). So too were studies of the crucial part played by the state in regulating sexuality and gender (Petchesky 1984; Luker 1985; Gordon 1988). The work of social historians such as Davidoff and Hall (1987) showed how definitions of public and private were historically specific, and validated, if it needed validation, the argument that the study of politics is a convention constructed by its practitioners.

Contesting disciplinary boundaries fits within a wider scepticism about foundational theories that arose as postmodern thinking became more influential and interest in poststructuralism, discourse theory, and deconstruction became more common in the social sciences. Even as the usefulness of studying women was affirmed and demonstrated, categories such as woman, man, male, female, masculine and feminine were being scrutinised, found wanting, and redefined.

Feminist intellectual concern about women and power was not confined to political scientists. Developments in the women's movements, in feminist theory, and in the growing and interdisciplinary women's studies movement had political dimensions and concerns. In the 1980s feminist activists became increasingly interested in political institutions and organisations. Feminism had a considerable impact on research in the arts, humanities and social sciences. The cognate fields of history, sociology, social psychology, literature, and cultural studies produced a substantial body of work about different aspects of women and power. In addition a significant field of 'new' men's studies examined masculinity as a category both of privilege and of oppression (Brod 1987; 1994; Connell 1994; Hearn and Collinson 1996). Analysis of masculinities has also received considerable attention from feminist theorists (Brown 1988; Cockburn 1983; di Stefano 1991; Segal 1990). Such writers affirmed the understanding that differences among women and men were at least as important as differences between women and men, that race, class, age, ethnicity, sexuality, and physical ability were, like sex, constitutive of political identity and therefore of political behaviour and power.

These developments were accompanied by a growing dissatisfaction with the analytical utility of the concept of sex, understood as a dichotomous variable separating the categories man and woman. Instead the term gender, defined primarily as the social construction of biological sex, was preferred. Over the course of the 1980s feminist anthropologists, historians, cultural theorists, psychologists and sociologists argued that the concepts of sex and gender were separate; hence the definition of gender was problemetised and complicated. A shift from a focus on sex to an interest in gender began, which, although not yet complete, became increasingly influential in feminist research into politics. Gender, understood as a characteristic of both women and men, is expressed in relations that are embodied in the sexual division of labour, compulsory heterosexuality, discourses and ideologies of citizenship, motherhood, masculinity and femininity (Orloff 1996: 51). Gender therefore is a concept that suggests another major re-examination of what we think we know about political life. Its implications are at least as insistent as the original second-wave feminist challenges to political science in the 1970s. The gender concept has been incorporated into research on politics, where its effects on the development of research questions are already substantial; I believe they will be increasingly productive, offering important understandings of how political life has developed and will change.

This essay examines some of the consequences and implications of the move from sex to gender in the study of women and politics.[1] First I describe the origins of the concepts of gender used by feminist social scientists. Second I discuss the implications of the shift from sex to gender for empirical research; third I illustrate my contentions with a discussion of recent research from North America and Western Europe on gender and politics that incorporates the concept of gender into its design, and fourth I identify the research strategies that produce the most successfully 'gendered' analyses. Finally, in the concluding discussion, I argue that feminist political science needs the concept of gender but must also retain the use of the dichotomous variable of sex.

Origins of the Shift from Sex to Gender

Gender is widely used as a synonym for sex. Inconsistent and contradictory uses of the term are a cause of considerable confusion in contemporary writing. As soon as the complexity of gender is considered, the difficulty of devising and organising an appropriate lexicon appears. It seems almost impossible to develop the vocabulary needed to discuss gender without already having that vocabulary available. Yet over the last twenty years or so, a distinct shift from a focus on sex to an interest in gender has been apparent in the feminist study of politics. Most often implicit, the shift has its origins in at least two sets of developments: (*a*) in women's studies and feminist theory and (*b*) in political behaviour and political science.

Women's Studies and Feminist Theory

The women's studies movement has provided a continuous flow of ideas, theories and other knowledge about women and political life. As the implications of the insight that gender is a social construction became more evident, and it became more widely understood that both women and men have gender, debates across disciplinary boundaries became a common feature of feminist scholarship. These debates are part of a continuing process of definition refinement and theory production that is relevant to political science. The central argument is that sex and gender are analytically distinct, gender is relational, and the concept of sex is meaningless except when understood in the context of theories of gender relations.

New research questions and possibilities from the sociology of organisations were raised in Savage and Witz's (1992) influential collection *Gender and Bureaucracy*. This collection coincided with a spate of publications on gender and organisations that placed gender at the centre of the analysis of power in organisations (Bologh 1991; Hearn 1991; Jones 1993; Davies 1994). The central insight of these studies was that all institutions are implicated in the shaping of gender relations, including not only those in the 'private' sphere but also public institutions such as workplaces and state organisations.

The elements of these analyses of gender and organisations are identity, sexuality, interaction, culture, and power. Davies (1994) argues that cultural codes of masculinity and femininity shape identity from earliest childhood and are encountered and reencountered in the 'frozen social relations' of institutions. In these accounts gender is relational; that is, masculinity and femininity are understood and can be understood only in relation to each other. Moreover the relation of masculinity to femininity, although dominant, is uneasy. There are numerous competing masculinities and femininities. The cultural codes of gendered behaviour do not match exactly the beliefs and behaviour of 'actually existing women and men'; they are cultural codes, hence complicated and idealised. The idealised cultural codes offer a theoretical separation of sex and gender with implications similar to those of Butler's contention that gender is performance rather than a biological given (*see* below).

The core theoretical problem is that the concept of gender immediately calls into question the givenness of sex. As Nicholson has written, although gender was developed and is often used as a contrasting term to sex, 'to depict that which is socially constructed as opposed to that which is biologically given...[the term]... has increasingly become used to refer to any social construction having to do with the male/female distinction, including those constructions that separate 'female' bodies from 'male' bodies' (1994: 79). In other words, as the inverted commas indicate, the body itself is seen through the mediation of social interpretation; hence sex is not separate from gender but subsumable under it. Butler (1990) goes further, questioning the notion of social construction itself and arguing that culture, not biology, is destiny. She argues that gender is performed rather than innate and is therefore radically independent of sex. This perspective separates gender from the human body and locates it in a set of beliefs about what constitutes masculine or feminine (Duerst-Lahti and Kelly 1995: 16).

Political Science and Political Behaviour

The argument has important implications for the study of politics. Notably it suggests that sex is more than just another variable to factor into otherwise unchanging research designs. Feminist political scientists are aware of this and have inevitably made efforts to contest narrow definitions of politics, to expand their research terrain to aspects of 'private' life, and to identify the role of government and the state in constructing and enforcing certain kinds of relationships between women and men. Research strategies developed to explore such interests were based in the canon of political science and reinforced by events in politics as feminist activists got more involved in mainstream political institutions

Recent feminist political science shows how useful it is to subsume sex under gender in empirical research. Although some fancy semantic footwork may be required, it is not necessary to deny biological sex in order to make use of gender as an analytical category (*see* Hacking 1997). Moreover there is ample space for gender analysis in the intellectual mainstream of political science. Institutional research traditions in political science require the close description of contexts, norms, processes and cultures to which a gendered vocabulary may be applied (Wellhofer 1994; Skocpol 1985). Such specification is necessary if we are to avoid essentialism. As historian Joan Scott (1988) has argued, attributes associated with men and women and deemed masculine and feminine vary across time, culture, and, important for this essay, institution. Separating sex and gender exposes the different meanings of gender according to class, race, history, and so forth, unmasking differences among women and allowing new ways of dealing with questions about difference. For feminist political science, the need to use an adequately theorised notion of gender became acute when it became necessary (and possible) to study the effects of women on previously male-dominated political institutions and organisations. Increasing numbers of women are present in legislatures, councils, and other representative bodies as well as in executive organisations and public administrations. Research strategies based on a dichotomous classification of sex have proved unsatisfactory and uninteresting. Increasingly, feminist political scientists question what else is happening when the numbers of women are changing, an interest that leads inevitably to the close study of political organisations and institutions. The question of what difference it will make to have more women in power is now a subject for empirical research in many countries at state, local, and national levels.

Implications of the Shift from Sex to Gender for Political Science Research

Using the concept of gender therefore involves (*a*) rejecting the definitions of politics implied by the conventions of the public/private split, (*b*) re-examining the productions of conventional political science for gender dimensions, and (*c*) constructing from *a* and *b* a political science that is gender-informed. The prospect of such an undertaking is unlikely to be universally welcome. It is difficult to think of an aspect of politics that would be unaffected by gender. The tidy and parsimonious models preferred by so many political scientists cannot easily accommodate embedded, ubiquitous variables. But if models of politics omit gender, serious mistakes will occur when they are used to explain political behaviour.

The use of sex as a simple, dichotomous variable will distort unless it is located in a gendered frame of reference. The effects of gender cannot be left to one side or held constant for the sake of other experiments. As it is coming to be defined, gender is embedded in individuals, relationships, institutions and organisations. A 'gendered' political science looks 'not just at particular theories and assumptions as they have been applied to women, but as they are constructed and apply in any case' (Sapiro 1991).

To gender feminist research into politics it is necessary to consider how masculinities and femininities interact in organisations, institutions and processes. Davies's (1994) exposition of cultural codes of masculinity and femininity are useful here. In contemporary Western democracies, cultural codes of masculinity stress autonomy; boundedness; responsibility to and for self; agency; abstract, rule-governed thinking; and instrumentality in relationships, characterised by decisiveness and competitiveness. In contrast, cultural codes of femininity stress connectedness; responsibility for others; concrete, contextual thinking; and selflessness in relationships, characterised by a style that is accommodating, group-oriented, and facilitating. Connell (1994), Stivers (1993), and Davies (1994) argue that the public world was designed to accommodate activity according to the codes of masculinity. The value cluster found in the masculine code inscribes the most influential vision of what it means to 'act in public'. In human terms the vision is incomplete, ruling out intimacy, emotion and affection from public institutions (Davies 1994).

Feminist writing on gender, professionalism and bureaucracy provides examples of how cultural codes of masculinity are built into public institutions. Using evidence from existing bureaucracies, Ferguson (1984), Bologh (1991), and Jones (1993) offer a critique of the theories of Max Weber on rational bureaucracy, professionalism, leadership and the institutionalisation of authority that focuses on its masculinism. They contend that Weber's professional, his rational bureaucrat, and his legitimate ruler are the same man; he is a construction of idealised masculinity, Weber's ideal man. According to Bologh, Weber's rational bureaucrat is a strongly bounded, 'agentic' individual who wishes to make a difference in the world. Such men, as bounded individuals, engage in autonomous action, each acting rationally in pursuit of individual interest. Relations to each other are aggressive and competitive in a public world of 'hostile strangers' in which collective action occurs only where power is exercised, where some men dominate everyone else. Other men are controlled through fear and loyalty institutionalised into hierarchy; women and femininity are underconceptualised (in the sense that, for example, women's unpaid work is not addressed) or invisible. Love and protection are illusory - among hostile strangers it is possible to accede to codes of femininity only by withdrawing. In the world of the rational bureaucrat, women remain in the private sphere under the protection of men. Femininity is inferior, lacking the discipline and constant struggle necessary to the development of intellect. The codes of masculinity and femininity are, as I have said, idealised and exaggerated. They are nevertheless ideologies that are central to the workings of public institutions and therefore to political life, conventionally defined.

At issue is whether it is necessary to perform masculinity in order to act in public. There is considerable debate among feminists and other theorists about the causes, stability, and results of gender differences in political activity. Especially powerful among both feminist activists and their opponents is the contention that women should not seek presence in powerful positions equal to men's because they will be incorporated and changed by it, will become unable to represent women because male-created institutions have turned them into political men. The counterclaim is that once a significant number and diversity of women occupy decision-making positions in institutions, the institutions will be transformed; their gendering will be altered.

This argument, so important in feminist debate, has echoes in the conventions of the study of political processes (Randall 1991). Once arrangements, practices and rules have been institutionalised, actors learn them, invest in them, and make decisions accordingly. Particular institutions become associated with particular behaviour and outputs. These insulate the positions of typical members and are notoriously difficult to change (Skocpol 1985; March and Olsen 1984). It takes only a short leap to see the gendered interests in such arrangements and to imagine that different forms of masculinity and femininity might be identified, classified, and mapped onto associated analyses of political processes and institutions.

But it is a step further to operationalise these insights for empirical research. A crucial characteristic of such research must be that sex is used as a dichotomous variable only in a closely specified, gendered context. In good research gender is always relational and is most simply measured on a continuum. With that proviso, it is impossible to imagine how gendered research can do without the dichotomous variable of sex. The uses of sex and gender must be explicit if effective research is to be designed. To support this contention I discuss three areas of feminist research into politics: political representation, public policy (using the example of welfare state research), and political institutions.

Political Representation

In the study of political representation, movement from a concern with categorical differences between women and men to the gendered analysis of institutions and processes was a long, slow development. It is far from complete. The term gender frequently appears as a synonym for sex, sometimes in publications that also use it in the more complex manner discussed above. A great deal of this work implicitly separates sex and gender but does not make the distinction explicit (Sapiro 1991; Lovenduski 1993). The most recent studies, informed by theoretical developments in the study of gender relations, make explicit distinctions and explore hypotheses based on gender (Duerst-Lahti and Kelly 1995).

Research into political representation includes women's political attitudes, behaviour, and participation in political elites. It is most developed in the USA, where extensive investigations of women's political roles began in the 1970s. Early studies (Kirkpatrick 1974; Diamond 1977; Githens and Prestage 1977) did not challenge disciplinary frameworks but attempted to locate women within them (Carroll and Zerilli 1993). By the end of the 1970s few researchers found evidence that the political orientations of women and men differed. This was partly because they took care to eliminate methodological biases that had previously tended to exclude women and partly because changes took place in the political behaviour of women as differences between men's and women's social roles, education, and employment decreased (Carroll and Zerilli 1993). Higher levels of education and working outside the home were shown to be positively related to women's rates and kinds of participation and levels of political efficacy (Sapiro 1983; Welch 1977; Baxter and Lansing 1980), while having children reduced participation for women and altered political orientations (Sapiro 1983; Jennings and Niemi 1981).

Changes in women's voting are well researched in the USA not least because the gender gap became important and interesting in electoral politics. However, cross-national comparative studies of men's and women's voting are scarce, and although there is some interest in and evidence of altering European gender gaps in voting, systematic comparison has not yet been undertaken.

Elite studies in the 1970s found women were less ambitious for public office than men. This research was sensitive to the constraints of gender norms and drew attention to the importance of traditional sex roles in keeping women out of electoral politics. There was a frequent implication that change would come through efforts by individual women. During the 1980s the emphasis of such research shifted and explanations of the underrepresentation of women focused more on the operation of the political system itself. Electoral systems proved important both in the USA (Carroll 1985, Darcy *et al.* 1987, Studlar *et al.* 1988) and in Western Europe (Randall 1987; Norris 1985; Lovenduski 1986; Haavio-Mannila and Skard 1985), where quota systems and proportional representation were found to affect women's chances of election. European research implicated political parties in the underrepresentation of women and showed how feminist interventions in party politics altered women's chances of election (Lovenduski and Norris 1993; Norris and Lovenduski 1995). Skjeie's imaginative and well-theorised work on the political integration of women in Norway used analysis of party documents together with in-depth interviews of women and men politicians to examine the relationships among organisational cultures, party political priorities, and the integration of women in the cabinet and legislatures (Skjeie 1991, 1993). Similar Swedish research shows the importance of cross-party groupings to the improvement of women's influence and power and offers evidence that more nearly equal distribution of parliamentary seats between women and men leads to more nearly equal distribution of the committee assignments that are so important to parliamentary influence (C Berqvist, unpublished data,). The Scandinavian research followed the appearance of numerous women representatives there and was enhanced by the availability of good source material including transcripts, party documents and parliamentary records, and good access to politicians. Politicians could be both located in their institutional contexts and questioned about their own understandings of gendered effects and changes. Understanding gender effects requires such combined strategies.

Duerst-Lahti and Kelly's (1995) recent collection of essays on gender and political leadership makes the most explicit use of the concept of gender in the empirical analysis of political representation. Duerst-Lahti and Kelly argue that gender needs to be understood as a category, as an attribute, and as normative, and they restate the contention that gender relations are relations of domination. Gender is therefore an attribute of power in which certain kinds of masculinity are dominant and privileged, a situation that is stable so long as dominant positions are strictly sex segregated. Once more than a token number of women become leaders, dissonance ensures that a process of reinterpretation occurs. Such interpretation may also occur when the idea that women might or should become leaders (representatives) is raised.

This is well illustrated by Duerst-Lahti and Verstegen (1995), who consider ways in which issues of political representation are gendered. They use Pitkin's (1967) distinctions among formal, descriptive, symbolic, and substantive representation and between 'standing for' and 'acting for' as modes of representation. Duerst-Lahti and Verstegen note the separation of the symbolic and substantive representation of women in studies of women and politics. They analyse the USA's 1992 'year of the woman' elections, explaining how the visual absence of women on the judiciary committee in the Hill- Thomas hearings raised American women's awareness of their lack of both substantive and descriptive representation; the hearings also provided a frame for discussions of gender in electoral coverage by the media and made possible a normalisation of the idea that women should become politicians (Duerst-Lahti and Verstegen 1995: 215–17).

In the same volume, Tamerius demonstrates how the use of dichotomous sex rather than gender as an explanatory variable may lead to misleading findings. She criticises the oversimplifications of numerous studies of congressional roll-call voting, which have shown minimal differences between women and men and have led to conclusions that women and men legislators have the same views on policy matters. Roll-call vote is actually a weak indicator of policy support because a legislator need only prefer a policy to its alternative to vote for it. Activities such as co-sponsorship, speech making, and sponsorship of bills indicate much higher levels of commitment, with sponsorship involving a significantly greater investment of effort in support of a bill than speech making or co-sponsorship. A parallel hierarchy of differences in awareness of issues is linked to these activities. Tamerius's study of support for women's issues in the 101st Congress found that although differences between women and men in roll-call voting on feminist issues were small, women were significantly more likely than men to co-sponsor feminist bills, to make speeches on behalf of feminist legislation, and to sponsor feminist legislation. Tamerius used a straightforward research design that made use of well-known facts about congressional behaviour. In looking beyond a simple measure of sex to processes and patterns of behaviour she was able to identify an important difference between women and men in Congress. '[C]ongresswomen tend to be leaders in feminist policy and congressmen do not.' Women legislators see women as a group with distinctive interests and needs and consistently represent the interests of women more than men do, and they do so regardless of party affiliation. Hence the power of gender is not only a symbolic influence, but a primary determinant of the types of issues around which representation emerges (Tamerius 1995: 110–11).

Public Policy

Interest in the gendered nature of political representation was accompanied by concern about the impact of participation by women on outcomes. Early feminist work on public policy addressed the impact of policy on women. Feminist critiques of public policy analysis followed a familiar pattern of exposing androcentrism and producing evidence that tacit gender biases routinely led policy analysts to bad science, in which they made contradictory claims about women that 'challenged the internal consistency of their arguments about human beings' (Hawksworth 1994: 110). Feminist policy studies offered critique, prescription, and evidence of gender biases and effects in policy making and delivery, paying particular attention to women's unique needs but also considering policies not normally regarded as within women's issue areas. Lewis (1992) showed how, across Western Europe, governments failed to value either the paid or unpaid work of women. Cockburn (1991) demonstrated how men's institutional advantage enabled them to resist government policies for equality between women and men, and Hoskyns (1996) traced the influence of feminist networks on equality policy in the European Communities. Discussions of feminist policy networks are an important part of feminist policy studies (Boles 1994, Abrar *et al.* 1998), but it is in examinations of particular policies that feminists have typically made the most sophisticated use of the concept of gender.

British studies of domestic violence policy have indicated how male predominance in police forces has led to problems of implementation. Not only do prevailing masculinities inhibit enthusiasm for policing male violence to women, but even where goodwill and willingness are present there are gender-based difficulties. One problem is that survivors of male sexual violence tend not to trust any men and hence are reluctant to turn to the police unless the latter have made great efforts to project a sympathetic image (Dunhill 1989, Hanmer *et al.* 1989). Another example of male-dominated policy making is the position of male local trade union representatives charged with the negotiation of maternity leave or child-care arrangements; without considerable direction and retraining they simply do not prioritise such policies either in their rhetoric or in their practice (Cockburn 1991).

The greatest volume of work on women and public policy has been on the development and impact of welfare states. A significant and sustained feminist intervention in this research area generated debates among feminists and between feminist and mainstream (gender-indifferent) researchers. Like the best research on political representation, feminist accounts of the welfare state take on the concerns of mainstream researchers while taking them to task for ignoring the ways in which state institutions of social provision and public service affect gender relations (Orloff 1996). The vast literature on welfare states for the most part ignores sex and gender in a canon that, feminists argue, distorts the design of research. In mainstream writing the welfare state is typically operationalised as the set of insurance and assistance programmes that protect or supplement the income of the family breadwinner. Feminists are prominent among those who argue for a broader use of the term to include the full range of provisions that states make to protect and assist citizens (Orloff 1996: 52).

The conceptual shift from sex to gender and the development of gender relations theories enabled a significant breakthrough in research on welfare regimes and on the state itself. Until the mid-1990s, two contradictory views of the relationship between the state and gender predominated: the welfare state was either responsible for the social reproduction of gender inequality or it ameliorated such inequality (Orloff 1996, 1997). According to social reproduction accounts, the development of modern welfare states constituted a shift from public to private patriarchy in which traditional gender relations were sustained in different ways (Holter 1984; Abramovitz 1988; Gordon 1988, 1990; Lister 1992; Land 1978; Waerness 1984; Ungerson 1990; Hernes 1987; Sassoon 1988; Finch and Groves 1983; Lewis and Aström 1992; Nelson 1984; Borchorst and Siim 1987) and in which states were explicitly implicated in the constitution of gender (Gordon and Fraser 1994; Knijn 1994;, Lister 1990; Saraceno 1994; Bryson 1992; Nelson 1989). This approach has the merit of showing how the welfare state maintains gender inequalities even where it improves women's material position. However, these largely single-country studies ignore cross-cultural and historical variations (Orloff 1996, 1997).

Amelioration advocates add consideration of the effects of the welfare state to more common assessments of effects on class inequality. These studies report variations in policy outcomes and demonstrate women's, particularly elderly women's, disproportionate poverty, implying that women have an interest in higher spending on welfare (McLanahan et al. 1989; Piven 1985; Kamerman 1986; Goldberg and Kremen 1990; Mitchell 1993; Ruggie 1988). These approaches show how state policies have benefited women. They have been widely criticised for their unsophisticated understandings of the bases of inequalities between women and men (Nelson 1984; Collins 1990; Quadagno 1994; Roberts 1995). They are open to criticism that they fail to understand how different policies evolve and ignore women's activities in policy making. Finally, they overlook the necessity for different policies to treat poverty for men and women (Orloff 1996, 1997).

In this area of scholarship the emergence of more sophisticated and convincing accounts resulted from both a greater use of comparative research strategies and a growing sensitivity to the effects of different gender regimes (Connell 1987). Recent feminist studies of the welfare state have been sensitive to the complexities of gender and, as a result, have offered both greater clarity and a more insistent challenge to mainstream work (Lewis 1992a, 1997; Langan and Ostner 1991; O'Connor 1993; Orloff 1993; Sainsbury 1993, 1996; Bussmaker and VanKersbergen 1994; Borchorst 1994; Daly 1994). A common point of discussion is regime typologies, which became controversial as attempts were made to adapt Esping-Anderson's (1990) three models of welfare for research on women and welfare policy. The problem is that '[a]nalysis using mainstream, regime-type frameworks to understand the relationships between welfare state and gender relations cannot fully explain important patterns, faltering partly *because they have made 'women' rather than 'gender relations' the targets of their enquiry* [and]...using gender-blind dimensions of a typology based around non-gendered characteristics' (Orloff 1997: 189, my italics).

An influential essay by Lewis (1992a) signalled efforts to 'gender' methodologies for studying welfare regimes. Her argument that policy regimes should be classified according to their different levels of support for male-breadwinner, female-dependent household types was, among other things, an attempt to design research around complex dimensions of gender rather than a simply defined dichotomous sex variable. Lewis's analytical separation of gender from sex facilitates consideration of differences among and between women and men and potentially enables a rebalancing of the study of welfare regimes, in which gender relations are an important (but not the only) means of structuring social relations. Her accomplishment is both to release feminist research on welfare states from an exclusive concentration on women and to show how important gender is to effective mainstream research. The point here is not that Lewis's is the ideal way to operationalise gender for empirical research but that her work demonstrates what is at stake. Gendered research into public policy should treat differences among women (and differences among men) as well as those between women and men. Modern welfare regimes do not necessarily have an emancipatory effect, and different types of regimes may enforce different forms of inequality. For example, paid employment does not necessarily improve the lives of all women, nor does state support for unpaid work (Orloff 1996).

Such insights have implications both for the way regimes are assessed and for feminist policy advocacy. What Molyneux (1985) described as the practical and strategic interests of women do not always coincide either with each other or with the interests of all women. Orloff (1996, 1997) argues that to make the best use of theories of gender relations in assessing what most enhances women's position, it is necessary to consider how state provision affects '*the capacity to form and maintain an autonomous household* ' (italics in original), 'a dimension which indicates the ability of...women...to survive and support their children...without having to marry to gain access to breadwinner 's income' (Orloff 1997: 195). Her argument is that such an indicator captures the effects on women both of access to paid work and cash benefits for unpaid work. Thus it highlights the crucial and often overlooked fact that gender is constitutive of the identities and political capacities of both women and men. Other recent studies of the state have similar potential as theories of gender relations are implicit in their approach (Pringle and Watson 1992; Hobson 1994; Sainsbury 1994, 1996; Langan and Ostner 1991; Ostner and Lewis 1995; Knijn 1994; Pederson 1993). However, this potential has so far rarely been realised in accounts that pay explicit attention to the range of gendered interests (for an exception see Skocpol 1992).

The obstacle to a full realisation of the concept of gender in research design is that it is so difficult, at this point, to design appropriate, focused, explicit questions. Research must incorporate gender at the design stage. It is also necessary to reformulate questions about other inequalities in order to thread gender through the research tapestry and to allocate to it an appropriate, important but not necessarily foundational place in the account. These are not problems that can be wholly resolved at the level of abstract theory. It is nearly impossible to develop universal questions about gender that are applicable to all empirical research. To be researchable, questions must be carefully devised and, ideally, constructed with attention to the conventions of study of the phenomenon under investigation. It is in refining and operationalising concepts in particular and well-specified contexts that their explanatory potential becomes apparent. This is the way empirical research takes account of theory, and it is on this terrain that feminist and mainstream research must engage each other.

Political Institutions

Feminist research on the welfare state is more extensively and explicitly gendered than is the study of women and political representation. Sociologists and social historians have led in a field that has attracted interest from only a few political scientists (Hernes 1987; Jenson 1986; Siim 1988; Sainsbury 1993, 1996). By contrast, feminist political scientists have produced path-breaking work in the gendered study of political institutions. Here the use of gender as an explanatory concept has, particularly in recent work, been explicit and imaginative.

Political institutions such as legislatures, parties, congressional committees, and social movements are all organisations, amenable to study *qua* organisations. They reflect gender biases that are likely to be specific to the organisation but that may be identified by counting the places occupied by women and men, considering the differences in positions occupied by women and men, and identifying the continuum of masculinity and femininity associated with various positions and processes within the organisation and in the organisation as a whole. Organisational masculinism implies that ideologies of masculinity are integral to the organisation, shaping its rules, values, norms, structures and outputs. Hearn (1989, 1991) has written at length about the development of masculinities in social life and in the spread of public organisations. Such developments both empowered men and sustained male power by increasing the quantity of sites on which it operated. The spread of public organisations was predicated on the existence of male power over women (and some men) in private life and private organisations; political organisations were not excluded from this process. Men in organisations were good at setting rules of the game that ensured that the qualifications of men were better valued and led more reliably to power and rewards. The historical association of state formation with physical strength, violence and war and the importance of the soldier to the formation of the modern state is an instance of such rule-setting processes. Diplomatic, colonial and military policy in most states is formed around a conception of masculinity that places a premium on toughness and force. The idealised separation of state and society parallels a division of labour that renders the contribution of women invisible. Organisational gender bias pervades political life.

Treating gender as an explanatory concept in the study of political institutions requires that it be explicitly theorised and that the ways in which institutions and processes are gendered be clearly specified. To argue that institutions are gendered requires at least four kinds of knowledge. First, it is necessary to be aware that everyone in the institution has a sex and performs gender. Recent research on organisations and institutions shows that women see themselves as women politicians, women civil servants, etc. that work constructs masculinity and femininity in different ways. In other words, the meaning of work to masculinity differs from its meaning to femininity, and various versions of masculinity and femininity incorporate work in various ways. Organisations are built around such masculinities and femininities. Therefore, second, the experience of individuals in institutions varies by both sex and gender (Epstein 1993). Third, sex and gender interact with other components of identity, such as race, ethnicity and nationality, and these too are interpreted according to cultural codes that have implications for masculinity and femininity as well as for institutional behaviour. Finally, institutions have distinctively gendered cultures and are involved in processes of producing and reproducing gender (Kenny 1996).

Gendered institutional research emphasises ideological and normative characteristics of gender (Acker 1992). It requires attention to the numbers of women and men, their placement in institutional hierarchies, and the nature of dominant and subordinate masculinities and femininities. The challenge for empirical researchers into political institutions and processes is to relate the complex variable of gender to organisational behaviour. Where gender is conceptualised as a continuum this means breaking behaviour and processes down into their separate, component acts, which can be considered for their masculine and feminine components, whether these be different interests, styles or resources. In practice this means reinterpreting and expanding research on the construction and operation of each institution we analyse.

Qualitative methodologies, such as in-depth interviews to learn life stories, may be combined with quantitative information on the position of women, attitudes, pay, and employment data to help identify the gender culture of an institution and the behaviour of men and women within it. Such studies show how important particular individuals are in achieving changes and also reveal great variations in individual responses to structural constraints (McGlen and Sarkees 1993; Cockburn 1991).

Feminist interest in state institutions followed the concerns of activists who advocated the expansion of state-directed social policy. By the 1990s a substantial feminist scholarship on different aspects of political institutions was available.

Pateman (1988) argued that the dominant public institutions were based on a fraternal contract. Phillips (1998) provided arguments that the sex of representatives was important, and Dahlerup (1988) showed that bringing more women into public institutions made a difference. Feminists claimed that political institutions institutionalised and privileged particular masculinities and substantiated such claims by examining gender biases in different organisations. Not only was the absence of women from the heart of government noted, but variations in the presence of women at different levels of government were detailed, discussed, and compared across different types of political systems (Lovenduski 1986; Haavio-Mannila and Skard 1985; Dahlerup 1988; Dodson 1991; Dodson and Carroll 1991; Karvonnen and Selle 1995; Stetson and Mazur 1995), and the roles of women in different types of welfare states were assessed (Lewis 1992b; Sainsbury 1996). Cockburn's (1991) study of masculinities, femininities, and equality in four British organisations was a model of its kind, tracing resistances to women at lower levels of organisational hierarchies. Stivers (1993) showed how, in public administration, both theory and practice privilege cultural masculinity at the expense of cultural femininity. Gender norms are incorporated via administrative theory and are replicated in sex-segregated occupational hierarchies and in sex-stereotypical interactions between bureaucrats and their clients (Stivers 1993: 4). By the mid-1990s research was becoming more detailed and, arguably, more gendered in the sense that purpose-designed investigations of institutional masculinities and femininities were undertaken (Duerst-Lahti and Kelly 1995; Watson 1994; Abrar et al. 1998).

Such work shows how important it is to know where women and men are located in institutions. It is also necessary to pay attention to how they act and what their actions mean; often performing the same act has a different meaning for women and men. King examined the barriers of expectations and preconceptions that underpinned preferences for masculinity in American state administrations. She found no significant differences in the decision styles of men and women. However, women in her study of high-level leaders and managers were more likely than men to identify with management styles that were normally regarded as masculine, suggesting that women were more likely than men to be constrained by gendered organisational norms. She speculates that leaders may not be able to show their femininity until after they have proved their masculinity, which men do by default but women must perform (King 1995). A dichotomous sex analysis would not have identified the force of norms of masculinity and would have offered explanations based on individual characteristics. Separating sex from gender allowed institutional characteristics to be identified and explanation to move beyond the attribution of decision-making styles to women and men.

Similarly Norton's study of congressional policy making on reproductive matters traces a labyrinth of committees, subcommittees, procedures, and conventions that disperse this area of policy making such that it has been almost impossible for a sufficient number of congresswomen to get into influential positions. She shows how the historical exclusions of women tend to prevent congresswomen from accumulating the power and resources necessary to shape policy in this area. Their impact on policy has been limited because, despite some numerical increase, women are not yet in a position to influence it. Roll-call analysis of sex differences in voting hides crucial differences in men's and women's legislative resources that have a significant bearing on their behaviour (Norton 1995).

Interactions between men and women give institutions their gendered characters. Kathlene's (1995) study of the Colorado state legislature used linguistic analysis techniques to demonstrate how men's sense of entitlement to more verbal and physical space supports their dominance of various proceedings. Kathlene measured differences in the speaking behaviour of members of legislative committees by sex, seniority, interest and party. She found that men's dominance of conversation, discussion, and meetings enhanced their power and undermined that of women even where the formal positions of men and women legislators were equal. Her research showed that women did better at controlling the dialogue and making themselves heard when other women were present, visible (sitting where they could be seen), and in positions of authority.

In summary, successful application of the concept of gender to the investigation of political institutions must acknowledge not only the complexity of gender but also the nature of the particular institution and the kinds of masculinities and femininities that are performed. In Britain, for example, the cultures of the Labour and Conservative parties both feature uneasy masculine dominations, but the kinds of masculinities that prevail and their relation to femininities in the parties are different, forged in different historical experiences according to different class, racial and organisational imperatives. It means little simply to say that both are male-dominated. The challenge to feminist political science is to produce empirical research that relates gender to political behaviour. This means disaggregating organisational processes into component acts to assess their masculine and feminine elements. It also means taking into account good mainstream research on institutions and reinterpreting and expanding it.

Conclusions

Feminist research on political representation, public policy and political institutions has undergone a significant, if incomplete, shift in method from the use of a dichotomous category of sex to a more complex and sometimes slippery category of gender. The shift is incomplete partly because many feminists are reluctant to give up on biologically determined categories of man and woman. Empirical work focusing on women has assumed that women share something politically that separates them from men. Researchers have believed that by controlling statistically for other variables (education, race, class, ethnicity, etc.), they can isolate the effects of sex; the category 'woman' can be more precisely defined, its essence identified (Carroll and Zerilli 1993). There is something in this view. Such variables as race, class and nationality all work together with sex in both women and men to shape identity, and they are so intertwined that it seems almost nonsense to try to separate them empirically by assigning numerical values; nevertheless, they are also identifiable components of political interest that may affect women and men differently. So long as this kind of empirical research is properly contextualised, and so long as its practitioners do not indulge in overgeneralisation, it is valuable and should continue. Probably there should be more of it. As Carroll and Zerilli write, 'The concerted focus by feminists on women and women's experiences has helped us as a discipline to see the biases and the blinders that characterised pre-feminist work and to improve our knowledge base by correcting for these biases and removing the blinders' (1993: 72).

Much of political science has been content to continue with its biases and blinders. Even in the USA, with a 'women and politics' group in the American Political Science Association and an established place in the curriculum, feminism is still marginal in the study of politics, where its normative ambitions provide reasons to suspect it of reflecting values rather than hard evidence. Moreover, feminist political science is regarded as marginal in women's studies because of its emphasis on the epiphenomena of political life and its unwillingness to take up the analysis of culture with the enthusiasm of feminists working in the arts and humanities academic fields (Sapiro 1991). This double bind poses problems for feminist political scientists in search of academic validation and may be the reason they place so much emphasis on electoral behaviour and other measurable participation. Such data are the stock in trade of mainstream political science, hence the terrain on which feminists must prove themselves - an instance of needing to perform masculinity, perhaps?

An important question is how hospitable political science is to feminist concerns. There has been relatively little research on the internal dynamics of nongovernment institutions and social relationships - even though power is implicated in such relationships, and their dynamics may be shaped and directly regulated by governments, have direct effects on public policy, and so forth. For example, when a political scientist refers to the family, s/he tends to see 'a corporate unity that produces new citizens or is the object of public policy' (Sapiro 1991: 17). Yet where, outside common law theory, are families unitary? Real families are sites of conflict, with divisions of labour and interest. These conflicts and divisions are important in the processes of constructing gender. Imposing a false unity on families for analytical convenience weakens our ability to see vital relationships between politics and personal life (Sapiro 1991: 171).

The preferences for parsimonious models, elegant, slender hypotheses, and measurable data are elements of political science that are inhospitable to the study of gender. Yet many political scientists share feminists' preoccupations with organisational culture, patterns of interaction, and the relationships between ideas and behaviour. The new institutionalism, the persistent interest in networks and coalitions of advocates and/or issues, and the interest in regime analysis are all examples of approaches that are amenable to and have been used in feminist scholarship.

Feminist research often calls into question the frameworks and assumptions it adapts, arguing that our dominant frameworks cannot accommodate the inclusion of women - that many of the frameworks, assumptions, and definitions central to political science must be reconceptualised (Carroll and Zerilli 1993: 1). The shift from sex to gender sharpens this argument as the new research exposes the incompleteness of accounts that leave out the relational dynamics of gender. It remains to be seen whether the shift will result in the paradigm change that feminist scholarship portends.

Notes

1. The literature generated by the study of women and politics is vast, far too extensive to report in an essay of this length. Its development has been closely monitored in the sense that a large number of state-of-the-field essays have been produced. These are cited along with the primary sources directly relevant to the issues I discuss. In preparing this essay I drew heavily on the overviews offered by Carroll and Zerilli (1993), Githens (1983) and Orloff (1996). The panel organised at the 1997 American Political Science Association Annual Meeting in Washington, DC, by Karen Beckwith, 'The Concept of Gender: Research Implications for Political Science', was extremely useful to both the stimulation and the organisation of my ideas.

References

Abramovitz, M. (1988) *Regulating the Lives of Women: Social Welfare Policy from Colonial Times to the Present*, Boston, MA: South End.

Abrar, S., Lovenduski, J., and Margetts, H. (1998) 'Sexing London: the gender mix of urban policy actors', *IPSR*, 19 (2): 147–171.

Acker, J. (1992) 'Gendered institutions: from sex roles to gendered institutions', *Contemporary Sociology*, 1: 565–569.

Acklesberg, M. and Diamond, I. (1987) 'Gender and political life: new directions in political science', in B. B. Hess and M. M. Feree (eds) *Analyzing Gender: A Handbook of Social Science Research*, Newbury Park, CA: SAGE, pp. 504–525.

Baxter, S. and Lansing, M. (1980) *Women and Politics: The Invisible Majority*, Ann Arbor: University of Michigan Press.

Boals, K. (1975) 'Review essay: political science', *Signs*, 1: 161–174.

Boles, J. K. (1994) 'Local feminist policy networks in the contemporary American interest group system', *Policy Science*, 27: 161–178.

Bologh, R. (1991) *Love or Greatness: Max Weber and Masculine Thinking: A Feminist Enquiry*, London: Unwin Hyman.

Borchorst, A. (1994) 'Welfare state regimes, women's interests and the EC', in D. Sainsbury (ed.) *Gender Equality and Welfare*, London: Sage, pp. 26–44.

Borchorst, A. and Siim, B. (1987) 'Women and the advanced welfare state: a new kind of patriarchal power?', in A. S. Sassoon (ed.) *Women and the State: The Shifting Boundaries of Public and Private*, London: Hutchinson, pp. 128–157.

Bourque, S. C. and Grossholtz, J. (1974) 'Politics an unnatural practice: political science looks at female participation', *Political Sociology*, 4: 225–266.

Brod, H. (1987) *The Making of Masculinities: The New Men's Studies*, London: Unwin.

Brod, H. (1994) *Theorising Masculinities*, London: SAGE.

Brown, W. (1988) *Manhood and Politics: A Feminist Reading in Political Theory*, Totowa, NJ: Rowman & Littlefield.

Bryson, L. (1992) *The State and Welfare*, London: Macmillan.

Bussmaker, J. and van Kersbergen, K. (1994) 'Gender and welfare states: some theoretical reflections', in D. Sainsbury (ed.) *Gender Equality and Welfare*, pp. 8–25.

Butler, J. (1990) *Gender Trouble: Feminism and the Subversion of Identity*, New York: Routledge.

Carroll, S. J. (1985) *Women as Candidates in American Politics*, Bloomington: Indiana University Press.

Carroll, S. J. and Zerilli, M. G. (1993) 'Feminist challenges to political science', in A. U. Finifter (ed.) *Political Science the State of the Discipline*, Washington, DC: APSA, pp. 55–77.

Cockburn, C. (1983) *Brothers: Male Dominance and Technological Change*, London: Pluto.

Cockburn, C. (1991) *In the Way of Women: Men's Resistance to Sex Equality in Organisations*, Basingstoke, UK: Macmillan.

Collins, P. H. (1990) *Black Feminist Thought: Knowledge, Consciousness and the Politics of Empowerment*, New York: Routledge.

Connell, R. H. (1987) *Gender and Power*, Stanford, CA: Stanford University Press.

Connell, R. H. (1994) *Masculinities*, Cambridge, UK: Cambridge University Press.

Dahlerup, D. (1988) 'From a small to a large minority: women in Scandinavian politics', *Scandinavian Political Studies*, 11: 275–298.

Daly, M. (1994) 'Comparing welfare states: toward a gender-friendly approach', in D. Sainsbury (ed.) *Gender Equality and Welfare*, pp. 101–117.

Darcy, R., Welch, S., and Clark, J. (1987) *Women, Elections, and Representation*, New York: Longman.

Davidoff, L. and Hall, C. (1987) *Family Fortunes: Men and Women of the English Middle Class, 1780–1850*, London: Routledge.

Davies, C. (1994) 'The masculinity of organisational life', Presented at Conference on Women and Public Policy, Erasmus, University of Rotterdam.

Diamond, I. (1977) *Sex Roles in the State House*, New Haven, CT: Yale University Press.

di Stefano, C. (1991) *Configurations of Masculinity: A Feminist Reading in Modern Political Theory*, Ithaca, NY: Cornell University Press.

Dodson, D. L. (1991) *Gender and Policymaking: Studies of Women in Office*, New Brunswick, NJ: Center for American Women and Politics.

Dodson, D. L. and Carroll, S. J. (1991) *Reshaping the Agenda: Women in State Legislatures*, New Brunswick, NJ: Center for American Women and Politics.

Duerst-Lahti, G. and Kelly, R. M. (eds) (1995) *Gender Power, Leadership and Governance*, Ann Arbor: University of Michigan Press.

Duerst-Lahti, G. and Verstegen, D. (1995) Making something of absence: the year of the woman and women's representation, in G. Duerst-Lahti and R. M. Kelly (eds) *Gender Power, Leadership and Governance*, pp. 213–238.

Dunhill, C. (1989) *The Boys in Blue*, London: Virago.

Eisenstein, Z. (1981) *The Radical Future of Liberal Feminism*, New York: Longman.

Elshtain, J. B. (1979) 'Methodological sophistication and conceptual confusion: a critique of mainstream political science', in J. A. Sherman and E. T. Beck (eds) *The Prism of Sex: Essays in the Sociology of Knowledge*, Madison: University of Wisconsin Press, pp. 229–252.

Elshtain, J. B. (1981) *The Public and the Private: A Critical Inquiry*, Princeton, NJ: Princeton University Press.

Epstein, C. F. (1993) *Women in Law*, 2nd ed., New York: Basic Books.

Esping-Anderson, G. (1990) *The Three Worlds of Welfare Capitalism*, Cambridge, UK: Polity.

Evans, J. (1980) 'Women and politics: a reappraisal', *Political Studies*, 38: 210–221.

Ferguson, K. (1984) *The Feminist Case Against Bureaucracy*, Philadelphia: Temple University Press.

Finch, J. and Groves, D. (1983) *A Labour of Love: Women, Work and Caring*, London: Routledge/Kegan Paul.

Githens, M. (1983) 'The elusive paradigm gender, politics and political behavior: the state of the art', in A. W. Finifter (ed.) *Political Science the State of the Discipline*, Washington, DC: American Political Science Association, pp. 471–499.

Githens, M. and Prestage, J. L. (eds) (1977) *A Portrait of Marginality: The Political Behavior of the American Woman*, New York: McKay.

Goldberg, G. and Kremen, E. (1990) *The Feminization of Poverty: Only in America?*, New York: Praeger.

Goot, M. and Reid, E. (1975) *Women and Voting Studies: Mindless Matrons or Sexist Scientism?*, SAGE Professional Studies in Contemporary Political Sociology, Vol. 8. London: SAGE.

Gordon, L. (1988) 'What does welfare regulate?', *Social Research*, 55 (4): 609–630.

Gordon, L. (1990) *Women, the State and Welfare*, Madison: University of Wisconsin Press.

Gordon, L. and Fraser, N. (1994) '"Dependency" demystified: inscriptions of power in a keyword of the welfare state', *Social Politics*, 1 (1): 14–31.

Haavio-Mannila, E. and Skard, T. (eds) (1985) *Unfinished Democracy: Women in Nordic Politics*, Oxford: Pergamon.

Hacking, I. (1997) 'Taking bad arguments seriously', *London Review of Books*, 19 (16): 14–16.

Hanmer, J., Radford, J., and Stanko, E. (eds) (1989) *Women, Policing and Male Violence: International Perspectives*, London: Routledge.

Hawksworth, M. (1994) 'Policy studies within a feminist frame', *Policy Science*, 27: 97–118.

Hearn, J. (1989) *The Sexuality of Organisation*, London: SAGE.

Hearn, J. (1991) *Men in the Public Eye*, London: Routledge.

Hearn, J. and Collinson, D. (1996) *Men as Managers, Managers as Men: Critical Perspectives on Men, Masculinities and Managements*, London: SAGE.

Hernes, H. (1987) *Welfare State and Woman Power*, Oslo: University of Norway Press.

Hobson, B. (1994) 'Feminist strategies and gendered discourses in welfare states', in S. Koven and S. Michel (eds) *Mothers of the New World: Maternalist Politics and the Origins of the Welfare State*, New York: Routledge, pp. 396–430.

Holter, H. (ed.) (1984) *Patriarchy in a Welfare Society*, Oslo: Universitetsforlaget.

Hoskyns, C. (1996) *Integrating Gender, Women, Law and Politics in the European Union*, London: Verso.

Jaquette, J. S. (1974) 'Introduction', in J. S. Jaquette (ed.) *Women in Politics*, New York: Wiley, po. XII–XXX.

Jennings, M. K. and Niemi, R. G. (1981) *Generations and Politics: A Panel Study of Young Adults and Their Parents*, Princeton, NJ: Princeton University Press.

Jenson, J. (1986) 'Gender and reproduction: or, babies and the state', *Studies in Political Economy*, 20: 9–45.

Jones, K. B. (1993) *Compassionate Authority: Democracy and the Representation of Women*, London: Routledge.

Jones, K. B. and Jonasdottir, A. G. (1988) 'Introduction: gender as an analytical category in political theory', in K. B. Jones and A. G. Jonasdottir (eds) *The Political Interests of Gender*, London: SAGE, pp. 11–32.

Kamerman, S. B. (1986) 'Women, children and poverty: public policies and female headed families in industrialized countries', in B. Gelpi, N. Hartsock, C. Novak, M. Strober (eds) *Women and Poverty*, Chicago: University Chicago Press, pp. 41–63.

Karvonnen, L. and Selle, P. (1995) *Women in Nordic politics: closing the gap*, Aldershot: Dartmouth.

Kathlene, L. (1995) 'Position power versus gender power: who holds the floor?', in G. Duerst-Lahti, and R. M. Kelly (eds) (1995) *Gender Power, Leadership and Governance* pp. 167–194.

Kenny, S. (1996) 'New research on gendered political institutions', *Political Research Quarterly*, 49 (2): 445–463.

King, C. S. (1995) 'Sex role identity and decision styles: how gender helps explain the paucity of women at the top', in G. Duerst-Lahti, and R. M. Kelly (eds) (1995) *Gender Power, Leadership and Governance*, pp. 67–92.

Kirkpatrick, J. J. (1974) *Political Woman*, New York: Basic Books.

Knijn, T. (1994) 'Fish without bikes: revision of the Dutch welfare state and its consequences for the (in)dependence of single mothers', *Social Politics*, 1: 83–105.

Land, H. (1978) 'Who cares for the family?', *Journal of Social Policy*, 7: 257–284.

Landes, J. B. (1988) *Women and the Public Sphere in the Age of the French Revolution*, Ithaca, NY: Cornell University Press.

Langan, M. and Ostner, I. (1991) 'Gender and welfare: toward a comparative framework', in G. Room (ed.) *Toward a European Welfare State?*, Bristol: School of Advanced Urban Studies, pp. 127–150.

Lewis, J. (1992a) 'Gender and the development of welfare regimes', *Journal of European Social Policy*, 3: 159–173.

Lewis, J. (ed.) (1992b) *Women and Social Policies in Europe: Work Family and the State*, Hants, UK: Edward Elgar.

Lewis, J. (1997) 'Gender and welfare regimes: further thoughts', *Social Politics*, 4: 160–177.

Lewis, J., and Åström, G. (1992) 'Equality, difference and state welfare: labour market and family policies in Sweden', *Feminist Studies*, 18 (1): 59–86.

Lister, R. (1990) 'Women, economic dependency and citizenship', *Journal of Social Policy*, 19: 445–467.

Lister, R. (1992) *Women's Economic Dependency and Social Security*, Manchester, UK: Equal Opportunities Commission.

Lovenduski, J. (1981) 'Toward the emasculation of political science: the impact of feminism', in D. Spender (ed.) *Men's Studies Modified: The Impact of Gender on the Academic Disciplines*, Oxford, UK: Pergammon, pp. 83–98.

Lovenduski, J. (1986) *Women and European Politics: Contemporary Feminism and Public Policy*, Brighton, UK: Wheatsheaf.

Lovenduski, J. and Norris, P. (eds) (1993) *Gender and Party Politics*, London: SAGE.

Lovenduski, J. (1993) 'Introduction', in J. Lovenduski and P. Norris (eds) *Gender and Party Politics*, pp. 1–15.

Luker, K. (1985) *Abortion and the Politics of Motherhood*, London: University of California Press.

McGlen, N. E. and Sarkees, M. R. (1993) *Women in Foreign Policy: The Insiders*, New York: Routledge.

McLanahan, S., Sørenson, A., and Watson, D. (1989) 'Sex differences in poverty 1950–1980', *Signs*, 15: 102–122.

March, J. G. and Olsen, J. P. (1984) 'The new institutionalism: organizational factors in American political life', *American Political Science Review*, 78: 734–749.

Mitchell, D. (1993) 'Sole parents, work and welfare: evidence from the Luxembourg income study', in S. Shaver (ed.) *Comparative Perspectives on Sole Parents Policy: Work and Welfare*, University of New South Wales: Social Policy Centre, pp. 53–89.

Molyneux, M. (1985) 'Mobilization without emancipation? Women's interests, the state and revolution in Nicaragua', *Feminist Studies*, 11: 227–254.

Nelson, B. J. (1984) 'Women's poverty and women's citizenship: some political consequences of economic marginality', *Signs*, 10: 209–232.

Nelson, B. J. (1989) 'Women and knowledge in political science: texts, histories, and epistemologies', *Women and Politics*, 9:1–25.

Nicholson, L. (1994) 'Interpreting gender', *Signs*, 20: 79–105.

Norris, P. (1985) 'The gender gap in Britain and America', *Parliamentary Affairs*, 38: 192–220.

Norris, P. and Lovenduski, J. (1995) *Political Recruitment: Gender, Race and Class in the British Parliament*, Cambridge, UK: Cambridge University Press.

Norton, N. (1995) 'Women, it's not enough to be elected: committee position makes a difference', in G. Duerst-Lahti, and R. M. Kelly (eds) (1995) *Gender Power...*, pp. 115–140.

O'Connor, J. (1993) 'Gender, class and citizenship in the comparative analysis of welfare state regimes: theoretical and methodological issues', *British Journal of Sociology*, 44: 501–518.

Okin, S. M. (1979) *Women in Western Political Thought*, Princeton, NJ: Princeton University Press.

Orloff, A. (1993) 'Gender and the social rights of citizenship: the comparative analysis of gender relations and welfare states', *American Sociology Review*, 58: 303–328.

Orloff, A. (1996) 'Gender in the welfare state', *Annual Review Sociology*, 22: 51–78.

Orloff, A. (1997) 'Comment on Jane Lewis's "gender and welfare regimes: further thoughts"', *Social Politics*, 4: 188–202.

Ostner, I. and Lewis, J. (1995) 'Gender and the evolution of European social policies', in S. Liebfried and P. Pierson (eds) *European Social Policy*, Washington, DC: Brookings, pp. 159–193.

Pateman, C. (1988) *The Sexual Contract*, Cambridge, UK: Polity.

Pateman, C. (1989) *The Disorder of Women*, Cambridge, UK: Polity.

Petchesky, R. P. (1984) *Abortion and Women's Choice: The State, Sexuality, and Reproductive Freedom*, New York/London: Longman.

Pederson, S. (1993) *Family, Dependence and the Origins of the Welfare State: Britain and France, 1914–1945*, Cambridge, UK: Cambridge University Press.

Phillips, A. (1998) 'Democracy and representation or why should it matter who our representatives are?', in A. Phillips (ed.) *Feminism and Politics*, Oxford: Oxford University Press, pp. 224–240.

Pitkin, H. (1967) *The Concept of Representation*, Berkeley/Los Angeles: University of California Press.

Piven, F. F. (1985) 'Women and the state: ideology, power and the welfare state', in A. Rossi (ed.) *Gender and the Life Course*, New York: Aldine, pp. 265–287.

Pringle, R. and Watson, S. (1992) 'Women's interests and the post-structuralist state', in M. Barrett and A. Phillips (eds) *Destabilising Theory*, Cambridge, UK: Polity, pp. 53–73.

Quadagno, J. (1994) *The Color of Welfare: How Racism Undermined the War on Poverty*, New York: Oxford University Press.

Randall, V. (1987) *Women and Politics: An International Perspective*, 2nd ed. Basingstoke, UK: Macmillan.

Randall, V. (1991) 'Feminism and political analysis', *Political Studies*, 39: 513–532.

Roberts, D. (1995) 'Race, gender and the value of mothers' work', *Social Politics*, 2: 195–207.

Ruggie, M. (1988) 'Gender, work and social progress: some consequences of interest aggregation in Sweden', in J. Jenson, E. Hagen, and C. Ready (eds) *Feminisation of the Labour Force*, Oxford: Oxford University Press, pp. 172–188.

Sainsbury, D. (1993) 'Dual welfare and sex segregation of access to social benefits: income maintenance policies in the UK, the US, the Netherlands and Sweden', *Journal of Social Policy*, 22: 69–98.

Sainsbury, D. (ed.) (1994) *Gendering Welfare States*, London: SAGE.

Sainsbury, D. (1996) *Gender Equality and Welfare States*, Cambridge, UK: Cambridge University Press.

Saraceno, C. (1994) 'The ambivalent familism of the Italian welfare state', *Social Politics*, 1: 60–82.

Sapiro, V. (1979) 'Women's studies and political conflict', in J. A. Sherman and E. T. Beck (eds) *The Prism of Sex: Essays in the Sociology of Knowledge*, Madison: University of Wisconsin Press, pp. 253–265.

Sapiro, V. (1981) 'Research frontier essay: when are interests interesting? The problems of political representation of women', *American Political Science Review*, 75: 701–716.

Sapiro, V. (1983) *The Political Integration of Women: Roles, Socialization, and Politics*, Urbana: University of Illinois Press.

Sapiro, V. (1991) 'Gender politics, gendered politics: the state of the field', in W. Crotty (ed.) *Political Science: Looking to the Future The Theory and Practice of Political Science*, Evanston, IL: Northwestern University Press, pp. 165–187.

Sassoon, A. S. (ed.) (1988) *Women and the State: The Shifting Boundaries of Public and Private*, London: Hutchinson.

Savage, M. and Witz, A. (eds) (1992) *Gender and Bureaucracy*, Oxford: Blackwell.

Scott, J. (1988) *Gender and the Politics of History*, New York: Columbia University Press.

Segal, L. (1990) *Slow Motion: Changing Masculinities, Changing Men*, London: Virago.

Siim, B. (1988) 'Towards a feminist rethinking of the welfare state', in K. B. Jones and A. G. Jonasdottir (eds) *The Political Interests of Gender*, pp. 160–186.

Skjeie, H. (1991) 'The rhetoric of difference: On women's inclusion in political elites', *Politics & Society*, 19 (2): 33–63.

Skjeie, H. (1993) 'Ending the male political hegemony: the Norwegian experience', in J. Lovenduski and P. Norris (eds) *Gender and Party Politics*, pp. 231–262.

Skocpol, T. (1985) 'Bringing the state back in: strategies of analysis in current research', in P. B. Evans, D. Rueschemeyer, and T. Skocpol (eds) *Bringing the State Back In*, Cambridge, UK: Cambridge University Press, pp. 3–43.

Skocpol, T. (1992) *Protecting Soldiers and Mothers*, Cambridge, MA: Harvard University Press.

Stetson, D. M. and Mazur, A. (1995) *Comparative State Feminism*, London: SAGE.

Stivers, C. (1993) *Gender Images in Public Administration*, London: SAGE.

Studlar, D., McAllister, I., and Asuci, A. (1988) 'Electing women to the British commons: breakout from the beleaguered beachhead?', *Legislative Studies Quarterly*, 13: 515–528.

Tamerius, K. L. (1995) 'Sex, gender, and leadership in the representation of women', G. Duerst-Lahti, and R. M. Kelly (eds) (1995) *Gender Power, Leadership and Governance*, pp. 93–112.

Ungerson, C. (ed.) (1990) *Gender and Caring: Work and Welfare in Britain and Scandinavia*, Brighton, UK: Harvester Wheatsheaf.

Waerness, K. (1984) 'Care giving as women's work in the welfare state', H. Holter (ed.) *Patriarchy in a Welfare Society*, pp. 67–87.

Watson, S. (ed.) (1990) *Playing the State*, London: Virago.

Watson, S. (1994) 'Producing the right sort of chap: the senior civil service as an exclusionary culture', *Policy Politics*, 22: 211–222.

Welch, S. (1977) 'Women as political animals: a test of some explanations for male-female political participation differences', *American Journal of Political Science*, 21: 711–730.

Wellhofer, S. (1994) 'Men make their own history, but...: the new institutionalism and the fate of liberal democracy in interwar Europe', *Democratisation*, 1: 323–342.

Conclusion: Does Feminism need Political Science?

The second wave feminism of the 1970s was, amongst other things, a massive challenge to prevailing ideas about politics. It was an intellectual project that broke with established disciplinary conventions. Many feminists were interested in the academy. Broadly they organised there in two ways: separately in the movement to establish women's studies courses, degrees, departments and networks and within disciplines with a view to reconfiguring them around acknowledgement of the importance of gender. Each approach had advantages and disadvantages. Within traditional departments, feminists might be marginalised but they would also have opportunities to influence the wider research agenda. Within women's studies departments, feminists could find employment and develop feminist theory but risked too much separation from other intellectual developments and were, as institutional newcomers, especially vulnerable to the successive financial cuts that affected so many universities. Each approach risked irrelevance on its own but at the beginning they gained strength in combination.

In the first years of emerging feminist research and the early days of women's studies, it was possible to imagine working across disciplinary boundaries. Before very long, however, the women's studies project struggled for resources and was soon marginalised, barely present except in the USA by the end of the twentieth century. Feminist challenges to established disciplines met with mixed responses. In some fields (especially history, sociology and political theory) scholars organised around claims to include and problematise the study of women's roles, hitherto invisible or poorly understood. Some disciplines were more hospitable than others. In sociology gender is a long established concept, in the disciplines of political, legal and social theory arguments about justice and 'the women question' had some considerable purchase, hence these fields were more open to feminist concerns than cognate subjects. Along with economics, the empirical and analytical branches of political science were more resistant to the incorporation of gender, both in Europe and the USA. But other influences were also in play. By the time of the feminist challenge political science was in some flux, fragmenting into the many subfields that characterise it today. Change was both internally and externally driven, part of a long process of moving away from a fairly dry legal and administrative focus to more concern with political action and behaviour, but also a response to challenges from the radical student, environmental movement and Civil Rights movements. At the same time a growing preoccupation with methodology and narrowly understood values of scientific research emerged which came to have a considerable influence on the research agenda. I discussed these processes in 'Toward the Emasculation of Political Science' which I wrote in 1981 and have included in this collection. During the 1970s, whilst there was some evidence of feminist challenge and signs of an embryonic women and politics fragment, such developments were limited. By then women were still only a small minority in the discipline, only a few of whom actually worked on gender and politics.

Gradually, first in the USA, the dominance of men and masculine concerns in political science was challenged both intellectually and strategically within professional associations by such organisations as the Women's Caucus of the American Political Science Association, the Women and Politics Group of the Political Studies Association and the Standing Group on Women (later Gender) and Politics of the European Consortium for Political Research. These groups encouraged research on gender and politics and shared resources across national boundaries. They also organised, monitored, mentored and reported on the inclusion of both women and gender research at conferences, in faculties, research grants and the publication of their work in academic journals. By 2014 the balance has shifted although nothing like parity has yet been achieved. In this world of ideas and institutions the struggle continues.

So, faced with the allure of more hospitable disciplines and the disdain of the profession, why did any of us continue with political science? Part of the answer must have been that we had already invested in it, but there were other reasons. It is worth saying that despite successive take-over projects (behaviourism, game theory, rational choice etc.) the political science of the 1970s and 1980s was wide ranging, accommodating to diverse approaches. Political scientists drew on a number of intellectual sources especially history and other social sciences. Political commitment often motivated research. Many political scientists worked in the service of important political goals. For example, comparative political scientists were much engaged in the post-war project to strengthen and extend democratic systems. Not only was this a worthy aim, it also demonstrated that the discipline could be (and frequently was) harnessed to the causes espoused by its practitioners. It is true that there was a long running and possibly harmful preoccupation with a 'value free' discipline, but that somewhat naïve goal soon came to be widely regarded as impossible.

I make these observations to set up the difficult question of whether feminism needs political science. While it is not hard to argue that political science needs feminism if only to get rid of its 'blinkers and biases', the argument that feminism should not abandon political science is more difficult to make, more finely balanced. I started to argue this case in the introduction by highlighting the importance of power to the study of politics. I want now to tackle it properly.

I will begin with a brief rehearsal of the easier argument, that political science needs feminism, and then continue to the case for a feminist political science. As I stated in the introduction, only with an understanding of gender can we identify and explain the outcomes of political processes and predict developments in the gender regimes that animate all political institutions. Such explanations entail the specification of contexts, the collection and analysis of evidence and the theorisation of political relationships, taking into account gender and gender relations. For feminists, institutions are inevitably gendered in some way, though sometimes invisibly so. Too often gender relations are not considered in studies of politics yet may be of crucial importance to understanding political phenomena. This effect has been well researched and widely written about and is the subject of two of the essays in this volume.

The more difficult argument to make is that feminism needs political science. Surely we can do without a discipline that seems so completely to rule out our concerns. It is tempting to accept this assertion. But to abandon political science would be to deny ourselves a resource, a major aid to understanding the apparatuses and processes that structure and maintain the domination of women.

Political science is the branch of the social sciences that seeks to understand power. Even if that focus has been left behind, or more likely so taken for granted that it has been forgotten by many of my colleagues, it remains to my mind the core of the enterprise. As a discipline it offers theories, definitions, approaches, methods and techniques that feminists can adopt when explicating the gendered nature of power.

However the argument that feminists need political science is not straightforward, turning as it does on tensions on both sides and depending on how one assesses these and the overall balance of such assessments. I have identified six arguments that illustrate the tensions in the two intellectual projects. The arguments are not equally important and point in different directions.

1. Feminists and political scientists have a common interest in understanding power, though many empirical political scientists have either drifted away from a focus on power or simply take it for granted.
2. On one hand, political science is fragmented, difficult to characterise as a discipline. This makes it prone to takeover bids and subject to internal arguments about its fundamentals that rarely appear to be settled, a situation that creates opportunities for interventions by feminists and others.
3. On the other hand, political science as a discipline is, like most disciplines, path dependent and difficult to change
4. Political science is gender biased.
5. Political science is plagued by scientism (or scholasticism) and methodological dogma.
6. Political science is part of the wider social sciences with its many resources.

Argument 1: A common interest in power

The centrality of power to its concerns makes political science worthwhile for feminists. The resources that political science offers feminists are not easy to access. The profession is hostile and training often ignores the analysis of gender. However the history of any discipline is one of struggles over definition and meanings that permit new understandings and theories to become established. Political scientists offer concepts, routines, techniques and definitions that structure research to illuminate the nature of power.

Feminists have long been interested in understanding power but have tended to examine it in the context of succeeding debates about essentialism, identity, sexuality and difference, hence there is no one explicit, widely accepted feminist theory of power. Moreover the concept has been contested and its understanding has changed. Over time feminist critics begin with, but lead away from, functionalist accounts of state organisations as the structural loci of power toward concern with understanding the techniques and apparatus of control and regulation. The most influential feminist power theorists were mainly academics who were much inspired by post structuralism and especially interested in Michel Foucault's understanding of political power. He saw political power as a perennially shifting omnipresent result of social interaction that instead of being repressive was productive. Subjects were created by the operation of power and then subjected to power. This notion of power as ubiquitous and productive was so influential that it became pretty much inescapable in feminist theory where numerous critics, converts, supporters, opponents and those who wanted to take it in different directions all used his work as a point of departure when they discussed power. I do not claim here to do Foucault's theories justice; I mention them because they were so influential. However Amy Allen (1999, 2005) describes these developments well and also reminds us that feminist theories of power are contextualised in successive debates about women's subordination. Subordination is illuminated by post structuralist notions of discourse as well as Foucault's notions of discipline and surveillance, but its understanding also depends on realising the importance of the economic and political power of the state.

Feminists have written extensively about power but while their insights are challenging, and important, they are too often implicit. To use feminist concepts of power it is necessary to excavate and explicate them, a weakness of feminist theory that Amy Allen's work attempts, largely successfully, to correct. Allen offers a tripartite typology of feminist concepts of power. She proposes that feminists theorise power as a resource, as domination and as empowerment (2005). In doing this she pays due attention to the fact that these approaches emerged during hotly contested debates in which advocates claimed the distinctiveness of their different positions. But for the purposes of the argument that I make here, they can also be read together. Arguably the different understandings have enriched each other to provide a sophisticated, if incomplete basis from which to draw a feminist conception of *political* power.

Feminist political scientists have built on feminist theories of power using their components in conjunction with discussions and debates about power among political theorists and empirical political scientists. This iteration has generated at least three interlinked dimensions to feminist readings of political power, each of which starts with a criticism and offers a modification of a once established view. The results constitute a plausible synthesis of feminist and political science theories of power. First, feminist analysis moves away from top down power theories toward formulations that stress the omnipresence of power as something that is produced in every social relationship. What is interesting about political power is how it is exercised rather than any notion that it is a finite resource stored in some state location. Hence, second, feminist accounts recognise that the interests entailed in gender difference do not somehow arrive fully formed at the state for representation, but are defined and redefined in various arenas including private life. Power is diffused throughout society but under conditions of the dominance of some kinds of masculinity. The third dimension of the feminist understanding of political power considers how the assumed 'masculinity' of politics excludes women from powerful institutions and underwrites a culture in which politicians are 'naturally' male. Aspects of traditional masculinity are institutionalised into the formal and informal rules, practices and customs that make it difficult for women to enter or function in 'democratic' politics. This resonates with Lukes' third dimension of power (1974) and Schattschneider's (1960) notion of the mobilisation of bias whereby an unfavourable status quo has been normalised as the common sense of a society.

Feminists share with political scientists a preoccupation with and history of analysing political power and institutions potentially offering each other insights, techniques and methods for their work. However as Moya Lloyd points out much of feminist discussion of power operates in isolation from the debates about power within political theory and political science. Such work is rich and diverse. It identifies the essential features of power, examines how it is exercised, and classifies the forms it takes, explores its relation to other concepts including autonomy, freedom, responsibility, and representation, and specifies its scope and range (Lloyd 2014: 129).

Through its engagement with theories of political power, feminist political science offers a corrective to the limitations of feminist theories of power. For example, feminist political scientists seek to answer questions about power inequalities in public life, a project to which social and especially political science provides substantial foundations. They bring to the table an appreciation of the institutional contexts that shape political power that pre-feminist researchers described. The rules of the game, the nature of the actors, the quality of the aspirants, the processes of decisions are all elements of the political process that we need to think about in terms of gender. While gender inequalities are largely unremarked in earlier accounts of political institutions, such accounts provide foundations that we can investigate for their gender biases with a view to constructing feminist alternatives. We can see this in the way Birgit Sauer's research into policy debates treats discourses, ideas and frames as sources of power, demonstrating how discursive strategies determine identities in processes of negotiation (Sauer 2014). Feminist political science places struggles over meaning at the centre of analyses of power relations and is a development of long-standing preoccupations of political scientists such as Schattschneider and Lukes (1974).

Argument 2: Political science is fragmented, difficult to characterise as a discipline

The timing of the feminist political science project coincided with an acceleration of disciplinary fragmentation that affected the context in which feminist political science emerged. However fragmentation left space not only for the development of feminist research but also (ironically) for the production and increasing domination of a corpus of political science research that was characterised by a fascination with method at the expense of theory. In fact, political science has continued to fragment in a way that seems to be driven both by methodological sectarianism and the blinkers and blinders that accompany many thematic objects of study. Fragmentation occurs both in ideas and research designs. While this process undoubtedly created opportunities, it also generated a loss of the sense of a disciplinary core. For many, instead of being understood as a critique of the (apparently disintegrating) subject of political science, the feminist study of politics came to be seen as one of the fragments.

Argument 3: Political science is path dependent, too difficult to change it.

Definitions of political science were established by early research that institutionalised some of its resources. Data availability offers a very good example of path dependence. Data are expensive – in financial and other terms - to collect and early decisions greatly affect what comes later. We can see this in largescale attitude surveys where for the sake of continuity, some question batteries, favoured by established researchers, get preserved even as meanings change but question wordings do not. The availability of data and the form in which it is collected and collectable too often determines what questions are asked by researchers. Such constraints impede the balanced study of politics. When feminists first started researching political behaviour they famously were frustrated by the absence of suitable data, by misinterpretations of existing data and by outright biases that arose from mechanistic understandings of power, especially power in institutions. (There are also examples of lost data, of arbitrary decisions about questions being dropped or not as ideas change or commercial or ideological interests intervene, but that is too complicated to go into here.) Path dependence contributed to the difficulties that feminists have found in their attempts to locate themselves in this discipline.

Argument 4: Political science is gender biased

The assumptions of the masculine norm in political science are often misleadingly described as gender blindness. Such assumptions are in fact the basis of a pervasive gender bias. This is a serious but not insurmountable problem. It stems from two related conventions. First is an artificial separation from other social sciences which has probably developed with the growth of universities as a result of professional position conflicts in the academy. The separation has no convincing intellectual justification, a point I develop below. Modern political science grew out of the intellectual study of law (especially public administration) and history as well as economics, sociology and political philosophy. The second convention is a fetishisation of the so-called public sphere and its consequent failure to recognise that public and professional relations depend on private and personal relationships. This point is well made in Carol Pateman's account of the fraternal nature of the social contract which describes how men have been able to consolidate and defend their power, to group and regroup as a fraternity using discourses that ignore and therefore deny the relevance of gender (Pateman 1988).The interests of the fraternities are also constructed in various arenas of the state in such a way as to evoke the notion that men alone are political actors, acting on behalf of the population as a whole. Moreover while differences among men such as class or religion were important elements of the analysis of political behaviour and attitudes, women tended to be treated as a unitary group. In this imperfectly imagined polity that underpins contemporary political science, men are constructed in relation to each other while women, if present, are always inferior, may be invisible and, if not, considered only insofar as they differ from men (Beauvoir's 'other') while the ways they differ from each other are ignored.

Argument 5: Political science is flawed by scientism and methodological dogma

Too often questions that are not researchable by a fashionable method are ignored. Approaches derived from economics (e.g. rational choice) or from the physical sciences (quasi-experiments) may be illuminating but too often overshadow or even determine substantive content. Method driven research is often detached from important ideas, from interest in the nature of power and also from concerns about establishing and maintaining democratic accountability and fair political representation. When feminists and others tried to place these traditional (but messy) questions on the table, their work was dismissed as insufficiently scientific and parsimonious, criticisms that were inspired by methodological rather than theoretical preoccupations. (Lovenduski 1998).

True, recent developments in the social sciences have tilted research back toward multi method, interdisciplinary approaches but sectarianism continues and there is some evidence that methods trump content in professional intellectual hierarchies. While some five decades after feminists began to organise in the academy there is now evidence that multi method research favoured by feminists is now more widely used than it was, there is not much evidence that, without feminist presence and intervention, gender issues will routinely be adequately considered in most subfields of political science.

Argument 6: The social sciences inform political science

As I argue above, political science emphasises the practice of power. It can be seen as a development that was part of a commitment to the understanding of the interplay of ideas, action and social life that runs across the social sciences. Because feminism is first and foremost a way of thinking, we should consider political science in the wider context of what social science in general offers to the understanding of ideas especially how ideas might be formed, developed, tested and advanced. The history of the social science is one of struggles over meaning, often of struggles over the meaning of *science* defined in terms of its predictive capacity (Steinmo 2008). Indeed, too often an obsession with prediction distorted research and obscured the importance of explanation. Steinmo's observation has resonance for feminist research into politics. On one hand, as a feminist political scientist I am interested in prediction but unwilling to pay the high cost of overlooking the complexity of gendered dimensions of institutions that is a risk when concentrating on prediction at the expense of explanation. But on the other hand, explanation and prediction require an ability to characterise the institutional context and environment in order to identify their most salient features. In general feminist political scientists are interested in power and more interested in explanation than prediction. That preference is one of the bases of a scholarly affinity between the institutionalist and feminist approaches that I first highlighted almost two decades ago (Lovenduski 1998).

The six arguments suggest opportunities as well as obstacles. Feminising political science is not an impossible dream, but is a feasible project that has considerable intellectual value. A good example of how the social sciences in general and political science in particular can inform the study of gender is found in feminist institutionalism. Feminist institutionalism[1] overcomes many of the research problems of illuminating gender. It draws on and is part of 'new institutionalism.' While not explicitly gendered, the rediscovery of institutions in the 1980s refocused social scientists on problems of explanation. In common with other new institutionalists, feminist institutionalism explicitly highlights rules and processes, inviting analysts to consider the institutions that form the public and private bases of political power. When applied to politics, the approach offers the opportunity to explain how power is created and recreated and operates in various institutional settings over time and across space. Such power is gendered. Feminist political scientists seek to answer questions about power inequalities in public life, a project to which social and especially political science provides substantial foundations. Feminist institutionalism permits the exposition of gendered processes, norms and rules and illuminates a feminist approach to the understanding of power (Mackay 2010).

Feminist institutionalism is an approach to the study of politics that enables us to locate the operation of different kinds of power and to identify and explain power relationships that are gendered. It offers the capacity to make sense of the notion of gender regimes as political processes that produce and reproduce gender inequalities. The approach draws heavily on political science. It would be a mistake to ignore it. Feminism requires that we rethink accounts of political power in terms of gender. To do this we design research that takes into account and reconfigures earlier work. It does not and should not mean that we need to start again from the beginning. Rather it interrogates, remodels and reuses foundational work and develops it into something more reliable that offers better explanation. While gender inequalities are largely unremarked in earlier accounts of political institutions, I am confident that it is easier to locate and explain them with the

---

1. For resources and information about feminist institutionalism *see* FIIN http://www.femfiin.com

knowledge of how the institutions were seen to work by previous generations of scholars.

Conclusion

So how do these arguments stack up when we consider if feminism needs political science? While there may seem to be no compelling imperative it is wasteful, if not profligate, to do without the discipline, however flawed, that is founded on the recognition of the centrality of power to political life. If as feminists we want to understand and transform politics, we make it easier for ourselves by using the tools, suitably adapted, that have already proved useful in our own work. Why reinvent the wheel when we can change the gearing? I reject the view that foundational accounts of institutions are so toxic with assumptions of masculinity that they cannot be rescued. I am confident that it is easier to locate and explain power in gendered institutions with the knowledge of how the institutions were seen to work by previous generations of scholars. The intellectual history and contribution of political science is too important to ignore.

In common with many of my contemporaries I owe many intellectual debts. Independent research came after years of reading institutional political science in the Department of Government at Manchester University at the end of the 1960s and the beginning of the 1970s. Like many of my contemporaries I read my way into the theories of Marx, Lenin, Trotsky, Luxemburg (on whose work I wrote my MPhil), and moved on to Althusser, Lukacs, Poulantzas, Gramsci and the later Marxists. My guilty pleasure was reading Simone de Beauvoir, Betty Friedan, Germaine Greer, Kate Millet, Shulamith Firestone, Jo Freeman, Sheila Rowbotham and any other feminist literature I could find. Forty plus years later, in retrospect, it seems inevitable that these would combine into the feminist materialist (in the Marxist sense), institutionalist approach that I now advocate and try to use. But in bringing the ideas I found in that reading into my research, I would not be without the work of the likes of E.E. Schattschneider, Robert Dahl, Stephen Lukes, Gabriel Almond, Stein Rokkan, Sidney Verba or Hannah Pitkin. Their pioneering studies established foundations on which succeeding generations of scholars have built. While none were/are feminists, their contributions are essential to the way I understand politics. Struggles to define and eliminate gender inequalities take place in established institutions that have been built and understood around long-standing political ideas and theories. These good political scientists of decades past mapped and assessed institutions and identified power relationships within them. While they were mostly gender blind/biased, they blazed a trail, describing and theorising arrangements and processes in which power was created and institutionalised. Such observations may be rethought from feminist perspectives. The gender inequalities that interest me are located in contexts that their work illuminates and helps to explain. Pioneering researchers identified and traced power inequalities that interact with gender.

It is not enough for us to know that political institutions may discriminate against women; we need also to know via what mechanisms and configurations the discrimination operates and what is at stake. The same argument holds for the study of politics more generally. The field of political science offers resources that we should use, albeit critically. When feminists gender research strategies, they also transform them by making gender relations visible, by making women visible. While feminists therefore make an original and important contribution to the study of power in institutions we nevertheless still owe an intellectual debt that I am increasingly happy to acknowledge.[2]

In summary, feminist political scientists want to discover and explain gender effects in political life, a project that inevitably leads them to focus on how political institutions are formed and sustained and how gender is embedded in them. Gender is an institution nested in other institutions, all of which embody power relationships and are sites of politics. The practice of politics is constrained by power in both the public and private spheres. Feminist political scientists see gender relations as an instance of power relations. Research on gender relations that fails to recognise its political implications is *not* feminist. Properly contextualised, feminist political science research is located in an integrated social science in which the study of politics draws on and informs the cognate disciplines of, *inter alia*, sociology, economics, social psychology, law, philosophy and political and social history. To me it is completely obvious that political science which fails to consider underpinning gender power relations is futile.

References

Allen, A. (1999) *The Power of Feminist Theory*, Boulder, CO: Westview Press.

Allen, A. (2005, 2011) *Feminist Perspectives on Power*, Available at http://plato.stanford.edu/entries/feminist-power/ (accessed 2 February 2015).

Lloyd, M. (2014) 'Power, Politics, Domination and Oppression' in Georgina Waylen, Karen Celis, Johanna Kantola and Laurel Weldon (eds) *The Oxford Handbook of Gender and Politics,* Oxford: Oxford University Press, pp. 111–134.

Lovenduski, J. (1998) 'Gendering Research in Political Science', *Annual Review of Political Science*, 1: 333–356.

Lovenduski, J. (2005) *Feminizing Politics*, Oxford: Polity Press.

Lukes, S. (1974) *Power: A Radical View*, London: Macmillan.

MacKay, F. (2010) 'Toward a Feminist Institutionalism', in Mona Lena Krook and Fiona Mackay (eds) *Gender, Politics and Institutions: Towards a Feminist Institutionalism*, Basingstoke: Palgrave, pp.181–196.

Pateman, C. (1988) *The Sexual Contract*, Cambridge: Polity Press.

Pitkin, H. F. (1967) *The Concept of Representation*, Berkeley, Los Angeles: University of California Press.

---

2. On this point I am aware that some feminist political scientists (Feree, private communication) think that political science is in and of itself sexist, hence untransformable. But try though I have, I cannot uncover the basis of this argument.

Sauer, B. (2014) 'Framing and Gendering', in Dorothy McBride and Amy Mazur *The Politics of State Feminism: Innovation and Comparative Research,* Philadelphia: Temple University Press.

Schattschneider, E. E. (1960) *The Semi-Sovereign People: A Realist's View of Democracy in America. Austin, Texas:* Holt, Rinehart and Winston.

Steinmo, S. [2008] 'Historical Institutionalism' in Donatella Della Porta and Michael Keating (eds), *Approaches and Methodologies in the Social Sciences*, Cambridge: Cambridge University Press.

Index

Page numbers in italics refer to items in figures and tables

Abbott, D. 178
abortion politics *71*, 72, 73, *76*, *77*, 81, 114, 195–8
  and issue definition 196–8
  strategies used in 196
accountability *22*, 32, 44, 63, 66, 85–7, 90
  and consultation 66
  of representatives 84–7
Acker, J. 145
advocacy coalition framework 265–8, 288 n.2
  belief system concept in 266, 267–8
    and deep core beliefs 267–8
  policy brokers, role in 279
  see also under domestic violence
affirmative action 114, 122
Allen, A. 340
Allen, P. 104
Almond, G. 298, 306
American Political Science Association 293, 304, 327
  and feminist research 327
  Women's Caucus of 303–4, 338
Annesley, C. 104
Appleton, L. 200ff., 208, 225 n.1
Apter, D. E. 293, 298
Aristotle 295, 306
Armstrong, H. 176
Ashe, J. 182
Astor, N. 145, 146
Australia
  Labor Party and gender 116
    affirmative action, use of 116
  women's representation in 48, 116
    and gender equality 25, 118, 206
Austria 34

Beckett, M. 179
Beijing Platform for Action (1995) 17, 30
Belgium 32, 37
belief systems, concept of 266, 267
  and deep core beliefs 267
Benn, M. 253
Blair, I. 250
Blair, T. 176, 179
Bologh, R. 316
Boothroyd, B. 149, 186
Boston, S. 252, 253
Bourque, S. C. 299, 302
British Candidate Study (1992) 49, 129
British Representation Study (2001) 43, *49–52, 54, 56,* 57, 134, 157, 166 n.1
Brown, G. 179
Brownmiller, S. 241
bureaucracy 200, 316
  theories of 147, 316
  gendered models of 147, 314
  masculinity as privileged in 325
  rational bureaucrat (Weber) 316–17
    as idealised masculinity 316–19
  women's representation in 200
Butler, J. 314
Buxton, F. 181, 183
Byrne, P. 13

Cameron, D. 101, 103, 131ff., 180, 182–3, 186–7
Campbell, B. 183
Campbell, R. 11, 102, 134

Canada 150
  job training strategy 70
  women's representation in 93, 101,
    117
    and candidate selection 119, 125
    and party ideological positions
      114
Carroll, S. J. 327–8
Casey, L. 221
Caul, M. 58
Celis, K. 4 n.i, 66
Centre for the Study of British Politics
  and Public Life 99
Childs, S. 4 n.i, 11, 47, 103, 104, *178*,
  186
Chile 150
China 150
Chowdhury, N. 151
cities 199, 200
  gender systems in 200–1, 204–5
    decentralisation, effect of 204–5
    gendered structure in 199, 204
    NPM influence in 205
    public/private realms of 201, 203
  see also gender systems; London
    (UK), local authority analysis
civil service 34, 69, 85, 269
  see also bureaucracy
Clark, K. 183
class inequality and women 101, 321
  state policy research 321
Clegg, N. 103
Cockburn, C. 126, 173, 176, 325
Commission on the Status of Women
  (CSW) 18
Conservative Party (UK) 57, 110, 115,
  117, 131–41, 157–60, 179–83
  Conservative Women's Forum 181
  Conservative Women's
    Organisation 132, 139, 179, 180
    candidate encouragement by 180,
      181
  culture/values in 132–3, 139, 152,
    158, 165, 183, 275, 326
    'set of dispositions' in 152

gender differences in *54*, 55, 131–2,
  134, 326
sexism in 183
women, encouragement of 115,
  131–41, 145, 152, 158–60, 165,
  166, 169, 172, 179–83
  Cameron's A-list strategy 181–3
  candidate increase 132, 135
  and critique/party tension 182,
    183
  CSI/primaries strategies 137–8,
    158, 171, 182
  effectiveness of 138–9, 158–60,
    165, 166
  historical development of
    179–80
  merit, issue of 138, 139
  'Minister for Women' 180
  positive action plan (2005) 131
  quotas, support for 134
  recruitment/selection strategies
    135–6, 137–8, 157–9, 165, 182
  rule/procedure changes 137,
    158–9
  supply/demand problem in 136,
    158, 159, 165
  2001 discrimination, reports of
    158–9
  2005 election numbers 131–2,
    138, 140, 179, 181
  2010 election numbers 179, 183
  and unwinnable constituencies
    138, 152
  Women2win campaign 132, 139,
    181
voter support and gender 102, 132,
  133, 135, 140, 152
  generation gap in 133–4, 140
  see also UK, women's
    representation
Costa Rica 29
Council of Europe 28
Coward, R. 255
Cowley, P. 47
critical acts 64–5, 79, 90, 123

'critical mass' debate 19, 64–5, 79, 80, 87–9, 212
  concept of 12, 19
  and critical acts 64–5, 79, 90
Croatia 24
Cyprus 36

Dahl, B. 35
Dahlerup, D. 12, 19, 31, 55, 123, 325
D'Ancona, H. 34–5
Davies, C. 146, 314, 316
deliberative democracy 64, 69
Denmark
  gender equality in 37
  parliamentary discourse changes 31
  rape advocates in 248
descriptive representation 3, 43, 57, 63, 64, 65, 66, 319
  definition of 68
  as leading to substantive 65, 87–9, 91
  and women's movements institutionalisation 80
  see also critical mass debate
domestic violence 218, 219, 221, 224, 225, 230, 235, 239–40, 262, 265–88, 320
  definition, disagreement of 275, 288 n.1
  Domestic Violence Act (1976) 236
  Domestic Violence Matters project (1991) 283–4, 286
  and female empowerment 231, 232, 233, 239, 240, 269–70, 271
  feminist policy influence 225, 233, 239, 265–88
    advocacy coalition in 265–8, 269–70, 271, 272, 276–88
    core beliefs in 267–8, 270, 284, 286, 288
    locality analysis 275–84
    and political action 276

policy, development of 268–9, 270, 272–88
  Home Office, role in 272, 273–4
  and the Inter-Agency Project 277–81, 285
  locality differences 275–84
  policy brokers, role in 279, 285
police, role/attitudes of 236–7, 238, 272, 274, 277, 281, 282, 283ff., 320
social-structural explanations of 233
traditionalists, coalition in 269, 270, 271, 272, 286–8
  core beliefs of 270, 271, 272, 286, 287
  see also refuge movement
Dorries, N. 101
Duerst-Lahti, G. 319
Duverger, M. 300–2, 306
Dworkin, A. 254, 256, 257, 258

Eagle, A. 101, 183
Easton, D. 297–8, 306, 307 n.7
Edwards, L. 103
Egypt 24, 31–2
electoral systems
  women's representation, effect on 43, 143, 171, 318
  PR systems 143, 144, 171, 318
Equal Opportunities Commission (UK) 13, 128, 206, 207, 215
  and private contract provisions 207
  sexual harassment judgements (1986) 252–3
Esping-Anderson, G. 322
Eurobarometer 104
European Consortium for Political Research 338
  Standing Group on Women (Gender) 338
European Parliament 32
Evans, L. 103, 104, 185

family, traditional form of 203, 272
  decline of (UK) 203–4, 208
  and domestic violence 270, *271*
Fawcett Society 159, 160, 166 n.1,
  183, 186, 214–15, *217*
  aim of 215
  manifesto analysis of 186
Featherstone, L. 185
feminist institutionalism 1, 3, 344–5
  see also Feminist Political Science
Feminist Political Science 3, 293,
  294, 295, 298, 303, 305–28,
  337–46
  case for a 338–46
  funding for 306, 311, 337
  gender, as explanatory concept in
    314–16, 320–3, 324, 326, 327–8,
    337, 338–9, 344, 346
    as a continuum 324
    and sex/gender separation
      313–16, 325, 328
  institutions, study of 316–17,
    323–6, 338–9, 344–5
    masculine/feminine cultural
      codes in 316–17, 324
    organisational masculinism
      323–4
    women as political men debate
      317
    see also welfare state and
      feminist research
  power, theory of in 341–6
    struggles over meaning in 341
  public policy analysis 320–3, 326
    advocacy, use in 322
    feminist policy networks in 320
  new study areas in 305–6, 311–12
  see also political science
Finland 24
  gender equality in 34, 37
Foucault, M. 340
Fox, R. 102, 103
France 24, 32, 34, 37, 300
  parties and gender claims 115
  parité debate (NA) (2000) 30

quota systems, use in 32
women's issues, support for 30
women's representation in 118, 150
  numbers in parliament 111, 118

Gains, F. 104
gender
  concept/definition of 4, 5, 199,
    312–13, 315–17
    role of power in 4, 312, 314, 319,
      342ff.
    use in academic disciplines 337
    use in political theory 313–28,
      337, 342ff.
    see also Feminist Political
      Science
  and concept of sex in 4, 5, 199,
    312–13, 314, 315
    feminist differentiation of 199,
      312, 314, 315
    shift from focus on 313–16, 325,
      328
  cultural codes of 314, 316–17
  and difference 5, 312, 315
  as relational 314, 317
  as a social construction 313–14
  and the women's studies movement
    313–16, 337
  see also identity
gender regime 200, 225 n.1
gender systems 199–200, 225 n.1
  in cities 200–1
  concept of 199
  main dimensions of 200
  see also analysis under London
    (UK)
Germany 37, 300
  gender equality in 112, 118–19
    and party changes 116, 117
    positive discrimination, use in 116
    procedural changes in 33
    quota systems, use in 32, 116,
      117, 118–19, 122
Githens, M. 11
Goode, J. 129

Gorman, T. 149
Gould, P. 176
Graef, R. 250
Grossholtz, J. 299, 302
Guadagnini, M. 11, 92, 119

Hague, W. 179
Harman, H. 176, 179, 189
Hayes, B. 134
Hearn, J. 148, 323
Hearne, A. 261
Hills, J. 11
Hodge, M. 176
homelessness policy and women
    218–22, *271*, 274
    Centrepoint group 220, 221–2
    discrimination in 221
    as 'hidden problem' 219
    Homeless Network 221
    Homeless Persons Act (1977) 219,
        232, 274
    Housing Act (1985) (UK) 219, 274,
        280
    Housing Act (1996) (UK) 275
        and domestic violence 275
    local authority, gender differences
        220
    1990s interest/funding decline
        220–1, 275
    Rough Sleepers Initiative 221
    Shelter group 219, 220
    women's initiatives (London)
        219–22
        voluntary organisations in 219ff.
    see also violence and women
homosexuality and censorship 259–60
Hunt, M. 260

identity
    components of 324, 326–7
    cultural codes, effect on 146–8,
        314, 316
        femininity/masculinity codes
            316, 317
        male citizen model (Lister) 147

and electoral attractiveness 35
    political 312, 324
    women as distinctive group 44
    see also gender
India 24, 34
Institute for Democracy and Electoral
    Assistance (IDEA) 12
    quotas project database 103
institutional theory 146, 151, 323–6
    and gender-bias 147–8, 151, 323–3,
        324, 325, 345
    male/female location in 325
    and organisational masculinism
        323–4
    see also political science
International Conference on
    Population and Development
    (ICPD) 31–2
Inter-Parliamentary Union 24, 101,
    124
    women legislator rankings 101
        numbers data 143
IPSA, Sex Roles and Politics Group
    306
Ireland 112
    abortion issue in 195, 196
    parties and gender in 112, 118
Italy 32, 79
    abortion politics in 195, 197
    and gender equality 34, 37
    parties and gender 111, 112, 118,
        119
        and candidate selection 119–20
    prostitution debate in 83, 84

Jackson, G. 25
Jeffreys, S. 229, 260, 261, 262
Jenkins, K. 105
Jenkins-Smith, H. 267
Jowell, T. 127, 176

Kanter, R. M. 45–6
Kantola, J. 4 n.i, 74
Kelly, R. M. 319
King, C. S. 325

Kinnock, N. 179
Kolinsky, E. 116, 118–19
Kuhn, A. 255
Kuwait 143

Labour Party (UK), women in 29, 47,
    48, 53, *54*, 55, 59, 103, 112, 116,
    118, 121–9, 131, 134, 135, 138,
    139, 152–3, 155–7, 165, 166, 169,
    171, 172–9, 186, 188
  all-women shortlist policy 55,
      121, 124, 128–9, 136, 156, 157,
      175–7
    critique of 176
    1997–2010 MPs elected *178*
  'Blair's Babes' critique 47, 48, 53
  cabinet membership 177–8
  class-based ideology of 152–3
  cultural change in 123, 125, 126,
      127, 152–3, 173, 176–7, 178, 326
  equality, commitment to 188–9
  historical periods of 172–9
    feminist influence 1980s 174
    quota introduction 174–5
  leadership elections 178–9
    rule change 103, 179
  1997 election change in 41–4,
      46–59, 99, 156, 176
    attitudes/values differences 41,
      43, 44, 46, 48–9, 53, 149
    and gender policy differences
      47, 53
  organisational change in 122, 156
  parity, achievement of 129, 188
  positive discrimination in 122
  quota policy in 103, 116, 121–9,
      134, 156, 161, 170, 173–4, 177
    and Constituency parties 122,
      123, 124, 125, 129, 155, 156
    discrimination in 161, 163–4
    goals of 123, 129
    implementation difficulties of 125
    and National Executive
      Committee 123, 124, 125, 153,
      174, *178*

  qualifications, question of in
      125–6
    resistance/backlash to 121,
      127–8, 189
    sex equality strategies in 122, 136,
      137, 157
    selection process in 155–7, 161–6,
      177, 178
      and gender-bias 156–7, 163
      and supply problems 178
    and trade unions 119, 122–3, 125,
      153, 173, 176–7, 178, 229, 252,
      253
    Equal Pay Act (1970) 173
  women as shadow ministers 29
  Women's Group Parliamentary
      123
  women's organisations in 173
  Women's Representation Taskforce
      156
  see also UK, women's
      representation
Lane, R. 303
Latvia 101
Lee, J. 170
Lees, S.
Lewis, J. 320, 322
Lincoln, D. 176
Lister, R. 146, 147
Lloyd, L. 176
Lloyd, M. 341
London (UK) local authority analysis
    199–200, 201–26
  age-sex/employment pattern in
      201–3, 208
    family statistics (1993) 203–4
  and feminist policy influence
      205–6, 208, 224–5
    black feminism, rise of 215
    councillor initiatives 205–6
    equality policy initiatives 205–6,
      208, 218, 224
    and Labour Party support 206
  Greater London Council (GLC)
      204, 205, 208, 289 n.5

homelessness policy in 208,
218–22, 224, 225
and domestic violence 218, 219,
221, 224, 225, 289 n.5
gender dimensions of 218–9,
224, 225
see also homelessness policy and
women
hospital reorganisation policy in
208, 218, 222–4, 225
gender issues in 222–4
Health 2000 223
NHS women staff numbers,
effect on 222, 224
Tomlinson report campaign
(1992) 222, 223
ILEA 204, 205, 212–13
breakup, effect on women of
212–13
local authority system in 199,
203–26
CCT/NPM changes in 204,
206–7, 225 n.3
'contract culture', effect of 206–7
council positions (women)
209–12
decentralisation, effect of 204–5,
208
elite feminisation networks in 213
employment patterns in 208
equal opportunity, decline in
207–8
equality policy controversy 206
as a gendered system 199, 204,
208, 224
women's committees in 205–6,
207–8
Women in Local Government
Network 213
women's movements in 199, 208,
214–18, 224
advocacy role of 218
financing/publicity of 215–16,
218
as networking agencies 216, 218

number of 216, *217*, 218
use of term 215
and voluntary groups 214, 219,
220
London Research Centre 201, *202*
Lucas, C. 185
Lukes, S. 341

McAllister, L. 104
McBride, D. 11, 70, 81, 186
Mackay, F. 104, 105, 149–50
McKechnie, S. 219–21
McKerrow, J. 220
MacKinnon, C. 256, 257, 258
Major, J. 180, 181
Malawi 101
Malley, R. 104
Mama, A. 234, 238
Mandelson, P. 179
Mansbridge, J. 59
Margetts, H. 11
Mattinson, D. 176
Mazur, A. 11, 186
May, T. 132, 158
media 26
gender balance in 106
women MP's use of 26, 38
and 'media-speak' 25
women's presence in 26, 319
Mercedes, M. D. 19
Metropolitan Governance and
Community Study (UK) 209,
210–11
Mexico 101
Miliband, E. 101, 177, 178, 189
Mishler, W. 66
MP attitudes/values UK study 41–59
data/measures used in 41–2, 46–53
BRS Survey (2001) 49–52, *54*, *56*
male/female differences in 43, 53–9
left-right issues 43, 53
party political divisions 43, 53,
54, 57
women's autonomy issues 43,
53, 56, 57–8

theoretical framework of 43
see also British Representation
    Study; 'politics of presence'
Murray, R. 103
Muslim women 69

National Council of Women of Great
    Britain 214
National Women's Aid Federation
    (UK) 231
Nelson, B. 151
Netherlands, the 24, 34, 37
    abortion discourse, changes in 31,
        195, 196, 197
    gender equality committees in 25
    women's issues committees in
        29–30
    women's recruitment in 24, 118
        'negotiable quotas', use in 117,
            122
        'shadowing' system 24
new institutionalism 2–3, 6
new social movements 109
New Zealand 25
Nicholson, E. 180
Nicholson, L. 314
Norris, P. 11, 13, 111, 120, 129, 166 n.1
Northern Ireland 144, 171
Norton, N. 325–6
Norway 37, 300
    gender attitudes, challenge to
        112–13
    party and gender in 113–14
        candidacy (women) 111
        quotas, use in 122
        and sex equality strategies 112,
            114
    women's representation in 110, 112,
        318
        percentage in government 110

Oman 143
organisational cultures 200, 327
    masculinism in 323–4, 325
Outshoorn, J. 74, 81, 83, 91

Panebianco, A. 119
parliament, women's impact in 17–39
    committee selection 28, 30
        and women's committees 30,
            32–3, 38
    enhancement strategies 36–8
        positive discrimination 37
        see also quota systems
    four areas of change 20–39
        discourse 21–2, 27–8, 31, 34–5
        impact/influence 20–1, 26–7,
            30–1, 36–9
        institutional/procedural 20, 21–2,
            23–4, 28–9, 32–3
        representation 20, 21, 25–6,
            29–30, 33–4
    gender equality committees 22, 25
    and 'institutional masculinity' 18
        and male behaviour 19, 26
    key positions, selection for 28, 29
    legislation, feminisation of 21
    measurement criteria of 35
        in women's issues 35
    numbers in 18, 19–20, 35, 134–5
    and political image 35
    rule changes in 22, 29, 31
        strategies used 20–2, 29
    and 'tokenism' 19
    and training/socialisation 21–2,
        23–4, 25–8, 38
        debating skills 28
        media, use of 26, 28, 38
        and mentoring 21, 24, 25
        networking, use of 22, 24, 25,
            26, 28, 31, 33, 38
        on procedural rules 30
        self-perception changes 35
        voice/image projection 21, 24–6
    see also critical mass
parties and gender 13, 109–20, 150–4,
    318
    candidate selection in 101, 102–3,
        109, 110, 115, 117, 135–6, 155
    class/gender interaction in 101
    and local office 118

and positive discrimination
116–17, 120
and 'qualifications'/eligibility
117, 118, 155
see also quotas
and change from within 113
equality rhetoric, use of 122,
127, 132, 136
positive action, use of 115–16,
120, 122
and positive discrimination 114,
115, 116–17, 120, 122, 124
programmatic/organisational
change 113–15
strategies used in 114–15, 122,
136–8
and ideological differences 114,
118, 119, 135, 150, 151–4
institutional sexism in 151–2
and party structure 119, 135
promotion/recruitment of women in
33, 43, 58–9, 110, 114–15, 135
rules/informal practices, effect of
118, 155
and women's demands/claims
110–13, 117, 120
development of 111, 113
strategies used in 111–12, 120
women's issues, promotion of 110
and women's organisations 115–16
and women's training 23–4, 136
cross-party alliances 24
Pateman, C. 342–3
Perrigo, S. 126, 173
Philippines, The 101
Phillips, A. 44, 58, 64, 325
see also 'politics of presence'
Phillips, M. 127
Pizzey, E. 231
Political Quarterly, The 99
political recruitment (women) 1, 17,
19, 135, 154–5
and candidate selection rules 22, 135
supply and demand framework 1,
135, 154–5

systemic context of 135, 137
see also party and gender; quota
systems
political representation (women's) 3–4,
12, 63–89, 109, 110, 139
and the contagion effect 132
dimensions of 110
and feminist scholarship 63–4,
66–7, 110, 318–20, 326
concept of gender in 319, 326
input/effectiveness analysis 67–92
actor motivation/opportunity in
81–4
and critical mass debate 87–90
issue debate intervention 72–3,
81, 84
and movement to the Left 82, 84,
86, 90
RNGS data, use of 67–89
measures used in 68
movement actor presence in
67–8, 87–9
questions posed/analysed in 69–89
see also Research Network on
Gender and the State's (RNGS)
male/female attitude differences
102, 143
cultural bias/constraints 147–50
ministerial/presidential numbers 143
1992 cross-national MP numbers *124*
opponent typology 101–2
Pitkin's typology 4 n.i, 63, 64, 319
and under-representation 99–106,
143–66
see also under-representation
(women)
and women's interests 3, 65, 66,
74–8, 110, 148
party discipline constraints 79
policy responsiveness to 66
policy subsystem openness 78–9,
80, 86, 87
see also descriptive representation;
substantive representation;
parties and gender

political science 1–6, 11, 293–308, 337–8
  American domination of 293–4, 302, 304
  definition, difficulties of 295–6, 339
    and feminist refinement 314, 315
  feminist contribution to 1–3, 4, 6–7, 11, 13, 293ff., 304–8, 337–47
  political representation research 3–4, 317–20
  power and gender focus of 3, 4, 5, 6, 312, 313, 315–16, 337, 338, 339–41, 344, 345, 346
  sexist bias identification 304, 305, 306, 311–12, 324, 325, 339, 342–3, 346
  women's studies movement 313–14
  see also Feminist Political Science
  and feminist institutionalism 344–5
  feminist need of, debate 338, 339, 345–6
  tensions/arguments between 339–46
  fragmentation of 337, 339, 341–2
  gender blindness in 12, 342, 345
  and method driven research 343
  object of study in 296–7
  as path dependent 342
  political institutions, study of 6, 315, 316–17, 323–6
  and political power 297–8, 299, 339–41, 342, 343, 345
  post-structuralist theory 340
  see also power, political
  positivism/scientism in 302, 304, 339, 343
  sexist biases in 294, 299–303, 304, 311, 320, 324, 327, 339, 342–3
  neglect of women in research 300–3, 311
  and policy-making 320–3
  as a social construct 297, 306, 312

Political Science Association (PSA) 1, 338
  Women and Politics Group 338
'politics of presence' theory 3, 41, 44, 45, 46, 64
  and cultural 'tipping point' 45
  effects, display of 45–6
  and women's shared interests 44
Polsby, N. 13
pornography 229, 230, 241, 253–60
  censorship views, differences in 254, 256–60, 262
  Dworkin/MacKinnon ordinance (US) 257–8
  and homosexual issues 259–60
  contested issues in 259
  definition contestation in 253, 254, 259, 262
  connection with violence 254, 255, 256, 259, 260, 262
  essentialist assumptions of 262
  representation position 255
  and feminist protest 240–1, 253–6, 258
  commodification of women 256
  and sexual identity, construction of 262
  policy response, problems with 254–8, 259, 262
  and power/domination 255, 256, 258, 259, 261
positive discrimination 37, 57, 114, 115, 116–17, 120, 122, 124
  opposition to 128
  see also quotas
power, political 4–5, 6, 297–8, 299, 339–40, 342ff.
  feminist understanding of 4–6, 312, 313, 315–16, 319, 337–40, 342ff.
  Allen's tripartite typology 340
  gender relations in 3, 4, 5, 6, 312, 313, 315–16, 337, 338, 339–40
  and institutional sexism 147–8, 341

masculine domination in 341
  struggles over meaning in 341
Foucault's theory of 340
and mobilisation of bias 341
see also Feminist Political Science;
  political science
prostitution *71*, 72, 73, *76*, *77*,
  81, 83
public/private distinction 200–1,
  342–3
  and gender relations 201, 203, 312,
    314, 315
  in violence issues 269, *271*
  masculine/feminine codes in
    316–17
Putnam, R. D. 151
Puwar, N. 100, 144–5

Qatar 143
quota systems 22, 32, 33–4, 37, 103–4,
  116–17, 120–9, 136, 318
  attitudes towards 104
  constitutionalisation of 104
  country numbers using 103
  and culture change 123
  effectiveness of 103, 104
  fast track models 37
  formal/informal types of 32
  goals of 123
  IDEA database of 103
  incremental model of 37
  mandatory/voluntary types 103,
    116–17
  monitoring of 32
  'negotiable quotas', use of 117
  types of 103
    legislative 103, 104
    party 103
  see also under Labour Party (UK)

Randall, V. 11
rape 229, 230, 240–51, 262
  counselling 244, 250
  Crimes against Women conferences
    251

and criminal law 246–8
  advocates proposal 248
  rape trials, critique of 246–8
  reform demands of 248
  women, humiliation of 247–8
crisis groups/centres 243, 244–5,
  246, 249
  funding of 244, 273
  London Rape Crisis Group 243,
    249, 250
and feminism
  action/movements 240–1, 242,
    244, 245–50, 277
  empowerment strategy of 245
  male sexuality argument 240,
    241–2
  masculinity construction
    argument 242
  policy/law influence in 246,
    247–8, 251
  and rage reaction 241
  and women's subordination 241,
    245
in marriage 248–9
media coverage of 241
and police issues 246, 249–50, 277
  feminist definitions, use of 249,
    251
  reforms/sensitivity changes
    250–1
prevalence of 241
and racism 242, 247
rape trauma syndrome 248
and sexual coercion as 241, 244–5
Sexual Offences Act (1976) 248
refuge movement 231–40, 245, 249,
  273, 274–5
  Asian women's 234–5, 279
  collective working principles in
    232–3, 273
  and feminist principles 232–3, 235,
    273
  and housing authority co-operation
    238–9, 274–5
  and official refuges 239

and policing issues 236–7, 273
race, issue of in 233–4, 235, 236,
    261
Women's Aid Federation (UK)
    231–40, 250, 268, *271*, 274, 279
    aims/feminist principles of 231,
        232–3, 235, 280
    autonomy, maintenance of 235–6
    black women's groups in 235
    management structure of 232–3
    New Right policy tension 239
    and provision erosion 238, 273
    racist issues, effect of on 234
representation and women 65–6
    and accountability measures 84–7,
        90
    and citizenship models 78, 80, 147
    and classic representation theory
        74–5
    feminist theory 66–7, 74, 90, 147–8
    non-elected contexts of 65
    movement/state alliances 66
    opponent typology 101–2
    policy agency intervention 66, 69,
        71, 80, 87
    and accountability 85, 86–7, 90
    RNGS data analysis 67–91
        discourse, gendering of 69, 74
        institution/issue intervention *71*,
            75–8
    see also political representation
        (women's); women's
        movements; quotas
Research Network on Gender and the
    State's (RNGS) 12, 13, 63, 65
    movement definition of 84
    policy debate analysis in 67–89,
        186
        debate tracing, use of 79
    Women's Movement datasets/
        resources 91–2
Reuben, E. 305
Ruddock, J. 149
Rumbold, A. 180
Russell, M. 177

Sabatier, P. 266, 267, 268, 269, 279,
    284, 285
Sainsbury, D. 11, 112
Sahgal, G. 234
Saudi Arabia 143
Sauer, B. 11, 91, 93 n.10, 341
Scandinavian countries 109
    gender equality in 37, 121, 123
Schattschneider, E. E. 341
Schwindt-Bayer, L. 66
Scotland
    Holyrood, open culture in 104
    Scottish Women's Co-ordination
        Group 29
    women's representation in 29, 41,
        42, 104, 144, 170, *172*, 177
    and constitutional change 29
Scott, J. 315
Seccombe, J. 180
Segal, L. 241–2, 263 n.1
sexual harassment 230, 251–3, 262
    and definition 252
    as male power assertion 253
    trade-union women's initiatives
        252, 253
        NALGO response to 252
    Victim Support organisation 273
    Women against Sexual Harassment
        (WASH) 252
    at work 251, 252
    see also sexuality; women and
        violence
sexuality 230, 262
    power, relationship to 230, 262
    and sexual difference 230, 312
    social construction of 262
    see also gender; violence and
        women
Shepherd-Robinson, L. 166 n.1, 183
Sherif, C. W. 305
Short, C. 46, 149, 176
Shvedova, N. 35
Skjeie, H. 113, 318
Smart, C. 246–7, 248
Smith, J. 175

South Africa 24, 32, 33, 34
    Commission on Gender Equality
        (1997) 33
    women's empowerment in 33
Spender, D. 13
substantive representation 3, 43, 57,
        63, 88, 319
    definition of 88
    and descriptive, relations with 63,
        64, 65, 87–9
Sweden 24, 37
    abortion politics in 197
    egalitarian ethos in 112
    incremental quota system in 37
    party candidacy (women) 111, 118,
        120
        and local experience 118
        targets set for 120, 122
        women's organisations, effect
            on 120
    Riksdag women's interests study 45
    women representatives 112, 118,
        318–19
        number in parliament 111
Sylvester, J. 158
symbolic representation 4 n.i, 57, 319

Tamerius, K. L. 3 19–20
Thatcher, M. 100, 128, 132, 174, 175,
        180, 183, 222, 237
    women, encouragement of 180–1

UK, women's representation 25, 30,
        31, 41, 44–59, 99–106, 110, 123,
        131, 135, 136–8, 139–41, 144–66,
        169–89
    activism and movements for 169
    all-women shortlists, use of 55,
        103–4, 136, 138, 158, 161,
        175–7, 182, 185, 187
    and argument from justice 102, 153,
        154
    constitutionalisation of 105
    historical development of 170–2
    institutional constraints of 47, 135

leadership positions of 58, 186–7
    in local authorities 199–201
        see also analysis under London
            (UK)
    1918–2001 42
    1992 election 175–6
    1997 election change in 41–4,
        46–59, 99, 156, 176
        attitudes/values differences 41,
            43, 44, 46, 48–9, 53, 149
        and gender policy differences
            47, 53
        see also MP attitudes/values UK
            study
    and parity 99, 101
    party politics, effect on 169, 187–9
        discipline, use of 47, 49, 58, 188
        selection barriers 162–3, 165, 166
        see also Conservative Party
            (UK); Labour Party (UK)
    quotas, use of 103–4, 105, 134, 140,
        153–4
    2001 election 55, 135, 156, 159
    2005 election 131–2, 135, 137, 140,
        179
    2010 election 99, 172, 179, 183,
        186, 188
    Sex Discrimination Candidates Act
        (2002) 30, 59, 103, 136–7, 158,
        177, 186
    under-representation, causes of
        100–5, 134, 140, 143–66, 169
        demand/supply-side factors 140,
            165–6
        Electoral Commission report 134
        expense of 162
        institutional sexism/racism in
            147–50, 162–3, 164–5, 166
        and masculine culture 144–5,
            146–50, 165, 185, 188
        minorities and racism 163–5
        opponent typology 100–2
        see also under-representation
            (women)
    voting patterns of 6

under-representation (women) 99–106,
    143–66, 301, 318
    and argument from justice 102
    electoral systems, effect of 143
    and embedded institutional cultures
        146–50
        masculinity in 146–7
        sexism in 147–50
    and legal constraints 143
    and social obstacles 143, 144
    Westminster analysis 144,
        148–66
United Arab Emirates 143
United Kingdom
    abortion politics in 195, 196, 197
    electoral system(s) in 121, 135, 144,
        170, 171, 184
    Equality Act (2010) 183
    gender equality in 34, 100–6,
        133–5, 151–4, 188, 205–6,
        207–8
        Inter-Parliamentary Union table
            101
        monitoring of 105
        opposition/resistance to 101–2,
            105, 153
        proposals for 105–6
        and voter preferences 102
        World Economic Forum rankings
            100–1
        see also UK, women's
            representation
    Green Party 185
    House of Commons 12, 58, 110,
        145–6, 169, 172
        culture in 59, 104, 144, 145–6,
            148–51
        discourse in 27, 31, 148–9
        and Prime Minister's Questions
            101
        sexism in 27–8, 100, 101, 144,
            148–50
        see also UK, women's
            representation
    House of Lords 100, 106

    Liberal Democrats 103, 135, 153,
        154, 165, 166, 169, 170, 172,
        183, 184–5
        Gender balance Task Force 161
        indirect discrimination in 161
        party culture 153, 185
        shortlist quota system of 160,
            161, 164, 184
        women's organisations in 185
        women's support in 184–5, 188
    National Health Service 222
        women's employment in 222
    public office, women in 42, 44
    suffrage, development of 170
    women's issues, support for 30–1,
        56
United States
    abortion politics in 195, 197
    congressional policy making 325–6
        women's influence in 325–6
    party and gender in 113, 117, 134
        candidate selection 117, 119–20
        and women's left preferences
            134
    policy making analysis 325–6
        male dominance in 326
    pornography debate in 254, 256,
        257, 258
        Dworkin/MacKinnon ordinance
            257–8
    primaries in 117
    welfare-to-work policy debate 70
    women's representation in 32, 46,
        47–8, 319–20
        feminist research in 318, 319–20,
            327, 337
        gender differences study 46, 53,
            325
        and gender equality 25, 118
        and party candidacy 111
        roll call analysis 46, 47, 319–20,
            326
        women's issues, promotion of
            47–8
    women's voting patterns 6, 318

Uosukainen, R. 24
United Nations 28
  Beijing Platform 17
Unwin, J. 221

Verstegen, D. 319
violence and women 229–63, 265–88
  black/Asian experience of 234–5,
    237, 238
    and family honour issues 234–5
    racism, complexities of in 235,
      261
  child sexual abuse 237
  feminist analyses of 229–63
    and empowerment 269
    and issue definitions 230, 252,
      260–1, 265, 275
    male sexuality argument 240,
      241–2, 269, *271*
    masculinity construction
      argument 242
    psychoanalytic thought 229–30
    Radical/Socialist differences in
      229–30, 260–1, 268, 269
  feminist policy influence 265,
    276–82
    advocacy coalition framework,
      use in 265–8, 269–70, 285
    belief systems, role in 269, 285
  see also domestic violence; rape;
    sexual harassment; pornography;
    refuge movement

Wales 25, 144, 157, 170, 171, 172,
  177, 201, 203, 204, *209*, 237
  mixed-member system in 170, *171*
  National Assembly, gender balance
    in 170, *171, 172*, 177
Wängnerud, L. 27, 44, 45
Warsi, S. 183
Watson, S. 266
Webb, P. 152
Weber, M. 147, 316
  ideal man in 316
Weldon, L. 65–6, 71, 92 n.4

welfare state and feminist research
  321–2, 323, 325
  welfare policy models 322
Wilson, E. 260
Wilson, H. 170
Wintringham, M. 145
Wolin, S. 296, 297–8
Women and Equalities Unit (UK) 69
women's issues (in parliament) 23, 24,
  26–7, 29–31, 34, 35, 44
  committees on 32–3
  and diversity of positions 74
  definition of 44–5
    'objective'/'subjective'
      relationship in 44
    'ghettoisation' critique 30
    and 'hard'/'soft' distinction 26, 33
    and male training 24
    and 'media-speak' 25
  recognition and politicisation 45
  RNGS analysis 72–4
    movement actor intervention 72–8
  women's perspective, distinction
    with 26–7
women's movements 27, 38, 66
  accountability in 85–6, 90
  autonomous/integrated distinction
    in 67, 80, 86, 89
  institutionalisation of 79–80, 82, 86
  and policy intervention 66, 71–2, 87
  RNGS definition of 67, 91 93 n.13
    datasets/resources 91–2
    intervention data analysis 67–92
  see also under London (UK)
Women's National Commission (UK)
  105, 214, 215, 268
Women's Refuge Movement 231
World Economic Forum
  Annual Gender Gap Reports 100–1
    UK ranking 100–1

Yoder, J. 46
Yugoslavia 300

Zerilli, M. G. 327–8

www.ingramcontent.com/pod-product-compliance
Lightning Source LLC
Chambersburg PA
CBHW072046020426
42334CB00017B/1407